*Reason after Its Eclipse*

# Other Books by Martin Jay

*The Dialectical Imagination: A History of the Frankfurt School*
*and the Institute of Social Research, 1923–1950*
(1973, 1996)
*Adorno*
(1984)
*Marxism and Totality: The Adventures of a Concept from Lukács to Habermas*
(1984)
*Permanent Exiles: Essays on the Intellectual Migration from Germany to America*
(1985)
*Fin-de-Siècle Socialism and Other Essays*
(1988)
*Downcast Eyes: The Denigration of Vision in Twentieth-Century French Thought*
(1993)
*Force Fields: Between Intellectual History and Cultural Critique*
(1993)
*Cultural Semantics: Keywords of Our Time*
(1998)
*La crisis de la experiencia en la era postsubjetiva, ed. Eduardo Sabrovsky*
(2003)
*Refractions of Violence*
(2003)
*Songs of Experience: Modern American and European Variations on a Universal Theme*
(2005)
*The Virtues of Mendacity: On Lying in Politics*
(2010)
*Essays from the Edge: Parerga and Paralipomena*
(2011)
*Kracauer l'exilé*
(2014)

# REASON
## after Its
# ECLIPSE

*On Late Critical Theory*

## Martin Jay

The University of Wisconsin Press

Publication of this volume has been made possible, in part, through support from the **George L. Mosse Program** at the University of Wisconsin–Madison.

The University of Wisconsin Press
1930 Monroe Street, 3rd Floor
Madison, Wisconsin 53711-2059
uwpress.wisc.edu

3 Henrietta Street, Covent Garden
London WC2E 8LU, United Kingdom
eurospanbookstore.com

Printed in the United States of America

This book may be available in a digital edition

Library of Congress Cataloging-in-Publication Data

Jay, Martin, 1944–, author.
Reason after its eclipse: on late critical theory / Martin Jay.
pages     cm. — (George L. Mosse series in modern European cultural and intellectual history)
Includes bibliographical references and index.
ISBN 978-0-299-30650-2 (cloth: alk. paper)
1. Reason.   2. Critical theory.   3. Philosophy, Modern.   I. Title.
II.  Series: George L. Mosse series in modern European cultural and intellectual history.
B833.J39        2016
190—dc23
2015010451

ISBN 978-0-299-30654-0 (pbk.: alk paper)

For Ryeland

# Contents

# Preface

Scholars are often asked what first inspired a new project and why. In most cases, the answer is a bluff, covering over the mysterious process by which inchoate and vague intuitions coalesce into an exigent scholarly question worth spending sizeable amounts of time and resources trying to answer. As anyone who has to compose under pressure a prospectus statement for a grant proposal knows, there is also a great deal of whistling in the dark about the contours of an argument still very much en route. Often the embryonic hypothesis we think we are trying to prove turns out to be stillborn, but if we are lucky, we discover that we have more or less successfully dealt with another question we never initially intended to address.

In the case of *Reason after Its Eclipse*, however, I think a plausible explanation of origins is possible, or rather a combination of distant and proximate explanations. I can vividly recall a conversation I had over forty-five years ago in Montagnola, Switzerland, with Friedrich Pollock, a central figure in the history of the Institut für Sozialforschung, when I was working on my dissertation on the Frankfurt School. The two of us were discussing the School's critique of instrumental, subjective reason based on the narrow imperative of self-preservation, whose import I thought I had grasped. But what, I asked Pollock, was the normative alternative against which it was pitted? What exactly was the substantive, emphatic, objective concept of reason that was now in peril and how could it be justified both as a philosophical concept and as a norm for human emancipation, without regressing to a discredited idealist metaphysics? Pollock, looking increasingly exasperated, tried to formulate a compact answer, but quickly abandoned the effort. Instead he resorted to reminding me that "Horkheimer has already devoted an entire book to addressing that question!" The book to which he alluded was *Eclipse of Reason*, which was published in 1947 in English, at about the same time Max Horkheimer's more celebrated joint effort with Theodor W. Adorno, *Dialectic of Enlightenment*, appeared in German.

I remember not being fully satisfied with this answer, as Horkheimer's book had perhaps assumed more than it really demonstrated about the emphatic notion of reason whose eclipse it bemoaned. With the passage of time and subsequent attempts by later generations of Frankfurt School theorists to develop a more plausible normative notion of reason, I have remained troubled by the nagging sense that my question of 1969 remained unresolved. The opportunity to address it more closely was afforded—and this is the proximate origin of this exercise—by the kind invitation of Steven Aschheim of the Hebrew University in Jerusalem to deliver the George L. Mosse Lectures for 2012. Mosse, like Horkheimer a distinguished refugee from Nazi tyranny, was a fellow intellectual historian, who devoted a great deal of his formidable energies to making sense of the "irrationalist" thought that fed fascism. "Like romanticism," he wrote in arguably his most influential book, *The Crisis of German Ideology*, "Volkish ideas showed a distinct tendency toward the irrational and emotional, and were focused primarily on man and the world. This outlook found a receptive audience. Rationalism had been discredited."[1] What more suitable an occasion, it seemed to me, than lectures in his honor to return to the question of reason and its limits? And so this modest book on a very big theme was born.

There is, of course, something not very reasonable in trying to write a history of reason in all its motley variety, even one confined to what has come to be called the "Western" tradition.[2] A nineteenth-century overview, like that written by the Anglo-Irish historian W. E. H. Lecky, could assume that the meaning of the term was settled, and confidently pen a secularist philippic against religious persecution, witchcraft, magic, and superstition, but twenty-first-century scholars are forced to wrestle with the deeply contested meanings that have only multiplied since the Victorian era.[3] Either one attempts a thousand-page, magisterial survey of different usages or confines oneself to what are merely suggestive essays rather than an exhaustive treatment. Happily, the former task has already been admirably performed by the German philosopher Wolfgang Welsch, whose *Vernunft* (Reason) came out in 1995.[4] Rather than seek to produce a condensed version of his narrative—which would sound a bit like the Reduced Shakespeare Company's presentation of *The Complete Works of William Shakespeare (Abridged)* in one evening—this modest book will begin with a selective and incomplete presentation of the long history of thinking about something called "reason" in the two millennia before the Frankfurt School began to develop its own ideas of its meaning and defend its vital role in Critical Theory.

Or rather, it will examine the sedimented history of overlapping but not always fully compatible meanings that accrued to the term and its cognates — rational, rationality, rationalization, rationalism, reasoning, reasons, reasonable, only to mention a few — over that period, paying special attention to moments when it came into crisis, either from internal or external pressures, and needed a self-conscious defense. Insofar as it is not an atemporal abstraction that can be disentangled from its usages, or a fully coherent concept either present at the origin of our story or serving as a telos at its end, there is a danger that the protagonist of our narrative is really a shape-shifting phantasm without an essential identity. But here Adorno's suggestion about the way to approach "philosophical terminology" in his 1962 lectures on this theme comes to our aid. Rejecting the imperative to define terms before using them or reduce concepts to a singular, stable meaning, he argued that "the task of a philosophical terminology can consist in nothing else than resurrecting the life coagulated in these *termini* [technical terms]."[5] Only through acknowledging the ambiguities, even contradictions, in the history of a term's usage can the nonconceptual excess that always escapes being subsumed under conceptual generalizations be appreciated. Significantly, his illustration for the resistance to binding definitions was Immanuel Kant, whose "philosophy was a critique of Rationalism as the philosophy that had believed it could resolve the most important questions of Being by beginning with pure concepts."[6]

When a philosophical term is also very much a part of everyday language, as is obviously the case with the one whose history is being traced, the imperative to eschew limiting, a priori definitions is even greater. Sometimes to tease out their meaning such terms have to be situated in a force field of oppositions that function in distinct ways; "irrational," after all, does not mean the same thing as "unreasonable." And as Max Weber famously argued, "rational-legal" authority can be counterposed to either "traditional" or "charismatic" alternatives, accruing in either case subtly different meanings. The oppositions can also manifest themselves on the level of an adjectival binary that nonetheless tacitly assumes an underlying common denominator, as when "objective" and "subjective," "substantive" and "formal," or "instrumental" and "communicative" notions of reason are pitted against each other. Nor is it wise to ignore the ways in which nouns like "reason" and "rationality" are subtly transformed when they become verbs like "to reason" or "to rationalize." And when the denotative and connotative slippages that inevitably occur when moving from one language to another are taken into account, the vanity of a quest to write a "definitive" history of an ideal, transcendental concept of "reason" becomes even more obvious.

If there is a guiding principle in the first half of this book, it is the exploration of those issues in the history of "reason" and its cognates that were to become most exigent in the Frankfurt School's struggle to harness its energies for their critical project. The second half of the narrative will slow down to explore the various ways in which Max Horkheimer, Herbert Marcuse, Theodor Adorno, and most extensively Jürgen Habermas sought to grapple with the challenge of salvaging a critical version of "reason" after the eclipse of more traditional versions. The book will conclude with a chapter filled more with questions than answers, a performative affirmation of an important lesson of the exercise as a whole: that reason is as much critique as it is system-building, as open-ended as it is complete, as fallible in its conclusions as assertive in its premises. And insofar as it illustrates the insufficiency of one individual's attempt to write its history, it will, I trust, solicit an intersubjective interaction that includes all who want to argue about its meanings, limits, shortcomings, and still unrealized promise.

# Acknowledgments

There can be few books as long in preparation as this one, whose distant origins can be traced back to the doctoral dissertation I began at Harvard in 1967. Any serious tallying of the debts I have accumulated over the years would have to start by replicating the acknowledgments to *The Dialectical Imagination*, the book that emerged from that effort six years later. It would also have to include the comparable expressions of gratitude in later works, such as *Marxism and Totality*, *Adorno*, *Permanent Exiles*, and *Songs of Experience*, where the Frankfurt School played major roles. As a result, to attempt an adequate recognition of all the people and institutions that enabled this book to appear would require a list almost as long as the book itself. Not only does it take a village to raise a book, but sometimes several generations of its inhabitants.

Rather than replicate in detail those earlier expressions of thanks, let me simply register once again how much I have benefited from the kindnesses of both friends and strangers, many, alas, no longer alive to be thanked again, without whose generosity my extended encounter with Critical Theory would not have been possible. I can, however, be more precise about the proximate help given in preparing this particular volume, and do so with undiluted pleasure. Let me begin by thanking Steven Aschheim for inviting me to give the George L. Mosse Lectures at the Hebrew University in Jerusalem in November 2012, which were the basis for the second half of this book. John Tortorice, who directs the Mosse Program in its incarnations on three continents, was no less gracious and enabling in seeing the expanded lectures into published form. I would also like to thank Rüdiger Schmidt-Grépály, Jan Urbich, and Claudia

Wirsing for asking me to speak on the theme of the book at the Kolleg Friedrich Nietzsche der Klassik Stiftung Weimar during the same month, as part of a series of talks on the Frankfurt School later published as *Der Ausnahmezustand als Regel: Eine Bilanz der Kritischen Theorie* (Weimar, 2013). Thanks also to Tong Shijun of East China Normal University in Shanghai for the Chinese translation of that essay, which appeared in *Philosophical Analysis* (Shanghai) 6 (2013), and for inviting me to speak on neoliberalism and rationality to the Department of Philosophy at his university. Here I drew on the talk I prepared at the behest of Catherine Liu for a 2011 conference at the Humanities Center of the University of California, Irvine, on "The Neo-Liberal Imaginary," which was ultimately published as "The Neo-Liberal Imagination and the Space of Reasons," *Salmagundi*, no. 176 (Fall 2012): 61–76. I also benefited from Peter Gordon's invitation to present my research to the Harvard Intellectual History Colloquium, thus returning to the setting where I began my work on the Frankfurt School almost a half century ago. Peter himself has engaged more and more with the work of Adorno and Habermas, and our conversations on these common interests have proved enormously valuable to me.

At Berkeley, where I have taught in the Department of History ever since I left Harvard, I have benefited from the intellectual collegiality for which the department is justly famed, as well as from the generosity of the Sidney Hellman Ehrman Chair. My fellow intellectual historians Jonathan Sheehan and David Hollinger were especially helpful interlocutors. I would also like to express heartfelt gratitude to my colleagues in the Critical Theory Program, in particular Judith Butler, Robert Kaufman, Wendy Brown, and Hans Sluga for their extraordinary intellectual comradeship during the time this book was written. The gifted and challenging graduate students in our interdisciplinary Designated Emphasis in Critical Theory, many of whom participated in seminars on the themes of the book, were also a constant source of stimulation. Let me single out Will Callison in particular for his careful and insightful readings of early drafts of the book, and Ari Edmundson and Abhijeet Paul for their thorough and reliable research assistance. I also owe a genuine debt of gratitude to Wolfgang Welsch, who shared his vast knowledge of the philosophical history of reason during the semester I spent at the American Academy in Berlin in 2010. I would also like to thank Michael Morgan and Maeve Cooke for their extraordinarily constructive responses to the manuscript, the former especially for guiding my efforts to make sense of Greek thought, the latter for vetting my attempts to present the arguments of Habermas and his critics.

My thanks also to the staff of the University of Wisconsin Press, which has produced many distinguished volumes in the George L. Mosse Series in Modern European Cultural and Intellectual History, a series I am honored to join. Let me single out in particular Raphael Kadushin, Amber Rose, Carla Marolt, and Marlyn Miller. The press is also to be thanked for soliciting two very helpful readers' reports from Anson Rabinbach and Michael Rosen, which immeasurably improved the final version. Let me also thank Umar Thamrin for performing the arduous task of preparing the index with such scrupulous care.

Finally, as always I have been sustained in the process of researching and writing by my loving family: daughters Shana and Rebecca and their respective spouses, Ned and Grayson; my grandchildren, Frankie, Sammy, and Ryeland; and most of all by my first line of defense against muddled ideas and murky prose, as well as a constant reminder that Blaise Pascal knew what he was talking about when he said *le coeur a ses raisons que la raison ne connaît point*, my wife, Cathy Gallagher.

# 1

# The Ages
# of Reason

Have but contempt for reason and for science,
Man's noblest force spurn with defiance,
Subscribe to magic and illusion,
The Lord of Lies aids your confusion,
And, pact or no, I hold you tight.

Mephisto, in Goethe's *Faust*, part I

# 1

# From the Greeks to the Enlightenment

Helios, the Titan god; Apollo, his Olympian counterpart; and Sol, their Roman equivalent, all came to represent not only the sun but also in varying degrees something called "reason."[1] The links between illumination, enlightenment, and rationality were thus ironically forged in the crucible of mythology. Recalling the mythic representations of reason in ancient Greece—and there are likely many other examples from different cultures around the globe[2]—alerts us to several recurring tensions in the history of the term. First is the vexed issue of the uneasy imbrication of mythos and what came in Greek thought to be called logos.[3] As the Platonic dialogue devoted to the origin of the universe, the *Timaeus*, shows, even the philosopher most often associated with an emphatic concept of reason had to resort to a myth of a divine craftsman to explain what otherwise remains beyond our ken. Indeed, many of Plato's other dialogues, such as the *Phaedrus*, rely on a complex interplay of philosophical argumentation and mythical evocation, which demonstrates the abiding force of mythic thinking in Greek culture.[4] Even the most resolutely anti-mythic thinkers of the era appreciated the difficulty of expressing ideas in language utterly purged of narrative, allegory, and metaphor.[5]

In most traditional accounts of the origins of reason, however, the emphasis has been put on the decisive and fateful emancipation of the latter from the former, an achievement sometimes called "the Greek miracle."[6] Although much doubt has been cast on the overly neat opposition of the two terms, the tacit teleological reading of the transition, and the extent of its actual penetration into the Greek populace as a whole, it is still heuristically useful to compare them as ideal types. Whereas both are ways to generate meaning and fend off the threat of absolute contingency and chaos, mythos does so by telling stories, often involving protagonists—gods or heroes—who may act to create change or be the victims of occult forces they do not control. Myth achieves its semantic power through narration and personification, concrete and particularized, which may then be available for symbolic or allegorical interpretation. Myth remains on the surface, content to retell what is handed down from the past, often through the oral tradition, while logos and the metaphysical tradition it spawned hurries past it to plumb the depths allegedly beneath. Whereas myths are not amenable to falsification by new evidence or the want of logical plausibility, logos invites disputation and the possibility of being discredited by the better argument as the basis for consent.[7]

The tenacity of myth is nonetheless hard to gainsay. In fact, its ability to survive its culture of origin and still in many cases speak to us today derives from its fecundity as a generator of fresh meanings relevant in new contexts (as, for example, Freud famously showed with the Oedipus myth and James Joyce with the Odyssey). But like all systems of meaning, it also can grow old and no longer function to satisfy human needs. As Stanley Cavell notes, "when myth and actuality cannot live together happily—when you keep wondering too much, say about where rules come from, then you have stopped living the myth."[8] Or as Rodolphe Gasché puts it, implicitly playing on the dual meaning of "wonder": "wonder, not before particular things, but before the whole—in the opening of which things come to light—both characterizes philosophy and separates philosophy from myth, which, unmindful of wonder, knows everything ahead of time."[9] From wonder comes wondering; from wondering comes questioning; from questioning comes philosophy and the supplanting of mythos by logos.

Although logos is also intimately tied to language—in certain contexts, including early Christianity, it means "the word" and sometimes was associated by the Greeks more with rhetoric than with unvarnished truth—it has a different emphasis from mythos.[10] Whereas the latter, as we have noted, uses storytelling and anthropomorphic personification to provide meanings, often frankly allegorical, the former depends more on impersonal discursive argumentation and inferential deduction to generate not only meanings but also knowledge.[11] That is, logos assumes at least the possibility of getting access to an objectively existing world beyond the one constituted entirely by culture and its meanings, and seeks to break through not only the constraints of language but also the imperfections of sense perception. Or to put it differently, whereas myth accepts polysemic indeterminacy and revels in metaphors and other rhetorical tropes—the inevitable ambiguity of words—logos seeks the singular meaning of "the word" and claims it can be entirely adequate to whatever it references in the world (or beyond it). Whereas myth tacitly acknowledges the unbridgeable gap between the form of presentation and the content of what is being presented, logos normally strives for a complete unity of the two, a desire that sometimes plays itself out as the search for a perfect metalanguage, such as mathematics, to overcome the chaos of Babel.[12]

Traditionally, the pre-Socratic philosopher Heraclitus (ca. 535–475 BCE) is credited with the first strictly philosophical use of logos as a principle of order, proportion, measure, and form amid the chaos of dynamic reality (although parallels have been sometimes noted in the Indian idea of dharma and the Confucian Tao).[13] For Heraclitus, the true *archē* (foundational principle) of the world was fire, while other pre-Socratics like Thales preferred water.[14] Whatever its ultimate character, this order is invisible to the physical eye and needs to be brought to speech for humans to grasp it. That is, they must be able to give an account—the Greeks came to call it practicing the dialectic—of the truths of knowledge. From the Greek verb *legein* (λέγειν), which means "to gather, collect, put together, or pick up" as well as "to say," logos implies an act of ordering a world of random chaos, and in so doing expressing rational truths. More than just a true belief, logos, for Plato, involved following a path that would lead through a network of relations to arrive at the essence of a thing, which understood the pattern amid the apparent accidental contingency of the world.[15] At times, that path involved acts of definition and description, but it also could mean direct and immediate acquaintance.[16]

Man, Aristotle taught, was a *zóon lógon échon*, which in Latin was rendered as *animale rationale*.[17] But the truths he could uncover are more than the projection of dialectical reasoning, more than the human act of gathering, collecting, or organizing. Underlying the experience of seemingly contingent sensible particulars, logos was understood by the Greeks, or at least a good number of them, to subtend experienced reality, existing ontologically and universally as the intelligible forms—or, as Aristotle would have it, essences manifest in particulars—comprising an ultimately harmonious, lawful cosmos. As Hans-Georg Gadamer put it, "the magnificence of Greek metaphysics was that it sought reason in the cosmos; it sought the *nous*, which is at work ordering and distinguishing in all the formations of nature. To see reason in nature, that was the Greek heritage."[18] Here we have the germ of all those theories of natural law or natural right, developed by Zeno and the Stoics and still defended by twentieth-century political theorists like Leo Strauss, from the right, and Ernst Bloch, from the left, which objectively express reason and can thus be discerned by rational humans.[19]

Contrasted with the apparent world of dynamic flux, which Heraclitus contended was the immediate, unreflective experience humans have of reality, logos implies something more permanent that transcends a world of mere contingency and survives the vicissitudes of change. Myths also evoke a temporality that differs from quotidian experience in the narratives it supports. As Cavell has noted, they "generally will deal with origins that no one can have been present at," a "once upon a time" that is not ours.[20] Because the moment of founding is lost to human memory, myths tend to diminish the role of actual humans in the legitimation or justification of the order they are asked to follow. In contrast, logos tends to bracket the question of origins, remembered or immemorial, and seeks timeless truths, which are amenable to at least some human understanding by those privileged enough to grasp them and perhaps even justify them. Plato, whose utopian Republic was built on an ideal of unchanging hierarchical order, was anxious to differentiate the eternal forms of logos from mythos, even if at times he smuggled the latter into his dialogues.[21] Myths, he insisted, were like childish fantasies, not allegories of a deeper meaning—what the Greeks called *hyponoia*—as later thinkers such as Aristotle and the Stoics were to claim. For Plato, resistance to the treacherous world of mere appearance and ephemeral change went hand in hand with resistance to the immature worldview of myth, in which abstract principles were embodied in the colorful form of fictional personae.[22]

Although ancient Greece may have originated the opposition between mythos and logos, comparable distinctions have been detected elsewhere in the ancient world. Thus, for example, the noted Egyptologist Jan Assmann has observed the use of discursive reason—logos understood not as immediate intuition but as argumentation—in theological texts composed by the nascent monotheists of a much earlier era, called the Ramesside Age (ca. 1300–1100 BCE). "By explicit theology," he writes, "I mean a discourse about God and the divine world that, in contrast to 'mythology,' is not structured according to the rules of narration but rather those of argumentation. . . . Judging from hundreds of preserved texts, ancient Egypt seems to have turned into a country of theologians, with explicit theology becoming the major concern of the time."[23] Even this starting point was doubtless preceded by others: "We must imagine," writes the philosopher Lawrence Cahoone, "that humans have engaged in reason at least since the development of 'symbolic culture' in the Upper Paleolithic age, and perhaps earlier, since the maturation of relatively complex natural languages."[24] If there is an evolutionary advantage to reason, its origins may indeed lie well before any self-conscious awareness of its distinction from other human contrivances for survival, such as myth, in a hostile environment.[25]

However difficult it may be to pinpoint the original fissure between mythos and logos and find the historical moment in which reason makes its entrance onto the stage of human history, the claim that such a split did finally occur and is still operative today is one of the most frequent assumptions made by defenders of reason's integrity. In modern times, the struggle to protect atemporal logic in particular from its being genetically dependent on mythic origins—as well as social, psychological, historical, or even, broadly speaking, natural ones— would be once again vigorously waged by those hostile to the reductionist contextualization decried as "naturalism," "historicism," "sociologism," or most frequently "psychologism."[26] Whatever the external ground or "other" of reason might be—myth, social customs, psychological emotions, the body, the feminine, even nature itself—the fear was that granting it genetic priority could dangerously undercut the claim that reason was eternal and self-grounding, its own cause rather than dependent on something outside itself.

Significantly, the disentanglement of reason from its mythic context was paralleled by a comparable distinction between mind and body, or more precisely *psyche* from *soma*, in the evolution of Greek attitudes toward humankind. As Anthony Long has argued, Homeric man, still inhabiting a world of myth, possessed what he calls a "psychosomatic identity," in which the death of the body entails the extinction of the spirit within it.[27] By the time of Plato, however, a dualistic distinction between a mortal body and an immortal soul began to permeate Greek thought. The latter, of course, found one of its greatest legacies in religious belief in the afterlife, but it also could underwrite a no less powerful faith in the ability of logos to outlive the finite mortals whose ability to reason had discovered it. And, just as fatefully, it could give rise to a hierarchical subordination of women—associated with the denigrated body, the senses, and the passions—to allegedly rational men.[28]

What came to be called "logicism"—a term coined in 1910 by the German experimental psychologist Wilhelm Wundt in opposition to "psychologism"— contended that the syllogistic rules of reasoning first meticulously codified by Aristotle were universally valid no matter the contexts in which they may have first appeared to fallible humans or were subsequently applied by them.[29] Judgment, the reasoning of actual people, was less important than the intrinsic, self-evident nature of the truths they were judging. Logical *validity* was not dependent, *pace* psychologism, on *genesis* or application; 2+2=4 and A=A were simply universally true no matter the context. Certain anti-psychologists, such as the German philosopher Max Scheler and the British cultural critic T. E. Hulme, even argued that substantive truths, including moral norms, enjoyed the same privileged status. "Rational mind," in other words, somehow transcended the fallible minds, refracted through their historical and cultural experiences, of those who were doing the reasoning. Reason was self-grounding, not other-grounded; disembedded, not embedded in the world; absolute, not relative to the capacities of those who reasoned. The exigent questions that provoked rational thinking in the first place were deemed less important than the answers provided by logical reasoning.[30] Justifications were less foundational than the self-evident truths being validated. The faculty of reason in individual minds was isomorphic with the rational world whose intelligibility it mirrored.

Whether or not the neat distinction between self-grounding logos and mythos based on origins lost in time immemorial—or logic as a consistent, monolithic system transcending the human-all-too-human logicians who discovered and applied it[31]—is persuasive, the claim that it had been successfully achieved had a demonstrably powerful impact on Western thought and the discourse of reason at its core. The autonomy of reason, its being self-sufficient and unpolluted by what might have preceded it, became, in fact, one of rationalism's most cherished convictions.[32] One can still find it defended by the contemporary American philosopher John Searle, who argues that "rationality as such neither requires nor even admits of a justification, because all thought and language, and hence all argument, presupposes rationality. One can intelligibly debate theories of rationality, but not rationality."[33]

Any anterior process of autonomization in which reason could be understood to have shed its origins in a nonrational matrix, such as myth, was repressed and forgotten. Any attempt to ground it naturalistically was seen, to invoke Bernard Williams's helpful distinction, as inherently unmasking rather than potentially vindicatory.[34] It is not by chance that another Greek Olympian often associated with reason, the Goddess Athena, emerged fully formed from the brow of Zeus. In Dante's telling metaphor, reason is like an impregnable "citadel," even if situated in the first rung of Hell because the virtuous pagans within it are not yet redeemed by divine grace.[35] Along with the abstraction of the sacred from the profane and the distinction of a creator from his creation, which culminated in the transcendent monotheism developed in what Karl Jaspers famously called the "axial age" from 800 to 200 BCE,[36] the positing of a rational sphere of intelligibility or eternal essences beyond or subtending experienced contingency, historical ephemerality, and cultural difference has often been celebrated as one of the decisive breakthroughs of human history. Or at least so it has by many champions of an emphatic and circumscribed concept of reason.

But from another point of view, the split between logos and myth could just as easily be lamented as the beginning of a tragic loss, the needless pitting of the allegedly eternal against the merely ephemeral, and the dangerously rigid separation of reason from its allegedly irrational "others," a category that could be extended beyond myth to signify a welter of different meanings. Rather than celebrate the alleged autonomy of reason as the triumph of disenchantment and disembeddedness, defenders of this second view could bemoan its costs. For them, the alleged "pollution" of reason by its inferiors—not only myth, but variously the body, emotions, history, language, the feminine, or faith—would better be understood as a salutary return of what had been problematically abjected in the quest for a dubious purity.

In pursuit of these opposing positions, two dominant strategies have been developed. The first identifies reason with certain core characteristics—for example, logical rigor, calculability, analytical discernment, discursive justification, and systematic organization—and condemns whatever fails to live up to these criteria as "irrational" or at least "arational." Here reason is understood either subjectively as one mental tool or faculty among others, set apart from perception, memory, imagination, fantasy, judgment, and other faculties, or objectively as one characteristic of a reality that contains many other dimensions, even if that reality might be construed as potentially becoming more and more rational. In either a subjective or objective sense, reason is set against and typically understood to be superior to its alternatives. Indeed, the imperative to extend its domain has become for some a warrant for the ongoing project that came to be called "rationalization," a deliberate expansion of reason's power and dominion as a tool of the "civilizing mission" of those who claimed already to possess it.[37] This might be called the "narrow church" version of rationalism, rigidly limited in its self-definition, even as it seeks to colonize what it construes as beyond its borders.

In contrast, the second, more ecumenical "broad church," strategy resists both the claim that reason should categorically distinguish itself from allegedly irrationalist "others," keeping them at bay to avoid pollution, and the project of aggressive rationalization, which implies—for these critics—dominating and colonizing what is construed as not yet civilized or even fully "human." Instead, it seeks to locate in those very "others" already existing ciphers of a more capacious version of reason, one that the restricted alternative fails to appreciate and indeed threatens to undermine. Rather than simply inverting the hierarchy of logos over mythos, a temptation to which Romanticism at its most antirational sometimes submitted, it posits a more robust and inclusive version of reason. For if reason can be understood as making sense of the world through discerning patterns of meaning, why not allow a broader notion of reason to encompass all such efforts, narrative as well as discursive?

Rather than being rigidly "logocentric," to use the familiar twentieth-century locution, this broader conception would even have room for myth, at least

understood allegorically.[38] While admitting that there have been many obscurantist, even sinister, evocations of myth, often accompanied by deliberate
attempts to fashion new ones for dubious political purposes, a number of critics
of the alleged impoverishment of exclusivist reason refuse to relinquish faith in
myth's abiding cultural value.[39] Like many of the twentieth-century anthropolo-
gists who rejected the problematic assumption that the mind of modern man
was inherently logical and the "primitive" mind was not, they posit a more
capacious concept of reason.[40] Myth, they argue, was not "prelogical" but
"heterological," and thus a variant of reason rather than its other.[41]

A comparable "broad church" expansion of the concept can be seen in
those who reject the alleged opposition between logic and rhetoric (itself a
simplification of the original Greek usage).[42] Hans Blumenberg, representing
this position in our own day, has contended that from an anthropological point
of view, "the axiom of all rhetoric is the principle of insufficient reason,"[43] a
way to cope with inherent human deficiencies that cannot be remedied by logic
or scientific method alone. He further explains that this principle "is not to be
confused with a demand that we forgo reasons, just as 'opinion' does not denote
an attitude for which one has no reasons but rather one for which the reasons
are diffuse and not regulated by method."[44] Against the identification of reason
solely with science, it shows that practical wisdom can sometimes take procedurally unrigorous forms, following no prescribed method. Thus, he concludes
that rhetoric may well be "a form of rationality itself—a rational way of coming
to terms with the provisionality of reason."[45] Rhetoric, like myth, should therefore not be simply denigrated as the inferior "other" of reason, a Trojan horse
of irrationality. Instead, it should be acknowledged as a different form of reason,
broadly construed, no better and no worse than, say, scientific or instrumental
rationality.

The defense of an expanded, ecumenical concept of reason has, in fact,
taken many different forms, and continues to animate many contemporary
thinkers. It is worth pausing with a few salient examples from disparate thinkers
to demonstrate how popular it has become. According, for example, to a recent
American philosopher, broad reason would include mythological thinking,

> for this is still the predominant way in which individuals put their world
> together. Therefore, the broad notion of reason bridges the gap between
> *mythos* and *logos*. In myth we see the "passive" interpretation of *logos*: the
> world and its order are already laid out by God or one of his agents, or
> simply just there. Humans then are exhorted to conform to this pre-
> established order.[46]

Such a capacious use of reason opens the door for a healing reconciliation, which will potentially restore some of the enchantment lost when logos vanquished mythos.

Another recent commentator from Germany urges us to reserve the word "reason" for its more capacious usage alone and adopt "rationality" to designate the more restricted version. For "reason," she writes,

> essentially perceives the unitary and the united, while rationality articulates and analyzes its objects into their constituent parts and elements. Truth for reason, aiming at the individual, is unconcealedness; for rationality it is the truth of judgment. Reason perceives what is original and originating; rationality deduces from principles through arguments—"rational" is synonymous with "justified" and "well-founded."[47]

Open to the world as it is disclosed, rather than intent on reforming it, the broad notion of reason, she argues, is not separate from and superior to the senses: "reason, analogously to sensuality, is determined and impressed by its object and thus lets it be and happen as it likes to be and happen; reason is passive and receptive. On the contrary, rationality defines and determines, processes and masters its object; it controls and dominates, rules and orders sensuality."[48]

Two other German critics of the limited, narrow church version of reason, which reduces it to mere rationality, see a repeat of the process of restriction in the late Enlightenment's retreat from fantasy and imagination. Focusing on Kant's demolition of Swedenborgian *Schwärmerei* (nonsense), they lament the loss of what they claim has been abjected:

> Reason, preparing to dominate, grew narrow. Enlightened reason in the eighteenth century is no longer the self-assured and far-reaching reason of a Leibniz, nor is it any more the radical and aggressive critique of a Bayle. The reason that wants to dominate limits itself. It leaves the Other outside and at the same time is codetermined with this Other. From this point on, defense and dread accompany the domination of reason. . . . Reason withdrew into itself and thereby withdrew from the Other. Traffic over the fortified borders became difficult. The Other became foreign and incomprehensible.[49]

Instead of abandoning the project of reason, it is necessary to expand it, for "what matters is the overcoming of our understanding of ourselves as an *animal rationale*. It is a matter of turning away from the ideal of the autonomous rational human being. It is a matter of developing a knowledge of how to orient ourselves in our bodily existence and our dealing with atmospheres of feeling."[50]

Comparable claims are offered by a Canadian commentator, who urges the recovery of the "world-disclosing" power of a reason that can transform the future, not merely criticize or judge what is already in existence. By opening our eyes to possibilities, alerting us to the latent meanings in the lifeworld, a broader concept of reason avoids its reduction to a mere tool of mastery and domination.[51] A complementary plea is made by an Australian philosopher, who laments the limitation of rationality to its discursive function and accompanying identification of truth with what John Dewey called "warranted assertability," and urges instead the inclusion of insightful encounters with revelatory events.[52] A final example, which alleges that cultural bias is at the root of the narrow version, comes from an Afro-Caribbean philosopher, who claims that Western reason—including the Habermasian communicative rationality to be discussed later—is blind toward the inherent "reconciliatory" reason included in mythic thinking. "Only in the rationality of mythic thought," he avers, "is it possible to find models for the type of discursive interventions that could internally transform the project of technocratic reason and address the problem of nonrenewable traditions."[53]

These recent protests from an international chorus of critics against the restriction and limitation if reason—or its problematic identification with mere "rationality"—have not gone unchallenged,[54] but it should be acknowledged that they have a long-standing philosophical pedigree. Friedrich Schelling's attempt to explore the mythic background of a reason that can never be fully self-grounded or able to integrate everything into its speculative system would be one salient example.[55] But perhaps its most influential recent expression can be found in Martin Heidegger's attempt to recover a relationship to "being" obscured by, among other things, philosophy's focus on rationality in its restricted sense. In *Der Satz vom Grund*, his 1955–56 lecture course translated into English as *The Principle of Reason*, Heidegger contended that the initial withdrawal of "being," when it no longer manifested itself as presence, was accompanied by a fatal misunderstanding:

> in its inaugural *Geschick* [destiny] as λόγος being conceals its belonging-together with ground/reason. But the withdrawing does not exhaust itself in this concealment. Rather, inasmuch as it conceals its essence, being allows something else to come to the fore, namely ground/reason in the shape of ἀρχαί, αἴται, of *rationes*, of *causae*, of Principles, *Ursachen* [causes] and Rational grounds.[56]

What has been forgotten is the more fundamental meaning in which reason does not mean grounds, causes, principles, reasons, but rather, following the etymology of *legein* as "a letting-lie-present that assembles."[57] The broader concept of reason entails a recovery of that original, more inclusive meaning, which had been lost when the Romans translated logos into the Latin *ratio*, the initial step in what Derrida was later to call the "puzzling scene of translation which has shifted *logos* to *ratio* to *raison, reason, Grund, ground, Vernunft*, and so on."[58]

But lest the champions of the broad concept of reason be seen primarily as latter-day Heideggerians, nostalgic for a world before the forgetting of "being" or natural right, it should also be acknowledged that a similar lament about the restriction of reason can be found among twentieth-century Marxists, including the first generation of the Frankfurt School.[59] For all their explicit disdain for the nefarious implications of Heidegger's philosophy, not to mention his politics, they shared his dismay at the reduction of reason to technological or instrumental rationality.[60] Thus, in "Reason against Itself: Some Remarks on Enlightenment," a lecture given in 1946, Max Horkheimer would write, "Reason's ability to render an account of its transformation from the power by which the meaning of all things is perceived, to a mere instrumentality of self-preservation, is a condition of its recovery."[61] And in *Dialectic of Enlightenment*, which appeared in the following year, he and Theodor W. Adorno would claim that the fatal split was already foreshadowed when the Greek gods came to be understood as merely allegorical signs of essential reality, and no longer immanent in it:

> The Olympian deities are no longer directly identical with elements, but signify them. In Homer Zeus controls the daytime sky, Apollo guides the sun; Helios and Eos are already passing over into allegory. The gods detach themselves from substances to become their quintessence. From now on, being is split between *logos*—which, with the advance of philosophy, contracts to a monad, a mere reference point—and the mass of things and creatures in the external world.[62]

In the mid-1960s, Adorno would continue to contend that "the element of enlightenment, the impulse towards demythologization," is "twinned with the domination of nature."[63] And he further lamented that

> this disappearance of origins, of the impulse behind thought in logic, conceals the fact that it is above all the logical form of organization that serves domination, that logical thought and the discipline that logic requires of human beings is itself dependent, conditioned by the power of

the will. Reason only becomes available as an instrument for every conceivable desire through its objectification, through its being uncoupled from desire.[64]

The implication is that a nondominating relationship to nature, one based on a benign version of mimesis, restores some of the openness to mythical thinking and pre-rational desire—what Adorno called the "additional factor" (das Hinzutretende) absent from a purely rational morality—that was lost with relentless disenchantment. And so, despite his abiding suspicion of attempts to re-enchant the world, Adorno could admit that

> when Heidegger refers to metaphysics as a kind of rationalistic decline from the original understanding of being in archaic philosophy, I cannot entirely disagree, from a phenomenological standpoint, with his characterization. On the one hand, metaphysics is always, if you will, rationalistic as a *critique* of a conception of true, essential being-in-itself which does not justify itself before reason; but on the other, it is always also an attempt to *rescue* something which the philosopher's genius feels to be fading and vanishing.[65]

The efforts of the first generation of the Frankfurt School to rescue what was lost with the separation of logos from mythos and heal the wound caused by the breach—or at least grudgingly affirm the scar that covered it over—will be treated later. But for now what is important to register is that like Heidegger, Blumenberg, and the other commentators cited above, they too embraced a broader notion of reason than the limited ones typical of the modern era. In fact, even Habermas, certainly no friend of Heidegger's version of broad reason, could protest against the simple distinction between an "inside" and "outside" of reason, which he saw as an effect of a "consciousness-centered" philosophy of the subject.[66]

¶

If the disentanglement of logos from mythos and the erection of a boundary between reason and its "others" unleashed cries for reunification on the part of some observers, no less controversial was another aspect of the classical legacy of reason: the distinction between what the Greeks had called "noetic" and "dianoetic" notions of reason.[67] Although there were many nuances in the usage of these terms,[68] in general the distinction was as follows. *Nóēsis* is the mental operation of nous (mind or intelligence), which differs from the mere sensual perception of an object in the world called *aisthesis*. For Plato, it was a function of the "eye of the soul," as opposed to the physical eyes of the body.[69] It identifies resemblances, proportions, and contrasts, penetrates to essences beneath appearances, and is able to discern the intelligible forms inherent in reality, or to use Plato's term, the *eidos* or eternal ideas. Sometimes it is understood as an intuitive grasp of the deeper truths denied to mere sense knowledge, truths that are disclosed, brought to light, made present, rather than the result of analysis, constitution, or reflection. At its heart is the assumption that our minds partake of the world of rational intelligible forms, rather than stand outside it, merely judging it from afar. The pre-Socratic Parmenides had even claimed that thought (*noeîn*) and being (*eînai*) are the same.[70] Intuition, drawn from the Latin *intueri* (which means to "look on"), implies the ability to know something immediately and directly, through a kind of instantaneous "apperception," to anticipate a word coined by René Descartes in the seventeenth century, going beyond the uncertainties of mere sensation and perception. In Latin, the verb *speculor* (the origin of our "speculation") served the same purpose as *noeîn*, signaling the link between visual intuition and theoretical distance, distinguishing both from mere physical perception. Noesis is, to introduce another term employed by both Plato and Aristotle, "anhypothetical," meaning a principle that does not need to be hypothesized and proven.[71] Whether it be the form of the Good or the logical principle of noncontradiction, it was prior to the process of reasoning itself as a demonstrative exercise.

In contrast, dianoetic thought, although more than mere opinion—*doxa*—nonetheless eschews the direct power of noetic intuition to access the absolute, a power that might well be reserved only for the gods. Tacitly acknowledging the gap between subject and object, it privileges judgment and justification as the essential tools of rational discourse. Rather than noetic intuition, it employs syllogistic logic and discursive argumentation, the inferential process of reasoning, in order to come to rational conclusions. The addition of the prefix "dia" ("through") suggested a temporal process of demonstration, argumentation, and inference, perhaps best exemplified for the Greeks by the successive steps of an inferential geometric proof.[72] Developed in Socrates's polemics with the Sophists, it emerged as the primary organon of thought in Aristotle, elaborated in the sixth book of his *Nicomachean Ethics*.[73] Dianoetic reasoning can buttress scientific *episteme*, knowledge for its own sake; *techne*, knowledge used to produce something; or *phronesis*, knowledge used to guide conduct. It tends to be more analytical than synthetic, and lacks direct access to eternal intelligible forms (although as the example of geometry shows, it can draw on noetic knowledge of their existence prior to the inferential proofs that derive logical implications from their relationships).

As Herbert Schnädelbach has pointed out, dianoesis is based on a "dispositional" notion of reason, in which the center of gravity is not the objective world or eternal forms but the acting subject, so that "'rationality' normally belongs to the language of persons and actions, persons, that is, who have at their disposal the possibility of using the faculty of reason or the practice of reasoning. The talk of 'system rationality,' then, is a category mistake in Ryle's sense."[74] Often dianoetic reason employs what the Greeks called dialectics and eristics—disputation and polemic. As such, it can move the locus of reasoning away from the individual subject, either having an immediate noetic intuition or deductively and inferentially drawing logical conclusions from true premises, to the intersubjective process of argumentation, in which questions and answers, challenges and justifications, making a case and listening with an open mind to the cases made by others, are paramount. It also has a more tenuous relationship to truth, which it may approximate but not fully capture. For some commentators, such as the early Ludwig Wittgenstein, the inadequacy of dianoetic reasoning based on the ambiguities of language, could, in fact, produce a counsel of silence before unanswerable questions. But for others, and here a prime example would be Jürgen Habermas, it led to a defense of communicative rationality as the only alternative to the authoritarian implications of monologic intuition.

Dianoetic reason lacks the ability to ground first principles, the absolute premises prior to a train of inferential reasoning from them. For all its stress on moving forward to a rational consensus, it cannot entirely avoid recalling a point of past departure, a foundation for the reasoning to follow. The danger of an infinite regress backward always haunts dianoetic reasoning, which can only move forward from an original premise that it cannot defend by argument alone or blissfully lose sight of, as complacent traditionalists might, in the fog of "time immemorial." Nor can dianoetic reasoning easily counter the reproach of those "logists" who believe in an objective sphere of truths beyond judgments that it leads down a slippery slope to "psychologistic" relativism. Thus, even champions of dianoetic reasoning such as Kant, aware of the dangers of psychologism, ultimately fall back on an allegedly incontrovertible "fact of reason," which is prior to the act of reasoning itself. It might be said that there is always a noetic moment even in the most stringently dianoetic attempt at discursive reasoning. Defenders of a strong notion of the self-sufficiency of reason, such as Baruch Spinoza and his followers, thus feel justified in jettisoning the search for origins or foundations and rejecting a concept of truth as made—Giambattista Vico's celebrated *verum-factum* principle—for an alternative notion that truth is its own sign, or *verum index sui et falsi*.

The potential tension between noetic and dianoetic knowledge can often be discerned in different idioms in the subsequent history of reason, although it is sometimes possible to glimpse one hidden beneath the façade of the other (or perhaps better put, to realize that one is the blind spot of the other).[75] In general, one might say that champions of the broader concept of reason felt more comfortable drawing on the power of noetic insight than did the advocates of the restricted, dispositional alternative. It can, for example, be seen at times in Adorno's negative dialectics, which has been called "a noesis of the non-identical."[76] The tension between noetic and dianoetic versions of reason was, in fact, explicitly discussed in a conversation between Horkheimer and Adorno in 1956, recorded by Adorno's wife, Gretel.[77] While chastising Heidegger for being against discursive argumentation, Adorno nonetheless conceded that "there is really something bad about advocacy. . . . Arguing means applying the rules of thinking to the matters under discussion. You really mean to say that if you find yourself in the situation of having to explain why something is bad, you are already lost." Horkheimer adds with a touch of scorn, "The USA is the country of argument," which Adorno then trumps by pronouncing—without providing a justification—that "argument is consistently bourgeois."[78]

Marcuse defended noetic reason even more vigorously in *One-Dimensional Man*, noting approvingly that in its search for the truth, "classical Greek philosophy relies largely on what was later termed (in a rather derogatory sense) 'intuition,' i.e., a form of cognition in which the object of thought appears clearly as that which it really is (in its essential qualities), and in its antagonistic relation to its contingent, immediate situation." And then he added, "It is not a mysterious faculty of the mind, not a strange immediate experience, nor is it divorced from conceptual analysis. Intuition is rather the (preliminary) terminus of such an analysis—the result of methodic intellectual mediation. As such it is the mediation of concrete experience."[79]

Perhaps an even more striking example can be found in the thinking of Marcuse's teacher, Martin Heidegger, whose successive ruminations on the distinction are helpfully described by Michael Inwood. "Early on," Inwood writes, "he took Parmenides to be a precursor of Husserl: real being is disclosed (but not idealistically *constituted*) by theoretical apprehension. . . . Later, he interprets *noein* differently. It is *Vernehmen*, combining its senses of 'to hear, perceive' and 'to examine, interrogate': a receptive bringing-to-a-stand of what appears. . . . Later still, *noein* is interpreted as *In-die-Acht nehmen*, 'taking into one's care,' and being as *Anwesend des Anwesenden*, 'presence of what presences'; again these 'belong together.'"[80] Whatever variations on noesis Heidegger might have discerned in pre-Socratic philosophy—or perhaps better put, whichever definitions he might have imposed from his own philosophical vocabulary— he was clear that it had been undermined when dianoesis emerged as a systematic process of inferential reasoning to challenge it. Again Inwood:

*Noein* deteriorated under the influence of Plato's interpretation of being as *idea*. It became *dialegesthai*, "to argue, etc.," thus converging with the parallel decline of Heraclitus's *logos* into "assertion." . . . Now it has become the REPRESENTATION of "objects": the liberation of man involved in the "unfolding of being as subjectivity" that accompanied the decline of religious authority.[81]

It would take too long to spell out all the ways in which Heidegger's interpretation and critique of representational thinking, the dualism of subject and object, and the elevation of humanism over the care of being were all implied by his hostility to dianoetic thought. But it should be noted that in *The Principle of Reason*, which is devoted largely to Gottfried Wilhelm von Leibniz's understanding of "the principle of sufficient reason" or the *principium rationis*, he criticized the slippage that occurred when the latter was transformed into the *principium reddendae rationis*. For this version involved the demand to render reasons, to ground cognition, to be accountable. *Vernunft*, he contended with his typical reliance on etymological origins, came from *vernehmen*, which meant "to hear." With scarcely disguised reference to his ostracism after the Nazi era, when he notoriously refused to explain, let alone apologize for, his support for the regime, Heidegger whined: "lately we have had the demand to render reasons all too oppressively in our ears" and added that "the unique unleashing of the demand to render reasons threatens everything of humans' being-at-home and robs them of the roots of their subsistence, the roots from out of which every great human age, every world-opening spirit, every molding of the human form has thus far grown."[82]

❧

Focusing on Heidegger's critique of the need to render reasons is admittedly getting ahead of ourselves, but what it shows is that the contrast between noetic intuition and dianoetic discourse, as well as the conflict between broader and narrower notions of reason, remained unresolved well into the modern era. Let us now back up a bit and clarify some of the intervening history. It would be fruitful to explore the complicated dialectic of reason and faith during the Middle Ages, in which an Augustinian tradition suspicious of the claims of reason was met by a renewed appreciation for the legacy of Aristotle. In the Scholastic theology of Thomas Aquinas, Peter of Spain, and Francisco Suarez, reason was understood to be inherently compatible with revelation.[83] The medieval Islamic contest between rationalists like al-Farabi and Avicenna and their opponents like al-Ghazali, who stressed the inability of reason to grasp the absolute or the infinite, would likewise repay attention. It would also be worth pausing with the recovery of classical humanist ideals during the Renaissance, which entailed a new appreciation for Greek philosophers like Plato and an embrace of Stoic principles of natural law.[84] A more complete history would also examine the slow erosion of Scholasticism in seventeenth-century England, where reason lost its connection with the soul and divinity, and became instead a function of the mind—ratiocination as reckoning—leaving some of its previous roles to sentiment and the senses.[85] More time might also be spent with the developments in probability theory and statistics in the early modern period by mathematicians, scientists, and philosophers, such as Blaise Pascal, Gottfried Wilhelm von Leibniz, Pierre-Simon Laplace, Christiaan Huygens, and Daniel Bernoulli, which led to sophisticated modes of reasoning from patterns of large numbers.[86]

But perhaps the best place to begin an analysis that would illuminate the Frankfurt School's attempt to wrestle with the question of reason would be the European Enlightenment, the modern era in which the struggle to emancipate—yet again—logos from mythos led to a full-throated exaltation of reason over its various others. That struggle did not always imply a simple either/or, as a number of thinkers in that era still sought a viable compromise between reason and faith. Progressive theologians—Protestant, Catholic, and Jewish—abandoned the aggressive denigration of reason that characterized the Reformation, exemplified by Luther's infamous characterization of it as "the devil's greatest whore."[87] Many philosophes likewise promoted such compromises with religion as Deism or Neology, which sought to shed the fanatic "enthusiasm" of antinomian irrationalism. But there were also many others who more stridently asserted "the sovereignty of reason," in which it came to serve, to cite the historian of philosophy Frederick Beiser, as "the highest authority, the final court of appeal, so that it takes precedence over *every* other source or standard of truth, such as inspiration, tradition or the Bible. . . . Reason has *complete* jurisdiction over faith, the intellectual capacity and the moral right to examine all beliefs, and to accept or reject them strictly according to the evidence."[88]

The "age of reason," to cite the title of Tom Paine's celebrated pamphlet defending Deism, could just as easily be understood as an age of critique.[89] However it might be defined—and the word has amassed many sedimented meanings—"critique" implied suspicion of authority, tradition, self-evidence, and emotional appeal, demanding instead a reasoned exploration of the unacknowledged conditions of possibility, both epistemological and social, that underpinned conventional wisdom. In the preface to the first edition of his *Critique of Pure Reason*, Kant defined his task as the "self-cognition" of reason, the creation of a "tribunal that will make reason secure in its rightful claims and will dismiss all baseless pretensions, not by fiat but in accordance with reason's eternal and immutable laws. This tribunal is none other than the critique of reason itself: the *critique of pure reason*."[90]

The judicial metaphor employed by Kant in linking reason with critique could, however, cut both ways. That is, reason could be the judge in the tribunal of last appeal but also the accused in the dock. Precisely how reason could be both the organon of criticism and also the object of that criticism, an ambiguity neatly captured in the genitive form of Kant's formulation, remained for many later commentators unresolved, allowing them to claim that its self-grounding was really a vicious circle. But not all accepted this dismissive judgment. Thus, for example, Adorno was to call it

> a curious affair: it is a tribunal in which the judge, the prosecutor and the accused are actually one and the same person. However, I believe it would be a little facile to ridicule Kant for this because what we might call this paradoxical idea is actually the heart of the Kantian conception and points to a feature that is a motivating impulse rather than a mere presupposition or even a logical error that can be lightly dismissed.[91]

Evident in this cautious exculpation is the same attitude that would allow Adorno (and Horkheimer) to argue for the necessity of still using the Enlightenment to criticize the problematic implications of the Enlightenment in *Dialectic of Enlightenment*.

The Enlightenment, it might be said, came to admit the limits of reason but could not come to a consensus about where those limits were. What made the search for them so challenging was the increasing intertwining of reason as a mental faculty, involving logic, argumentation, calculation, and the like, with its complicated practical role in an early modern Europe undergoing many radical changes. Here the destructive impulse of critique was transformed into a positive platform for changing the world. It was a while before those changes came to be explicitly characterized as "rationalization" and desired—at least by some—as such, but in retrospect it is impossible not to acknowledge that more than just philosophical issues were involved in the debate over reason and its limits. Protocols of thought, tools of logical proof and discursive argumentation, could be translated into formal procedures of social, political, and economic organization. Accompanying the successes of scientific reason based on the mathematicization of nature and the application of rigorous methods of research went a desire for the scientific management of practical problems. The ongoing struggle to free logos from mythos was transformed by some into a conscious campaign for secularization, both of worldviews and the power of the church in the world. The absolutist state of enlightened despotism and the nascent capitalist marketplace could be interpreted in terms of processes—wrought by hands both visible and invisible—that substituted one or another version of rational order for the messy world of ad hoc institutions and practices inherited from what became known as "traditional" society.

Although some thinkers, such as Leibniz, remained faithful to the ancient Greek belief that reality, understood correctly, was always already rational and thus not in need of perfection, others, such as the Marquis de Condorcet and Kant, came to believe that rationalization was an ongoing project whose progressive realization was a desideratum to be sought, not an eternal truth to be disclosed. Many of the Greeks had also understood the disclosure as an active task, which required vigilance against the domination of mere opinion (*doxa*) or the seductions of sophistic rhetoric. Plato prescribed and performatively exemplified the anamnestic and maieutic exercises necessary to recall and help in the recovery of a reason that had been somehow forgotten.[92] He also tied the recollection of reason to the ability to lead a good life, a life in which ethics and reason were united in the struggle to tame the unruly forces of the body.[93] Plato explicitly analogized from the authority of wise political rulership to the role of reason over the passions—Anthony Long calls it his "politicized concept of rationality"[94]—to stress its responsibility as a bulwark against both a politics and a personal life of impulse and desire.

The identification of reason with self-controlling virtue, in fact, remained a frequent feature of classical thought—the Roman Stoic philosopher Seneca would famously claim that "virtue is nothing else than right reason"[95]—and then found its way into Christian theology as well. For the Greeks, the historian William Bouwsma notes,

> manhood was specifically associated with the rule of reason, which was at once the spark of divinity in man, his access to the higher rationality of the divinely animated cosmos, and the controlling principle of human behavior; the function of reason was to order the personality into conformity with the larger order of the universe as it was apprehended in the mind. The principles of reason thus come from "above," and the ideal man is therefore a fully rational being who pits his reason against the chaotic forces both within himself and in the world. The assimilation of this conception into historical Christianity has been responsible for its tendencies to an idealism in which the religious quest is understood as a commitment to higher things, with a corresponding contempt for the lower.[96]

The quest for individual perfection in medieval Christianity thus owed a great deal to pagan sources, however much it may have couched itself in the rhetoric of "imitating Jesus."

But the deliberate, collective project of rationalizing social, cultural, and political institutions beyond the life of the single individual or the isolated monastic community had to await what came to be called the modern age. Indeed, one plausible definition of modernity is the unprecedented assumption that such a totalizing project—combining will with reason—was in fact both possible and desirable. And if classical modernity has had a successor—which seemed plausible in the heyday of so-called postmodernism, but now less so—it would be marked by the uncomfortable realization that the project could become self-sustaining, no longer entirely a product of deliberate intention but rather a force of its own. And, of course, because it could become such a force, increasingly unmoored from the control of those who unleashed it, the question inevitably arose of whether or not reason might itself be a function of self-aggrandizing power. This question was to be most insistently posed by Friedrich Nietzsche and Michel Foucault, but in some ways it duplicated the perennial battle between psychologism and logism. In other words, could the rationalization of society be understood as a self-generated project of reason itself or a function of the external conditions and interests that reason tried so much to forget?

However one answers this question, there is one conclusion that inevitably follows. Any history of reason must acknowledge the accompanying, if not always parallel, processes of what came to be called rationalization, both as a personal and social project, sometimes intended and sometimes not. For there was a reciprocal feedback loop connecting the theoretical idea of reason, however it might be understood, and the multiple practices of rationalization. Without trying to determine whether or not theory more frequently guided practice or vice versa—there is doubtless evidence to support either alternative—what cannot be ignored is the mutually reinforcing effect of reason in both registers, or put more precisely, what has to be understood is the complicated entanglement of theoretical and practical rationalization, for although sometimes mutually reinforcing, they could also be at odds, depending on which variant of reason was in play.

Although the project to impose reason on the world has a long pedigree, perhaps as old as the competing claim that the world was always already rational, it was not until recent times that it became an object of self-conscious inquiry and critique. The German sociologist Max Weber (1864–1920) was arguably the pioneering diagnostician of modernizing rationalization in the West, providing as well a template for comparable developments elsewhere in the world. Despite his inevitable limitations, exacerbated when his theories formed the basis of Eurocentric and anticommunist "modernization theory" during the Cold War, spending some time with Weber's theories will help us make sense of the dialectic of theoretical and practical rationalization.[97] Several points in particular need to be emphasized before returning to the Enlightenment attempt to draw on reason as the ultimate intellectual tribunal, while at the same time submitting it to a self-critique.

First, as in the case of the ancient world's emancipation of logos from mythos, the rationalization that concerned Weber emerged from within the matrix of what it was often understood to have definitively superseded. That is, as demonstrated by his celebrated, if still controversial, thesis about the "elective affinity" between the Protestant ethic and the spirit of capitalism, Weber understood reason and faith as intertwined rather than simply opposed.[98] Likewise, the "ascetic activism" of certain sects dedicated to bringing the kingdom of heaven down to earth had an effect on later, more secular movements seeking to make the world more rational.[99] Although he did not see reason as a mere secularization of religious content—indeed, his well-known observation about the disenchantment of the world implies that a shared belief in ultimate meaning was lost, not transfigured by the rationalization process—he emphasized the importance of institutional organization, doctrinal codification, and practical, rule-bound ascetic activity as religious anticipations of secular rationality. Indeed, he understood substantive religious rationalization, which he identified with theological systematization and ethical reflection, to have occurred in the great world religions well before the onset of secularized modernity. Thus, as in the case of the impure origins of reason in the Greek period, rationalization in the modern world may have only imperfectly shed the residues of its pre-rational, or in some ways proto-rational, past. Whether or not they were a constraint—as, for example, has been argued in the case of the early eighteenth-century English Enlightenment[100]—or a resource for the recovery of a broader notion of reason, one that includes the traditions that have allegedly been left behind, has been debated ever since.[101] So too has the role of new sources of the "irrational" or at least nonrational as reactions to the limits of what Weber himself recognized as the "iron cage" of modern rationalization.

Second, Weber was sensitive to the modern differentiation and pluralization of reason into a number of relatively autonomous subvariants—indeed, he saw differentiation as itself a mark of modern rationalization—without seeking to elevate one above the others as the most normative, authentic, or legitimate version. Employing a method of ideal typical categorizations that frankly acknowledged its abstraction from the complexities of history, he distinguished among, inter alia, substantive, formal, instrumental, bureaucratic, and value rationality.[102] In addition, he posited discrete processes of rationalization within the differentiated value spheres—generally speaking, cognitive, ethical, and aesthetic—which may have shared certain characteristics but were not merely expressions of a single narrative of reason understood to underlie the process as a whole. Weber, moreover, did not claim that rationalization in whatever form could entirely displace other modes of social, cultural, and political legitimation, which he identified in his *Theory of Social and Economic Organization* with traditional and charismatic authority.[103] Nor could rational choice entirely replace the role of emotion and affect in human behavior. As a result, it might be said that Weber embraced a narrow and heterogeneous rather than broad and homogeneous notion of reason (as befitting someone who was more indebted to Immanuel Kant than Georg Wilhelm Friedrich Hegel), and one that moreover focused on subjective action or intersubjective procedures rather than the functional needs of the system as a whole, or, to recall an earlier distinction, dispositional rather than nondispositional reason.

Third, despite his stress on dispositional action rather than function or structure, Weber appreciated the linkages between whatever variants might be discerned conceptually or from the perspective of the individual actor, on the one hand, and more general practices and institutions in the social world, on the other. In particular, he was a keen analyst of the rise of impersonal, rule-bound, bureaucratic modes of administration in virtually all arenas of modern life, economic, political, cultural, military, and educational. Although some traditional societies had developed decentralized patrimonial organizations in which authority was delegated to subordinates and the arbitrary power of the ruler was curtailed, they lacked "(a) a clearly defined sphere of competence subject to impersonal rules, (b) rational ordering of relations of superiority and inferiority, (c) a regular system of appointment and promotion on the basis of free contract, (d) technical training as a regular requirement, (e) fixed salaries, in the type case paid in money."[104] Separating personal attributes and connections from impersonal office-holding and expert qualifications, rational bureaucracy meant the formalization of statuses, the training in specialized skills, and the circumscription of responsibilities and spheres of competence. Above all, bureaucratic administration involved technical training and "the exercise of control on the basis of knowledge. This is the feature of it which makes it specifically rational."[105]

Although bureaucratic rationalization was an outcome of the intentions of those with the power to challenge traditional procedures in the name of efficiency, Weber observed that it also could gain an impersonal momentum of its own. What was designed as a means could become its own end, especially when it was severed from any consideration of the substantive rationality of the ends or values it might serve. What might be called "functionalist rationalization" functioned largely in the service of its own expansion, colonizing not only areas of the social whole that were not yet rational but also those striving to realize other versions of rationality. The most obvious example of this tendency can be seen in the widely remarked, and frequently bemoaned, momentum of technological rationalization, the imperative to develop new technical tools whose ends were uncertain, an expansion whose inexorable power to shape our lives seemed to recognize no limits.

Rather, however, than characterizing such functionalist rationalization as a single monolithic domination of the world, Weber argued that autonomous processes understood in ideal typical terms can take more than one form. No less significant as an institutional embodiment of modern rationality than bureaucratization or technologization, as Weber saw it, was the differentiation of the rule of law from substantive moral and ethical contexts, as well as from the social, political, religious, or economic power of those who promulgated or were subject to it. If bureaucratic rationalization was depersonalized and formal, so too was its legal counterpart, which was informed by a faith in the law's "rational grounds—resting on a belief in the 'legality' of patterns of normative rules and the rights of those elevated to authority under such rules to issue commands (legal authority)."[106] As opposed to traditional notions of authority based on allegedly immemorial practices and the ascribed status of those with the power to enforce them or charismatic notions of exceptional personal qualities that are unique to a leader, rational-legal authority understood that laws were made, not found, and that they could be changed only by procedures that were themselves rule-bound.[107] The rationalization of law meant systematization into a consistent corpus of binding rules, which were abstract and applicable in consistent ways to particular cases that fell under them. Although there was room for the exercise of judgment about how to interpret the relationship between abstract rules and concrete cases, as well as the exceptional possibility of mercy suspending rules (the circumscribed right of the sovereign to pardon), the fundamental assumption of rational-legal authority was impersonal and universal justice on the basis of equality before the law.

It would, however, be misleading to conclude from Weber's analysis that rationalization was a simple process in which a uniform notion of reason gradually replaced discredited traditional alternatives. The modern world was never fully disenchanted—for good or for ill—and secularization, as any twenty-first-century observer can quickly attest, could be effectively resisted and even reversed.[108] There was, moreover, as Weber himself recognized, a potential tension between bureaucratic rationality and its legal counterpart, at least insofar as enlightened despots were still despotic enough to think they were unconstrained by legal rules and thus able to administer rationally "from above." Here the doctrine of the "reason of state," anticipated by Niccolò Machiavelli and fully developed in the wake of the liberation of the state from universalist

religious authority after the Treaty of Westphalia in 1648, could provide a justification. "Reason of state" could, moreover, complement the idea of a "rational
state," one that would put an end to the incessant confessional violence that
had torn Europe apart since the Reformation. It led, as Foucault was later to
put it, to the belief that "the art of governing is rational, if reflection causes it to
observe the nature of what is governed—here, the *state.*"[109]

In the case of eighteenth-century Germany, what became known as the
*Polizeistaat* (an administrative state) reached its apogee in the Prussia of Frederick
the Great.[110] It employed a strong version of administrative rationalism underpinned philosophically by a no less confident version of substantive reason. It
was not by chance that the absolutist state arose in the wake of disastrous religious wars, just as rationalism was undermining the primacy of revelation and
scripture. As the bitter struggle over Christian Wolff's rationalist philosophy in
the years 1723–40 shows, it was a combination understood to threaten traditional modes of philosophizing and governing alike, and it took a while to
sweep away the obstacles to its triumph.[111] But once they were overcome, a
direct link came to exist between the ideal of benevolent administrative rule, at
least in a number of German states, and the early Enlightenment's emphatic
rationalism. As one observer puts it, "The principle of the common welfare
pragmatically developed in *Polizeiwissenschaft* was sublimated in the philosophical
systems of Leibniz and Wolff. They allied the principle with one of metaphysical
perfection, seeking to establish a 'rational jurisprudence' based on the perfection
of being which would unite logic, metaphysics, and law in a comprehensive
philosophical system."[112]

The ideal of the "police-state," it should be made clear, must not be confused with our contemporary conception of the police as merely a coercive law
enforcement agency, but rather with the benevolent promulgation of rational
rules of good government aiming at the happiness and security of the population. Combining, as Foucault noted, both ancient Greek and Christian notions
of pastoral care, it developed technologies of allegedly benign control.[113] The
secularized, postconfessional state should tolerate different religions rather
than enforcing conformity to one. What in other contexts would be called the
"common weal" was to be achieved by the application of a rational "political
science," the enlightened rule of experts able to know what was best for the
population as a whole. Cameralist economic policies, developed by such academic proponents of *Kammerwissenschaft* as Johann Heinrich Gotlob Justi, aimed
at increasing efficiency and productivity, fostering population growth and
consumption. The soft control of "governmentality," as Foucault was to call it,
began to supplement the harsher applications of coercive state power.[114]
Management of individuals through surveillance and discipline complemented

control of mass populations through statistical analysis of regularities and patterns of biological health and illness, economic prosperity and cyclical decline,
cultural emergence and cultural decay. What at the time was called a "tutelary
state" and in our own day the "soft paternalism" of "the nudge"—or by its critics
the "nanny state"—arrogated to itself the right and responsibility to guide
those in its care, based on the possession of rational truths.[115]

❦

It was against this background of rationalization in the political, legal, and social
spheres, which they also helped to stimulate and justify, that developments
internal to philosophy occurred during the so-called Age of Reason. The work
of the major philosophers who have come to be called Rationalists—René
Descartes, Nicolas Malebranche, Baruch Spinoza, Gottfried Wilhelm von
Leibniz, and Christian Wolff—cannot be reduced to a single coherent program.[116] They differed, for example, over such basic questions as whether God
transcended the world or was immanent in it—the former leading to Deism,
the latter to pantheism—and whether mind was dualistically distinct from
body or ultimately one with it, which pitted Cartesians against Spinozists (who
saw "thought" and "extension" as "attributes" of the same "substance"). They
often heatedly debated the merits of mechanism, fatalism, and materialism.
Some stressed radical discontinuities and ruptures within "being"; others were
advocates of continuity and incremental transformation. Some subordinated
will entirely to reason; others allowed a certain role for the former, at least
when it came to its divine expression. Some began their analyses with the
subject of reason, others with the object, still others with an indifference point
of equiprimordiality prior to that very differentiation. Nor were all major
philosophers of the era devoted followers of the Rationalist position.[117]

  But at least they shared a sufficient number of "family resemblances" to
allow us to continue grouping them together. All were unapologetic metaphysicians, hostile to skepticism and fideism and concerned with absolute rather
than relative knowledge. With few exceptions, they were convinced that reason
in its deductive, intuitive, and noetic form was prior to observation or sense
experience.[118] Virtually all valued universal truths over idiosyncratic differences,
what endured over what was ephemeral, the general over the particular or
individual.[119] Ideas in the mind, they all claimed, were essentially innate rather
than derived from the senses, and knowledge could therefore be certain rather
than merely probable. Even the existence of God could be demonstrated
through rational proofs. For the Rationalists, science—both natural science
and in the broader German sense of *Wissenschaft* as true knowledge—was more

than mere experimentation and inductive or inferential reasoning.[120] Following Descartes, they extolled the virtues of rational method to sweep away the accumulated superstitions, prejudices, and delusions of the past. Its findings, moreover, could be organized in systematic form and ultimately expressed in the rigorous language of mathematics, which cut through the ambiguities of rhetoric and the idiosyncrasies of vernacular tongues.[121] With Leibniz they sought to free formal logic from its embeddedness in ambiguous natural languages and sought to express it in mathematical terms. They adhered to what Pascal had famously called the "spirit of geometry" rather than the "spirit of finesse," in Spinoza's case going to the extreme of even expressing his ideas in geometric form. At their most ambitious, they folded mythos back into logos, embracing that broadest notion of "reason" without worrying that its pedigree might taint its purity.[122] Whatever the nuances of their distinct positions may have been, the early Enlightenment Rationalists assumed that metaphysics and good government, reason and rationalization, were intimately intertwined. Substantive or what might be called an "emphatic" concept of reason and governmental rationalization could be comfortable bedfellows (although as the case of Spinoza shows, it could also foster a protoliberal distrust of strong governmental control).

Or at least they remained so until some time in the late eighteenth century, when the story was complicated by two major developments in the history of reason. First, the critical power of substantive reason was increasingly marshaled to challenge rather than support enlightened despotism. As the intellectual historian Reinhart Koselleck has noted, the critic "enters into competition with a rational State that sets itself above the religious groupings. . . . The alliance between reason and the existing State had disintegrated. . . . The pro and con of criticism, which had followed its non-political course within the Republic of Letters, turned into a trial between the *Règne de la Critique* [the reign of criticism] and the rule of the State."[123] What has been called "the radical Enlightenment" by Margaret Jacob, sometimes understood as a result of the underground diffusion of Spinoza's ideas in particular, could be turned against the elitist assumption that only those with the right educational credentials and political status could serve as the rational tutors of humankind.[124] Institutions outside the purview of the state or the university, such as the Masonic Lodges, could act as the disseminators of rational ideas. The Baron d'Holbach, materialist, atheist, believer in the universal applicability of the scientific method, may have still harbored a residual faith in established authorities to further political rationalization, but far more subversive figures like Denis Diderot and Joseph Priestley could advocate the restriction of the Church's interference in politics and the implementation of popular sovereignty and individual human rights.[125]

   Tellingly, the French Revolution drew on the same metaphoric link between reason and the sun that can be traced all the way back to the Greeks and that so often underpinned the Enlightenment praise of clarity and transparency.[126] Wresting away solar glory from divine monarchs like Louis XIV, the "Sun King," the philosophes transferred it to historical processes of a more secular kind. As Jean Starobinski has observed,

> metaphors of light triumphing over darkness, life being reborn out of death, and the world being brought back to its beginning were to be found everywhere in the period leading up to 1789. For these simple similes and ageless antitheses, charged from time immemorial with religious values, that age seemed to have a special and passionate predilection. Once the old order had been reduced to the semblance of a dark cloud or cosmic scourge, the struggle against it could, by the same process, represent its object as the advent of light. Once the self-evidence of reason and feeling took on the force of a law of light, any relationship of authority or obedience that was not based upon it was bound to belong to darkness.[127]

For a brief period during the Revolution, at the height of its campaign of de-Christianization, there was even an attempt to establish a new "Cult of Reason," which celebrated a national holiday on November 10, 1793 (or the twentieth Brumaire, Year II of the Republican calendar). The ultra-left, sans-culotte-supported faction around Jacques Hébert, Antoine-François Momoro, Pierre-Gaspard Chaumette, and Joseph Fouché reconsecrated churches, including Notre Dame in Paris, as "temples of Reason." Inscribing "To Philosophy" over the door of the cathedral and lining the entrance with busts of famous philosophes, the organizers went so far as to direct their devotion to the "goddess of Reason" (or perhaps "the goddess of Liberty," according to some accounts). To avoid any hint of superstitious idolatry, she was embodied in an actual live woman, a kind of homecoming queen for the festival of "reason."[128]

   Although the Hébertists were to lose a deadly power struggle in the spring of 1794 with Maximilien Robespierre, who promoted a more cautious Deist "Cult of the Supreme Being," the link between "reason" and revolution they had so avidly promoted allowed critics of the French Revolution, at least from Edmund Burke on,[129] to argue that it was the evil spawn of Rationalist metaphysicians imposing abstract theory onto the messiness of the real world in a vain utopian hope of rationalization from below. The alliance between the counter-Enlightenment and political conservatism, already brewing in the *ancien régime*, was solidified in opposition to the identification of revolution with the resurgence of an emphatic conception of substantive reason, which ironically could justify violence and terror. Indeed the seeds for this outcome were sometimes discerned even earlier by latter-day defenders of the virtues of corporatist traditions, when enlightened despotism justified the *Polizeistaat's* modernization from above through a putatively benevolent *Polizeiwissenschaft* promoting the welfare of all.[130]

The second important innovation in the second half of the eighteenth century was the emergence of several alternative models of reason to challenge— although never completely replace—the hegemony of the substantive, metaphysical version underpinning the absolutist *Polizeistaat* and the radical Enlightenment alike.[131] If, after all, the proponents of that emphatic version could not themselves agree on what "reason" dictated, the door was open for still other possibilities to emerge. Just as the alliance between "reason," understood in its strongest substantive guise, and the Enlightened *Polizeistaat* became strained, so too the simple equation of "reason" and critique underwent a reconsideration, at least so far as the former was identified with the metaphysical certainties of the Rationalist tradition. Critique, that is, could be applied by figures like Pierre Bayle in the name of another, more skeptical concept of reason, which disdained the dogmatism it saw in the metaphysical systems it could no longer support. With the onset of the so-called pantheism dispute in the 1780s surrounding the allegedly fatalist and atheistic implications of Spinoza's legacy, the crisis of metaphysical rationalism came to a head.[132]

One alternative drew on the nascent field of aesthetics, articulated by theorists like Alexander Baumgarten in Germany and Anthony Ashley-Cooper, the third Earl of Shaftesbury, in England, in which judgment about matters of taste resisted being deductively subsumed under general rules or principles.[133] The most influential development of aesthetic theory came in Kant's third critique, *The Critique of Judgment*, published in 1790. Here he first formulated a crucial distinction between reflective and determinant judgments, the former based on analogical reasoning and paradigmatic cases, the latter on subsumptive principles applied to examples of those principles. Each could underpin distinct modes of reasoning. The reason based on reflective judgments was more intersubjective and fallibilist than the model informing *Polizeiwissenschaft*. Aesthetic reasoning also worked to overcome the gap between mind and body, which more logical and deductive notions of reason had widened; the senses and the pleasure they might foster were not necessarily understood as one of the "others" of rational thought.[134] The "animal" in the *animal rationale* need not be suppressed, as aestheticians rediscovered the virtues of play and sensual fulfillment, and ceased seeing them as the antitheses of reason. Indeed, the materialist tradition of the late Enlightenment in general, perhaps best exemplified by Diderot, celebrated the senses and corporeal desires as compatible with reason.

A second alternative to the *Polizeistaat* supported by Rationalist metaphysics reflected the increasing power of the economic market and civil society in which reason could be located primarily in individual decisions rather than mandated by an all-knowing, benevolent state administration with its cameralist paternalism. Reason had long been identified with reckoning or calculating in the service of self-preservation, which came especially to the fore when ratiocination as a profane mental operation supplanted reason as a faculty of the soul, a subjective, strategic activity, not a holy thing.[135] Thomas Hobbes, for example, had defined it this way in his *Leviathan* of 1651, although employing it to generate a social contract theory that culminated in a strong, absolutist state to preserve the peace.[136] When anxiety about security waned in Britain, as it did after the end of the religious and political turmoil of the seventeenth century, it was possible to retain the emphasis on individual rational calculation but diminish the importance of a strong state to maintain order. Bernard de Mandeville's early eighteenth-century *Fable of the Bees*, a poem first published in 1705, advanced the then scandalous claim that "private vices" could really be "public virtues." Now an underlying rational harmony was assumed to exist between those individual rational choices and the rational functioning of the system as a whole. Here the assumption of inherent self-organization, a principle historians have recently discerned in a wide range of intellectual and cultural phenomena, de-emphasized the need for intentional intervention.[137] The growth of a relatively autonomous economic sector in society meant that bureaucratic rationality, involving rationalization from above, could be challenged by a functional rationality in which individual, self-interested rational choices—or indeed, choices driven by desires that were unnecessary to justify rationally—could be understood as leading, albeit indirectly, to a rational outcome for society as a whole. What in our time returned as "rational choice theory" had its roots in this period.[138]

By the time of Adam Smith's *Wealth of Nations* in 1776, the scandal had died down, as individual "interests" were substituted for "vices" as the motor of collective rational outcomes (understood as increasing abundance and productivity).[139] Rationalization of the economy could mean creating a free space for the operation of allegedly natural economic laws, which were no longer thwarted by the welter of historically inherited or administratively imposed constraints—tariffs, monopolies, corporations, guilds, and the like—that impeded free markets in labor and capital investment. Although in the British Utilitarian tradition identified with Jeremy Bentham and James Mill, faith in the unimpeded workings of the market wavered for a while and administrative rationality enjoyed a brief revival, by the heyday of "Manchesterite liberalism" in the mid-nineteenth century, it had once again regained momentum.

Yet a third alternative to the administrative rationalization of the *Polizeistaat* allied with the systematic rationalism of the early Enlightenment appeared in the growing circumscription of absolute power through the increased pressure to adopt constitutional and legal procedures limiting the arbitrary will of even the most enlightened and benevolent of despots. An uneven process, varying from state to state, often ironically enabled by violent rebellion, the growth of what Weber called "rational-legal authority" meant the identification of reason not so much with administrative efficiency or the functional outcomes of individual rational choices as with the accretion of formal legal rules and procedures applicable to all in the society, no matter their status or function. Although the idea of "the rule of law" can be traced as far back as Aristotle, and was popularized as a slogan by the British legal theorist A. V. Dicey only in the nineteenth century,[140] it was already a force in the Enlightenment in parts of Europe. Ironically, it could function as a means to temper the arbitrary will of absolute sovereigns, who were no longer allegedly "enlightened" despots "above" the law, as well as serve as a check on the potential for exploitation and injustice in the marketplace. Although important antecedents can be found as early as the Roman Empire, where a system of justice was developed based on equity for all free citizens, only the modern era came to believe that laws were made, not found.[141]

In the German context, the transition occurred from a *Polizeistaat* to what was called a *Rechtsstaat* (State under the rule of law) during the Reform Era (1807-19), associated with Karl Freiherr vom Stein and Karl August Fürst von Hardenberg in Prussia, after the Napoleonic Wars. The "state of laws" differed from Leibniz's "rational jurisprudence" in its reluctance to mandate substantive laws designed to assure human happiness. Instead, it stressed constitutional constraints on absolute power, the importance of a healthy civil society in balance with the state, and judicial review of legislative decisions. Because of its proceduralist emphasis, the *Rechtsstaat* tended to bracket the issue of the ultimate rational purpose of the laws, as well as their putative source in an allegedly rational *Polizeiwissenschaft*. Although it too relied on the *ultima ratio* of state coercion—the "force" in "law enforcement"—it hoped that internalized adherence to laws that were at least formally rational rather than arbitrary (and ensuing, for a few who dared to dream, from the democratic practice of legislation, made by the people's representatives themselves) would diminish the role of external power in producing compliance.[142]

A final alternative to the alliance of substantive reason and administrative rationality from above or political radicalism from below was the looser identification of it with the "common sense" of the average citizen. From the ancient Greeks to Giambattista Vico, *sensus communis*, once literally meaning a common sense combining the other five, had accrued a variety of different denotations and connotations.[143] Although reason and common sense, like reason and experience, were often opposed, they could also be blended together, if somewhat uneasily. Tom Paine, after all, was the author not only of *The Age of Reason* but also of the enormously influential pamphlet *Common Sense* of 1776. As the intellectual historian Sophia Rosenfeld has argued,

> there existed more than one kind of reason, and during the years of the so-called High Enlightenment, the very basic, low-level, quotidian form of reason associated with "good sense" often found itself pitted against the system-building Scholastic logic of theology or Cartesianism, as well as against pedantry of all kinds. What made *le bon sens* distinct as a subset of the larger category "reason" was that it was understood to be premised neither upon scholarly erudition nor upon contemplative leisure time given over to complex thinking. Rather, it depended solely upon the experiences and observations common to everyday life.[144]

Although experience and utility could be turned against reason *tout court* rather than be understood as compatible with it, as was the case with a conservative like David Hume in his more skeptical moments, they could also become potent allies in the struggle against superstition, dogmatism, and revelation.[145] Rather than seeing reason as the preserve of the educated few or those with the gift of noetic intuition, it might be possible to understand it as disseminated among the population as a whole, even if underdeveloped and always in competition with other impulses and mental faculties. Rather than a monologic tool of either syllogistic logic or scientific observation, it could be understood as a dialogic practice of intersubjective, public communication in which all might participate. As in the case of the scientific method, broadly understood, it favored inductive over deductive reasoning, learning from experiences rather than imposing a priori categories on them. But rather than disdaining the ambiguities of seductive rhetoric, as was the case with stringent defenders of *episteme* against *doxa* ever since Plato, it acknowledged the virtues of oral eloquence and metaphor, allowing it to play an important role in the aesthetic theorizing of Shaftesbury and Kant. Resisting the privileging of the eyes, typical of rationalism from Plato to Descartes, it took seriously the claims of the ear in the process of reasoning, the role of listening to the opinions and arguments of others. Indeed, in the guise of "reasonableness," implying a willingness to compromise and consider with an open mind the reasons of others, "common sense" could become a weapon against the allegedly unrealistic, even utopian fantasies of arrogant rationalizers bent on imposing their understanding of reason on a recalcitrant world.

All of these alternative concepts of reason—aesthetic, economic, legal, commonsensical—cumulatively undermined the hegemony of the metaphysical giants of the seventeenth century. Whether or not they had ever really believed in a fully rationalist "heavenly city" no less scholastic than that of their Christian predecessors, as the American intellectual historian Carl Becker famously asserted, may be debatable, but clearly their successors did not.[146] As the next century dawned, so Ernst Cassirer contended in his celebrated account of the Enlightenment—a work, let it be noted, by a neo-Kantian philosopher who came to understand the importance of history—the mood had radically changed. The ambitious *esprit de système* of the earlier Rationalists was succeeded by a more modest *esprit systématique*, in which reason lost some of its hubris, backed away from the love of systems for their own sakes, and began to acknowledge its fracturing into a pluralism of meanings.

In the entry on reason in the great *Encyclopedia* of Denis Diderot and Jean le Rond d'Alembert, there is an expression of that transition, if with residues of the previous era. In it, reason is variously defined as (1) "simply and in the broadest sense that natural faculty with which God endowed men to know truth, whatever light it follows, and to whatever class of subjects it applies"; (2) "this same faculty considered, not absolutely, but only inasmuch as it functions in accordance with certain notions, which we bring with us at birth, and that are common to all men of the world"; (3) "that very natural light by which the faculty that we refer to by this name is guided. It is in this way that one ordinarily understands the term when one is speaking of a proof, or of an objection taken from reason, and which one wants to distinguish in this way from proofs and objections grounded in divine or human authority"; and (4) "the sequence of truths that the human mind can attain naturally, without being aided by the light of faith. The truths of reason are of two types: some are what one calls eternal truths, which are absolutely necessary, to the point that the opposite would imply contradiction. Such are truths of which the necessity is logical, metaphysical, or geometric. One could not overturn these truths without being led to absurdities. There are others that could be called positive truths, because they are the laws that it pleased God to give to nature, or because they depend on nature. We learn them either by experience, that is to say, *a posteriori*, or by reason, and *a priori*, that is to say by considerations of convenience that caused them to be preferred."[147]

The Encyclopedists may have advocated the supremacy of reason over faith bestowed by nature and shared by all humans—"we are men," they insisted, "before we are Christians"[148]—and thought it was applicable everywhere, but it is clear that they saw it only as a dispositional faculty of human knowledge, enabling the quest for truth, and not an inherent quality of the world. Paraphrasing d'Alembert and Étienne Bonnot de Condillac, Cassirer wrote that the eighteenth century came to understand reason "not as a sound body of knowledge, principles, and truths, but as a kind of energy, a force which is fully comprehensible only in its agency and effects. What reason is, and what it can do, can never be known by its results but only function."[149] That function came, as previously noted, to be identified primarily with critique, the imperative to dissolve the residues of illegitimate authority, tradition, and revelation.

Cassirer's characterization of the Enlightenment has itself been subjected to many criticisms since its appearance in 1932.[150] But his insight that an early metaphysical rationalism, optimistic about discovering the inherent rationality of the universe, had given way to a more modest critical reasoning, which increasingly accepted the limits of what might be known by even the most rigorous of rational or scientific methods, has stood the test of time. So too has his insight that the age of critical reason was itself soon to end, as the oscillation between rationality's critical or even destructive impulses and the urge to construct anew, between analysis and synthesis, went through another cycle when the Enlightenment itself declined. In the nineteenth century, Cassirer observed, the pendulum swung once again in the opposite direction, for "reason cannot stop with the dispersed parts; it has to build from them a new structure, a new whole. But since reason creates this whole and fits the parts together according to its own rule, it gains complete knowledge of the structure of its product. Reason understands this structure because it can reproduce it in its totality and in the ordered sequence of its individual elements."[151]

In the evolution of German Idealism in particular, which passed from a critical to a speculative stage, occurred a mirror reversal of the Enlightenment pattern, in which a deflationary concept of reason, one conscious of its limits, now gave way to an inflationary one, in which those limits were eagerly transgressed. A "broad church" notion of reason now prevailed. Even though it too, in turn, lost its momentum and was succeeded by an even more radical disenchantment, even a frank embrace of irrationalism, the legacy of the German Idealist discourse of reason still resonated for the Frankfurt School and indeed remains potent well into the twenty-first century. Its elaboration in the work of Kant and Hegel must be examined before then turning to its legacy in the work of Idealism's avowed foe, Karl Marx.

# 2

# Kant

## Reason as Critique; the Critique of Reason

By any measure, the most penetrating critical reconsideration of the foundations and limits of reason in the late Enlightenment came from the pen of the
Königsberg philosopher Immanuel Kant. He had begun his career under the
spell of Wolffian rationalism at its most emphatic, and then lost his faith, having
being awakened, in his celebrated phrase, from his "dogmatic slumber" by
reading the skeptical David Hume.[1] But rather than accept the defeat of reason
as final, he sought to establish a more viable alternative that would resist
Hume's withering criticisms. Refusing, we might say, to loiter in the shadow of
an eclipsed metaphysical rationalism, he emerged, as Habermas was likewise to
do two centuries later, once again into the light when it had passed. His "critical
philosophy" rejected both dogmatic rationalism and skeptical empiricism,
seeking to build a securer foundation for a still undetermined metaphysics of
the future.

In political terms, Kant also rejected the enlightened despotism that had
been supported by deductive rationalism at its most paternalistic. If Leibniz
and Wolff could be understood as the philosophical apologists of the *Polizeistaat*,
it was Kant who best articulated the principles of what came to be called the
*Rechtsstaat*, with its more limited notion of reason as formal and procedural.
Although he was an unqualified admirer of the Frederick the Great who could
warn his subjects *"argue* all you want and about whatever you want, *but obey!"*[2]
and could himself deny citizens the right to rebel against authority in the name
of mere happiness,[3] his exaltation of the value of autonomy and stress on the
role of critique led Reinhart Koselleck to argue that Kant had "clearly spelled

out the claim of criticism to pre-eminence over the State."[4] As we have seen, he tellingly employed the metaphor of reason as a tribunal, which ruled by formal laws that were universally applicable. Kant's defense of the rule of humanly created positive law against the arbitrary will of even the most benevolent of enlightened despots was no less influential.

In addition, to return to the other alternatives to the *Polizeistaat* we explored in the previous chapter, the distinction he made in *The Critique of Judgment* between reflective and determinant judgments, which was a cornerstone of aesthetic reasoning, could later become a model for democratic politics as well.[5] Likewise, Kant's acquaintance with the economic and moral theories of the Scottish Enlightenment—and its epistemological skepticism articulated best by Hume—meant that he was no stranger to the arguments for the beneficial effects of free markets.[6] His stress on individual judgment and responsibility could be seen as compatible with Adam Smith's notion of individual choices in the marketplace following more than mere unmediated desire.[7] And finally, although he scorned the "Common Sense" school of philosophy associated with figures like Thomas Reid, James Beattie, and James Oswald, he reintroduced the old notion of *sensus communis* in his analysis of aesthetic judgment.[8] His commitment to the public, intersubjective use of reason rather than a purely monological one has sometimes been seen in *The Critique of Pure Reason* (1781) as well.[9]

It is, of course, to the first Critique that we must turn to appreciate fully Kant's contribution to the discourse of reason in the modern world, including its exploration in the later work of the Frankfurt School. Although attempts are still made today to resurrect the emphatic metaphysical variant promulgated by the Rationalists of the early Enlightenment—Spinoza in particular continues to have his passionate defenders[10]—it is with Kant's first Critique that any serious self-critical account of reason must begin. Before grappling with his attempt to defend a more modest version of reason that would survive the withering criticism of skeptics like Hume, we should make clear what separates him from the emphatic concept of reason so prevalent in the early Enlightenment. Kant was not opposed to metaphysics—in fact, he entitled his 1783 précis of the argument of the first Critique *Prolegomena to Any Future Metaphysics That Will Be Able to Present Itself as a Science*—but he was sharply critical of the Rationalist metaphysics that had been developed before him. In this sense, he was a member of the narrow rather than broad church of reason, determined to build defensible walls around an enclave that was endangered from without. Deductive reason, innate ideas, noetic intuition, the identity of rational thought and rational being, rational proofs for the existence of God—all of these had been left behind when he awoke from his dogmatic slumber. So too was the belief, fundamental to the rationalizing project of the *Polizeistaat*, that reason could provide any guidance for the realization of human happiness, which was too idiosyncratic to follow any rule.[11]

Perhaps the most fundamental difference between the Rationalists and Kant was their attitude toward the "principle of sufficient reason," *nihil est sine ratione* (nothing is without a reason) or sometimes *nihil fit sine ratione* (nothing comes to pass without a reason). Spinoza, Malebranche, and, above all, Leibniz had made it into a cornerstone of their philosophies, although versions of it can be detected in all of the Rationalists.[12] Noetically intuited, rather than dianoetically justified, it was derived from the ancient Greek word αἴτιον (*aition*), which in Latin became *causa*.[13] Originally it implied responsibility, and thus suggested an agent who acted intentionally, but by the time it became a more general term, "cause" came increasingly to imply unintended, even impersonal forces, which were nondispositional rather than strictly dispositional. Both causes and purposes—the latter defensible by reasons—could serve as explanatory grounds. Thus, Aristotle's famous four "causes" (efficient, formal, material, and teleological) went beyond what today we would more narrowly construe as a cause.

In the thirty-first and thirty-second sections of his *Monadology*, Leibniz had claimed that all of our reasoning is based on two fundamental principles: the principle of contradiction and the principle of sufficient reason, the former serving to ground necessary truths, the latter contingent ones. That is, not only could logic be understood to have a firm foundation in a rational principle, but so could the seemingly random and haphazard facts of the experienced world, which were not, despite appearances, unmoored from rational intelligibility. For Leibniz, every contingent occurrence, every particular fact, had a reason-cum-cause; none was ungrounded. Here the nominalist impulse in his philosophy, his belief in the individuality of monads irreducible to general principles or intelligible forms, led him to claim that there was sufficient reason even in apparently inexplicable and meaningless events and facts. Not only generic categories but also individual proper names with all of their idiosyncratic experiences were rationally grounded.[14] To deny this truth would be to say that some things cannot be explained or interpreted, even by God. But we cannot imagine, he argued, an effect without a cause, even if we may not immediately understand all of them. The principle of sufficient reason served many purposes for Leibniz's philosophy. According to Amos Funkenstein,

> On the ontological level, it is both a criterion of reality (possibility and compossibility) *and* a criterion of God's choice (existence). The latter, inasmuch as it is reasonable (but strictly speaking it need not be), has the same reasons as the former. On the epistemological level, it is a criterion of

objectivity of the phenomenal world, by which we assess the relative degree of reality . . . of our mental representations and constructs. On the methodological, scientific level, it is a criterion of choice among hypotheses.[15]

The principle of sufficient reason, according to some commentators, may itself be based on an analytic notion of truth as identity of subject and predicate, which presupposes the principle of contradiction.[16] But whether or not this was the case for Leibniz is less important for our purposes than an even more basic premise of his argument, which he spelled out in his 1710 *Theodicy*: the omnipotence, omniscience, and benevolence of a rational, rather than willful or capricious, God, a God who has created the "best of all possible worlds."[17] Like Descartes with his faith in a beneficent God who cannot by his nature deceive or be inconsistent, but going beyond the Frenchman's stress on the initial importance of arbitrary divine will, Leibniz posited a divinity whose very nature was to be in accord with reason. Otherwise he would not be a God worthy of our devotion. Natural causes are merely the reverse side of the coin from divine reasons. Events are thus rationally grounded as well as caused.[18] The fact that reality can be understood in the universally valid language of mathematics — Leibniz himself was a brilliant mathematician and the inventor of integral calculus — testifies to its inherent intelligibility.

The moral implications of this argument were also profound. For even seeming evil could be justified, or at least understood, as serving a larger good. Unlike Spinoza, Leibniz stressed the importance of final causes as a key explanation of the intelligibility of reality. Indeed, that intelligibility, he argued, was the ultimate reason (final cause) for the existence of the world, because it allowed us to appreciate the constitutive power of reason itself. The circularity of this argument did not bother Leibniz, nor did its latent anthropomorphic underpinnings. Human reason blessed with innate ideas was in harmony with the divine mind, but only because Leibniz's version of the latter was implicitly modeled on the human capacity to act purposely on the basis of consciously intended goals. The harmony of the cosmos was like the harmony of a musical composition. Whichever was the prior model, the theodicial lesson was clear: we should learn to accept even apparent evil as part of a larger beneficent plan.

But when that optimistic premise came under fire, as it famously did when Leibniz's theodicy was challenged by events like the War of the Austrian Succession (1740–48), the Seven Years War (1756–63), and most spectacularly by the devastating Lisbon earthquake of November 1, 1755,[19] the intuitive self-evidence of a rational *meaning* — a plausible justification as more than just a natural *cause* — for even the most contingent of events seemed harder to support. Faith in benign Providence or pre-established harmony wavered, although some of it was displaced onto the invisible hand doctrine of the classical economists.[20] As Werner Hamacher has suggested, the shaking of the literal ground in the earth-quake rattled faith in the rational grounding of metaphysics and ethics.[21] Or rather it did so for most philosophers, while allowing some adherents of religious belief to this very day to invoke "God's plan" or the ineffability of his "mysterious ways" as a consolation for disaster.

Two major conclusions were drawn by critics of the more emphatic Rationalist notion of reason, one for epistemology, the other for morality. Hume argued that causality could not be intuited or proven as an underlying rational principle in the natural world, even if there were correlations between what appeared to be a cause and its effect.[22] Or more precisely, he said that while there may well be causal grounds for events, we fallible humans cannot know them with any certainty. We can admittedly use "probable reasoning" to orient ourselves in a world in which predictions about the regularities of events were often right, but we cannot fall back on the intuitive belief that our minds and the divine mind are ultimately one.[23] "Reasonable" men may act *as if* the principle of sufficient reason obtained and natural science could be based on occult causes, but there can be no rational certainty that we are right. Conversely there could be no certainty that we are wrong either, as some things are simply beyond human ability to prove or disprove. In this sense, not only does the noetic faculty fail us; so does dianoetic reasoning show its limits. We are left to cope as best we can with habit, experience, faith, and probability. Kant drew on Hume's critique of the metaphysical grounds of the principle of sufficient reason to deny certain knowledge of intelligible causes, although, as we will see, he rejected his more skeptical conclusions.

Secondly, the moral implication of the unraveling of Leibniz's optimistic theodicy drawn by many was that we cannot discern an inherent justice in the playing out of contingent events. Teleological purposes, if they exist, are not amenable to human ken; and if they do exist, they are so unfathomable, so occult, that they contradict our normal sense of justice. Not only does this mean that we have to question the certainty and universality of our moral judgments, which may be culture-bound rather than absolute, but it also means that the conflation of causes with reasons under the umbrella term "ground," which was assumed by the principle of sufficient reason, is harder to sustain. For although there may be *causal* explanations for the earthquake, to which our science can give probable if not certain access, there are no plausible *reasons*, no meaningful excuses, and no moral justifications why a benevolent God could unleash so much suffering on the innocent. Kant thus had to find another ground for morality than the Rationalists' confidence that a greater good could emerge out of lesser evils (even if it was to reappear in some of his more marginal writings).

Although the explicit distinction between cause and reason had to await Arthur Schopenhauer's *On the Fourfold Root of the Principle of Sufficient Reason* of 1813,[24] its presence can be felt in the difference between the idea of reason in Kant's first and second Critiques. Ironically, the young Kant, twenty-four and still a metaphysical Rationalist when the Lisbon earthquake struck, had taken a very keen interest in the debate over its causes and meaning. Not only did he attempt a scientific account of its origin—no less a commentator than Walter Benjamin was to call it "the beginnings of scientific geography in Germany. And certainly the beginnings of seismology"—but also directly contributed to the debates about optimism and theodicy.[25] Here he resisted Voltaire's disillusionment and upheld a still benign view of rational nature. In his pre-critical works, in fact, he staunchly defended a metaphysical concept of the principle of sufficient reason.[26]

But after his life-changing encounter with the skeptical challenges of Hume, Kant came to very different conclusions. As he pondered the collapse of his earlier metaphysical assumptions, but resisted the full implications of Humean skepticism, he formulated the remarkable alternative to both that became known as his "critical" philosophy, drawing explicitly on the original Greek word *krinein* for separating and judging.[27] We live, he argued, in an "age of critique," to which even religion, despite its sanctity, and legislation, despite its majesty, must submit, for only if they do so will they earn genuine respect rather than blind obedience. Merely to assert or intuit truths dogmatically was not enough; they must become the object of unflinching scrutiny.

Indeed reason itself, not in the sense of mere book-learning but rather as our very power or faculty (*Vermögen*) of reasoning, the ability to draw inferential conclusions using logical means, must also open itself to critique (or more precisely, reflexive self-critique). For an overweening rationalism, a rationalism optimistically grounded in the principle of sufficient reason, led to contradictions, antinomies, paralogisms, and aporiae. Rather than falling back on a dubious assumption that human minds somehow shared with divine intelligence innate ideas that needed no experiential source or confirmation, he took seriously the challenge to defend a more modest dispositional notion of rationality that would not depend on the principle of sufficient reason. Whereas the latter tacitly turned humans into passive participants in a heteronomous process based on the inherent rationality of a world divinely created, the former attributed to them the autonomy of those whose reason was ultimately their own.

Adorno would see in Kant's delicate balancing act—his self-reflexive division of reason into both an organon of criticism and its target, at once tribunal and accused—not an inconsistency or hesitation but rather "the sign of an extraordinary seriousness. That is to say, the Enlightenment can only achieve fulfillment if its own meaning, which is the idea of truth, is retained, and if, in the midst of the dialectical movement to which these concepts are subjected, the concepts still survive. This glorious insight is present in Kant."[28] Or to put it another way, Kant's appreciation of the limits of reason never led to his being tempted by a return to mythic thought or intuitive mysticism, as was the case with so many of his compatriots,[29] but rather to a sober attempt to work within those limits with as much self-critical rigor as his powers would permit. Both a vindication and critique of reason, his work was a delicate balance that always seemed in danger of going too far in one direction or the other.

There can be few texts in the history of philosophy as exhaustively analyzed as *The Critique of Pure Reason*, in which some seventeen distinct uses of *Vernunft* have been distinguished, and it would serve no useful purpose to present yet another detailed account of its arguments or elaboration of its strengths and deficiencies.[30] But there are some general points that warrant emphasis. One, as we have suggested, is Kant's attempt to limit the cognitive use of reason in order, not merely "to make room for faith,"[31] as he famously admitted in the preface to the second edition, but also to justify a more viable notion of reason itself, to make room, in the words of Hannah Arendt, "for thought."[32] As the celebrated opening of the preface to the first edition of the *Critique of Pure Reason* acknowledged, "human reason has a peculiar fate in one kind of its cognitions: it is troubled by questions that it cannot dismiss, because they are posed to it by the nature of reason itself, but that it also cannot answer, because they surpass human reason's every ability."[33]

Although it took Kant almost three hundred pages to arrive at his elaborated critique of the Rationalists' "transcendental illusions," where he spelled out the ways in which those questions were erroneously answered, his target from the beginning was the unreflective dogmatism he saw in Rationalist metaphysics: "the pretension that we can make progress by means of no more than a pure cognition from concepts (i.e., philosophical cognition) in accordance with principles—such concepts and principle as reason has been using for a long time—without inquiring in the manner and the right by which reason has arrived at them."[34] The fundamental flaw of Rationalist metaphysics was its noetic, unjustified assumption that there were no limits to reason's ability to *know* the world. It was a version of reason that arrogantly called itself "pure," because it refused to credit the role of sense experience in our acquisition of knowledge about a world that was external to our minds: "pure reason is that reason which contains the principles for cognizing something absolutely *a priori*."[35] It was "speculative" because it narcissistically assumed a perfect mirroring of a sufficiently rational world, guaranteed by a nondeceiving God, in the minds of the fallible humans who claimed to know it. "Pure reason," Kant charged, "is in fact occupied with nothing but itself. Nor can it have any other business. For what are given to it are not objects for the unity of the experiential concept, but cognitions of understanding for the unity of the concept of reason, i.e., for the unity of coherence in a principle."[36] In other words, Kant argued, "human reason is by its nature architectonic,"[37] seeking to build a coherent, self-contained system on firm foundations.

In the place of a constitutive notion of architectonic, systematic, grounded reason, in which the world was its outcome, reason was best understood only as a regulative principle, guiding our attempts to understand that world. For knowledge to be more than solipsistic, it must get beyond the radical immanence of speculative reflection and conceptual self-sufficiency and encounter a coherent world outside the knower. But for it to be more than mere acquaintance with isolated sense impressions of that world, it had to assume something it could not justifiably know: that reality was a system of regularities that were discernable by scientific investigation.

Following Hume, Kant argued that we do have to begin by drawing on sense experience, albeit rightly understood, as the alternative to speculative reflection, for "there can be no doubt that all our cognition begins with experience."[38] In one sense, this also meant returning to Descartes's starting point, which was the subject of experience, although Kant did not then follow Descartes in going all the way back to a full-fledged positive metaphysics based on the inherent rationality of the world. Kant's celebrated metaphor of a "Copernican Revolution" in philosophy suggested that he was reversing the priority of reason as inherently existing in the world—an assumption that could no longer be taken for granted—to reason as a critical tool of the mind.[39] In so doing, he hoped to prevent slipping down the Humean slope to uncertainty, probability, opinion, and philodoxy (the uncritical love of creed).

To avoid that outcome, Kant contended that although cognition begins with experience, it does not entirely arise from it, as empiricists since John Locke had contended with their image of the mind as a blank tabula rasa passively recording impressions from without. Instead, he argued that there was indeed a crucial role for the a priori faculties of the mind in cognition, although not as the source of substantive ideas. Instead, they were structuring principles, ways of organizing the data of consciousness into coherent "objects of experience," but, *pace* the Rationalists, not objects in themselves. Because these principles were shared by all humans—and this was the basic premise that allowed Kant to avoid subjectivist relativism and individual solipsism—he called them "transcendental," which he defined as "all cognition that deals not so much with objects as rather with our way of cognizing objects in general insofar as their way of cognizing is to be possible *a priori*. A *system* of such concepts would be called *transcendental philosophy*."[40] That is, deeper than the individual psychological subject merely registering what came from the senses, or what would be worse, a self that was made up solely of those sense impressions, was a unifying mental faculty structuring our experiences. Not only did it provide a sense of meaningful continuity for the integrated and enduring subject doing the cognizing, but it also allowed him to identify objects in the world that also survive the moment of fleeting impressions of their existence. As in the case of logical operations with concepts, inferential reasoning is employed to enable the judgments we make about our sensory experience. And it does so as our perceptions are being registered, not through belated reflection on them.

Kant remained enough of a traditional Rationalist to value coherence and systematicity, and to believe that the transcendental structuring power of the mind could be organized architechtonically, that is, based on firm foundations or grounds like those undergirding a stable building; foundations, as we will see shortly, that included a weaker version of the principle of sufficient reason. The building, however, should avoid trying to rise too high and reach truths we cannot know in the manner of metaphysical rationalism. As he put it with an allusion to the Tower of Babel, "we found, to be sure, that although we had in mind to build a tower that was to reach to heaven, yet our supply of materials sufficed only for a dwelling just spacious enough for the tasks that we perform on the level of experience, and just high enough for us to survey these tasks."[41] But validated by what he called a "transcendental deduction," the categories of the knowing mind were, Kant claimed, impervious to doubt.[42] The terra firma of understanding or intellect (*Verstand*) is, however, "an island, and is enclosed by nature itself within unchangeable bounds. It is the land of truth (a charming name), and is surrounded by a vast and stormy ocean, where illusion properly resides and stray fog banks and much fast-melting ice feigns new-found lands."[43] Thus for Kant, as Adorno was to note, "the task facing reason is not to discover whether it is internally coherent—for the validity of logic is every-where taken for granted and reason itself is held to be identical with logical thinking. Instead the meaning of Kantian reason is always that reason should reflect on its own possible relationship with objects of different kinds."[44] In particular, when extended too far in the effort to discern rational grounds for objects in themselves, not just objects of experience, as in the metaphysical "principle of sufficient reason," it led to the "transcendental illusions" of dialec-tical *Vernunft*, dangerously allowing us to "stray into intelligible worlds."[45] It was wrong, for example, for mortal humans to claim *knowledge* of the immortality of the soul, which could never be an object of experience open to synthetic a priori judgments while we were alive, although of course we can have a *thought* of an immortal soul after our deaths. Our cognitive judgments can neither affirm nor deny the validity of such thoughts, which we can justifiably hold only as matters of faith.

But when it came to objects of experience, Kant held on to a modified version of the principle of sufficient reason, which he redescribed entirely in epistemological rather than ontological terms, equivalent only to the variant called *ratio cognoscendi* (ground of knowledge) in his pre-critical days. Like Leibniz, he sought to find a rational principle underlying contingent realities, those that were not tautological identities but rather events in the temporal world in which causes were antecedent to their effects and not, as Spinoza had contended, simultaneous *causa sui* (self-caused). Real grounds should not be confused with logical ones. But unlike Leibniz, he sought to justify the former not in ontological or substantial terms but rather in ones derived from our shared cognitive structuring capacities, or as Béatrice Longueness puts it, "the *objective unity of self-consciousness* (namely . . . the unity and numerical identify of the self-conscious act of combining representation), which is now the *transcendental ground (Bestimmungsgrund)* of grounds (reason*s*) and of the principle of sufficient reason itself."[46] It was, in other words, in the propositions or assertoric judgments we make about the world, rather than in the world in itself, that reason plays a role. Whether or not his depiction of that role was itself exaggerated—especially because he seems to have believed that judgment itself followed transcendental rules when it applied general principles to specific cases—was an issue that emerged after the linguistic turn in the twentieth century with the development of transcendental pragmatics.[47]

Crucial to the defense Kant made of the limits of the principle of sufficient reason to objects of experience was the emphasis he placed on the distinction between analytic and synthetic judgments. One of the most controversial premises of his argument—perhaps the most authoritative rebuttal to which came in W. V. O. Quine's 1951 paper "On Two Dogmas of Empiricism"[48]— the distinction opposed judgments whose predicates were contained in their subjects with ones whose predicates were not. The identitarian impulse in metaphysical rationalism should be confined entirely, Kant argued, to analytic judgments, in which tautologies (e.g., A=A or triangles are three-sided figures) meant that reason was inherent both in the judging subject and in the object of judgment. Kant was an ardent opponent of psychologism when it came to the universal truths of logic, which were formal rather than substantive, and binding whether or not fallible men assented to them. They could be identified by seeing if negating them led to a contradiction (A≠A is a contradiction in terms; a triangle cannot have more or fewer sides and remain a triangle). Involving both noetic intuitions (the immediate, timeless apprehension that a triangle has three straight sides and three angles) and dianoetic inferences taking place in real time (the calculation that those angles always total 180 degrees), the location of analytic truth is in the ideal object as well as in the mind of the rational subject. As far as analytic judgments go, Kant remained true therefore to the metaphysical tradition, for although we might have empirical evidence of specific triangles to help us concretize the geometrical abstraction "triangle," the latter existed ideally and atemporally beyond mere sense data. The validity of logic or geometry had nothing to do with its genesis in human reasoning or its verification by contact with the empirical world.

But Kant distanced himself from the assumption of such earlier Rationalists as Leibniz that mathematics was the universal language of all reality, arguing instead that 7+5=12 is a synthetic, not analytic, judgment. Unlike the analytic tautologies of ideal geometric abstractions, synthetic a priori judgments about objects of experience could not be ontologically grounded in a strong version of the "principle of sufficient reason." Leibniz, it will be recalled, had claimed that every contingent event was explicable by a cause or reason in the real world. Kant, however, followed Hume in admitting that although that might be the case, we cannot *know with certainty* what those causes or reasons might be on the ontological level. Reason, he warned, overreached itself in seeking a priori principles operating in the real world outside of human understanding. There were neither innate ideas nor innately rational principles in the world available to our cognition, and a fortiori no perfect correspondence between them.

But unlike Hume with his recourse to mere probability and habit, Kant did not abandon the claim that causes were operative in the understanding of objects of experience, objects that did obey the laws that were discerned by natural scientists like Newton, whose work he revered. These objects and the laws determining their behavior were cognizable through synthetic judgments, insofar as they gave us new knowledge of the world that went beyond mere formal tautologies. Syllogisms alone can tell us nothing new about the world, nor can geometry and mathematics, based as they are on axioms, definitions, and demonstrations.[49] To achieve that end, we must investigate and verify predicates that are not contained in their subjects, as is the case in analytic judgments, but go beyond them (e.g., this triangle is made of metal, which does not become a logical contradiction if we say it is not made of metal, but of wood).

Kant warned, however, that strictly a posteriori judgments based on the senses alone, which empiricists since Locke had assumed were all we could hope for, were no more compelling, even when their imperfections were corrected by impersonal instruments, than solely a priori ones based on pure reason. Against the inductive empiricists and outright skeptics, he claimed that synthetic judgments might also have an a priori component, in which the mind contributes universally shared structuring principles that allow us to get beyond the disorganized chaos of sense impressions. For human cognition, both sense data and a priori principles were crucial; new knowledge, in short, comes only from the amalgam of passivity and activity, receptivity and spontaneity, that were synthetic a priori judgments. Although Kant postulated a range of such structuring principles, including the intuitions of time and space and the categories of substance and accident, it was cause and effect that was most relevant to his case, as it had been Hume's main target. Kant sought to salvage the integrity of causation by arguing it was a transcendental premise of human consciousness as a condition of the possibility of all knowledge. Objects of experience or "phenomena" were neither figments of imagination nor effects of mere habit, although they were also not equivalent to the objects "in themselves," or "noumena." To put it in another way, even though we cannot know essences or even particular objects as such, our knowledge of appearances was sufficient to ground both our everyday and scientific judgments about the world. The objectivity of the latter was grounded not in access to ontological laws but rather in our regulative use of reason to make sense of the phenomenal world.[50] When a priori reasoning claimed certain knowledge of non-experienceable objects "beneath" or "beyond" appearances, however, it led us off the dry land of justifiable knowledge into the stormy, foggy, ice-strewn seas of transcendental illusions.[51]

Reason does, however, have a place in carrying us beyond our immediate sense impressions, beyond even the synthetic a priori judgments of the understanding, whose categories are constitutive of objects of experience, to the deeper truths of science. As a number of commentators have stressed, although Kant denied its *constitutive* role in making the world as well as any concomitant knowledge about its intelligibility, he did see reason's capacity to serve as a *regulative* ideal as enabling our investigation of the natural regularities discovered by science, those laws of nature that can be discerned only if we assume that nature is a systematic and continuous unity.[52] This is so because only reason can move us beyond the empirical understanding of what we experience and give us the goal of making sense of nature as a whole as a coherent and consistent system. As Susan Neiman puts it,

> the capacity to demand explanations of experience requires the capacity to go beyond experience, for we cannot investigate the given until we refuse to take it as given. To ask a question about some aspect of experience, we must be able to think the thought that it could have been otherwise. Without this thought, we cannot even formulate the vaguest *why*. This thought is unavailable to understanding, whose whole content is experience.[53]

Even if the quest for the "unconditioned" as the ultimate ground of reality is doomed to failure, searching for it enables the scientific project to move forward.

In short, there is a link between critique and science, as both express the uniquely human capacity to do more than passively affirm the status quo.

A great deal more can be said about Kant's imaginative response to both dogmatic rationalism and skeptical sensationalism, which remains a remarkably nimble attempt to *reculer pour mieux sauter* (draw back to make a better jump). But as Kant himself came to realize, the first Critique left a number of essential questions still open. The most urgent were: (1) what was the role of reason in moral action, and (2) how did reason function in the course of human history? To address the former was the task Kant set himself in his second Critique, *The Critique of Practical Reason*, published in 1788. To deal with the latter, he published a number of essays, among which "Idea for a Universal History with a Cosmopolitan Aim" of 1784 is the most consequential. I will take each in turn.

Kant's release from the coils of his pre-critical metaphysical rationalism was due not only to the influence of Hume but also to his anxiety that it provided no plausible ground for human freedom. That is, a universe in which every contingent event had an antecedent ground threatened to be a determinist nightmare, at least when it came to the issue of moral choice. Kant, whose Pietist religious background left an indelible mark on his understanding of the human condition, had found a way to salvage causation when it came to the natural world and our place in it, but he was deeply reluctant to extend it to our role as moral agents. As is also often stressed, his early reading of Jean-Jacques Rousseau left a profound impact on both Kant's belief that moral dignity involved obeying self-imposed rules and his egalitarian conviction that all men were capable of autonomy.[54] Attempts by Rationalists like Leibniz to distinguish between "absolute" and "hypothetical" necessity, and thus find a way to square the certainty of God's foreordained knowledge with the apparently free actions of men, he found wanting.[55] Nor did he accept the distinction between external causes and internal ones, which allowed earlier thinkers like the Lutheran pastor Christian August Crusius to claim that believing in the latter was equivalent to valorizing human freedom.[56] It was, however, Spinoza's philosophy that presented the most powerful threat to human freedom, as became apparent to him during the celebrated "pantheism controversy" that roiled German philosophy for a generation and more after F. H. Jacobi claimed to disclose Gotthold Ephraim Lessing's Spinozism in a quarrel with Moses Mendelssohn in 1783.[57] Jacobi had concluded that any attempt to impose reason on the world led down the path to atheism, and so he made an impassioned plea for faith against the entire program of the *Aufklärung*. For Kant, although agreeing that Spinozan determinism could ultimately lead to atheism, it was still imperative to defend a limited notion of reason against its obscurantist detractors in order to meet Jacobi's irrationalist challenge.

In fact, to do so it was necessary to embark on those dangerous seas against which he had warned in the first Critique, leaving our safe harbor on the "island" of the understanding. The goal was not to rescue a pure theoretical concept of reason, which was still mired in transcendental illusions, but rather to find a "practical" one instead. That is, Kant still limited theoretical reason—there was no metaphysical *knowledge* to be had of substantive moral laws as noumenal things in themselves, nor could they be explained by synthetic a priori judgments of the causal laws of nature—in order to make room for another kind of reason, one that could inform our actions in the world and thus have an implication for practice. The questions were now "what ought I to do?" and "how should I act?" rather than "what can I know?" and "what is the validity of my experience?" Dissatisfied with the appeal to an innate moral sentiment combining benevolence, sociability, and kindness made by Scottish Enlightenment thinkers like the Earl of Shaftesbury and Frances Hutcheson, he insisted that reason could be enough to guide our actions. Unlike the more radically anti-Enlightenment Jacobi,[58] he did not seek to undermine reason in the service of faith but rather to salvage a defensible notion of it.

By "practical," it has to be understood, Kant did not mean instrumental reason, the most efficient means to achieve whatever goal we might hope to realize, but rather a way to select, justify, and realize the goals themselves. Against the more passive implications of a purely noetic or intuitive notion of reason, his stress on practical reason went even further than the limited epistemological constructivism of his Copernican Revolution in the first Critique. As John Zammito has noted, "the heart of Kantian philosophy is the idea of consciousness—of reason—as *act*."[59] Here we have one of the first pluralizations of reason, however much Kant may have sought a unifying principle underlying its varieties. In the preface to the first *Critique*, Kant had alluded to reason's "common principle,"[60] but nowhere did he spell out what it might be. The resulting pluralization was one many later postcritical German Idealists sought mightily to overcome but, as we will see, was accepted by twentieth-century Critical Theorists like Habermas.

Kant's initiative was to turn to the will, to whose importance he had been alerted by earlier theorists like Crusius and Rousseau, the latter of whom he admiringly called "the Newton of the moral world." In so doing, he might have seemed on first glance to be taking sides in a long-standing dispute within the Western tradition between those who privileged divine voluntarism over reason. Ever since the nominalists of the fourteenth century had disputed the existence of intelligible forms as a constraint on God's omnipotence, morality seemed for many believers ultimately dependent on the unfathomable intentions of a God who was above reason.[61] Any rational limits were dismissed as incompatible with a God whose absolute power and ineffability were part of his very identity. Antoine Arnauld before Kant and Søren Kierkegaard after him were examples of the continuing allure of this position. Metaphysicians in the Age of Reason like Spinoza, Malebranche, and Leibniz, by contrast, had generally downplayed the importance of will, understanding moral principles as something discovered by reason, not mandated by arbitrary divine decisions.

Kant's great innovation—although there had been a precedent of sorts in the ancient Greek notion of *prohairesis* (deliberate choice)[62]—was to combine will with reason in the concept of autonomy or self-legislation. Significantly, he confined the term "autonomy" to reason, ethics, principles, and will, rather than to individuals as holistic persons. From one perspective, as Steven Nadler has claimed, "the true, albeit secular, heir to the rationalism of Leibniz and Malebranche is . . . Kant. According to Kantian ethics, the moral law is reason's law, and it has nothing to do with subjective inclinations. Reason alone can see whether an action is right or wrong—mainly by determining through an *a priori* logical procedure whether it is the kind of action that can in principle be commanded of everyone without exception."[63] Even God was for Kant subordinate to reason, not above it.[64] The ground of human morality, he came to argue, was itself far more than mere sentiment, habit, or worst of all, blind obedience to authority. Although religious piety might yield virtue, Kant, very much the admirer of Rousseau, insisted that genuine morality brooked no servility among rational beings. Nor did it flow from selfish personal motivations like the hope of salvation or fear of damnation. It was instead a "deontology"— from *deon*, the Greek word for duty or obligation—in which the good intention to follow the call of duty was alone the decisive factor.

Where then was the role of the will in answering that call, especially if moral imperatives have nothing to do with "subjective inclinations?" The latter Kant identified with the irrational desires and whims of humanity understood as part of the natural world, the world of mechanical causal determination, and as such could not really be the ground of moral obligation. Synthetic a priori judgments directed at understanding objects of experience cannot therefore give us knowledge of the moral law, contrary to the hopes of some rationalist metaphysicians to unite cognition of what *is* with the imperative to do what *ought* to be done. Instead, Kant argued, we were also endowed with a deeper moral compass, which he located in the noumenal essence of our humanity. We possess the ability for moral self-governance in which the will can freely choose its actions, even if they contravene our desires. We even have the power to interrupt the causality of nature—including our own bodily desires and inclinations—and initiate a new causality, one expressing our free will. This was the great gift of autonomy, a power, Kant audaciously asserted, that made us like God in our ability to exert our will and freely give ourselves the law that we then can choose to follow. Also like God, we do so not capriciously but through adherence to a law that is inherently rational. As Schneewind puts it, "Kant embeds his conception of autonomy in a metaphysical psychology going beyond anything in Hume or Rousseau. Kantian autonomy presupposes that we are rational agents whose transcendental freedom takes us out of the domain of natural causation. It belongs to every individual, in the state of nature as in society."[65] Reason, as Kant's vivid metaphor put it, was like a vault whose keystone was freedom.[66]

As many subsequent critics have noted, Kant, despite his disdain for the intuitionism of a Jacobi, was here embracing an essentially noetic understanding of our noumenal selves, which no amount of empirical evidence or discursive justification could establish. We have only an "idea" of our freedom, and not "knowledge" amenable to explanation as part of the natural world of determined causation, a world in which heteronomy reigns. Although we often do experience a tension between natural desire and moral duty, and can choose to act on the one rather than the other, there is nothing to prove or verify the existence of our noumenal selves; indeed by definition there could never be such verification beyond a kind of faith in their existence. Nor is there a deduction to ground the claim that such morally obliged selves are "transcendental" in the same way that the a priori constitutive self of the knowing subject is. "How *pure reason can be practical*," Kant wrote, "is beyond the power of human reason to explain and all the labor and pains of seeking an explanation for this are in vain."[67] Instead, Kant chose to talk simply of the "fact" (*Faktum*) of reason—not meaning merely the passive "given" of reason, but something "made" by it[68]—insofar as we could not escape the force of feeling a moral obligation. But at the same time he conceded that it could not be itself rationally justified. Thus, as Beatrice Longueness has noted, we have moved from the *ratio cognoscendi* of the first Critique to a tacit *ratio credendi* (ground of faith) in the second.[69] Like the immortality of the soul or the existence of God, we can only rely on faith to orient ourselves in such matters beyond human cognition. But it was, Kant argued somewhat cryptically, a *Vernunftglaube* (a reason-belief or faith in reason), which was not the same as a dogmatic religious faith.[70]

Faintly audible in Kant's dualism was the echo of the old Christian distinction between the eternal *corpus mysticum* (the mystical body) and the finite profane body of Christ, which, as Ernst Kantorowicz famously argued, was given a political reinterpretation in the medieval notion of the king's two bodies, one mortal, the other not.[71] This notion, in turn, was available for a humanist reading in Dante, which transformed it into the opposition between *homo* and *humanitas* (individual man and humankind), *Adam mortalis* and *Adam subtilis* (mortal Adam and spiritual or immortal Adam), which could then be transfigured into the distinction in democratic theory between the will of all—the people as it empirically existed—and the general will—the ideal people, so critical to Rousseau and later normative political theorists. Kant's redescription of these oppositions in terms of the phenomenal human body, enmeshed in the coils of natural determinism, and the noumenal human soul, free to transcend nature and choose, allowed him both to limit reason and to celebrate it.

Wherein lay the rationality of the law that autonomous beings gave to themselves and then followed? It took a while for Kant to shed the sentimentalist moral belief that reason needed such feelings as self-love and benevolence to buttress its power to guide our actions to a moral end.[72] But when he wrote the second Critique, he had arrived at the conviction that practical reason alone could suffice, indeed that only reason could provide the universal imperative to move all of us in the right direction. "Moral law," he wrote, "is given as a fact by pure reason of which we are conscious *a priori* and which is apodictically certain, even though it is granted that no example of its exact fulfillment can be found in experience. Hence the objective reality of moral law cannot be proved through a deduction by any efforts [on the part of] theoretical reason, whether speculative or supported empirically."[73] Able to begin a new chain of freely chosen causality in the empirical world, practical reason thus left the transcendent realm and became immanent, "itself an efficient cause in the field of experience."[74] If we have any sentiment associated with the moral law, Kant conceded, "the word *respect* [*Acht*] alone offers a fitting expression of the esteem in which a rational being must hold it."[75] It was because of that respect that we were motivated to honor our obligation to obey it.

Reason, however, could not be understood to provide substantive commandments for moral behavior; it was not a set of positive rules or principles like the Decalogue. Nor was practical reason to be judged by its consequences, such as the achievement of human happiness, a criterion based on merely empirical interest. Accordingly, a paternalist *Polizeistaat* of the type advocated by Enlightenment Rationalists seeking to assure the welfare of its citizens would be "the greatest conceivable *despotism*, having a constitution which suspends all the freedom of the subjects who thereby have no rights whatsoever."[76] Even the "golden rule," implying that we should act morally to be the recipient of others' moral behavior, was corrupt because of its grounding in self-interest. Instead, pure practical reason mandated only a formal procedural principle, a law-like imperative that all rational beings felt categorically and without exception, but which, as befitting their inherent dignity as free men and women, they could choose to follow or not. More than just a prudential maxim helping us instrumentally to achieve an end we desire for other reasons, it gives us a way to orient ourselves by testing the ends themselves. That test, significantly, was like the one Kant had introduced to distinguish an analytic from a synthetic cognitive judgment: it invoked the logical law of contradiction. The categorical imperative imposed upon us the obligation to ask whether or not our moral actions could become a universal maxim. If not, they were not rational and cannot be judged moral. A second expression of the categorical imperative is that all humans should always be treated as ends rather than means, and a third is that we should work to create a "kingdom of ends" in which all rational beings form a union and obey the moral law.

Whether or not these variations were all fully commensurable has been much debated in the literature on Kant's moral philosophy, but what is important to note is that he never attempted a logical, deductive proof of their validity, as many previous metaphysical Rationalists might have done. Rather, as Onora O'Neill has pointed out, he proposed a "*justification* or *vindication* of reason, rather than a *proof* or *foundation* for reason. Justification differs from proof in that it is directed to some audience, and unconditional justification must be directed to audiences without assuming that they meet any specific conditions, so must be directed to all agents. . . . Kant calls it *public* or *autonomous* reasoning."[77] Here we have an anticipation of the crucial role of intersubjective justification aiming at universal consensus in the work of Habermas and his followers, which will be discussed in the second half of this study.

Much more can be said about Kant's discussion of practical reason, whose primacy in his philosophy has been underlined by many subsequent commentators. Unlike pure speculative reason, which led into dangerous waters when extended to objects in themselves, pure practical reason was not limited in its application. Unlike cognitive judgments, which depended on an impure mixture of a priori categories and sense data, moral judgments, unconditional in their claims over us, were made without regard for the mediation of our fallible, creaturely bodies with their finite selfish interests.[78] Here the genitive in the phrase "critique of" meant more critique *by* than critique *aimed at*. For some critics, the uncompromising quality of Kant's practical reason, its refusal to admit that any other version of morality—for example, the positive commandments of Jewish law—deserved respect, meant that it was ominously coercive. Nietzsche, for example, could famously claim that "the categorical imperative smells of cruelty."[79] Hannah Arendt would level a similar charge in claiming that "the inhumanity of Kant's moral philosophy is undeniable," because the absoluteness of the categorical imperative contradicts the relativity of human relationships:

> the inhumanity which is bound up with the concept of one single truth emerges with particular clarity in Kant's work precisely because he attempted to found truth on practical reason; it is as though he who had so

inexorably pointed out man's cognitive limits could not bear to think that in action, man cannot behave like a god.[80]

And yet, *pace* Nietzsche and Arendt, Kant did come to acknowledge that even in the case of practical reason, there was ultimately a limit on rational comprehension for humans that could not be surpassed. In the conclusion of his *Metaphysical Foundations of Morals*, written in 1785 while preparing the second Critique, he conceded that reason always looks for an ultimate source of its justifications, seeking the unconditional ground of its arguments. Although Rationalist metaphysicians beholden to the principle of sufficient reason thought they had found this Holy Grail, Kant was less certain. Not even the idea of a beneficent God would suffice, as he is himself beholden to practical reason. This is not to say that in a temporal or even logical sense, God comes after reason, but rather that they are equiprimordial.[81] Neither can be the cause of the other, leaving the question of the absolute ground unanswered. But "reason cannot be blamed for refusing to explain this necessity by a condition; that is to say, by means of some interest assumed as a basis, since the law would then cease to be a supreme law of reason. Thus we do not comprehend the practical, unconditional necessity of the moral imperative, but we comprehend its *uncomprehensibility* which is all that, in fairness, can be demanded of a philosophy which aims to carry its principles to the very limit of reason."[82]

Kant's philosophy, we might say, moved relentlessly toward that limit but never transgressed it. In many of his moods, this meant establishing and maintaining boundaries, warning against illegitimate attempts to undermine them, and chastising those who failed to heed the warning. But Kant was never merely a policeman of order, who thought he had arrived at the destination of a system whose self-sufficiency would withstand all challenges. Instead, his critical impulse was extended to his own efforts to build such a system on firmer grounds than the shaky foundations of previous metaphysics. Not only did this lead him in his third great Critique, the *Critique of Judgment* of 1790, to investigate the realms of the aesthetic, in which morality and sensuality were intertwined, and nature understood teleologically rather than merely mechanically. It also allowed him to introduce the issue of historical change into the very heart of metaphysics itself. Significantly, the first Critique ends with a short chapter called "the history of pure reason," which is designed to "mark a place in the system that still remains and that must be filled in the future."[83] In the second edition of the first Critique he even talked of the "*epigenesis*, as it were, of pure reason," borrowing a term from the biological debates of his day.[84] In his 1784 answer to the question "what is Enlightenment?," he had explicitly denied that his was an already enlightened age, arguing instead that it should be understood as one in which enlightenment was still an ongoing process, one in which humankind was still struggling to leave behind its "self-incurred immaturity."[85] This new historical note, so Michel Foucault came to argue, made Kant's work the first genuinely modern philosophy.[86] Habermas agreed that for the first time "the philosophy of history itself was to become a part of the enlightenment diagnosed as history's course."[87] That is, Kant understood his own project not merely to be at the culmination of past historical developments in the investigation and application of reason but also as still in the middle of an ongoing process that had not yet reached its conclusion, if indeed it was ever to do so. Not only was there a "space of reasons," to invoke the American philosopher Wilfrid Sellars's celebrated phrase,[88] but also a "time of reasons," in which rationality was understood as involving intersubjective deliberation, argumentation, adjudication, and education.

What is so perplexing about this claim is that it was implicitly in tension with Kant's "logist" denial that rational principles had emerged at any one moment rather than being eternal. If reason had not even been the issue of God's will, but somehow always already bound that very will, then why did it have to emerge over time in human affairs? Or was it merely the human inclination to follow reason that was strengthened, while reason itself remained constant? If the categorical imperative were not in the service of a prior interest, such as self-preservation or power, and should always engender the same respect to obey it, then why did it not have a constant obligatory force in human affairs and need to be nurtured over time rather than merely always obediently followed? If reason were eternal, how could it also be an ideal, serving as an inducement to move into a future in which it would be increasingly, if never completely, realized, in the actions and institutions of men? Such questions have bedeviled Kant's interpreters ever since. And yet, despite the instability it created in the architectonic unity of his system, in a number of his occasional writings, most notably his remarkable essay of 1784, "Idea for a Universal History with a Cosmopolitan Aim," Kant pondered the implications of situating reason in history, or to put it in terms that anticipated Weber, to understand the relationship between reason understood philosophically and the concomitant cultural, social, and political processes of rationalization.[89] Here, we might say, the narrow churchman of reason showed that he could cautiously hope for an expansion of its reach into territories not yet under its dominion.

For a long time, the apparently irrational contingencies of historical change had been understood to be ruled by apparently capricious "fortune," whether explained by the whims of the gods in Greece, ineffable divine Providence in the Middle Ages, or natural forces beyond our will in the Renaissance and baroque.[90] But it was also possible to read religious notions of Providence optimistically as based on a hidden plan, which suggested the world was improving in ways that might be construed as rational.[91] Here the religious claim that nothing happens without a reason, which had provided comfort for those whose suffering might seem unearned or capricious, could survive increasing secularization. It had already appeared in pagan notions of fate or destiny, which attributed the mysterious workings of human affairs to some higher, impersonal force, whose reasons were ineffable.

Once the Moderns had won their battle with the Ancients and older notions of degeneration from putative golden ages in the past lost their allure, the way was open for a full-throttled notion of historical progress, which implied the inexorable realization of reason in the affairs of men.[92] Such a belief was dependent on the audacious conceit that all of humanity could be understood to have a single history, which could be narrated as a coherent and intelligible tale of the species as a whole.[93] As a result, it was possible to locate reason at its most robust not in the individual mind but in the collective journey of humankind, which was not finite, as in the case of the mortal individual, but infinite and open-ended. Even more significant was the waning of faith in the automatic realization of a hidden plan, based on purposes that were beyond our ken, which created an opening for more active human intervention. A dispositional notion of reason could once again be elevated to nondispositional status, but now as a potentiality or possibility rather than an actuality, a project in time — historical time — not an inherent reality.

Although cautiously adopting this position, Kant was nonetheless suspicious of strong Enlightenment notions of progress, which understood history as a narrative of inevitable ascent based on objective, developmental laws capable of being discerned by human cognition. He did not want to replace the religious notion of hidden purposes with a mechanistic notion of causality, in which history operated as did nature only in terms of first causes. Like Hume and the historians of the Scottish Enlightenment, Kant preferred what Dugald Stewart had called "theoretical or conjectural history."[94] Significantly, the first word in the title of his essay was "idea," which in his special vocabulary meant a concept of theoretical reason, not of the understanding; a speculative, "as if" conjecture, which was not the same as an a priori synthetic judgment about the world, held with cognitive certainty and empirically verified. He developed his "idea" in nine "propositions," which were less noetic axioms than tentative thought experiments. At one point, he even compared the results to a novel, although one with a practical purpose in helping to bring about what it speculatively describes.[95]

In positing this speculative "idea" with a practical intent, Kant was tentatively advancing a fiction that might reunite the two modes of the Rationalist principle of sufficient reason, which were differentiated in his first two Critiques: natural causes and rendered reasons. Or put slightly differently, he attempted to find in nature the ground for the moral imperatives of practical reason, which were themselves then increasingly realized in the institutions and practices of the species as a whole. Or put in yet another way, which anticipates the similar effort made by Habermas in more linguistic terms, he sought to locate a transcendent imperative immanently in nature and history rather than hovering above them in a realm entirely outside of the messy contingencies of the world.

The key to this effort was his new willingness to think of nature—or at least organic nature—teleologically and not just causally, or in Aristotle's language, through final as well as efficient causes.[96] Humans, he argued, do not simply follow instinct, as do other animals, which would situate them entirely in the realm of efficient causes. Nor are they perfect angels who can exert their conscious wills to plan society rationally. But since nature is not wasteful and does not create any organ without a purpose, and since men possess the faculty of reason, they are destined, so Kant anthropocentrically argued, to realize it in its highest form: "Nature has willed that the human being should produce everything that goes beyond the mechanical arrangement of his animal existence entirely out of himself, and participate in no other happiness or perfection than that which he has procured from himself free from instinct through his own reason."[97] The most rational state of human interaction—rational understood in terms of practical reason—will be reached when a perfect civil constitution is achieved within a state and a cosmopolitan, peaceful federation between states.[98]

How does nature intentionally work to bring about this innate purpose? Here Kant introduced a device that recalled Leibniz's theodicy, in which partial evil was part of a larger good, albeit one reconfigured in temporal terms. As in the case of the "invisible hand" of the classical economists, turning intersubjective competition into general prosperity, and what Hegel was later to call the "cunning of reason" (List der Vernunft) negating negation into a higher affirmative harmony, the mechanism reconciling individual action and general outcome, revealing the hidden plan of nature, was antagonism. Kant named it, following Michel de Montaigne, "unsocial sociability" and proclaimed "thanks be to nature, therefore, for the incompatibility, for the spiteful competitive vanity, for the insatiable desire to possess or even to dominate. For without them all the excellent natural predispositions in humanity would eternally slumber undeveloped. The human being wills concord; but nature knows better what is good for his species; it wills discord."[99]

Relying on such a mechanism, working behind the backs of men, may well seem an affront to the values of autonomy, maturity, and freedom, which Kant so insistently trumpeted elsewhere. It certainly marked a step away from the dispositional identification of reason entirely with persons and their actions, allowing instead the possibility that reason can also exist outside of individual human intention or even intersubjective discourse. In this essay, in fact, Kant acknowledged that humans will never be fully rid of their creaturely limits, or as he put it in a frequently cited metaphor, "out of such crooked wood as the human being is made, nothing entirely straight can be fabricated."[100] Philosophies like Stoicism, which idealized the "sage" capable of angelic moral perfection, were missing the animal in *animal rationale*. Because of his imperfections, man is, in fact, an animal that needs a master, but that master, Kant concluded, can only be the species itself. That is, rationality exists in the learning process of humanity, which can progressively tame, if never entirely obliterate, the selfish, instinct-driven animal in us and overcome all conflict. Each child, to cite Axel Honneth's gloss of Kant's work on pedagogy, "is required to appropriate for himself or herself reasons that are stored up in his or her cultural environment. The child's reason [*Vernunft*] is formed through the internalization of the social reserve of knowledge that is amassed in the society in which the child grows to maturity."[101] Kant understood that such collective learning is uneven and often discontinuous. But what does increase, at least potentially, is the ratio of morally rational, freely chosen actions to those determined by impersonal circumstances or our hedonistically motivated animal natures. We can see an intimation of this outcome in the emergence of aesthetic disinterestedness, in which human appetite is sublimated rather than directly sated, an advance that he was to link directly in the *Critique of Judgment* with morality.[102] And when the cosmopolitan federation is achieved, unsocial sociability will no longer play the key role it once played in producing the progressive outcome that rational discussion can now deliberately foster.

Kant did not, however, entirely give up his preference for a dispositional or action-oriented notion of reason over a nondispositional or functional one. He hoped that by speculating on the possible history that he outlined, justifying nature's historically revealed purposes to man, we can better enable the realization of those very purposes. As in his positing of reason's regulative role in orienting scientific knowledge toward a greater and greater grasp of the systematic inner workings of the world, he extended its sway to our action as historical agents. For "although we are too shortsighted to see through to the secret mechanism of its arrangement, this idea should still serve us as a guiding thread for exhibiting an otherwise planless *aggregate* of human actions, at least in the large, as a *system*."[103] Not only does such an insight provide a consoling view of a future that will be better than the past, but it also gives us practical guidance and moral inspiration in our attempt to realize it. And perhaps most important of all for the concept of reason, it allows us to appreciate the subtle linkages that tie our noumenal selves to our phenomenal selves, situating the obligations we feel through practical reason amid the natural laws we discern through our cognitive capacities (or at least a teleological perspective on the organic nature out of which we have emerged). And in so doing, it restores some of the confidence in reason's fate that Kant himself had lost when he had been awakened from his dogmatic slumber by Hume; for now that fate was no longer understood to be in the hands of mortal, finite individuals, who, *pace* earlier Rationalists, did not share in the divine mind but rather in the species as a whole, whose naturally bestowed telos was infinitely progressive enlightenment.

Perhaps Kant's greatest achievement, at least from the perspective of the story I am telling in this book, was his making "reason" as much an exigent question for philosophy as a comforting answer. His relentless struggle to defend it against its skeptical or irrationalist detractors, while resisting the dogmatic fallacies of many of his metaphysical predecessors, was heroic but not fully successful. He never fully resolved the tension between his claim that from one perspective reason could be construed as timeless and irreducible to ephemeral circumstances, while from another it was an ongoing project in the world still awaiting its realization. His hope to find a unifying principle underlying the distinction between theoretical and practical reason, cognition and morality, remained unfulfilled. But by sharpening the distinctions and rigorously exploring their implications, he raised the level of the discussion about reason to a height never before achieved, and bequeathed to us questions that still demand answers in the twenty-first century.

# 3

# Hegel and Marx

Although "Idea for a Universal History" was only a marginal essay in Kant's vast oeuvre, it anticipated a number of subsequent developments in the tradition that came to be called German Idealism, a tradition that took seriously the challenge of fashioning a new metaphysics on postcritical foundations and often looked to history for answers. For many of Kant's readers, however, his more general effort to salvage a viable concept of reason by limiting it had not been persuasive.[1] Attempting a metacritique of his critical philosophy, they hoped to avoid the pitfalls of dogmatism and the positing of arbitrary premises, while recovering the certainties of a more traditional metaphysics with systematic pretensions. Yearning to overcome the intolerable dualisms in his thought, most notably between phenomena and noumena, transcendent and immanent, finite and infinite, is and ought, universal and particular, and subject and object, they sought a way to reunite in a monistic holism what he had left sundered. A few reverted back to the empiricism of Locke and Hume, while others, made anxious by the "nihilism" they saw in Kant's denial of access to ontological truth, sought answers in frankly irrationalist faith.[2] Although many bemoaned the solipsism they saw in his Copernican Revolution with its stress on the constitutive subject of knowledge, others turned that subject into an ontological, rather than merely epistemological demiurge, an autopoetic metasubject who made the world that it came to know. Some endorsed his defense of Enlightenment natural science, while others derived a more romantic version of "natural philosophy" from his musings on the teleological moment in organic nature.[3] Whatever new interpretation of reason and its role in the world might be offered,

Kant's legacy needed somehow to be addressed, absorbed, and, if possible, surmounted.

To do justice to this extraordinarily creative and fertile period would require detailing the contributions of a host of challenging thinkers, including Moses Mendelssohn, Friedrich Heinrich Jacobi, Johann Georg Hamann, Johann Gottfried Herder, Karl Leonhard Reinhold, Salomon Maimon, Johann Gottlieb Fichte, and Friedrich Wilhelm Joseph Schelling, not to mention the lesser-known figures who attempted to return to Wolff or Locke. But because this is a history of the Frankfurt School's later struggle to defend a viable concept of reason, we can move more expeditiously to the single figure who is so often seen as the culmination of the German Idealist tradition and its most powerful defender of a robust notion of reason, Georg Wilhelm Friedrich Hegel. For it was in works such as Marcuse's *Hegel's Ontology and the Theory of Historicity*, and *Reason and Revolution*, along with others like Adorno's *Hegel: Three Studies*, that the vital importance of the Hegelian tradition for Critical Theory was made clear.[4] Although unexpected traces of Schelling's critique of Hegel can be found in Adorno's work and the profoundly anti-Hegelian Schopenhauer was a stimulus to Horkheimer's thinking, it is impossible to understand their concept of reason without working our way through Hegel's audacious attempt to transgress the limits set by Kant's more cautious critical philosophy.[5] Even though it would be misleading to characterize their approach, as did some hasty early readers of their legacy, merely as a variant of Hegelian Marxism, when it came to the question of reason, Hegel served as a vital stimulus.

Their motivation for being attracted to Hegel was not merely philosophical. Marcuse was most explicit in linking Hegel's philosophy to the ongoing project of making society and politics substantively rational. "Robespierre's deification of reason as the *Être suprême*," he baldly asserted (while conflating the Hébertists and Robespierre), "is the counterpart to the glorification of reason in Hegel's system. The core of Hegel's philosophy is a structure the concepts of which— freedom, subject, mind, notion—are derived from the idea of reason."[6] Although other commentators have pointed to Hegel's nuanced critique of the Jacobin Terror as an expression of the tyranny of reason at its most abstract or interpreted his ambivalent response to the Revolution's legacy as an act of working through a traumatic loss, they maintained the conviction that his thought was ultimately tied to the politically progressive movements of his day.[7] In fact, a latter-day defender of Critical Theory has conjectured that Hegel found inspiration, at least in his description in *The Phenomenology of Spirit* of the dialectic of master and slave, in the Haitian Revolution in which the issue of emancipation from slavery was directly addressed.[8] While acknowledging that Hegel's attitude toward the French Revolution was ambivalent, Habermas also concluded that

however much he may have feared actual revolutionaries, the great German
Idealist still "desires the revolutionizing of reality."[9] Whatever the precise relationship between specific historical events and the realization of reason in his
thought, the Frankfurt School understood that Hegel continued and deepened
Kant's insight in the "Idea for a Universal History" that there was rationality
latent in the course of contingent historical events, a rationality that nonetheless
had to be actively fostered rather than merely passively observed in the hope
that it would somehow manifest itself in time.

There is no easy way to condense into a few pages the gist of Hegel's post-
Kantian defense of a reason that was dialectical and absolute rather than critical
and limited, as it was never expressed in straightforward principles or defended
by entailed arguments. Instead, it was manifested holistically in the totality of
his writings, which rejected the method of beginning with firm foundations and
moving inferentially to persuasive conclusions. Appropriately, as in the totality
we call reality, here too, "the True is the whole."[10] In fact, as Adorno noted
with some sympathy, Hegel explicitly eschewed formal argumentation: "Hegel
distrusts argument deeply, and with good reason. Primarily because the dialectician knows something that [Georg] Simmel later discovered: that anything
that remains argumentation exposes itself to refutation. For this reason Hegel
necessarily disappoints anyone who looks for his arguments. . . . The Ideal is
non-argumentative thought."[11] In other words, Hegel's reason can perhaps be
judged more noetic than dianoetic, based on a nondiscursive presentation of
apodictic truths or description of their manifestations in the world rather than
assertoric claims that need proofs to persuade. Here he seemed to echo the
early German Romantics, who embraced an intuitive Platonic notion of reason,
which was more mystical than discursive.[12]

But for all his disdain for clarity of expression, he did not follow the lead of
linguistically oriented thinkers like Hamann and privilege poetic language and
rhetoric over logic as the locus of truth.[13] Nor did he dogmatically identify the
noetic grasp of truth with an immediate rhapsodic intuition, preferring instead
to stress its slow and deliberate appearance over time, its manifestation in
dynamic "becoming" rather than static "being," and the importance of "tarrying
with the negative" rather than jumping to immediate conclusions. In his vivid
metaphor, "truth is not a minted coin that can be given and pocketed ready-
made."[14] But what he did do by disdaining argumentation was to suspend the
strictures against contradiction in traditional logic, preferring instead to valorize
contradiction itself as an inevitable and indeed productive quality of reality and
thought alike. Kant had denounced as transcendental illusions any attempt to
use reason to adjudicate claims about the existence of God, the immortality of
the soul, or the choice between freedom and determinism, because it could

equally support contradictory positions. Hegel, in contrast, substituted the logic of "both/and" for traditional logic's "either/or" and folded contradiction into the truth, rather than damning it as its enemy.

In addition, Hegel moved the center of gravity of philosophy from self-reflective epistemology back to ontology, and disdained the primacy of critical judgment, which privileged the judging subject or intersubjective discourse, in favor of a kind of autonomous conceptual self-assertion.[15] Access to ontological truth came not through a reflective critique of the conditions of knowledge but rather through a presuppositionless phenomenological description of consciousness and its representations, which led inevitably out into the world represented in consciousness.[16] Although early in his career he had explored the dialectic of intersubjective recognition underlying an ethical community, he replaced it with a more monologic notion of self-objectifying Absolute Spirit.[17] His was a fully nondispositional notion of reason, or perhaps more precisely, he displaced the active agent of reason from humans to the more impersonal *Geist* (spirit or mind). The Kantian metaphor of reason as a stern "tribunal" was left behind, as Hegel imbued that Absolute Spirit with the indulgent characteristics of an all-forgiving, merciful father.[18] Against the belief that mental representations of an objective reality—the German *Vorstellung* (representation) implies an object placed before a subject—should be the focus of philosophy, he embraced a dynamic philosophy of relationality in which subjects and objects were mutually constituting. Or to put it in terms we have already encountered, he disdained, as had Kant, not only psychologism, in which thought was conditioned by extra-intellectual forces or circumstances, but also transcendental cognition, in which objects of experience were conditioned by universal mental categories. Instead, he defended a full-blown pan-logicism based on the belief that reason permeates all realms of reality, objective as well as subjective. Although careful to distinguish his position from Spinozan pantheism, which he argued led to an "acosmism" that denied the reality of the created world with all of its not-yet-rational qualities, he nonetheless claimed that the task of philosophy is "to comprehend what is. . . . Because what is, is reason."[19] Reason, for Hegel, was neither solely an organon of subjective thought nor an inherent quality of reality; it was both at once, at the deepest level an "identity of identity and non-identity." As Gadamer put it, "Hegel defines reason as the unity of thought and reality. Thus, implied in the concept of reason is that reality is not the other of thought and, hence, that the opposition of appearance and understanding is not a valid one."[20] Where Kant cautiously posited limits to the reach of reason, Hegel countered: "the very fact that we know a limitation is evidence that we are beyond it, evidence of our freedom from limitation. . . . To know one's limitation means to know of one's unlimitedness."[21]

"That reason rules the world," Hegel unapologetically acknowledged, "is our presupposition and faith."[22] Although he did reject the "rapturous enthusiasm which, like a shot from a pistol, begins straightaway with absolute knowledge" and defended the "strenuous effort of the notion"[23] that effort produced more of an imaginative metanarrative than a carefully reasoned discourse rebutting counterarguments at their strongest. Hegel's stress on "dialectic," a word with considerable baggage in the history of philosophy,[24] implies the temporality of "dia" (the Greek, as we noted, for "through"), but his was not a genuinely inferential method of reasoning involving questions and answers, as in the original Socratic use of the term. Consequently, it has been easy for critics of Hegel to fault him for never rigorously addressing the careful arguments that Kant had made to warn against the improper use of *Vernunft* to transgress the limits of *Verstand* and make dubious claims to absolute knowledge.[25] "Is it rational," they have wondered, "to give up the Kantian enterprise of sorting and validating in favor of a 'higher' understanding in which the false comes to be reintegrated as a 'moment' of the true? Surely philosophy's function in deciding disputed claims to knowledge is too important to be eliminated in this way."[26] Is the overcoming of the traditional principle of contradiction ironically a capitulation to a kind of irrationalism, despite Hegel's insistence that a more capacious notion of reason follows, as we have noted, the logic of "both/and" rather than "either/or?"[27]

And yet, however inadequately justified by careful argumentation or grounded in traditional logic, Hegel's more emphatic and capacious "broad church" notion of reason clearly struck a chord with those dissatisfied with what were perceived as the deficiencies in Kant's position. Take, for example, the question of history and reason, which was especially pressing in the light of modernity's shattering of what seemed for a long time a coherent order embodied in the hierarchy of a timeless "great chain of being." Where Hegel differed from Kant was in his transgression of the limit placed by Kant's distinction between a mere "idea," a speculative "as if" conjecture with possible practical implications, and a full-blown, cognitively self-confident philosophy of history. The latter, he maintained, could take the form of a synthetic and systematic *Wissenschaft*—the German word for a science more capacious than its English equivalent—which went beyond the limited judgments of Kant's understanding.[28] The ground of his confidence lay in his disdain for what he saw as the overreliance on subjective epistemological constructivism in Kant, leading to a number of lamentable dualisms, as opposed to his own belief that "reason" (*Vernunft*) could go beyond mere "understanding" (*Verstand*), and once again claim access to ontological truths by dialectically reconciling what Kant had considered in perpetual opposition. Setting such oppositions in motion and undermining their static rigidity could mediate and reconcile the distinctions Kant had constructed through the analytic "understanding," as well as sublate the contradictions of dialectical "reason" he had insisted were eternal antinomies. Rather than conceiving the immanentization of reason—in particular, practical reason—in the world as an endless process only asymptotically reaching fruition because of human frailty (that crooked wood Kant thought could never be made fully straight), Hegel in certain of his moods saw it as always already achieved or in others as inexorably en route to that end point.

Rejecting the residue of otherworldliness in Kant and with it such dualisms as noumenon and phenomenon, spirit and flesh, transcendence and immanence, Hegel took his cue from what he understood to be the realization of religion in the practices, mores, and institutions of daily existence, in what he called an ethical form of life (*Sittlichkeit*). Against the Enlightenment belief in a dry "religion of reason" or formal moral principles (*Moralität*), which he saw as merely the abstract negation of unreflective cultic idol-worship, he celebrated the realization of reason in the emotional life of a concrete religious community, whose myths, rituals, and practices were positive, objective manifestations of reason in the world. Here the primitive religious cult and the Greek polis served as models for what in the modern world he came to acknowledge could no longer be fully realized. As Hegel matured, he recognized that it was impossible—and indeed undesirable—merely to restore the naïve, communal unity that might once have existed in the premodern world. Individualized subjective interiority, which came into the world largely with the Reformation and had been so important for earlier German Idealism, had also to be valorized. Otherwise, reason would remain an external force, as it had been in determinist naturalism and the mechanical *Polizeistaat* tradition supported by the Rationalists of the pre-Kantian era.

As the German historian Friedrich Meinecke once noted, the early Enlightenment idea of reason, which, as we have seen, undergirded the *Polizeistaat*, was more completely developed by German Idealism: "Compared with the idea of humanity which was later to arise out of a profoundly stirred and ennobled inner life—namely, that of German Idealism—this older concept of humanity (which merely continued to develop the basic ideas of the old Stoic and Christian Natural Right) was simpler, plainer, more general and more lacking in content. For it was directed principally towards the practical aim of making oneself and other men happy."[29] This limited notion of reason, Hegel charged, had been satisfied to know the automatic laws governing nature, equating them with external causes, and thus underplaying the no less vital role of subjective consciousness and interiority. In the period of classical Greek philosophy, a similar opposition had occurred, with Anaxagoras defining reason in terms of external natural laws, and Socrates appreciating the importance of conscious human reasoning.

But Hegel, unlike Kant in his major writings, abhorred dualism and sought to find a way to bring together the two, combining, as it were, the insights of Anaxagoras with those of Socrates. While denying that mere happiness rather than freedom was the telos of rationality—world history, he soberly observed, "is not the soil of happiness. The periods of happiness are blank pages in it"[30]— he also resisted the idea that reason and freedom were exclusively interior qualities of our higher moral selves, while happiness was relegated to our lower creaturely existence as animals ruled by natural laws. Desire—for recognition as well as bodily pleasure—was an essential motor in the process of realizing reason in the world.[31] But desire, although necessary, was insufficient, as it had to be satisfied in the actual world, an effortful process that he identified with labor. As he put it in the *Phenomenology*, labor "is desire held in check, fleetingness staved off; in other words, work forms and shapes the thing."[32] Thus, it was the dynamic dialectic of desire and labor, interior freedom and exterior realization, subjective reflection and communal solidarity that allowed reason to realize itself in history.

Hegel's choice to write a "phenomenology" rather than a "noumenology" reflected his conviction that reason was manifest in the seemingly contingent, "phenomenal" world of the finite, suffering, desiring human being and the disparate institutional forms of life—social, political, and cultural—he had created through his labor. Correctly understood, the apparent messiness of that concrete world revealed a dynamic system with its own inherent logic, a system in which universality was not an abstraction counterposed to particularity, hovering above the world, but rather immanent in its mundane particulars. Kant's distinction between unknowable, albeit thinkable things-in-themselves and knowable objects of experience was therefore wrong-headed, Hegel insisted, as phenomenology was a fully rational science (*Wissenschaft*) of apparently contingent experiences, not merely of intelligible essences.

That science, moreover, was fully historical rather than transcendental. Combining Leibniz's notion of a theodicy with Kant's defense of the inadvertently benign consequences of "unsocial sociability," Hegel saw in the seemingly haphazard narrative of dialectical development "the cunning of reason." Even "world-historical individuals" who had a certain sense of what they were trying to realize were tools of forces larger than themselves.[33] Understood in this way, history is a meaningful story, which becomes clear only retrospectively (arriving, in his celebrated metaphor, only with the owl of Minerva at dusk) but can also allow us to justify proleptically what appear to be current imperfections as necessary episodes of that narrative.

Valorizing all that seemed contingent and partial as necessary "moments" in the dynamically developing totality—an authentic rather than dubious effort to "save the appearances"[34]—was, we might say, his version of the principle of sufficient reason. "To understand that which exists is the task of philosophy, for what exists is reason. . . . To recognize and know reason as the rose within the cross of the present and thus to enjoy the present, this sort of rational insight is the *reconciliation* with actuality which philosophy provides for those who have received the inner demand to understand."[35] Despite the crucial role of negation and contradiction in his understanding of dialectics, indeed because they were recuperated as valuable in themselves, Hegel's ultimate standpoint was thus as optimistic as Leibniz's, indeed "comic" in its validation of a happy ending despite the "tragic" or "ironic" fate of the individuals whose micro-stories were fragments of the whole.[36]

Whether Hegel's "comic" rationalism was successful in dialectically overcoming the various dualisms, antinomies, and contradictions bequeathed to Idealism by Kant—let alone evident in the real history whose underlying coherence he claimed to decode—was, of course, a source of considerable dispute in his day, and continues to be so today.[37] For example, he did not entirely jettison the ideal of the categorical imperative that every man should be treated as an end and never a means, writing in *The Philosophy of History*: "Man is only an end in himself (or final end) through what is divine in him—by what from the beginning has been called reason and, insofar as it is active in itself, what has been called freedom."[38] But how this credo could be plausibly reconciled with the opposite claim, reminiscent of Leibniz's theodicy, that "the cunning of reason" sometimes used men for its own purposes was left open (a danger that has also troubled critics of Kant's essay "Idea for a Universal History").[39]

Nor did Hegel make clear how the dynamic system as a whole, understood from a position immanent in it, could be grasped as inherently rational, while at the same time contending that reason was the telos of the historical process understandable only after it was completed. Because of this uncertainty, he opened himself to the charge that for all his stress on freedom, there was something determinist about his insistence that history could be read as the autobiography of a rational World Spirit. As the skeptical Habermas was to put it, "as absolute knowledge, reason assumes a form so overwhelming that it not only solves the initial problem of a self-reassurance of modernity, but solves it *too well*. The question about the genuine self-understanding of modernity gets lost in reason's ironic laughter. For reason has now taken over the place of fate and knows that every event of essential significance has *already* been decided."[40] Habermas himself, as we will see, offered a "rational reconstruction" of the past as a meaningful evolutionary narrative but, contra Hegel, explicitly ascribed to it only a heuristic status without any guarantees of realization or perfect embodiment in the messiness of actual historical occurrences.

There was, however, enough ambiguity in Hegel's system, enough play in his richly articulated narrative of reason's immanence in the world, for his successors to take his ideas in many different directions. Perhaps the most succinct expression—and certainly one of the most widely debated—of that ambiguity came in his celebrated remark in the preface to *The Philosophy of Right*, that "philosophy is, because it is the *exploration of the rational*, by that very fact the *prehension of the present and the actual (Wirklichen)*, and not the construction of something *otherworldly* that might be God knows where. . . . *The rational is actual; And the actual is rational.*"[41] The ambiguity is evident in the very language he used in that final chiasmic formulation. In this rendering into English, the term "actual" is chosen for the German *wirklich*, which is also sometimes translated as "real." The former term implies something that is merely current, something that is happening, something that now exists. The latter suggests an ontologically deeper, truer state of affairs, which is the opposite of an illusory appearance. This latter connotation can, in fact, also be discerned in one of the other meanings of actuality, when it is counterposed, as it has been ever since Aristotle's notion of final causes, to the idea of potentiality. According to Marcuse, "Hegel's philosophy is in a large sense a re-interpretation of Aristotle's ontology, rescued from the distortion of metaphysical dogma and linked to the pervasive demand of modern rationalism that the world be transformed into a medium for the freely developing subject, that the world become, in short, the reality of reason."[42]

If Hegel is interpreted as saying that what is currently the state of the world is already inherently rational, he can be characterized as a conservative upholder of the status quo, providing a patina of rationality for what by any plausible criteria was still far from it. In this reading, his support for the Prussian state of his day, which once fueled the problematic belief that he was an apologist of the authoritarian state, can be given a philosophical justification.[43] But even if we acknowledge that the state to which he was referring was the Reformed post-*Polizeistaat*, a complexly articulated modern state of checks and balances, not the top-down enlightened despotism defended by metaphysical Rationalists, the "right-wing" Hegelians could still appropriate him as an affirmative justification of the status quo. Against the Kantian *Rechtsstaat*, which was a mere *Verstandesstaat* based on abstract, ideal universals always in tension with their imperfect realizations, he could be read as legitimating the "emphatic institutionalism" of a *Vernunftstaat* in which the actually existing state was a living community concretely embodying substantive reason.[44] Against Fichte's ideal of a communal "realm of reason" in which the state would be overcome and morality would no longer need the sanction of law, he had always resisted the utopia of sanctionless ethical life.[45] Hegel's praise for the rational function of the state civil service, which he understood in terms that anticipated Weber's ideal type of bureaucratic rationality, valorized the actually existing form of political universality. Here the open-ended Kantian "ought" was folded back into a living "is." As Dieter Henrich has put it, for Hegel, "the rational state whose good constitution respects the freedom of its citizens" is "the *structure* in reality that corresponds to the internal structure of the will. . . . The will is the *comprehensive* structure that *includes* the subjective will and the objective constitution."[46] Overcoming the tension between Kant's stress on the obligation to obey the law and the always threatening possibility of not doing so, between duty and desire, there seemed to be a built-in harmony, at least for Hegel's disciples on the "right," between the subjective choice that led us willingly to obey the law and the rationality of the law that was being obeyed. Freedom and necessity are one.

But if the actuality or reality in the chiasm "what is real is rational, what is rational is real" is understood instead as a state of affairs not yet attained, what does exist can be understood as still only potentially rational and not yet fully there. For those who prized the critical impulse in Hegel's dialectics—the "left Hegelians," as they came to be called—this was the reading that seemed most potent, and remained so for many years after. Take, for example, the extensive discussion of the passage at the beginning of Friedrich Engels's 1888 tract *Ludwig Feuerbach and the End of Classical German Philosophy*. Quoting—or rather slightly misquoting—the passage as "all that is real is rational; and all that is rational is real," Engels acknowledged that "no philosophical proposition has earned more gratitude from narrow-minded governments and wrath from equally narrow-minded liberals" for being a "sanctification of things that be, a philosophical benediction bestowed upon despotism, police government, Star Chamber proceedings and censorship."[47] But then he noted that this was the wrong interpretation, for "according to Hegel certainly not everything that exists is also real, without further qualification. For Hegel the attribute of reality belongs only to that which at the same time is necessary."[48] In fact, Engels went on, citing the case of the *ancien régime* before the French Revolution, what had existed had lost its claim to reality and thus also its rationality: "in the course of development, all that was previously real becomes unreal, loses its necessity, its right of existence, its rationality. . . . Everything within the mind which is rational in the minds of men is destined to become real, however much it may contradict existing apparent reality. In accordance with the rules of the Hegelian method of thought, the proposition of the rationality of everything which is real resolves itself into the other proposition: All that exists deserves to perish."[49] While

Engels conceded that the substance of Hegel's system may have contradicted this conclusion, he argued that the dialectical method he had bequeathed to Marx inevitably led to it.[50]

Engels's gloss on the passage is significant for several reasons besides its typification of an enduring left Hegelian reading. It is worth pausing with them now because Engels provided a foil for later Western Marxists, beginning with Georg Lukács and including the Frankfurt School, who read Hegel differently. First is its conflation of reality and reason with a putative "right to existence," which contradicts Hegel's argument—his temporalized theodicy—that even the most apparently irrational moment in the ongoing dialectical totality is part of the comprehensive narrative of rational historical development and thus its existence is in some sense justified. That is, rather than saying that what fails to live up to absolute reason should simply perish, Hegel had used the verb *aufheben*, a pun that suggested more than mere cancellation or abolition. The English term of art "to sublate" is often introduced to translate it, as we have already done, although sometimes it is left in the original and defined as containing multiple meanings, including "to abolish," "to transcend," "to supersede," "to pick up," "to raise," "to keep," "to preserve," "to end," and "to annul." However it may be rendered, it is clear that it has more complex resonances than the "perish" that Engels borrowed from a famous line of Mephistopheles in Goethe's *Faust*.[51] Acorns that become oaks do not simply "perish"; they are incorporated into the mature tree, which of course itself then generates more of them. Potentiality becoming actuality is not the same as one social or political order utterly perishing in order for another to be born. As Charles Taylor puts it, "at earlier stages reason will be imperfectly realized; in this sense the real will also be irrational, or not fully rational. But since these stages themselves follow necessity, since they are dictated by reason, we can say that the stage of relative imperfection that reason has reached at any given time is itself according to reason."[52]

Second, Engels's identification of reason with necessity alone reduces the former to the causal determinism that we have seen was only one aspect of the principle of sufficient reason. The link between reason and freedom so cherished by Kant and continued by Hegel was severed with Engels's unnuanced claim that rational ideas are "destined to become real." As Adorno was to note, the notion that the real is rational is "not merely apologetic. Rather, in Hegel reason finds itself constellated with freedom. Freedom and reason are nonsense without one another. The real can be considered rational only insofar as the idea of freedom, that is, human beings' genuine self-determination, shines through it."[53] Although that self-determination had to be rational to be truly free rather than the outcome of random impulse or unreflected desire, it could not be reduced for Hegel to mere conformity with external laws, such as those that ruled nature.[54] In contrast, Engels endorsed a determinist view of dialectical development that implicitly bracketed the importance of the deliberate, freely chosen act in realizing reason, as well as the giving of reasons and judging them as reasonable that was also a critical component of the tradition (itself a source, as we have seen, of chagrin for later commentators like Heidegger, but also positive for others like Habermas).

Engels's treatise *Feuerbach and the End of German Classical Philosophy* was, to be sure, written after Marx's death in 1883 and has often been interpreted as one of the early expressions of what Marxist humanists came to lament as the scientistic "betrayal of Marx."[55] Although there were moments in Engels's own subsequent consideration of these issues when he retreated from a strictly determinist position, he was generally taken to be its advocate.[56] What, we have to ask, was Marx's own attitude toward reason in history, and how successful was he in extending it beyond the limits posited by Kantian critical Idealism? To do full justice to this question would be to open the vexed issue of the continuities between Hegel and Marx, or the lack thereof, which exercised a generation of Western Marxists in the late twentieth century.[57] It might also require a serious evaluation of attempts to find Spinoza's rationalism an even more potent source, which inspired such twentieth-century Marxists as Louis Althusser.[58] Instead, we can only focus on some of the ways in which Marxism held on to and transformed the rationalist project of the left Hegelians, and try to unpack his understanding of reason itself.

In many respects, Marx sought to go beyond German Idealism, in both its critical and speculative guises. His embrace of an explicitly materialist position — understood more in terms of historical than dialectical materialism, the latter being a term developed only by certain of his followers[59] — meant that he eschewed the claim that thought in general and reason in particular could be the motor of history. From the beginning of his career, as evidenced by his dismissal of Rationalist ontological proofs for the existence of God in his dissertation and his mockery of Pierre-Joseph Proudhon's vulgar Hegelianism in *The Poverty of Philosophy*,[60] he had no use for an abstract rationalism that hovered above the world, stressing instead economic modes of production and the relations between social classes. Nor did he have any patience for the comforting Hegelian claim that apparent unreason in history was in reality a form of reason, a claim he scorned as "Hegel's *false* positivism" and "merely *apparent* criticism."[61] He would have endorsed Engels's mockery in the influential 1880 tract *Socialism: Utopian and Scientific* of the Enlightenment's universalist rationalism as "in reality nothing but the idealized understanding of the eighteenth-century citizen, just then evolving into the bourgeois."[62] It was not, *pace* Hegel, the "labor of the concept" that he celebrated but labor of a more physical/social kind, albeit one that could also move beyond alienated toil to become an expression of human spirit as well.

Nor did Marx ever rest content with a retrospective view of the past as the narrative of realized reason. As has often been noted, he replaced an Epimethean emphasis on the completed past with a Promethean one on a future still to be made, an outlook that underlay his hope that collective rational planning might one day supplant the unintended consequences of competitive individual decisions under capitalism. Here, we might say, he harbored the hope that a fully dispositional view of reason would ultimately replace a nondispositional one, when men made history rather than being the victim of a process outside of their control. The "invisible hand" of the market would become the visible hands of real men and women deciding their own fate. But because his materialism took seriously the demands of the body and the cultivation of the senses, it went even further than had Hegel's Idealism in validating desires, or at least the legitimate expansion and satisfaction of human needs. In *Reason and Revolution*, Marcuse could even go as far as to claim that "Marxian theory has developed a full contradiction to the basic conception of idealist philosophy. The idea of reason has been superseded by the idea of happiness. . . . Hegel had emphatically denied that the progress of reason would have anything to do with the satisfaction of individual happiness. . . . The Marxian theory consequently rejected even the advanced ideas of the Hegelian scheme. The category of happiness made manifest the positive content of materialism."[63] There was also, he continued, an important distinction between their concepts of totality: "For Hegel, the totality was the totality of reason; a closed ontological system, finally identical with the rational system of history. . . . Marx, on the other hand, detached dialectic from this ontological base."[64]

And yet, *pace* Marcuse, it is clear that reason still played a pivotal role in Marx's progressive narrative of historical development toward the realization of a society in which happiness would be finally achieved. As early as his 1842 polemic against "the Historical School" of Karl von Savigny and Gustav Hugo, he mocked the deification of positive, irrational historical fact as a value in itself. Of Hugo, he wrote, "the *skepticism of the eighteenth century* concerning the *rationality of existing conditions* becomes *skepticism* concerning the *existence of reason*. . . . *In what is positive he no longer sees anything rational, but only so that he won't have to see in what is rational anything positive*."[65] Marx's investment in reason was also evident in his strong attachment to scientificity—however that might be defined—in his method of understanding the world. Although acknowledging what he saw as the bourgeois underpinnings of the Enlightenment, Marx shared its commitment to the link between freedom and reason, and, after recovering from his youthful infatuation with Romanticism, he had little patience for the various "others" of reason, such as myth, emotion, faith, or rhetoric, however much he may have valued literature and often employed vivid metaphors in his own writing.[66]

For a brief time in the 1980s, some Marxists even attempted to integrate Marxism into the then fashionable "rational choice theory," which had its roots in Cold War liberalism.[67] Because its exponents sought to purge Marx entirely of his Hegelian roots and reconcile him with twentieth-century analytic philosophy, it was a marriage that was ill-starred from the beginning. For it is impossible to understand the rationalist dimension of Marx's thought without acknowledging his debt to German Idealism in general, and Hegel in particular, however much he may have criticized them.[68]

With Hegel, Marx resisted the claim that reason was a transcendent standard of cognitive or moral perfection hovering ahistorically above the actual world. Instead, it was immanent in the world, embedded in the institutions and practices of human life, although still more on the level of latent potentiality than fully manifested actuality. As he put it in a frequently cited letter of September 1843 to his friend Arnold Ruge, published shortly thereafter in the *Deutsch-Französische Jahrbücher*,

> Reason has always existed, only not always in a rational form. The critic can therefore start out by taking any form of theoretical and practical consciousness and develop from the *unique* forms of existing reality the true reality as its norm and final goal. Now so far as real life is concerned, precisely the *political state* in all its *modern* forms contains, even where it is not yet consciously imbued with socialist demands, the demands of reason. Nor does the state stop at that. The state everywhere presupposes that reason has been realized. But in just this way it everywhere comes into contradiction between its ideal mission and its real preconditions.[69]

With typical Left Hegelian faith in the ultimate capacity of the world to make manifest its latent rationality, the young Marx pointedly directed his fire at the Right Hegelian claim that the modern state, independent of the social and economic conditions on which it was founded, could represent a fully realized reason. Unlike Hegel himself, he had no illusions about the rationality of a state bureaucracy claiming universal disinterestedness above the conflicts of civil society.[70]

Although as he matured Marx reduced his explicit entanglement with Hegel's philosophy—so much so that some interpreters such as Althusser could even claim he underwent an "epistemological break" with his early involvement

when he became truly "scientific"[71] — the residues were apparent in the rationalist underpinnings of historical materialism. Many generations of Marxists
repeated his celebrated imperative in *Capital* to turn Hegel "right side up again,
if you would discover the rational kernel within the mystical shell,"[72] although
they may have disagreed about what precisely that kernel contained. Marx
may well have been more tacitly indebted to Hegel's *Lectures on the History of
Philosophy* than his *Lectures on the Philosophy of History*, because the former offers a
narrative of progress in philosophical reasoning as a succession of inadequate
and insufficient but partially true and thus necessary positions, which were
sublated into Hegel's own culminating system. Allan Megill goes so far as to
argue that

> the *History of Philosophy* is the one dialectical history Hegel wrote. There is
> no other. Hegel's rationality-criteria are displayed in his other works also,
> but only in this work did he come close to exemplifying these criteria in a
> historical work. . . . Marx takes as his model for history-in-general a particu-
> lar history that is rational by definition, since philosophy, which is the
> object of the history of philosophy, is itself aimed at the rational apprehen-
> sion of reality.[73]

Insofar as dialectic had once meant the give and take of philosophical argumentation, we might conclude that there was a latent dianoetic component in
Marx's depiction of historical development, which suggested intersubjective,
communicative interaction among participants in the making of history. But if
such a potential existed in Marx's thought, it was blunted by his adoption of the
proletariat, understood as a potentially universal class both for-itself and in-itself,
as a surrogate for the singular metasubject that Hegel had identified with the
Absolute Spirit.[74] Although building on Ludwig Feuerbach's anthropological
inversion of Hegel's problematic claim that Spirit was the subject and Man the
predicate, Marx did, to be sure, argue that the abstract human subject should
be situated more concretely in history. That is, there were only men (and pre-
sumably women), not Feuerbach's "Man," and despite his early adoption of
the phrase "species being," no universal essence lurked behind or beneath
actual social relations.[75] And yet, Marx still understood reason largely in terms
of a monologic "consciousness philosophy" writ large, in which Hegel's "expressivist" view of the metasubject of history was now identified with the praxis of
the proletariat. This assumption may have uncomfortably jostled with the
functional rationality of Marx's more structuralist argument about the ways in
which capitalism operated on autopilot, as if it were a second nature. But in
either case, a dialogic notion of reason was largely absent. In each instead,

there was a residue of Hegel's pan-logicism in Marx's emphasis on the role of objective "contradiction" in history, an inherently logical concept that is not the same as a difference of opinion or opposition between views, which might be reconciled through dialogic interaction.[76]

It was this notion of monologic rationality that has allowed Marx to be accused of underestimating the virtues of political pluralism and fallibilism, and unwittingly enabling the rise of an elite, soi-disant vanguard party that asserted its right to represent the general interest of the universal class, and thus of humankind as a whole. It was this belief in the central role of labor and production, whether of the concept or the commodity, that led the mature Marx to marginalize the rationality in communicative interaction, at least according to Habermas:

> The parallels between Hegel and Marx are striking. In their youth, both thinkers held open the option of using the idea of uncoerced will formation in a communication community existing under constraints of cooperation as a model for the reconciliation of a divided bourgeois society. But later on, both forsake the use of this option, and they do it for similar reasons. Like Hegel, Marx is weighted down by the basic conceptual necessities of the philosophy of the subject.[77]

It was also this notion of rationality that fueled Marx's disdain for the "irrationality" of the capitalist marketplace and his faith in rational economic planning as an antidote to the anarchy of exchange relations left unregulated.[78] And finally, it was this notion of subject-centered rationality that allowed a relatively smooth transition from the Hegelian valorization of totalizing *Vernunft* to a scientific notion of reason as an organon of domination over the natural world. As one commentator has put it, "for Marx, freedom simply means the extension of the modern world's *rational* organization of its technical mastery of nature (against *irrational* practices imbedded in capitalism), so that abundance is assured. This sets the parameters for all other freedoms."[79]

In this reading, what the Frankfurt School later decried as "instrumental rationality" leading to the domination of nature was already ominously present in Marx, whose Promethean faith in the power of "the forces of production," once they were liberated from the shackles of capitalist "relations of production," could lead inadvertently to the fetishism of technology.[80] This is not the place to engage in yet another polemic over whether or not Marx relied too heavily on the intrinsically emancipatory function of technological progress.[81] But it is worth pausing to acknowledge a counterargument, based on the similarity of Marx's claims with ones we have already encountered in Kant's

"Idea for a Universal History with a Cosmopolitan Aim." The most obvious parallel was his stress on the ultimately positive consequences of class conflict, which echoed Kant's claim that "unsocial sociability" had unintended benefits, as well, of course, as Hegel's belief that "reason" had the capacity to be "cunning" in its use of apparent negation to produce affirmative outcomes.

But more important for the larger question we are addressing is the fact that Marx at times also shared Kant's strategy to avoid choosing between the two notions of reason, dispositional and nondispositional, that had emerged with the breakdown of Leibniz's overly homogenous "principle of sufficient reason." Kant, it will be recalled, had attributed a teleological impulse in nature to make manifest what was a latent potential in it, the capacity for reason given only to humans. Here the functional nondispositional notion of an impersonal *system* rationality was understood to be ultimately in the service of a burgeoning *practical* rationality involving free choice and the ability to reason intersubjectively. Reason was thus historical, collective, and immanently realized in an open-ended learning process both theoretical and practical, cognitive and moral, in the world of human institutions and interactions. Lest this be construed as an implausible transformation, let the maturation of an irrational child into a (more or less) rational adult serve as its rough equivalent. Kant, to be sure, denied a triumphant conclusion for his "as if" narrative, in which a rational society was fully realized, and decoupled individual, material happiness from the species project of collective rationalization. But—and this was the critical anticipation of Marx—he posited the gradual transition from one form of reason to another, the blind reason of the system to the self-conscious, practical reasoning of the human beings who were both its agents and its beneficiaries. That the transition was not a simple before and after is shown by his adoption of the seemingly oxymoronic phrase the "causality of freedom" to describe the way in which will can intervene in the impersonal chain of causes and initiate something new in the world, which itself can lead to a fresh causal chain.

The logic of Marx's argument was similar, even if he were less inclined to a teleological view of nature and saw the transition as a more abrupt process than Kant, although not one that was entirely lacking in gradual but cumulative transformations in the objective possibilities presented by a system increasingly in crisis. There was evidence in his writings—beginning with his 1841 doctoral dissertation on the distinction between Democritus and Epicurus[82]—that could be read as an endorsement of the view that nature, and perhaps history as well, was ruled by objective causal forces, even if there were also textual evidence to the contrary. Because of his general inclination in much of his published work toward causal explanations of the kind defended by Democritus, Marx's followers after his death could easily understand his social theory as equally determinist. I have already mentioned Engels's contribution to this outcome.

What was often forgotten, however, was that Marx has also employed the concept of an artificially constructed "second nature" to describe the ways in which history—in particular the system of capitalist social relations—had developed seemingly natural institutions, practices, and relations that operated "as if" they were as causally binding as the first nature. Moishe Postone succinctly describes the implications of this distinction:

> The historical development of capitalism, then, of a society based upon an abstract quasi-natural form of social domination entailed not only the supersession of direct, personal forms of social domination but also the partial overcoming of the domination of humans by nature. In other words, to the degree that, with the development of capitalism, humanity freed itself from its overwhelming dependence on the vagaries of its natural environment, it did so by the non-conscious and unintentional creation of a quasi-natural structure of domination constituted by nature, a sort of "second nature"; it overcame the domination of the first, of the natural environment, at the price of constituting the domination of this second nature.[83]

Because Marx conceived of capitalist social and economic relations operating as if they were an impersonal, dominating "second nature," he thought he could treat them in terms of automatic laws of development, whose contradictions would produce fatal crises that could be delayed but not indefinitely forestalled. A rational "scientific" analysis of these laws would allow the theorist to understand processes that "worked behind the backs and against the wills" of men in the way that "unsocial sociability" and the "cunning of reason" had for Kant and Hegel. Although the term "reification" (*Verdinglichung*) was not introduced until somewhat later to the Marxist tradition by theorists like the Hungarian Georg Lukács, it expresses the spirit of Marx's analysis of capitalism, in which humanly created processes appear as natural laws, and commodities produced by human labor for human use are converted into self-sufficient objects or things to be exchanged in the marketplace.[84]

But what is crucial to note and what some of his followers did not fully appreciate is that Marx, like Kant before him, believed that free human activity—the revolutionary praxis he identified preeminently with the proletariat—could somehow liberate itself from those causal chains and undo the grip of second nature, which was not beholden to immutable laws. It was, in fact, precisely the historically specific ideological effect of capitalism to produce such apparently natural laws (e.g., the law of supply and demand). As in the case of Kant's "idea" of a universal history, which was itself intended as a spur to bring it about, those who possess the scientific knowledge of capitalist laws—or to give

Kant's more cautious formula, adopt the regulative ideal of such knowledge—and are able to see through their pseudo-naturalist surface also have the potential to change them. As Charles Taylor puts it,

> while Marx takes up Hegel's concept of the cunning of reason, this fails to apply to the last great revolution. In Marxist thought, the bourgeois, and earlier political actors cannot understand the significance of their acts; they do more and other than they think. But this is not true of the proletariat. These have in Marxism a scientific view of things. In this case the significance of their innovative action is understood by the actors.[85]

After the revolution, at least Marx implied, a different version of rationality would prevail, not one that passively contemplated natural laws—or the law-like forces that determined social relations as if they were a "second nature"—with the external eye of a scientist but rather a reason that was what we have called fully "dispositional," based on the intentions and deliberations of a collective community of free actors, a universal society beyond class distinction, no longer driven by structural contradictions beyond their control. As Marx put it in the third volume of *Capital*, "freedom in this field can only consist in socialized man, the associated producers, rationally regulating their interchange with Nature, bringing it under their common control, instead of being ruled by it as by the blind forces of Nature."[86] This was not the "randomization of history and politics" that some orthodox Marxists feared but the hope that the causality of material conditions would be a spell that one day might be broken.[87]

Or so the humanist reading of Marx came to argue. But what if this liberated humankind still operated with a concept of reason that was uncomfortably close to the Hegelian idea of a single metasubject whose rationality and that of the world he had created were identical? What if such a version of reason were based on a consciousness-philosophy model of monologic rationality writ large, which underestimated the value of unsublated pluralism in human affairs? What if this type of reason, always yearning for a Promethean "subject of history" to serve as a surrogate for Hegel's "Absolute Spirit," also neglected to acknowledge the costs of subduing first nature, and in so doing continued the process of domination that occurs under capitalism with the construction of "second nature"? What if the reason it promulgated was a distorted and partial variant, which had crowded out its more benign alternatives? What, in short, if the well-intentioned project of rationalizing the world had produced not emancipation but a new tyranny?

In response to these and similar questions (as well as their reading of the uncertain fate of class struggle), some later Marxists came to realize, it might be

worth revisiting the limits of reason in its several varieties. Perhaps it was necessary even to return to Kant rather than hoping for a Hegelian sublation of all of
them into a comic narrative of benign reconciliation. The so-called Revisionists
in late nineteenth-century Germany, typified by the German Social Democrat
Eduard Bernstein, were perhaps the best-known advocates of a Kantian socialism, although more for moral than cognitive reasons. Undoing the immanent
dialectic of is and ought, lamenting the widening gap between the world of
surface "facts" and the allegedly objective forces beneath them, skeptical of the
deepening crisis of capitalism posited by more orthodox Second International
theoreticians, they fell back on a frankly ethical imperative to change a world
that was not heading by itself in a rational direction.

But even after the revival of a more Hegelian Marxism had taken place in
the 1920s, a Marxism that drew on the renewed hope produced by the Soviet
revolution and then spawned a more "Western Marxism" that found in Hegel
rather than Lenin its major inspiration, the ghost of Kant could still return to
haunt Marxist theory.[88] Let us finish this section with one suggestive example,
which involves the Frankfurt School. In the lectures he gave in Frankfurt on
Kant's first Critique in the mid-1960s, Adorno pointed out what he saw as a
productive contradiction in the work. On the one hand, the Copernican Revolution that privileged the subjective structuring of cognition brought a new kind
of identity thinking into philosophy, one in which objects of experience were
decisively formed by transcendental subjectivity. Here we can see an anticipation
of the strongly constitutive subject beloved by Marxist humanists, who expanded
it beyond the transcendental subject of epistemology to an ontologically creative
actor who actually made the world through both its labor and political praxis.
But in tension with this impulse in Kant was the philosopher's recognition that
there was always something ontologically real in excess of those constituted
objects. This latter recognition continued the late Enlightenment project of
questioning the overweening claims of demythologized, overly anthropomorphic reason in which men had been wrongly given the unlimited powers once
attributed to the gods. "The greatness of the *Critique of Pure Reason*," Adorno
argued, "is that these two motifs clash. To give a stark description we might
say that the book contains an identity philosophy—that is, a philosophy that
attempts to ground being in the subject—and also a nonidentity philosophy—
one that attempts to restrict that claim to identity by insisting on the obstacles,
the *block*, encountered by the subject in its search for knowledge."[89]

Adorno, as we know, came to embrace a negative dialectics, critical in
nuanced ways of both scientist and humanist Marxism alike, which privileged
nonidentity over identity and defended the preeminence of the object over the
subject. He warned against the coercive potential in a dialectical thought that

sought to impose the "cunning of reason" on a world that was always in excess of it.[90] But while valorizing the stubborn resistance of "the block," he did not entirely repudiate the claims of reason or abandon the utopian impulse he saw in the Marxist project, as I will show in a later chapter. There were, however, many other ways in which the "block" to a capacious and emphatic notion of reason could be more dogmatically conceived, even ultimately undermining *any* trust in its emancipatory or even critical power. The danger of total disillusionment, in fact, always shadowed measured efforts to curtail the ambitions of a reason that seemed a bit too excessively "sufficient." For the revenge of its various marginalized or excluded "others" could unintentionally turn into a wholesale repudiation of reason *tout court*. Kant himself had warned against this very threat, and even identified it with a term he resurrected from Plato's dialogue *Phaedo*, "misology."[91] Hegel echoed his warning, while extending the charge of misology to all those who denied dialectical reason and thus by implication to Kant as well.[92]

But from the heights of Hegel's pan-logist redemption of reason, the only direction was down. Coming too close to the blazing sun, as the Greeks knew when they imagined Icarus falling from the sky to his death in the sea, has its dangers. As in the case of the seventeenth-century Rationalists, many functional equivalents of the Lisbon earthquake conspired to undermine confidence not only in ours being the best of all possible worlds but also the faith that history was somehow progressing, even fitfully, toward that goal. The struggle to make it happen was, to be sure, not entirely abandoned, even well into the twentieth century. For unlike in the famous ekphrastic poem by William Carlos Williams, reflecting on Pieter Breughel's landscape depiction of the Icarus legend, the decline of reason did not produce a "splash quite unnoticed."[93] Instead, it was accompanied by a thundering clash between those who gleefully celebrated its tumble and those who sought to rescue the drowning boy before he went entirely under.

# 4

# Reason in Crisis

When did the inevitable Icarian fall from rationalist hubris happen? Or to stay with our dominant metaphor, when did the eclipse begin?[1] Was it a function of obstacles that could ultimately be overcome or was there something problematic in the very project of rationalizing a world that was so recalcitrant to that goal? According to one commentator, the German philosopher of religion Georg Picht, the descent began in the late Enlightenment: "at the moment in which reason, knowing itself, achieves enlightenment concerning the fact that the historically existing subject of reason cannot postulate its identity with the absolute subject of transcendental reason. At this point the history of the decline of reason begins."[2] Humean skepticism was an early indication of its vulnerability, even if Kant's response seemed for a while to meet the challenge. But despite the efforts of Kant, the young Hegelians, and Marx to turn the existing distinction between the transcendental and the empirical into a historical imperative to make the imperfect actual subject ultimately live up to the regulative ideal of absolute reason, the opposite conclusion could also be drawn. That is, the existing flawed subject of reason—culturally bound, linguistically limited, motivated by unreflective desires, unshakeable prejudices, and unjustifiable passions—could be understood as the hidden truth behind the fantasy of an unrealizable ideal subject, which was then understood to be merely an ideological cover for the promotion of less exalted ends. In this debunking mood, reason was disdainfully turned into a tool of power, understood as inherently beyond rational justification.[3] Psychologistic reductionism trumped the effort to ground reason in a logism that transcended the fallible judgments of the mere mortals who exercised it. Validity became entirely an effect of genesis. Whether called the hermeneutics of suspicion, the genealogical method, or just aggressive contextualism, the critique of reason—or rather, to employ a term already in play at the time of Hamann's attack on Kant, the "metacritique" of reason[4]—led to widespread disenchantment with its elevated status.[5]

The optimistic metanarrative of impersonal, nondispositional rationalization, which we have seen animating much of the German Idealist and Marxist traditions, stalled with the growing suspicion that it had become an autonomous process no longer serving human emancipation, a fear that led in particular to alarm about the dangers of unchecked technological rationality becoming an end in itself. The souring of radical political hopes in 1848 worked to sharpen that disillusionment with a history that resisted a comic narration. Not surprisingly, a recent intellectual history of the period from 1848 to 1914 could call itself—without pausing to explore what "reason" might have meant—"the crisis of reason."[6] Although it was anything but a smooth ride down—there was, after all, a vigorous "return to Kant" movement in European philosophy after 1860 that survived even into the interwar era,[7] and the "psychologistic" onslaught against "logicism" lost its momentum after the war[8]—anything that might remotely be called the "age of reason" had clearly passed. It was easier to speak instead, to cite the title of a recent study of French culture from 1914 to 1940, of "the embrace of unreason."[9]

The manifestations of this erosion of confidence in reason, which had practical as well as theoretical implications, were legion, and it would take another volume to do them justice. We would have to look at religious and aesthetic, as well as social and political, trends, and detail many arguments within the tradition of philosophy itself. We would have to examine the ways in which rationalization in one sphere could be coupled with its reversal in another, thus complicating any simply Weberian notion of modern society as having entirely superseded its traditional predecessor. We would need to explore the crisis of the humanist notion of the subject or self—either understood transcendentally or individually—as a bearer of rational judgment.[10] We would have to probe the links between the crisis of faith in history as the arena of the realization of reason and the undermining of Western history as a story of progressive civilization and widening enlightenment, with such turning points as the failed revolutions of 1848 and the outbreak of war in 1914 serving as decisive junctures in the declension narrative. We would have to summarize the subtle and controversial arguments and chart the checkered fortunes of such major figures as Jacobi, Kierkegaard, Nietzsche, Henri Bergson, and Heidegger, as well as more dubious purveyors of an aggressive anti-rationalism, such as Oswald Spengler, Ludwig Klages, and Carl Schmitt.

Instead, we will confine ourselves to only two aspects of the larger story: the rise of *Lebensphilosophie* (philosophy of life) or vitalism, and, perhaps more surprising, the triumph of positivist scientism as an alleged successor to rational philosophy. The first represents the revenge of one of the most potent "others" of reason: embodied, material, desiring, energetic life, with all of its apparent irreducibility to the constraints of the rational mind and the mechanical causality of physical nature. The second expresses a tendency within reason itself to turn anything that does not accept those constraints into its abjected "other," to be expelled into outer darkness or brought under control.

I will take each of them in turn, and then conclude with a few thoughts on the unexpected ways in which vitalism and positivism could themselves be combined with more than just theoretical implications. Broadly defined, vitalism valued the flourishing of organic life—with all of its metaphorical social, aesthetic, political, and cultural connotations—over the mortifying dissection of analytic reason.[11] Moving beyond the traditional dichotomy of matter and spirit, it posited something between them with properties reducible to neither. The opposition of life and reason had not always seemed self-evident. Indeed, for Hegel, "life" was understood to be an early example of the unification of contradictions that was the hallmark of reason itself.[12] The *animal rationale* was, as we have noted, not traditionally considered an oxymoron. As Paul Harrison has pointed out, the figure of Socrates had traditionally been understood as an exemplary instance of the "life of the mind": "the mythical embodiment of the *bios theoretikos* [theoretical life] illustrates that unity of life-conduct and philosophical practice that made the life of reason more than simply a metaphor and that is now no longer possible in modernity."[13] The Enlightenment had already seen the rise of protovitalist interpretations of nature.[14] But the now seemingly obvious contrast between organic and natural, on the one hand, and mechanical and artificial, on the other, was not, as it were, in full flower as a cultural opposition until the nineteenth century.[15] Indeed, "organic" was not yet fully differentiated from "organized," with its explicit connotation of rationally planned, until that period.

Vitalism as a self-conscious philosophy expressed precisely those distinctions. Whether understood biologically or aesthetically, whether applied to nature or history, the organic privileged the integrity of wholes over parts, spontaneous growth over mechanical tinkering, relational interdependence over isolated entities, the ultimate source of energy as internal rather than external, and the assimilation of matter into an organized "vital" system beyond mechanical contrivance. Instead of stressing substance, vital materialism privileged force and energy. As we have noted in the case of Kant's increasing fascination with nature understood teleologically (at least as a regulative idea), the premise that meaning was inherent in the development of potentiality into actuality was a powerful alternative for those who were no longer sure of providential intervention in nature or history. For those impatient with the universalizing abstraction and formalism of rationalist thought, valorizing the overflowing plenitude and infinite variety of teeming life seemed a compelling remedy.

For some observers, vitalism could also lead in dangerous directions, especially when it was simply counterposed as a simplistic antidote to reflective thought or calculating reason. When the faculty of intuition lost its connection to noetic reason and instead became a way to grasp in a flash of holistic illumination an alleged truth that analytic and discursive reasoning could not appreciate, as it did most explicitly in Bergson's vitalism, it risked becoming a warrant for incommunicable and unverifiable nonsense. In Goethe's *Faust*, it should be recalled, it was the devil who utters the typical vitalist claim: "Gray, my dear friend, is every theory, and green alone life's golden tree."[16] Turning "life" into a value unto itself could be directed not only against reflective thinking but also against attempts at moral valuation. Defending biological "mere life" as a self-sufficient value avoided the question, as old as Aristotle and the ancient Greeks, of how to identify the "good life." Often appealing to a crypto-normativity in which life—sometimes understood on the individual level, sometimes on that of the species—was somehow its own justification or "survival of the fittest" the measure of ultimate value,[17] vitalism could lose the critical edge that so often accompanied defenses of reason and become a warrant for abandoning any hopes for improving the human condition.

And yet, at a time when the costs of modernizing rationalization—however that might be understood—were becoming increasingly apparent, it was tempting to turn to "life" for an alternative to what seemed the shortcomings of reason. Although there are many obvious examples, such as the Sturm und Drang poets, the Romantics, Herder, and the naturalist Johann Friedrich Blumenbach, as well as later figures such as the sociologist Georg Simmel,[18] it will be most useful to focus on one particularly influential voice in the chorus of antirational celebrants of something called "life": Arthur Schopenhauer.[19] For in many respects, Schopenhauer illustrated both the promise and dangers of vitalism. Spurning the optimism of Leibniz and other Enlightenment Rationalists, he was a dogged pessimist who denied that this was the best of all possible worlds or, more importantly, that it could possibly get better through human action. "If the act of procreation were neither the outcome of a desire nor accompanied by feelings of pleasure, but a matter to be decided on the basis of purely rational considerations," he sardonically asked, "is it likely the human race would still exist? Would each of us not rather have felt so much pity for the coming generation as to prefer to spare it the burden of existence, or at least not wish to take it upon himself to impose that burden upon it in cold blood?"[20] Against Kant, he once again separated the will from reason and turned the former into more than an individual faculty of choice. Instead, it became the name for the irrational desire that coursed unsatiated through all of existence without ever finding a place to rest. Scorning the elevation of practical reason as binding not merely on men but on all conceivably rational beings, he substituted a morality of compassion and pity. The primacy of practical reason, he contended, violated Kant's own injunction against the illegitimate extension of reason to answer metaphysical questions; it was as useless in determining deontological imperatives as it was in establishing ontological truths. No less hostile to Hegel, whom he vituperatively defamed as a charlatan, Schopenhauer mocked the claim that reason was immanent in history, preferring instead to see the latter as an arena of blind, directionless striving with no telos in sight. Reason for Schopenhauer was not autonomous or self-sufficient, nor a handmaiden of human freedom, but merely a functional expression of the will to live.

Although Schopenhauer's vitalist impact was most explosive in the post-1848 climate of pessimistic disenchantment with both reason and revolution, it is worth remembering that in his dissertation, written in 1813 at the University of Jena when he was twenty-six, before his mature philosophy was fully fashioned, Schopenhauer had defended the "principle of sufficient reason" as "the mother of all sciences" and the "*principle of all explanation.*"[21] Endorsing Kant's reluctance to extend the principle of sufficient reason into a metaphysical assurance that reason underlies everything that exists, the mistake of earlier Rationalists like Leibniz and Wolff, Schopenhauer stressed that it was solely a principle of human cognition. Thus Kant was right to question the validity of ontological or cosmological proofs for the existence of God and the immortality of the soul, neither of which could be known by us. He was also right to reject the search for a first cause and the belief, held by Spinoza, that something could ever be a self-sufficient *causa sui,* an unconditioned "absolute," independent of a human faculty to realize it. Against the efforts of post-Kantian Idealists like Fichte and Hegel to reassert the ontological basis of rationality, Schopenhauer firmly located it in the judgment of the knowing subject, not in reality as such. His was an even more radical subjectivism when it came to knowledge than Kant's critical idealism. Rejecting the Kantian thing-in-itself as an unnecessary concession to our need for a limit to knowledge (and as an expression of an unwarranted fear of being called a Berkeleyan solipsist), he argued that only representations exist, not the things represented. "*To be object for the subject,*" he contended, "*and to be our representation or mental picture are the same thing. All our representations are objects of the subject, and all objects of the subject are our representations.*"[22] The regular connections that exist among objects are the result of our a priori reasoning, and can be distinguished according to four different classes of represented objects. In other words, at a time when speculative Idealism was seeking to extend the ontological reach of reason in ways that Kant had denied were possible, the young Schopenhauer was content to explore the way it functioned in human interaction with various objects of knowledge, while denying its ontological import.

In short order, however, Schopenhauer left behind the relatively cautious formulations of his dissertation and embraced a forthright metaphysics of the irrational will in which he conflated it with the Platonic idea, the Kantian noumenon, and virtually anything else that previous philosophers had assigned the role of ultimate ontological truth. He thus moved closer to the position of later critics of rationality like Heidegger, who said that both seeking causes and giving reasons were not as profound as being open to a deeper truth that revealed itself to the thinker able to receive it.[23]

Although Schopenhauer was overshadowed by Hegel for most of his career, his time would come in the second half of the nineteenth century, as the vitalist tradition grew increasingly impatient with the claims of reason in whatever guise. As a recent observer put it with reference to one of its major exponents, "in the thought of Nietzsche, the rose of reason does not wither; rather it is crushed."[24] Even if sometimes that crushing was less total than its detractors allowed, it nonetheless fueled the impression that defending reason was somehow on the side of life-denying decadence.[25] Schopenhauer's *On the Fourfold Root*, however, is useful to recall because it reminds us of a moment when a future metaphysician of the irrational will was still able to produce a sympathetic account of one of the cornerstones of rationalist thought. As such, it helps us avoid any simple opposition between rationalism and irrationalism, and allows us to appreciate the ways in which the two could be intertwined once the more robust and emphatic notion of reason still apparent in German Idealism and Marxism had lost its allure.

In fact, a combination of vitalism and at least one variant of reason was also often evident in the other major intellectual development that came into its own during the era of disillusionment with reason in the second half of the nineteenth century: positivism. For all his advocacy of aesthetic contemplation as a way to escape the meaninglessness of existence, Schopenhauer was himself a close follower of the empirical science of his day, and incorporated physiological findings into his worldview.[26] His belief in a "vital force" underlying life may have become an embarrassment to later followers—they have preferred to call it a kind of "emergentism" that resists the reduction of biology to chemistry[27]—but it expresses his involvement with the cutting-edge science of the time. Well after his passing from the scene—he died in 1860—vitalism and positivism could in fact forge an uneasy alliance as well as confront each other as alternatives. And in certain respects, that alliance could paradoxically head in an ultimately antirationalist direction.

The relationship between science and reason is, of course, itself by no means a settled question.[28] We have noted, for example, that Kant defended synthetic a priori judgments producing new knowledge about the world against an analytic, a priori rationalism that gave too much power to what Hegel would praise as "the labor of the concept." Because of his acknowledgement of the critical role of the a priori moment in cognition, Kant had maintained his distance from a purely empiricist and inductivist version of the scientific method. Indeed, as I have noted in discussing his faith in the ultimate unity of theoretical and practical reason, he maintained the claim that nature as a rational system must function as a regulative ideal underlying all scientific inquiry. But he was still firm in his belief that pure reason was too tautological and self-referential to provide new knowledge about the world. His speculative Idealist successors were, however, less cautious in their claims for the power of reason. When their theories were empirically refuted, they notoriously replied—the phrase is variously attributed to both Fichte and Hegel—"*desto schlimmer für die Tatsachen*" (so much the worst for the facts).[29] As a result, as Gadamer has noted, "such a patronizing attitude on the part of the a priorism of reason had to evoke the resistance and the mockery of the empirical sciences."[30]

When a more aggressively positivist conceptualization of science emerged, the distance between knowledge—putatively based on nothing but inductive inference from experimentally verified evidence—and pure reason increased. Positivism itself generated many different varieties after the term was introduced by Auguste Comte in the first half of the nineteenth century, some less modest than others in their cognitive reach. The label itself became more an imprecise pejorative than a precise designation, as the squabble over its meaning in the so-called positivist dispute in German sociology of the 1960s still demonstrated.[31] But one common denominator shared by all varieties was a questioning of the metaphysical residue they saw in rationalist philosophies of nature.

Ironically, however, the more self-limiting impulse in positivism, its deflation of metaphysical pretensions, could be overwhelmed by an inflated faith in science's ability to solve all problems, including ones that were more moral than cognitive. What its critics came to call "scientism" sought to apply the same analytical tools that had proved their mettle in advancing knowledge of the natural world to cultural and historical questions. The only reasoning its advocates took seriously was that of the scientific method, whose reach they extended even into areas, such as religious faith, that more prudent figures like Kant knew could be neither confirmed nor refuted by science (as well as rational argument). Ironically, in debunking traditional metaphysics, scientism ended up by replacing it with a system no less overweening in its pretensions.

But even the defenders of a more modest notion of positivism were vulnerable to criticism. Those still yearning for an emphatic and robust notion of reason beyond that informing natural scientific inquiry could charge that the latter was beholden to a purely technological or instrumental version of rationality. That is, positivism's hostility to metaphysics of any kind, nominalist disdain for real universals, phenomenalist (n.b., *not* phenomenological) impatience with anything beyond the level of surface phenomena, and strict separation of facts and values meant that it had reduced reason to a tool in the service of ends that were irrationally chosen only in terms of efficiency. Experience, which in Hegel's vocabulary had been a word for the journey over time of the rational spirit, was reduced to unmediated sense impressions and controlled scientific experiments. *Vernunft* had been replaced entirely by *Verstand*, dialectical reason by analytical understanding, critical or humanist Marxism by its scientistic alternative.[32] As a result, the Polish philosopher Leszek Kołakowski, then still in his Marxist humanist phase, could bluntly title his 1966 history of positivist thought "the alienation of reason."[33]

The political implications of this alienation were troubling to those who saw reason as an indispensable tool of critique. In *Reason and Revolution*, for example, Marcuse included German philosophers like the later Schelling and Friedrich J. Stahl along with Comte as the founders of a tradition that explicitly targeted the progressive implications of both critical and speculative Idealism. "Positive philosophy," he wrote, "was a conscious reaction against the critical and destructive tendencies of French and German rationalism, a reaction that was particularly bitter in Germany. Because of its critical tendencies, the Hegelian system was designated as '*negative philosophy*.' . . . The political aims thus expressed [by Comte and Stahl] link the positive philosophy with the doctrines of the French counter-revolution: Comte was influenced by De Maistre and Stahl by Burke."[34] Auguste Comte's positivist sociology, Adorno added, had "an apologetic, static orientation," which was revealed in its intolerance not only for metaphysics but also for fantasizing an alternative social order.[35] If positivism had any political inclinations, they were toward supporting a technocratic elite that administered a world beyond partisan politics, a fantasy already made manifest in Comte's antirevolutionary search for a way to combine order and progress.

This critique of positivism, as not merely philosophically dubious but also politically problematic, was extended by other Marxists like Georg Lukács to aesthetic movements such as naturalism, which they saw as an expression of the positivist mentality but ironically imbued at the same time with many of the values of vitalism. Still later, in the work of a very different thinker no longer beholden to Marxism, Michel Foucault, the links between technological or instrumental rationality and vitalism were explored in a new register, one that investigated the ways in which governments had attempted to harness "bio-power" for the disciplining and normalization of their populations.[36] At its most sinister—and this was Horkheimer and Adorno's main point in their explanation of the rise of fascism in *Dialectic of Enlightenment*—the combination of vitalism and positivist reason could even lead to the nightmare politics that had forced them to flee from Nazi persecution. By employing modern techno-logical means to facilitate the revenge of dominated nature against the very instrumental rationality that had been responsible for the domination in the first place, fascism combined the worst of both responses to the retreat from an emphatic concept of reason.

It would, of course, be wrong to tar all of the variations of positivism and vitalism as protofascist, a problematic conclusion drawn in Lukács's weakest book, *The Destruction of Reason*, published at the height of the Cold War in 1952.[37] Some twentieth-century exponents of logical positivism, such as Otto Neurath, were in fact politically progressive.[38] Many early twentieth-century thinkers, as H. Stuart Hughes pointed out in his classic study of the "reorientation of European Social thought," *Consciousness and Society*, presented a more judicious response to the overweening extension of positivism from the natural to the cultural or human sciences.[39] Not all antipositivists, he shows, also turned against the Enlightenment, or at least not against its more cautious embrace of limited rationality associated, as Cassirer argued, with the critical *esprit systéma-tique*. The heroes of Hughes's story are not the neo-Hegelians like Lukács or Benedetto Croce, who sought to restore a more emphatic concept of reason against the dangers of unchecked empiricism,[40] but rather Max Weber and Sigmund Freud. Weber explicitly defended a methodological principle of "ideal types" in which subjective reason was posited heuristically as the default motor of individual action: "for the purposes of a typological scientific analysis it is convenient to treat all irrational, affectually determined elements of behav-ior as factors of deviation from a conceptually pure type of rational action."[41] And Freud, despite his debts to Schopenhauer (via his reading of Eduard von Hartmann) and other exponents of the power of the unconscious, nonetheless argued that psychological health involved bolstering the capacity for autono-mous rational judgment, or in his oft-cited phrase *"Wo Es war, soll Ich werden"* (where id was, there ego shall be). Indeed, as the following sentence indicated, he saw it as more than a merely individual task: "It is a work of culture—not unlike the draining of the Zuider Zee."[42]

And yet, both Weber and Freud were suspicious of any emphatic concept of reason that sought to use it to establish or even vet values.[43] They were no less cautious when it came to assigning history the redemptive task of realizing reason, even if Weber could characterize modernity as the progressive triumph of bureaucratic and rational-legal authority, understood formally and procedurally. Their post-positivist push-back against both scientistic positivism and the celebration of irrational vitalism had no intention of restoring reason to the place it had occupied in earlier, more optimistic times. Although both still were more or less loyal to a liberal politics that was rapidly losing its grip on intellectuals and nonintellectuals alike, they were too aware of all the ways in which nonrational factors—charisma, libidinal attachments to leaders, mass hysteria—could influence human behavior to champion it with much confidence. In fact, they came to appreciate that reason itself, if carried to an extreme in its quest for the absolute, can be a sign of folly, even of a paranoid inclination to find causes and meanings where none really existed.[44]

Perhaps no better indication of this diminished status is the role that the concept of "rationalization" came to play in psychoanalysis. Although the insight behind it was certainly not new—it had been noted as early as the Roman rhetorician Quintilian and traced in many other figures, such as the Romantic poet William Wordsworth[45]—the new label bespoke a heightened suspicion of reason itself. Introduced by Freud's Welsh collaborator Ernest Jones at the first Psychoanalytic Congress in Salzburg in 1908 and quickly adopted as a term of art by the movement, rationalization came to signify an excuse given by individuals attempting to justify their unacceptable actions or irrational beliefs through a pseudo-rational explanation.[46] Rapidly entering the popular vocabulary, it was understood to be not as pathological as a full-fledged delusion, or even a neurotic defense mechanism, but rather a familiar feature of normal human behavior. Although "rationalization" retained other meanings, for example the streamlined organization of capitalist industry during the interwar era and the maximization of workers' productivity through scientific management,[47] the negative connotation implied in Jones's psychological coinage was hard to overcome.

Even for those who resisted other aspects of psychoanalytic theory, the suspicion that many apparently rational arguments masked another agenda, unconsciously or not, fueled a general cynicism about reason. Weber's argument about the Protestant ethic and the spirit of capitalism could serve the same purpose, as it reinforced the conclusion that religious motivations and psychological anxieties were at the root of the allegedly "rational self-interest" of modern *homo economicus*. For a wide range of skeptics, defensive "rationalization" was not understood merely as a personal tactic; it was a broad cultural one as well. With the general crisis of Western culture that followed the unassimilable trauma of World War I, reason seemed to many a quaint relic of a fast receding liberal bourgeois age, whose humanist premises and universalist pretensions were no longer self-evident.[48] Desperate advocates of a disinterested reason above the fray, such as the French philosopher Julien Benda, flailed in vain at those intellectuals who had "betrayed" their true vocation and descended into the partisan politics of race, class, and nation.[49] The momentum seemed to the dwindling band of reason's champions to be going in the direction of a vitalism that had grown increasingly coarse, fueling a politics that was no less problematic. Prewar intellectuals like Georges Sorel, who had promulgated a vitalist, "romantic anti-capitalist" politics that frankly advocated the redemptive power of violence and myth, all the while blurring the distinction between left and right, seemed prophetic with the rise of fascism.[50] Their interwar successors such as the surrealist Georges Bataille explicitly sought to undermine the solar myth of reason, writing transgressive celebrations of "the solar anus" and the "rotten sun," in which the Western logocentric tradition was violently demolished.[51]

Even many of reason's defenders grew less confident of their cause. The reigning "*Ratio* of the capitalist economic system," the Weimar culture critic Siegfried Kracauer conceded in his celebrated 1927 essay "The Mass Ornament," "is not reason itself but a murky reason," which needed to be succeeded by a clearer and more genuine alternative that would encompass ends as well as means. But what that might be he could only identify unconvincingly with something that vaguely "arises from the basis of man."[52] Understood by others as little more than a "hygienic" procedure for consciousness to rid the mind of extraneous ideas, reason lost its critical and productive edge and became merely a defensive way to avoid dealing with things it could not fully understand. As the German philosopher Peter Sloterdijk described it in his widely discussed *Critique of Cynical Reason* of 1983, "a certain intellectual shrinking process can be observed within the strictly rationalist camp, so that the impression is given that the sanitary and defensive function of rationalism has won the upper hand over the productive, researching, clarifying function." And then turning to later movements, such as the "critical Rationalism" of Karl Popper and his followers, he added, "they emphasize their rational methods so much because there is a lot they simply do not understand, and so, with clever resentment, they cover up their lack of comprehension with methodological rigor. Here, however, a merely negative, filtering, defensive function, inherent in rationalism from the beginning, is revealed."[53] Even such a latter-day defender of the rational underpinnings of liberalism as Isaiah Berlin would throw up his hands and recoil from the ideal of rational ends or purposes as "to me not intelligible."[54] The cautionary example of the Soviet Union, which purported to advance a substantive rationalization of society, reinforced long-standing fears of reason's hubris, and not only among relativist pluralists like Berlin.[55]

More, much more, could be said about the erosion of confidence in reason in most of its more robust forms in the interwar era and beyond. But it is time to conclude this rapid tour d'horizon of the long history of reason's vicissitudes by turning to a summary of the state of the question by Max Horkheimer, the main Frankfurt School theoretician in the period just after he and his colleagues were forced into exile in New York. In 1934, he published a lengthy essay in the *Zeitschrift für Sozialforschung*, the Institute of Social Research's house organ, titled "The Rationalism Debate in Contemporary Philosophy."[56] By spending some time with it, we can appreciate the complicated role reason played in Critical Theory in the decade before they lamented its putative "eclipse."

At this time, Horkheimer identified broadly with historical materialism and was hostile to the pretensions of idealist philosophies to have transcended the social conditions out of which they arose. His essay opens with a straightforward claim that modern rationalism began with Descartes, whose dualistic division of the world into mind and matter led to an identification of reason with an entirely mental process of pure thought. Applied to a static concept of an already given reality, this process ignored the role of human practice in creating that world outside of it. It also was grounded on a notion of the sovereign individual subject, capable of rationalist cogitation, a subject who endured even when the empiricist critique of rationalist metaphysics replaced sense impressions with innate ideas as the source of valid cognition. "Just like the Cartesians," Horkheimer argued, "the English empiricists view human existence as comprised of individual processes of consciousness, of *cogitations.* . . . In these controversies of modern philosophy, the closed individual consciousness is set on a par with human existence."[57] Such a view mirrors the bourgeois subject, autonomous, self-interested, isolated, and allegedly free from any ties of dependence on prior social relations.

Because Horkheimer himself was suspicious of consciousness philosophy in its individual guise, he has been credited with anticipating Habermas's explicit critique of it a generation later, a critique that will occupy us later in our narrative.[58] But the essay does not tarry to elaborate a different version of reason, focusing instead on the threat of other more wholesale rejections. Whether in the name of tradition, history, or life, these alternatives threaten to throw out the critical baby with the affirmative bathwater. Whereas the earlier critiques of bourgeois rationalism and the humanist self—Horkheimer cites Nietzsche, Bergson, Simmel, Wilhelm Dilthey, and the Impressionists[59]—were also progressive protests against the stifling of individuals by capitalist modernization, the later ones, for example Klages and Spengler, capitulate to it, thus legitimating a sinister transition in modern society: "the rejection of rationalism that has steadily risen in the last decades—and that seems already to have passed its zenith—reflects the history of the transition from the liberal to the monopoly capitalist period of the bourgeois order."[60] Instead of seeing individual men as ends in themselves, as Kant had, modern irrationalism glorifies their obedient self-sacrifice in the name of the organic whole.

But here too there are hidden commonalities between older notions of consciousness philosophy, whether rationalist or empiricist, and their irrationalist opponents: "the contemporary debate concerning rationalist and anti-rationalist thought leaves untouched the idealist notion that human beings can gain access to the primordial ground of being in the world—and thus can derive the norm of their actions—through internal capacities."[61] Instead, materialism understands that the abstract reasoning of pure thought must itself be rescued from its status as the property of the isolated individual consciousness. For all its regressive hostility to conceptualism, in which it wrongly conflates *Vernunft* with *Verstand*,[62] *Lebensphilosophie* has been so successful because it exploits a major weakness in traditional rationalism, the latter's overestimation of the power of pure thought. But it sins in the opposite direction, failing to understand that "all knowledge is codetermined by the people who bring it about. Lacking insight into the indissoluble tension between knowledge and object, it takes on the character of an identity philosophy that remains every bit as ahistorical as the doctrine it criticizes."[63] Replacing the effort it takes to comprehend the world, which Hegel made clear, and failing to appreciate the necessary, if insufficient, role of analysis, it seeks immediate intuitive insight into organic wholes. Although justifiably resistant to the lifeless abstraction of the purely rational subject and praiseworthy for its stress on the emotional and sensual dimension of human existence, vitalism goes too far in deifying the unconscious and substituting the causality of historical rootedness or biological advantage for critical reason. Although it rightly calls into question the bourgeois fetish of individual self-preservation, it falsely replaces it with a mindless self-sacrifice of the individual to the organic whole. "While rational thought cannot be narrowed—as extreme liberal ideology would have it—to the standard of egoistic ends, rational justification of any action can ultimately be related only to the happiness of human beings."[64] Materialism, in contrast to vitalism, agrees with Hegel that "analytically derived concepts could be made fruitful for the intellectual reconstruction of living processes," but unlike Hegel, it has no faith in the existence of a "suprahistorical subject which alone could grasp reality."[65] Instead, as Feuerbach understood, "it is man who thinks, not the ego, not reason,"[66] or in less anthropological terms, the concrete men living in specific historical circumstances.

All of these, it has to be conceded, are standard historical materialist arguments, and it is clear that Horkheimer was unable to express much hope that the concrete men of 1934 in the concrete circumstances in which they find themselves were on the road to realizing a more rational society. The essay nears its end with a vague and general statement that "rational action is oriented to a theory of society that . . . is no mere summation of abstract conceptual elements. Rather, it is the attempt, with the aid of all the various disciplines, to reconstruct an image of the social life process that can assist in understanding the critical condition of the world and the possibilities for a more rational order."[67] But rather than concluding with a ringing plea for the virtues of rationalism, Horkheimer indicts it along with irrationalism for assuming "the function of accommodating human beings to things as they are. . . . Rationalism and irrationalism both provide the service of mystification."[68] Thus, "materialism supports neither side in the controversy between rationalism and irrationalism. . . . In the present, rationalism becomes easy prey for its opponent; history has long since left behind the era of rationalistic systems. The reason inherent in rationalism lives on today in the theory whose method was developed by rationalism itself under the rubric of dialectics."[69]

But was it possible for dialectics to find in the historical developments of the day warrant for optimism about the realization of a reason that was not transcendental or universal by nature? Were there concrete forces whose actions might help that realization occur? Was there a meaningful arena for the democratic practice of a dianoetic version of reason, in the workers' movement or elsewhere, that could prove a check on the catastrophic decline of liberal culture into its authoritarian successor? Was there any basis for the hope that reason could be discerned in the systematic unfolding of historical development, a nondispositional reason that worked behind the backs and even against the wills of individuals whose dispositional reason was impotent to stem the tide of irrationalism? Was the sun of reason, in short, still shining brightly or was it in the process of being eclipsed by changes in society that were blocking its rays from reaching those who needed their warmth and light the most? Or perhaps no less troubling, was reason itself in need of a radical reconceptualization to reignite its capacity to shed light on times that were becoming increasingly dark?[70] In the years that followed, Horkheimer and his colleagues at the Institute of Social Research grappled with these questions, coming to a wide spectrum of answers, which we will try to spell out in the second part of this study.

# II

# Reason's Eclipse
# and Return

I feel that Max Weber's question regarding the paradoxes of
rationalization is still the best key to a philosophically and scientifically informed diagnosis of our time. . . . There is neither a
higher nor a lower reason to which we can appeal, only a procedurally sobering reason—a reason that proceeds solely on
sufficient grounds; a reason that puts itself on trial. That is what
Kant meant: the critique of reason is reason's proper task.

Jürgen Habermas, A Berlin Republic

# 5

# The Critique
# of Instrumental Reason

*Horkheimer, Marcuse, and Adorno*

In 1941, arguably one of the bleakest years in all of modern history, the Frankfurt School reluctantly acknowledged for the first time the crisis of the emphatic concept of reason that had been a mainstay of its work for much of the previous decade.[1] The disillusionment was abrupt. Although in his earliest days Max Horkheimer had in good historical materialist fashion denounced the dualism and idealism he saw in Cartesian rationalist metaphysics, he had come staunchly to defend a dialectical notion of reason against the irrationalist alternative he identified with the threat of fascism.[2] While acknowledging that rationality in its liberal, bourgeois form was tied to egoistic self-preservation rather than the general good, he had resisted the conclusion that reason *tout court* inevitably led in this direction. As a result, one commentator has gone so far as to posit a "rationalist turn" in Critical Theory around 1937 in which concrete political hopes were replaced by more philosophical concerns.[3] In an essay of that year, "The Latest Attack on Metaphysics," Horkheimer could still insist, as noted at the end of the previous chapter, that "rationalism uses existing objects as well as the active inner strivings and ideas of man to construct standards for the future. In this regard it is not so closely associated with the present order as is empiricism."[4] In the same year, Herbert Marcuse could add in the pages of the *Zeitschrift für Sozialforschung*:

> Reason is the fundamental category of philosophical thought, the only one by means of which it has bound itself to human destiny. Philosophy wanted to discover the ultimate and most general grounds of Being. Under

the name of reason it conceived the idea of authentic Being in which all significant antitheses (of subject and object, essence and appearance, thought and being) were reconciled.[5]

Four years later, Marcuse's spirited defense of Hegel against his alleged support for statist authoritarianism, *Reason and Revolution*, could even more vigorously celebrate the critical energy of universal reason. In its dialectical guise, which emphasized the power of negation, reason had resisted the affirmative implications of positivism in all of its forms. Going beyond the limits of the analytic understanding (*Verstand*) that Kant had posited for cognition, reason (*Vernunft*) was a synthetic faculty able to incorporate the moral norms Kant had relegated to practical reason alone. According to Marcuse, Hegel's idea of reason, with which he clearly identified, "has retained, though in an idealistic form, the material strivings for a free and rational order of life. . . . The core of Hegel's philosophy is a structure the concepts of which—freedom, subject, mind, notion—are derived from the idea of reason."[6] Capitalist rationalization, tied to commodity fetishism, the domination of exchange value, and what Lukács had called reification, was a pathological distortion of this ideal. As Marx had famously said in 1843, "reason has always existed, but not always in rational form."[7] Despite sub rosa tensions between Marcuse and some of his colleagues at the time, the book was proudly dedicated to "Max Horkheimer and the Institute of Social Research,"[8] whose theoretical stance he thought he shared.

But in a new essay of 1941 by Horkheimer, "Reason and Self-Preservation," which first appeared in a private volume to mourn the recently perished Walter Benjamin, a very different note was struck. When it appeared in the final issue of the Institute's journal, which coincided with Horkheimer's move from New York to California and the growing importance of his partnership with Adorno, it was retitled in more apocalyptic fashion "The End of Reason."[9] "The fundamental concepts of civilization are in a process of rapid decay," Horkheimer began ominously. "The decisive concept among them was that of reason, and philosophy knew no higher principle."[10] The decay of reason, Horkheimer then suggested, was due not only to the failure to realize itself in the world but also to a fatal characteristic of the concept itself. Ironically, the inherent connection between reason and critique could ultimately be carried to the point that reason might undermine its own legitimacy. "Rationalism itself had established the criteria of rigidity, clarity and distinctness as the criteria of rational cognition. Skeptical and empirical doctrines opposed rationalism with these selfsame standards. . . . Skepticism purged the idea of reason of so much of its content that scarcely anything is left of it. Reason, in destroying conceptual fetishes, ultimately destroyed itself. . . . None of the categories of rationalism has survived."[11]

There is a withered residue of reason still left in human behavior, Hork-heimer conceded, but only in its instrumental guise: "its features can be summarized as the optimum adaptation of means to ends, thinking as an energy-saving operation. It is a pragmatic instrument oriented to expediency, cold and sober."[12] Was this an aberration or the working out of a sinister potential always lurking in reason? Marcuse had been inclined to blame it on the increased power of technological rationality in the modern world.[13] But Horkheimer, at his most pessimistic, asserted that "as close as the bond between reason and efficiency is here revealed to be, in reality so has it always been."[14] To the extent that reason claimed universal, ahistorical validity, it was based, moreover, on a lie, because all previous societies were divided along class lines. As the universality of reason became more frankly formalistic, it resigned itself to the separation of thought and object, the ideal of universality betrayed by the reality of class division. The increasing influence of nominalism, which meant the loss of any hope for a substantive concept of reason as inhering in the actual world, also ratified the separation of facts from values and the hegemony of calculation. "The triumph of nominalism goes hand in hand with the triumph of formalism. In limiting itself to seeing objects as a strange multiplicity, as a chaos, reason becomes a kind of adding machine that manipulates analytical judgments."[15]

Along with this decline of reason into the instrumentality that was always lurking under the surface of the substantive concept went a concomitant erosion of the individual subject who was supposed to be its bearer. Although in the past a dialectic of self-preservation and self-sacrifice meant that there was some rough balance between individual and community, now the former was in total disarray:

> The destruction of rationalistic dogmatism through the self-critique of reason, carried out by the ever renewed nominalistic tendencies in philosophy, has now been ratified by historical reality. The substance of individuality itself, to which the idea of autonomy was bound, did not survive the process of industrialization. Reason has degenerated because it was the ideological projection of a false universality which now shows the autonomy of the subject to have been an illusion. The collapse of reason and the collapse of individuality are one and the same.[16]

The result is the political horror that was now sweeping over Europe, which must be understood as more than an expression of atavistic irrationalism: "the new order of fascism is reason revealing itself as unreason."[17] Holding on to a faint hope that fascism might not have the last word, Horkheimer concluded his jeremiad with a modified evocation of the famous alternative Rosa Luxemburg had posed in her World War I Junius Pamphlet: "the progress of reason that leads to its self-destruction has come to an end; there is nothing left but barbarism or freedom."[18]

Throughout the 1940s, Horkheimer still desperately attempted to salvage something from the wreckage of reason. But even the end of the war and defeat of fascism did not lessen his dire conclusion in 1946 that reason itself "today seems to suffer from a kind of disease," the cure of which is uncertain.[19] Only digging deep into its past might provide some potential relief: "reason must reconstruct the history of its vicissitudes—try, as it were to recollect its origins and understand its own inherent self-destructive trends and mechanisms. . . . Reason's ability to render an account of its transformation from the power by which all things are perceived, to a mere instrumentality of self-preservation, is a condition of its recovery."[20] Only by facing the sources of the "self-liquidation of reason" can the process of enlightenment continue, a process, despite its paradoxical implications, needing to be encouraged: "the hope of Reason lies in the emancipation from its own fear of despair."[21]

Struggling against that fear while at the same time not flinching from the despair were the motivations behind Horkheimer's two subsequent works, *Eclipse of Reason* (1947) and *Dialectic of Enlightenment*, the latter of which he wrote jointly with Adorno (1947). Together, they represented the summa of the Frankfurt School's thesis of the self-liquidation of reason. This is not the place to hazard yet another detailed summary of their complicated arguments, especially those in the more familiar *Dialectic of Enlightenment*, which also contained extensive discussions of other issues such as the culture industry and the sources of anti-Semitism.[22] Because *Eclipse of Reason* was more specifically devoted to the theme I am examining in this book, it will be the focus of what follows.

The subtle shift from a title proclaiming reason had ended to one suggesting it was merely in eclipse signaled the stubborn refusal of the Frankfurt School's first generation to believe all was lost.[23] *Eclipse of Reason*, while no longer strongly defending an explicitly Hegelian notion of totalizing reason, nonetheless was careful to distance itself from the alternative presented by Max Weber's frank dismissal of any substantive, goal-setting rationality that went beyond mere instrumental or functionalist alternatives. Weber, Horkheimer charged, "adhered so definitely to the subjectivistic trend that he did not conceive of any rationality—not even a 'substantial' one by which man can discriminate one end from another. If our drives, intentions, and finally our ultimate decisions must *a priori* be irrational, substantial reason becomes an agency merely of correlation and is therefore essentially 'functional.'"[24]

Against the functionalist and subjectivist reduction of reason, Horkheimer pitted what he termed an "objective" alternative, which meant "reason as a force not only in the individual mind but also in the objective world—in relations among human beings and between social classes, in social institutions, and in nature and its manifestations."[25] It had first appeared in ancient Greek philosophy and was revived in post-Kantian German Idealism. This emphatic concept of reason, however, had been undermined not only by subjectification and functionalization but also by formalization. "In the end, no particular reality can seem reasonable *per se*; all the basic concepts, emptied of their content, have come to be only formal shells. As reason is subjectivized, it also becomes formalized."[26]

How do we get access to objective reason, an inherent reason that is not projected onto the world by a subject bent on self-preservation or control of nature? How can we restore what Socrates had called a reflection of "the true nature of things"? How do we restore meaning to a world in which ends are arbitrary and only means considered rational? In *Eclipse of Reason*, Horkheimer could only offer a vague and unsatisfactory remedy: "This structure is accessible to him who takes upon himself the effort of dialectical thinking, or, identically, who is capable of *eros*. On the other hand, the term objective reason may also designate this very effort and ability to reflect such an objective order."[27] Marcuse in *Reason and Revolution* could still defiantly identify reason in a left-Hegelian manner with the radical negation of the status quo, implying that there was a force in history that might become its carrier. But Horkheimer now only mentioned negation sparingly, while conceding that it would be wrong to equate truth, goodness, and reason with reality as it was now experienced. It was moreover impossible, he stressed, to restore an outmoded notion of metaphysical reason, as advocated, for example, by contemporary neo-Thomists, for "such undisturbed confidence in the realism of the rational scholastic apparatus was shattered by the Enlightenment."[28] But the Enlightenment's own alternative was deeply problematic, including the reduction of reason to mere reasonableness, which implied adjustment and "conformity with reality as it is."[29]

As he had argued in his earlier essays, the shattering that climaxed in the Enlightenment was an outcome of the self-liquidation of reason, not something brought to it from the outside. "If one were to speak of a disease affecting reason, this disease should be understood not as having stricken reason at some historical moment, but as being inseparable from the nature of reason in civilization as we know it. The disease of reason is that reason was born from man's urge to dominate nature,"[30] a charge that was also extensively developed in *Dialectic of Enlightenment*. It was as if the mortal illness of reason was already latent in its genes. Born of the self-sacrificial cunning needed to survive in a hostile environment, it never lost its original taint, what one observer has called its "mark of Cain."[31] Indeed, "the transition from objective to subjective reason was not an accident, and the process of development of ideas cannot arbitrarily at any given moment be reversed. If subjective reason in the form of enlightenment has dissolved the philosophical basis of beliefs that have been an essential part of Western culture, it has been able to do so because this basis proved to be too weak."[32] Not even Kant, whose formalism earned him a comparison with the Marquis de Sade in *Dialectic of Enlightenment*, had found a way to reverse the downward slide of reason.[33] Once the primordial mimetic relationship between man and nature—still preserved in the sympathetic magic of the world of myth—was replaced by a more rationalist one, the road to domination of nature and conformity to the status quo was already paved. Rebelling against reason in the name of an injured nature was also insufficient, as the Nazi example clearly demonstrated. Fascism, in fact, revealed itself as "a satanic synthesis of reason and nature—the very opposite of that reconciliation of the two poles that philosophy had always dreamed of."[34]

*Eclipse of Reason*, for all of its lamenting of the withering away of objective reason and insistence on anamnestically preserving what had been lost, sought to resist the temptations of nostalgia. "The transition from objective to subjective reason," Horkheimer concluded, "was a necessary historical process."[35] Attempts to return to earlier expressions of objective reason may be well intentioned, but they run the risk of "lagging behind the industrial and scientific developments, of asserting meaning that proves to be an illusion, and of creating reactionary ideologies. Just as subjective reason tends to vulgar materialism, so objective reason displays an inclination to romanticism, and the greatest philosophical attempt to construe objective reason, Hegel's, owes its incomparable force to its critical insight regarding this danger."[36] Rather than pitting one version of reason against another, one should work to "foster a mutual critique and thus, if possible, to prepare in the intellectual realm the reconciliation of the two in reality."[37] But at present, and these are the final words of *Eclipse*, "denunciation of what is currently called reason is the greatest service reason can render."[38]

In retrospect, it is clear that *Eclipse of Reason*, along with *Dialectic of Enlightenment*, left Critical Theory with a genuine dilemma. Not only had the triumphalist historical narrative derived from Hegel and adopted by Marx proved wrong, but reactionary attempts to restore a metaphysical notion of reason that had existed before the fall into instrumentalism, subjectivism, and formalism were also discredited. Or more precisely, Horkheimer scorned such attempts, while himself still tacitly drawing on an emphatic ideal of reason that was scarcely less metaphysical than those defended by neo-Thomists.[39] As a result, to quote one later commentator, his critique is "burdened from the outset with an uncertainty regarding the validity of its standard."[40]

There was another equally problematic issue. Horkheimer had disparaged the functionalization of reason he saw in Weber, and which could be traced even earlier to nineteenth-century figures like Schopenhauer, Kierkegaard, and Nietzsche.[41] For them reason was little more than a tool in the service of power or the will or the hubris of the subject. While rejecting their sweeping claims, Horkheimer came, however, perilously close to the same conclusion. From Schopenhauer in particular, he had learned that a rational theodicy, such as that defended by Leibniz in terms of the "principle of sufficient reason" or Hegel in terms of the "cunning of reason," meant that suffering could be complacently turned into an affirmative function of totalizing reason. The historical materialist in him also balked at the idealist sublation of creaturely misery into a necessary moment in this best of all possible worlds or a historical narrative of redemption.

Indeed, not only should reason in this strongly affirmative sense be prevented from justifying partial evil as part of a general good, but it also should be understood itself as complicit in causing the very suffering that it cannot redeem. Thus when he argued that "reason was born from man's urge to dominate nature," Horkheimer was implying that the ur-function of reason—the genetic origin that had caused the "disease" from which it now suffered—was the preservation of the self and mastery of the natural world that ultimately led to the hegemony of subjective over objective reason in modernity. Rather than an act of anamnestic totalization, "the self-reflection of reason upon the conditions of its own possibility now means," as Seyla Benhabib was to put it, "uncovering the *genealogy* of reason, disclosing the subterranean history of the relationship between reason and self-preservation, autonomy and the domination of nature."[42] Many years later, Adorno would continue to express a similar point in *Negative Dialectics*, arguing that "*ratio* is no more to be hypostatized than any other category. The transfer of the self-preserving interest from individuals to the species is spiritually coagulated with the form of the *ratio*, a form that is general and antagonistic at the same time."[43] Because the universality inherent in reason from the very beginning produces an abstraction that dominates particulars, "all-governing reason, in installing itself above something else, necessarily constricts itself."[44]

To resist that constriction paradoxically requires that the dialectic remain negative, renouncing the claim to totality that allowed Hegel in his more triumphalist moods to reconcile what was in fact antagonistic. The antidote to the functionalization *of* reason was not functionalization of suffering *by* reason. Adorno never fully renounced the critical reading of Hegel's notion of reason that had animated earlier Frankfurt School texts like Marcuse's *Reason and Revolution*. But he did so by trying to locate in Hegel a way beyond the potential domination in a totalizing rationality of self-reflective reconciliation. Invoking the concept of mimesis, derived in large measure from Benjamin's earlier thoughts on the mimetic faculty,[45] Adorno developed it in the 1940s as a beleaguered redoubt of benign nurturance outside the functionalization of reason as a tool of self-preservation: "the speculative Hegelian concept rescues mimesis through spirit's self-reflection: truth is not *adaequatio* but affinity, and in the decline of idealism reason's mindfulness of its mimetic nature is revealed by Hegel to be its human right."[46]

Whether or not this generous reading of Hegel was persuasive, Adorno was pointing to one of the ways that after the "eclipse" of reason, Critical Theory sought to locate a more viable alternative that might resist the full triumph of instrumental, formal, and subjective rationality. Before we try to spell out their attempts, it is worth pausing with the implications of the eclipse metaphor itself. At its root is a loose historical narrative, in which at a certain point the light of reason progressively illuminating the world—reason defined emphatically as an organon of universal human freedom, a beacon of emancipatory enlightenment—was occluded. Although some sort of historical rationalization did occur, a process that Weber had masterfully described, it was a dimmer version of reason, subjective rather than objective, formal rather than substantive, and concerned only with means rather than ends. Why the shadow had fallen was not, however, explicitly spelled out. The mathematicization of nature, the triumph of the exchange principle, capitalist reification, the fetish of technology, bureaucratization, positivist thought—all were plausible candidates for the celestial body that had passed before the rational sun. Or to return to another of Horkheimer's metaphors, all were plausible pathogens for the "disease" of reason.

But at times, it bears repeating, Horkheimer seemed to assume the eclipse or degeneration was inevitable—"the transition from objective to subjective reason was not an accident"—as the germ of reason's self-liquidation was present at the origin. Its disease was thus a form of autoimmunity run amok. For all its self-congratulatory leaving behind of the world of myth, rationality had revealed itself to be entangled with it from the beginning and was still entangled at the end. Although lurking behind the larger narrative was a tacit acknowledgment of the failure of the working class to be the engine of an emancipation that Marxist theory had assumed it would be, it almost seemed as if reason would have self-destructed even with a successful revolution (as was, in fact, the case in the Soviet Union). For the domination of nature was by no means a goal that Marxism itself had eschewed. It was thus hard to avoid the conclusion that the functionalization of reason as a tool in the primal struggle for self-preservation lamented in *Eclipse of Reason* was not all that far removed from Michel Foucault's later debunking of the Enlightenment project as no less a ruse of power than a vehicle of emancipation.[47] Although both the astronomical and biological metaphors did hint at the possibility of a better future—eclipses, after all, pass and one can recover from a disease—the first generation of the Frankfurt School, deeply traumatized by the lessons of the Holocaust and the misfiring of the Soviet experiment, were anything but optimistic in their reading of the enlightenment's dialectic.

With such a bleak view of the prospects for a benign version of the rationalization of the world, it is no surprise that Critical Theory in its classical form grew increasingly unable to generate a plausible immanent point d'appui from which to launch its critique. One possible resource was a reading of psychoanalysis against the grain, which tried to rescue it from the pessimistic conclusions reached by Freud himself.[48] As Axel Honneth has pointed out, it could be understood as positing the "frankly anthropological thesis that human subjects cannot be indifferent about the restriction of their rational capacities. Because their self-actualization is tied to the presupposition of a cooperative rational activity, they cannot avoid suffering psychologically under its deformation. This insight—that there must be an internal connection between psychological intactness and undistorted rationality—is perhaps the strongest impetus that Freud provides for Critical Theory."[49]

Of all the original members of the Frankfurt School, it was Marcuse who most doggedly maintained a faith in Hegelian dialectics and infused it with that power of eros that Horkheimer had fleetingly invoked in *Eclipse of Reason*.[50] As he put it in his 1955 *Eros and Civilization*: "Eros redefines reason in his own terms. Reasonable is what sustains the order of gratification. . . . Repressive reason gives way to a *new rationality of gratification* in which reason and happiness converge."[51] Imaginatively reconceptualizing Freud's instinct theory, finding a virtue in the narcissism Freud had seen as regressive, and valorizing the perversions as a protest against the tyranny of genital sexuality, Marcuse pushed the utopian impulse in Critical Theory to its extreme. The compromises of ego psychology and neo-Freudian revisionism, exemplified by the Institute's former colleague Erich Fromm, need not be tolerated.

In addition, Marcuse also tacitly echoed his teacher Heidegger's yearning for a version of logos that antedated its transformation into an organon of conceptual domination: "whatever the implications of the original Greek conception of Logos as the essence of being, since the canonization of the Aristotelian logic, the term merges with the idea of ordering, classifying, mastering reason."[52] Under capitalism, it had degenerated further into what he called "the performance principle," in which instrumental rationality and capitalist self-interest rule. Only with a new "logos of gratification" could the promise of another reason at its most liberating be revived.

But could such a sunny redescription of Hegelian rationality, infused with Heideggerian nostalgia for being and vitalized by libidinal energy, really suffice to provide a viable positive notion of reason after its eclipse? Although Freudian theory might still be mobilized for critical purposes, as Jürgen Habermas later demonstrated, it could not be as easily combined as Marcuse had hoped with a Hegelian notion of reason, which extended beyond individual human pleasure to the historical world and its institutions. Celebrating the instincts as an archaic source of rebellious subjectivity did not, alas, easily fit with the cultural work done by reason in dealing with the less laudable effects of unleashed desire. As Joel Whitebook noted, Marcuse lacked an appreciation of the need to tame infantile demands for omnipotence and the fantasy of overcoming separation from the mother: "any scheme for radical transformation that does not include a mechanism for decentering infantile omnipotence stands condemned of utopianism in the pejorative sense."[53] There might even be unintended consequences in a utopianism that undervalued the imperfect achievements of more modest notions of rationalization. As the American philosopher Richard Bernstein put it in his critique of Marcuse's legacy, "what concretely does this mean? . . . We must not only comprehend what we are talking about, but ask ourselves what type of social institutions in a 'post-industrial' world can embody such a 'rationality of gratification.' We are confronted here not only with the anger of vacuity, but the more ominous danger where the demand for absolute liberation and freedom turns into its opposite—absolute terror."[54]

Broadly speaking, the two most plausible alternatives were developed by Adorno, who turned to aesthetic theory, and Habermas, who favored a more general theory of communicative interaction. Both reworked rather than repudiated the Enlightenment tradition, although with a different understanding of its implications.[55] Both still found in Hegel some inspiration for a reason that would go beyond the limits of Enlightenment rationality, while also conceding the value of Kant's more modest acknowledgement of reason's limits.[56] Both came to appreciate the potential of religion or at least theology as a resource for a more capacious notion of reason than the instrumental variant that Critical Theory feared was crowding out all alternatives.[57]

Although Habermas came to feel Adorno's solution was inadequate, he could nonetheless acknowledge that in comparison to Horkheimer,

> Adorno, faced with the aporia of the self-referential critique of reason, was better able to keep his composure because he could bring another motif

into play. He did not need to depend solely upon the enlightening power of philosophical criticism but could let his thinking circulate within the paradoxes of an identity logic that denies itself and yet illuminates from within. That is, for him the genuine aesthetic experience of modern art had opened up an independent source of insight.[58]

Habermas would, in fact, continue to characterize Horkheimer's position as more consistently hostile to reason than Adorno's, chastising him, for example, in an essay from 1991, for his "profound skepticism concerning reason. What for him is the essential substance of religion—morality—is no longer tied to reason. Horkheimer praises the dark writers of the bourgeoisie for having 'trumpeted far and wide the impossibility of deriving from reason any fundamental argument against murder.' I have to admit that this remark irritates me now no less than it did almost four decades ago when I first read it."[59]

In contrast, Adorno distanced himself from the more despairing pronouncements of the 1940s and returned to a more robust defense of reason. Indeed at certain moments, such as his 1958 critique of religious attempts to re-enchant the world, "Reason and Revelation," he could fall back on what sounded suspiciously like the traditional Marxist project of rationalizing the world, claiming that "the excess of rationality, about which the educated class complains and which it registers in concepts like mechanization, atomization, indeed even de-individualization, is a lack of rationality, namely the increase of all the apparatuses and means of quantifiable domination at the cost of the goal, the rational organization of mankind, which is left abandoned to the unreason of mere constellations of power."[60]

While Habermas may no longer himself have had much faith in such a grandiose project, he did admire Adorno's effort to overcome the simplistic distinction between philosophy and art, finding in the latter, supplemented by a theoretical appreciation of its implications, a place for a kind of reason irreducible to its instrumental variant. Perhaps the most succinct expression of Adorno's mature theory of the relationship between art and reason came in the paralipomena to his posthumously published *Aesthetic Theory*. Here Adorno repeated his general warning against the potential of abstract universal reason to overwhelm particulars: "rationality would become rational only once it no longer repressed the individuated in whose unfolding rationality has its right to exist."[61] An emancipated particular would not, however, be in simple opposition to the universal, a kind of Kierkegaardian absolute of its own, but somehow able to embody it while not extirpating its individuality. Against Hegel and with Marx (and Marcuse), he insisted on the need to reconcile—or rather, place in a mutually beneficial constellation—happiness with reason:

> Hegel hypostasizes rationality and falls into the trap of thinking of ratio-
> nality as the logic of things independently of their *terminus ad quem* in
> human beings, the very thing he had expressly called for with his realist
> interpretation of the concept of reason. The rationality of the universal,
> then, if it is to be rational at all, cannot be an abstractly self-standing
> concept, but must consist in the relation of the universal to the particular.[62]

It was to stress the importance of actual gratification that he, like other members
of the Frankfurt School, so often invoked the phrase of Stendhal adopted by
Nietzsche against the cold Kantian ideal of aesthetic disinterestedness: "art is
*une promesse de bonheur* [a promise of happiness]."[63]

For Adorno, the dialectic of enlightenment had led, as J. M. Bernstein puts
it, to "the *rationalization* of *reason* itself. The rationalization of reason is the process
through which the sensory—the contingent, contextual and particular—is first
dominated, and then repudiated as a component of reason, and the remnant, the
sensory rump, dispatched into the harmless precinct of art and the aesthetic."[64]
But rather than abandoning this sensory rump as inherently outside of reason
narrowly construed and thus an external threat to be dominated or merely reversing the hierarchy and celebrating the "other" of reason, Adorno argued
that art can overcome without fully collapsing the distinction. It finds a way to
juxtapose in a benign constellation universal and particular, spirit and matter,
form and substance, while resisting the full autonomy of the creative or dominating subject. Both a memory of a time before the separation and a foretaste
of what might be a future reconciliation, art is therefore not the betrayer of
reason but rather its salvation.

Complementing its prefiguration of a happiness to come, art could also
implicitly protest against suffering, both human and natural. Modern art in
particular, with its refusal of organic wholeness and harmonious form, voiced
this protest. Horkheimer had always resisted a theodicy that would justify or
redeem past suffering, preferring Schopenhauer's pessimism to Hegel's too
easy optimism about the alleged cunning of reason. Past suffering could not be
made into an instrument of future happiness. Adorno also avoided any hint of
a sublation of misery in a narrative of redemption. But he stressed that suffering—
or better put, the surplus suffering that extended beyond the mortality and
vulnerability of the human condition—was itself not a permanent quality of
all societies. And although reason in some of its guises may have abetted that
suffering it was also a necessary weapon in the struggle to create an alternative
future. Aesthetic rationality was a prefigurative placeholder for that possible
outcome.

Significantly, the promise of happiness was expressed not only in the sensual gratification provided by artworks and their implicit protest against suffering but also in the type of rationality they embodied, a rationality that resists the dominating implications of the homogenizing concept. "Reason in artworks," Adorno explained,

> is reason as gesture: They synthesize like reason, but not with concepts, propositions, and syllogisms—where these forms occur in art they do so only as subordinated means—rather, they do so by way of what transpires in the artworks. Their synthetic function is immanent: it is the unity of their self, without immediate relation to anything external given or determined in some way or other; it is directed to the dispersed, the aconceptual, quasi-fragmentary material with which in their interior space artworks are occupied.[65]

It is because of this gestural synthesis that art "reminds us of an objectivity freed from the categorical structure. This is the source of art's rationality, its character as knowledge."[66] In Terry Eagleton's concise gloss on Adorno, it is art in which "the hidden irrationality of a rationalized society is brought to light; for art is a 'rational' end in itself, whereas capitalism is irrationally so. Art has a kind of paratactic logicality about it, akin to those dream images which blend cogency and contingency; and it might thus be said to represent an arational refutation of instrumentalized rationality."[67]

However, rather than turning art into a sacred enclave actually embodying the healthy rationality that overcomes the "disease" spelled out in the work he and Horkheimer composed in the 1940s, Adorno conceded that "artworks participate in the dialectic of enlightenment. . . . Windowless, artworks participate in civilization. That by which artworks distinguish themselves from the diffuse coincides with the achievements of reason qua reality principle."[68] As a result, art cannot entirely escape the oppressive potential of reason: "in themselves, artworks ineluctably pursue nature-dominating reason by virtue of their element of unity, which organizes the whole."[69] Art therefore can never occupy a utopian space unto itself, with no echo of what happens outside. Even the most seemingly autonomous of modern artworks registers, if indirectly, what is beyond its apparent borders.

But if art were not a realized, full-throated embodiment of a benign rationality smoothly reconcilable with the principle of happiness, a truth that prevented it, *pace* certain aesthetes, from serving as a genuine escape from the depredations of real life, at least it opened up the possibility of the ultimate attainability of that reconciliation. It was this hope, after all, that allowed art to be called "a promise" of happiness, if not its actual realization. Despite art's inevitable registering of the dark side of the dialectic of enlightenment, it also evinces a subtle resistance to the external reality principle: "Whereas the unity of artworks derives from the violence that reason does to things, this unity is at the same time the source of the reconciliation of the elements of artworks."[70] An important shift occurs when that violence is rendered symbolic rather than literal and turned immanently toward the work rather than directed to the actual world: "the rational shaping of artworks effectively means their rigorous elaboration in themselves. As a result they come into contrast with the world of the nature-dominating *ratio*, in which aesthetic *ratio* originates, and become a work for themselves."[71]

The key to the shift is the expression in works of art of the mimetic impulse in our interaction with the world and other people, an impulse that is very different from the domination of nature engendered by the drive for self-preservation. Rather than a subject actively mastering a threatening other, it enacts a more passive and benign assimilation of otherness itself. The rational moment in works of art follows from the need to give mimetic comportment an objective embodiment. But their relationship is more of a constellation of juxtaposed elements—here the influence of Benjamin on Adorno was palpable—than that full Hegelian *Aufhebung* (positive dialectical sublation) for which Marcuse still seems to have yearned. The distinction was expressed in Adorno's willingness, *pace* Marcuse, to call the demand for happiness frankly "irrational." As he acknowledged in one of the most important sentences in *Aesthetic Theory*, "if the telos of reason is a fulfillment that is in-itself necessarily not rational—happiness is the enemy of rationality and purpose, of which it nevertheless stands in need—art makes this irrational telos its own concern."[72]

In other words, however necessary reason in its most benign, gestural form might be, it is never sufficient. Even when liberated from its identification with instrumentalization, formalization, and subjectivization, reason cannot alone be the standard of utopian redemption. Even when it no longer functions to serve self-preservation and the exchange principle or is disentangled from its bureaucratic institutionalization, reason needs to make room for something else to atone for its original sins of dominating nature and universalizing nonidentical particularity. In short, even a revived substantive notion of reason would have to concede that the ultimate values it affirms come from elsewhere. Art, for all its service as a placeholder of a possible future utopia, does not really function as a model of that benign rationalization of the world envisioned by Hegelian dialectics. A negative dialectics knows, among other things, the limits of reason, even in its most benevolent form. As such it reveals itself as indebted more to Kant—who also denied the ability of reason to account for individual happiness—than Hegel, for whom all of its limits were to be overcome.

Despite his skepticism about a positive dialectical overcoming of oppositions, Adorno thus never simply pitted reason against its "irrational" others, whether understood as happiness, bodily pleasure, material reality, imagination, emotion, the id, violence, mimesis, perhaps even madness.[73] Indeed, Axel Honneth goes so far as to claim that mimesis was itself necessary in the origin of rationality, which was not solely derived from the need for self-preservation: "Only through imitative behavior, which for Adorno originally goes back to an affect of loving care, do we achieve a capacity for reason because we learn by gradually envisioning others' intentions to relate to their perspectives on the world."[74] There is thus no inherent tension between rationality and mimesis, despite Adorno's having called the happiness derived from the latter "irrational." Adorno, he writes, "sees our special, imitation-based capacity for reason precisely in experiencing the adaptive goals of speechless beings, even things, as intentions demanding rational consideration. He is therefore convinced that any true knowledge has to retain the original impulse of loving imitation sublimated within itself in order to do justice to the rational structure of the world from our perspective."[75]

Against the privileging of the intersubjective variant of mimesis—the child, say, imitating its nurturing parent—the inclusion of "speechless beings, even things" in Honneth's formulation comports with Adorno's call in *Negative Dialectics* for "the object's preponderance."[76] Another way to make the same point, but now with reference to value questions, is to acknowledge that pure reason can never be the sole source of norms, for reality outside the rational subject can also be normative. As J. M. Bernstein puts it, "it is this which the disenchantment of nature denies and what Adorno thinks is necessary in order to contest the hegemony of rationalized reason. It is equally just this which artworks exemplify through their nondiscursive meanings."[77]

Mentioning the importance of meanings that are nondiscursively expressed in works of art, meanings that also register the normative claims of objects against human domination, raises the question of the proportion of noetic and dianoetic moments in Adorno's noninstrumental variant of reason in the aesthetic sphere. At the end of *Negative Dialectics,* he had expressed a certain "solidarity . . . with metaphysics at the time of its fall,"[78] which may indicate his nostalgia for a time when reason depended less on inferential argument and more on deductive intuition. We have already cited the contention of Herbert Schnädelbach that Adorno was a "noetic of the non-identical."[79] In *Minima Moralia*, in fact, Adorno explicitly defended a way of thinking that goes beyond argumentation where the goal is always to be right: "the very wish to be right, down to its

subtlest form of logical reflection, is an expression of that spirit of self-preservation which philosophy is precisely concerned to break down. . . . To say this is
not, however, to advocate irrationalism, the postulation of arbitrary theses
justified by an intuitive faith in revelation, but the abolition of the distinction
between thesis and argument."[80] Performatively, the very aphorisms of *Minima
Moralia* reinforced this claim, as did the paratactic quality of Adorno's prose in
some of his longer works, where assertion follows assertion with little inferential
reasoning tying them together.[81]

The comparative virtues of noetic and dianoetic versions of reason continued
to occupy Horkheimer and Adorno in a conversation they had in 1956, the notes
of which were taken by Gretel Adorno.[82] While chastising Heidegger for being
too one-sidedly against discursive argumentation, Adorno nonetheless conceded
that "there is really something bad about advocacy. . . . Arguing means applying
the rules of thinking to the matters under discussion. You really mean to say that
if you find yourself in the situation of having to explain why something is bad,
you are already lost." Horkheimer added with a touch of scorn, "The USA is
the country of argument," which Adorno then trumped by pronouncing—
without providing a justification—that "argument is consistently bourgeois."[83]

But was a concept of reason that remained more noetic than dianoetic a
sufficiently compelling placeholder for that emphatic notion of rationality on
which the early Frankfurt School had placed its hopes before the eclipse? Not
all observers were convinced. Thus, for example, Christoph Menke, a leading
member of what is sometimes called Critical Theory's third generation, would
charge that "Adorno's efforts to conceive of an experience that encounters,
beyond reason, the infinite claims of reason as satisfied, are either metaphysical
(utopian cognition), empty (atopian cognition), or theological or heteronomous
(projections onto aesthetic experience). The teleological variant of the grounding of the negative dialectic of reason from without is thus unconvincing."[84]
Habermas himself would come to worry about the problematic implications of
the aphoristic form in *Minima Moralia*, which privileged noetic over dianoetic
reasoning.[85]

Other pressing questions also emerged. Did focusing excessively on art
cede too much ground to the "diseased" versions of reason—instrumental,
formal, subjective—that Critical Theory had feared were now almost totally
hegemonic in the modern world, and as a consequence betoken a retreat into a
beleaguered aesthetic sanctuary that had little chance of ever expanding its
territory? Had Adorno identified any concrete, institutional embodiments
outside that enclave that might allow a reading of history as suggesting a
more benign rationalization that could challenge the one decried in *Dialectic of
Enlightenment*? Was mimesis too "fuzzy" a concept to provide a "real alternative

to relations of domination?"[86] Did Adorno's version of aesthetic rationality, based on a constellation of nontotalized forces, depend too much on the model of the modern artwork, which was itself as much in danger of passing into history as the bourgeois subject that had been its precondition? Did it fully escape the aporias of a subject-centered philosophy, which tacitly posited a notion of reason as a transcendental faculty, in a world in which competing communities of historically variable subjects resisted being subsumed under a single, universal model? Was there, in short, another, more promising way to reestablish reason's power after its eclipse? It is to the attempt to do so by the Frankfurt School's most eminent second generation theorist, Jürgen Habermas, that we now must turn.

# 6

# Habermas and
# the Communicative Turn

With so many unanswered questions about the status of reason after its eclipse, it is no surprise that the Frankfurt School's most gifted second-generation theorist, Jürgen Habermas, felt compelled to seek a radically new foundation—or better put, a functional equivalent of one—for noninstrumental rationality, in the hope of salvaging the critical energies of the Enlightenment tradition. To do so required what might be called a metacritique of the critique of instrumental reason, one that would avoid the alternatives of irrationalist skepticism and metaphysical rationalism. Habermas's point of departure was a broad feeling of solidarity with the earlier Frankfurt School's yearning for a viable concept of reason able to serve the cause of radical social change.[1] No theory that could justifiably call itself critical could dispense with the cognitive insights and normative force that had been developed under the rubric of reason. Like Horkheimer and Adorno, Habermas absorbed the Hegelian lesson that reason, however it might be defined, had to be realizable in history, rather than conceived naturalistically or transcendentally. What he liked to call the "desublimation" of reason meant that he understood the imperative to realize reason practically in the actions and institutions of the lifeworld, which meant situated amid the inevitable diversity of particular cultures and specific bodies with all their accompanying desires and vulnerabilities. Thus the question of reason was not a question for philosophy alone but also for social relations in the everyday lifeworld of pre-reflective practices and beliefs, and even more so in the specialized institutions and differentiated value spheres that emerged from it. Habermas thus shared and even intensified Horkheimer and Adorno's suspicion of a subject-centered notion of reason, one derived from a monologic, Cartesian notion of the punctual self abstracted from the world. Such a self, he agreed, was the correlate of the isolated, asocial individual whose own preservation was its primary goal.

But unlike the first generation of Critical Theorists, Habermas did not pine for the restoration of anything that might be called objective or substantive reason in the emphatic, even quasi-metaphysical, sense of the term. While lamenting with them the hypertrophy of instrumental, technological rationality, which he saw as "mirroring the objective one-sidedness of the capitalist modernized lifeworld,"[2] he cautioned against reducing it to no more than an expression of reification and domination. Nor did he allow the apparent lessons of the Holocaust to turn him away from the rationalizing "project" of the Enlightenment, despite all its potential for domination.

Instead, Habermas boldly promoted a paradigm shift, which, as his student Herbert Schnädelbach was succinctly to put it, involved "the replacement of the critique of pure reason by the critique of linguistic reason."[3] The audacity of this move is hard to gainsay. Ever since the Sophists challenged Plato, thinkers who focused on language were generally skeptical of the exorbitant claims of reason.[4] Although as I noted in the opening discussions, modern defenders of rhetoric such as Hans Blumenberg could see it as a weaker form of "insufficient" reason, albeit one that was necessary, most devotees of logical rigor, clear and distinct ideas, and the scientific method sought to limit its power to obfuscate and confuse. Demanding strict definitions, scorning metaphoric excesses, seeking to root out ambiguity and vagueness, they yearned for a language that was transparent and precise. In response, critics of Enlightened rationalism, such as Hans Georg Hamann, the great scourge of Kant, mobilized all of the poetic resources of language—indeed a macaronic riot of different languages, ancient and modern—to demonstrate performatively that ideas, however internal to the mind they may seem, were always dependent on the medium of their expression.[5] When such later critics of rationality as Kierkegaard and Nietzsche mounted their attacks on Hegelian metaphysics, they too drew on the polysemic, rhetorically excessive potential of language used more poetically than scientifically for the same end. Following the so-called linguistic turn in the twentieth century, exemplified by Wittgenstein's ordinary language philosophy, the hermeneutics of Heidegger and Gadamer, and the deconstruction of Derrida and de Man, close attention to language seemed to erode still further surviving beliefs in the strong claims of reason.[6] Even for those like Horkheimer, who resisted that erosion, language remained "a mere tool in the omnipotent production apparatus of modern society."[7] And as for Adorno, although he did take seriously the power of language, including his own, the few times he addressed its intersubjective, communicative potential, he dismissed it for still privileging subjects over objects.[8]

Habermas, however, turned to language, understood in terms of what he called "universal pragmatics," to bask in the sunlight of reason as it emerged from its eclipse. In so doing, he sought to avoid the paradoxical recourse to a mere "faith in reason," a tacit concession to irrationality, which he had lamented in the philosophy of science promoted by the soi-disant "critical rationalist" Karl Popper.[9] At the same time, he wanted to find in the world of concrete human practices a vantage point of rational critique that would survive the discrediting of dubious transcendental foundations. Against those who would seek to build a barrier between scientific reason, purified of the dross of linguistic mediation, and the alleged "sophistry" of mere rhetoric, he would warn that

> one who uses "sophist" as an insult, so as to spare oneself arguing, must first explain the sense in which procedural rationality developed in the modern age and spelled out by modern philosophy can be so ominous; one must show, second, that in science or philosophy there can today still be found truths whose validity is based in the final analysis on something other than agreement brought about through argumentation.[10]

Although ultimately elaborated as a full-blown theory of "communicative rationality" with anthropological, sociological, and philosophical underpinnings, Habermas's linguistic turn was initially stimulated by a concrete historical analysis developed in his *Habilitationschrift* (second doctoral dissertation) in Marburg, written under the direction of the leftist political scientist Wolfgang Abendroth. Although his theoretical interest in language developed only in the course of the 1960s—one account credits his editorial involvement with a Suhrkamp Press series of books by Noam Chomsky, John Searle, Gregory Bateson, and others[11]—it is already evident in his empirical study of what he called "the bourgeois public sphere." In any account of Habermas's gradual dissatisfaction with Horkheimer, Adorno, and Marcuse's concepts of reason, *The Structural Transformation of the Public Sphere*, published in 1962, must be accorded a primary role.[12] Its own roots in Habermas's personal narrative—the challenges he felt trying to communicate as a child with a cleft palate, the horrors of growing up in a totalitarian society where the public sphere was non-existent, the fragility of the postwar German democracy—are also unmistakable.[13]

Although concluding with a rueful account of the contemporary withering of a robust public sphere, which anticipated the similar argument Marcuse was to make in *One-Dimensional Man* two years later, the book began by tracing the origins of a virtual space between the state, the economy, and the family in which individuals could meet and argue about their opinions on equal footing without the assumption of superiority tied to ascribed roles or innate traits. Whether in salons, coffee houses, Masonic lodges, voluntary reading societies, or learned academies, the power of the better argument based on evidence and logic could produce a consensus through persuasion rather than seduction, coercion, or deference to the status of the speaker.[14] Or rather as an ideal type, this was the telos of the nascent public sphere, as Habermas understood it. Because of its critical potential, its impulse to reflect on rather than merely obey tradition, authority, and revelation, it paradoxically often had to be conducted in secret to avoid persecution, but its inherent logic was to become more transparent and available for public scrutiny, thus realizing the "publicity" of the public sphere. Ultimately, it would have an impact on the realm of politics, even in a nondemocratic context: "The medium of this political confrontation was peculiar and without historical precedent: people's public use of their reason (*öffentliches Räsonnement*)."[15] In legal terms, this abetted the rise of what Max Weber had called rational-legal authority over its traditional or charismatic rivals. In both the political and legal arenas, the emergence of the public sphere meant at least potentially that the will of the community was reached through intersubjective discourse, and not, as later anti-liberal irrationalists like Carl Schmitt had contended, by the arbitrary decision of a singular sovereign above the law: "Public debate was supposed to transform *voluntas* [will] into a *ratio* that in the public competition of private arguments came into being as the consensus about what was practically necessary in the interest of all."[16] Although clearly the participants in that debate were still limited—it was, after all, a specifically "*bourgeois* public sphere"—there was no obstacle in principle to the ultimate inclusion of all who wanted to join in.

Here we have a more optimistic version of the Enlightenment tradition that seemed to escape the dialectic of domination and mastery, self-preservation and self-sacrifice, described with such despair by Horkheimer and Adorno. Here subjects were not primarily looking at objects in order to dominate them or treating other subjects as if they were objects to be instrumentally manipulated, but rather addressing and listening to other subjects as their equals. Here the concepts of rational thought were not simply vehicles for the suppression of nonidentity and difference, as Adorno and Horkheimer had feared in *Dialectic of Enlightenment*.[17] The "disease" of reason, we might say, had not affected all organs of the *animal rationale* for Habermas.

It was ironically perhaps Hans-Georg Gadamer, with whom Habermas had many disagreements,[18] who best expressed the spirit behind his hope for a renewal of reason, when he noted that from the time of the Greeks, reason was understood not to be like other goods, whose possession could be hoarded by some:

> in contrast to all other goods it is not diminished by being shared and so is not an object of dispute like all other goods but actually gains through participation. In the end, this is the birth of the concept of reason: the more what is desirable is displayed for all in a way that is convincing to all, the more those involved discover themselves in this common reality; and to that extent human beings possess freedom in the positive sense, they have their true identities in that common reality.[19]

A corollary of Habermas's cautious optimism about the public sphere as a space for the sharing of reason was a tacit critique of the first generation of the Frankfurt School. Habermas explicitly rejected a full-throated Hegelian notion of dialectical *Vernunft*, defended by Marcuse in particular, as an antidote to the analytic *Verstand* that went along with technological, instrumental rationality. Whereas Kant could still employ "reasoning" and "rational argument" in the Enlightenment sense of rational argumentation, the more authoritarian Hegel, Habermas warned, had wrongly feared that

> reasoning thought (*das räsonierende Denken*), as mere use of the understanding (*Verstandebestrachtung*), did not penetrate to the concrete universality of the concept; Hegel, faithful to the Platonic tradition, found its most exemplary development in the Sophists. . . . Hegel downgraded the use of rational arguments, especially their public use, in order to justify political authority (with which the reasoning public, of course, was involved in a polemical way) as an element on a higher level.[20]

Locating the remnants of noninstrumental rationality in an aesthetic enclave, in the manner of Adorno, was also problematic, reflecting what Habermas impatiently called a defensive "strategy of hibernation."[21] If there were an aesthetic dimension to the emergence of discursive rationality in the public sphere, it was expressed not so much internally in the work of art itself, through gestural resistance to the domination of concepts, as externally in the public judgment of such works conducted without conformity to pregiven rules or standards. What Kant had called "reflective judgments" based on paradigmatic exemplars and revealing analogies were a more promising locus of rational argumentation than either "determinant judgments" based on subsumptive conceptual logic or the flashes of insight produced by artistic experiences.

For a number of years, however, Habermas's tacit critique of the first generation on the issue of reason remained somewhat muted. In his 1963 collection, *Theory and Practice*, he still invoked the traditional Frankfurt School critique of the positivist exclusion of normative questions from their cramped definition of reason, which left the way open to an arbitrary decisionism:

> from the mainstream of rationality the pollutants, the sewage of emotionality, are filtered off and locked away hygienically in a storage basin—an imposing mass of subjective value qualities. Every single value appears a meaningless agglomeration of meaning, stamped solely with the stigma of irrationality, so that the priority of one value over the other—thus the persuasiveness which a value claims with respect to action—simply cannot be rationally justified.[22]

At the 1965 German Sociological Association conference at Heidelberg commemorating Max Weber's centenary, Habermas joined with Horkheimer and Marcuse in criticizing Talcott Parsons's benign reading of Weber's legacy, lamenting the latter's "decisionist self-assertion in the midst of a rationalized world" and noting a sinister link with Carl Schmitt.[23] In his seminal essay of 1968, "Technology and Science as 'Ideology,'" Habermas excoriated yet again Weber's split between facts and values and bemoaned his abandonment of a substantive notion of reason. Likewise, in the ongoing "positivism debate" between the followers of Karl Popper's "critical rationalism" and Critical Theory that roiled German sociology in the late 1960s, he remained clearly on the side of Adorno, even defending Hegel against Popper's caricatured version of him.[24]

At the same time, however, Habermas's growing dissatisfaction with certain aspects of the older Frankfurt School's legacy slowly emerged into the light. He grew skeptical of the utopian goal of entirely overcoming the human domination of the natural world, based on a new and more benign version of technology. Nor did he hold out much hope for the dedifferentiation of various value spheres in culture through a dialectical reconciliation of contradictions.[25] And perhaps most important from the perspective of the restoration of a robust notion of reason, Habermas also began to distinguish between two concepts of rationalization, each of which had certain virtues. As he put it in his seminal 1968 essay distinguishing labor from symbolically mediated interaction:

> At the level of the subsystems of purposive-rational action, scientific technological progress has already compelled the reorganization of social institutions and sectors, and necessitates it on an even larger scale than

> heretofore. But this process of the development of the productive forces can be a potential for liberation if and only if it does not replace rationality on another level. *Rationalization at the level of the institutional framework* can occur only in the medium of symbolic interaction itself, that is, through *removing restrictions on communication.*[26]

In other words, rather than demonizing instrumental rationality per se, which he saw as inevitable in the realm of "labor," he only worried about its colonization of the separate sphere of what at that time he called "symbolic interaction."

And while he applauded Marcuse's resistance to the status-quo-affirming, "one-dimensional" mentality of contemporary society, Habermas was not convinced that instinctual rebellion could provide a plausible antidote to its domination. Even in the generous tribute to Marcuse he wrote shortly after the latter died in 1978, he could express his doubts: "this theory has the weakness that it cannot consistently account for its own possibility. If rebellious subjectivity had to owe its rebirth to something that is beyond—a too deeply corrupted—reason, it is hard to explain why some of us should at all be in a position to recognize this fact and to give reasons in defense of it."[27] In short, the threat of positivism, one-dimensionality, and the hypertrophy of instrumental reason could not be met by recourse to discredited metaphysics, libidinal experience, or retreat into the enclave of the aesthetic.

By the late 1970s, a far more potent threat to the rationalist tradition than positivism in its various guises had emerged, which broadly speaking came to be called either poststructuralism or postmodernism. Unlike positivism, it took the linguistic turn seriously but came to very different conclusions from Habermas about its lessons. Alarmed by its penetration of leftist culture in the wake of Marxism's decline, Habermas hastily conflated it with the "young conservative" critique of modernity derived from thinkers like Carl Schmitt and Arnold Gehlen, which was feeding the *Tendezwende* or turn to the right in German politics of that era.[28] Derived in large measure from the counter-Enlightenment tradition that culminated in Nietzsche's restitution of the claims of mythos over logos, it seemed to signal the exhaustion of all previous varieties of rationalism.[29]

Not only did Habermas perceive this development as a politically dangerous challenge to a viable critical theory, but also began to read Horkheimer and Adorno's writings of the 1940s, in particular *Dialectic of Enlightenment*, as an anticipation of the ideas of Foucault, Derrida, Jean-François Lyotard, and others in the poststructuralist camp. Habermas now concluded that they too had "found political institutions, all social institutions, and daily practices as well, completely void of all traces of reason. For them, reason had become utopian in the literal sense of the word: it had lost all its locations and thus ushered in the whole problematic of negative dialectics."[30]

In the lectures that were published as *The Philosophical Discourse of Modernity* in 1985, Habermas spelled out more explicitly than ever before the dangers he saw in their one-sided analysis of the crisis of reason. Undeterred by their half-hearted attempts to gesture toward an emancipatory alternative, he focused with alarm on Horkheimer and Adorno's claim that "*from the very start* the process of enlightenment is the result of a drive to self-preservation that mutilates reason, because it lays claim to it only in the form of a purposive-rational mastery of nature and instinct—precisely as instrumental reason."[31] Reducing all science and technology to its positivist caricature, ignoring the healthy implications of the differentiation of value spheres noted by Weber, and abandoning their earlier nuanced appreciation of the achievements of bourgeois modernity, they ended by allowing ideology critique to undermine its own foundations. Their total, self-referential ideology critique, Habermas warned, is "turned not only against the irrational function of bourgeois ideals, but against the rational potential of bourgeois culture itself, and thus it reaches into the foundations of any ideology critique that proceeds immanently. . . . As instrumental, reason assimilated itself to power and thereby relinquished its critical force—that is the *final* disclosure of ideology critique applied to itself."[32] The result was a performative contradiction—critique drawing on a reason that was itself also the object of the critique—with no way out: "Adorno's *Negative Dialectics* reads like a continuing explanation of why we have to circle about within this *performative contradiction* and indeed even remain there."[33]

Such a skepticism about reason in general threatened to align Horkheimer and Adorno, despite their intentions, with other critics of subject-centered reason, such as Heidegger, the focus of the next chapter in *The Philosophical Discourse of Modernity*, entitled "The Undermining of Western Rationalism through the Critique of Metaphysics."[34] Refusing to distinguish between *Vernunft* and *Verstand*, which had been so crucial for the Enlightenment and German Idealism, and conflating humanist universalism with fascist particularism, Heidegger had damned all aspects of the project of modernity: "No matter whether modern ideas make their entry in the name of reason or of the destruction of reason, the prism of the modern understanding of Being refracts *all* normative orientations into the power claims of a subjectivity crazed with self-aggrandizement."[35] Although he sought to go beyond the modern philosophies based on the consciousness of an empirical or transcendental subject and privileged world-disclosure over the domination of nature, his analysis of an allegedly intersubjective "being-with" remained trapped in the struggle for authenticity waged by the isolated *Dasein* (being-there) posited in *Being and*

*Time*.[36] Ultimately, Habermas concluded, Heidegger was unable to go beyond a cognitive relationship of subjects to objects, or of *Dasein* to *Sein* (being).

What Horkheimer, Adorno, Heidegger, and the French poststructuralists all lacked, according to Habermas, was an appreciation of what speech act theorists had called the illocutionary dimension of language, which moved its center of gravity away from the subject of enunciation and the object of reference to the intersubjective action intended pragmatically by every linguistic utterance.[37] Instead of focusing on the "I-he, she, or it" function of utterances, it stressed the "I-thou or you" function. It was to this neglected dimension of linguistic practice, which operated above the level of deep structures, that Habermas turned to flesh out the insights he had had in his earlier work on symbolically mediated interaction and the public sphere, whose current incarnation he no longer read as fully exhausted.[38] No less was at stake than a radical reformulation of the ground of critique in a version of reason that the first generation of Critical Theorists had not sufficiently taken into account.

Drawing on an astoundingly wide range of old and new sources—inter alia, Humboldtian linguistics, Gadamerian hermeneutics, the pragmatism of C. S. Peirce and George Herbert Mead, Karl-Otto Apel's transcendental pragmatics, Weber's theory of the modern differentiation of value spheres, and Stephen Toulmin's work on argumentation, in addition to the speech act theory of J. L. Austin and John Searle—he fashioned a revived version of Critical Theory, which sought to avoid the Scylla of historicist contextualism and the Charybdis of ahistorical transcendentalism or naturalism. In the place of the untenable "objective" or "dialectical" reason of the first generation, extending beyond Adorno's aesthetic alternative, was what Habermas called "communicative" reason.[39] In the terms I have introduced in the narrative of reason's earlier adventures, it was more "narrow church" than "broad"—no attempt here to fold mythos back into logos—more dianoetic than noetic,[40] and more "dispositional" than situational, while nonetheless being dialogical rather than monological and allowing for the institutional and systemic embodiment of certain versions of reason as well. Although reminiscent of Kant's critical project in its acknowledgment of the limits of reason, its ambitious scope invited comparison with the holism of speculative Idealists like Hegel.[41] Unlike Adorno and Benjamin, he did not retreat into the micrological analyses, *Denkbilder* (thought-images), or aphoristic pronouncements that performatively expressed the claim that "the whole is the false."[42]

Habermas's audacious attempt to restore the light of reason after its eclipse also involved several salient departures from traditional notions of reason, including a number that continued to inform classical Critical Theory. Let me enumerate them now and spell out their implications in greater detail in what follows: (1) *the desubstantialization of reason*: jettisoning an emphatic idea of objective reason inherent in the world either actually or potentially, and thus abandoning an ontological faith in the principle of sufficient reason; (2) *the detranscendentalization of reason*: refusing to ground it in the forms allegedly hard-wired in the mind of a universal subject prior to shifting historical contexts and evolving natural languages; (3) *the linguistification of reason*: seeking in communicative interaction or "universal pragmatics" its foundationless foundation as a normative vantage point for Critical Theory, but without positing a fully rational form of life as the telos of critique; (4) *the desublimation of reason*: situating it concretely in the practices and institutions of the social world, while acknowledging rationalization as a perpetually incomplete or "impure" process rather than a fixed state of completion; (5) *the pluralization of reason*: resisting its comprehensive integration into a singular meta-category, while holding out hope for a productive and balanced interaction between all of the local variants, including instrumental; (6) *the proceduralization of reason*: seeking discursive protocols of reasoning and argumentation that can be applied to both cognitive as well as normative questions; (7) *the temporalization of reason as an infinite project*: jettisoning a strongly anamnestic notion of a reason recoverable from the past in favor of one that sees it as a regulative ideal to be ever more closely approximated, but never fully realized in the future; (8) *the "as if" narrativization of reason*: employing a "rational reconstruction" of a species-wide learning process as a standard by which to measure the potential realization of that future, without reviving a discredited objective philosophy of history.

Let us slow down and take each of these dimensions in turn.

(1) *The desubstantialization of reason*. While Adorno could still talk of solidarity with metaphysics at the moment of its fall and Horkheimer could nostalgically recall the objective reason that had prevailed prior to its "eclipse," Habermas adopted a position he could forthrightly call "postmetaphysical."[43] Above all, this meant abandoning the assumption that rationality might be an inherent quality of the world, either actually or potentially. Although his elaboration of the communicative, intersubjective dimension of language meant going beyond the nominalists' radical individualism, he shared their suspicion of rational essences or intelligible forms. Moving away from the Hegelian underpinnings of earlier Critical Theory, he rejected the idea that concepts could be understood ontologically as latent in a world that was not yet adequate to them on the level of actuality.[44] There was, in other words, absolutely no residue of pantheism in his worldview, no yearning for the reuniting of mythos and logos into a grand synthesis of meaningful plenitude.

Whereas Horkheimer had tied the nominalist belief in the unconstrained will to the domination of nature and the formalization of reason, Habermas

also stressed that the nominalists had performed a crucial function in undermining the assumption that real universals existed both in the world and in the
minds of men. "From its inception," he wrote, "idealism had hidden from itself
the fact that the Ideas inconspicuously include within themselves the merely
material and accidental moments of individual things, from which they had indeed only been abstracted. Nominalism exposed this contradiction and demoted
substances or *formae rerum* to mere names, to *signa rerum* that, as it were, the
knowing subject tacks on to things."[45] But rather than abandoning reason
entirely for faith—nominalism, it should be recalled, began as a fourteenth-
century Franciscan theology[46]—Habermas sought to locate it elsewhere than
in the objective world of intelligible forms or natural laws, while avoiding the
nominalists' excessive reliance on subjective will, either divine or human, in
constituting the world.

(2) *The detranscendentalization of reason.* Reason should also not be located in a
universal, species-wide, timeless mental capacity, in the sense, say, of Kant's a
priori epistemological categories. Even more than his Frankfurt School predecessors, Habermas sought to make a clean break with the "consciousness philosophy" "or "mentalism" that understood reason as inherent in the mind of the
thinking subject and/or congruent with the external world represented in that
mind. Reason understood logocentrically, based on the privileging of concepts
and representations of the world as objects for cognitive purposes alone, was
actually an impoverished version of it, and not equivalent to reason per se.[47]
When it only adopted the perspective of first or third persons—the dualism of
subject and object, I and It—it neglected the second-person relationship of
reciprocity between subjects, recognizing each other as such. Subject-centered
rationality was indeed a function of that drive for self-preservation that Horkheimer had seen as leading to the domination of what was construed as external
to it, but it was not the only alternative in the modern world.

Rather than a faculty of the individual mind representing an object external
to it, reason should be understood more capaciously as an intersubjective
procedure of validity testing. As Habermas put it in one of his more succinct
articulations of the difference:

> Subject-centered reason finds its criteria in standards of truth and success
> that govern the relationships of knowing and purposively acting subjects to
> the world of possible objects or states of affairs. By contrast, as soon as we
> conceive of knowledge as communicatively mediated, rationality is assessed
> in terms of the capacity of responsible participants in interaction to orient
> themselves in relation to validity claims geared to intersubjective recog-
> nition. Communicative reason finds its criteria in the argumentative

procedures for directly or indirectly redeeming claims to propositional truth, normative rightness, subjective truthfulness, and aesthetic harmony.[48]

Even when rationality might seem to be a personal disposition of a self-reflective subject, it expresses a self-relation that is "due in each case to the adoption and internalization of the perspective on me of other participants in argumentation,"[49] in which the second person stance of "I-thou" is internally mirrored.

Another implication of detranscendentalization was the replacement of a Kantian notion of the necessary character of the presuppositions inherent in all attempts to communicate with a Wittgensteinian one. Reason, Habermas explained, "does not have the transcendental meaning of universal, necessary, noumenal (*intelligiblen*) conditions of possible experience, but has the grammatical meaning of an 'unavoidability' stemming from the conceptual connections of a system of learned—but for us inescapable—rule governed behavior."[50] Because of this redefinition, the Kantian distinction between reason (*Vernunft*) and intellect or understanding (*Verstand*) is blurred, as is the opposition of noumena and phenomena.

Indeed, the full sway of even those rules set by the more contingent processes suggested by Wittgenstein was limited, as they did not extend to the judgment necessary to apply general principles to specific cases. Kant's attempt to provide a transcendental deduction that would not only establish a priori categories but also the ways in which they determined specific judgments was untenable. For a transcendental pragmatics, in contrast, there is always a hermeneutic component in the application of rules, which defies formalization. "One cannot represent language," according to Schnädelbach's gloss on Habermas's position, "in rules of formal logic, and no transcendental deduction of impure concepts of the understanding is possible; therefore there can also be no transition to a 'transcendental doctrine of judgment,' which would allow one to formulate *a priori* rules of linguistic reason."[51] In the familiar terms of Kant's third Critique, the application of reflective rather than determinant judgments extended beyond the realm of aesthetic rationality to inform all transitions from abstract rules to concrete cases.

(3) *The linguistification of reason.* Abandoning Kant's belief in the transcendental deduction of rule-bound categories of judgment did not, however, require jettisoning his hope for a limited role for rationality in cognitive terms. Communicative competence implied the possibility of reasoning about one's beliefs, not merely asserting them, and also listening to the reasoning of others. "Detranscendentalization," Habermas wrote, "leads, on the one hand, to the embedding of knowing subjects into the socializing contexts of a life world and on the other, to the entwinement of cognition with speech and action."[52] It was in

the interpersonal, communicative function of language—which, *pace* his post-structuralist critics, Habermas freely acknowledged was not the only way it might be approached—that a nonmentalist rationality might be located. Whether implicitly or not, all speech acts entail giving reasons and making arguments to support their claims for validity, although some do so more expressly than others. "There is a sense in which any interpretation," he went so far as to argue provocatively, "is a *rational* interpretation,"[53] because it depends on the reasons offered for its plausibility. Especially when there is an explicit disagreement or problem to be solved, tacit assumptions need to be reflexively or discursively validated. They enter what the American philosopher Wilfrid Sellars would famously call "the space of reasons," where intersubjective arguments among interlocutors, normative claims to rightness, and inferential reasoning subtend any claims about the state of reality.[54] Not only was it necessary to argue for a position rather than merely present it assertorically, but there is also an equal obligation to listen to the arguments of others, which might persuade you by their evidentiary, logical, or rhetorical power. Even those beliefs that had once been unquestioningly accepted as divine commands could become available for validity testing by those who held them, a process Habermas designated with the inelegant phrase the "linguistification (*Versprachlichung*) of the sacred."

In fact, if there is any one criterion to identify modernity it would be the increased accessibility of what was previously held sacred to the test of argumentative justification. There was, of course, an ever-present threat of regressive "delinguistification" and the restoration of authoritarian traditions or the emergence of charismatic authority. Even when those alternatives were avoided, the steering mechanisms of money and administration could bypass communicative rationality in favor of a functionalism that ran on autopilot (an especially chilling example being the fad of game theoretical decision-making during the height of the Cold War).[55] But by and large, postconventional societies no longer bound together by unquestioned cultural assumptions increasingly needed to justify their decisions discursively, if they were to avoid arbitrary violence. Although there had never been, contrary to Benjamin's postulation of an Adamic language before Babel, a universal metalanguage that might be seen as the basis for all natural languages or serve as its potential telos, there was in every language a latent imperative at the deepest level to supply reasons for whatever assertions, beliefs, commands, and so on might be uttered by speakers to their listeners. Modernity, if it meant anything at all, implied increasing recourse to that imperative in making actual decisions.

Accompanying the widening of the "space of reasons" was what might be called a comparable extension of the "time of reasoning," the deliberative process that allowed all the relevant arguments and available evidence to be considered before acting. Unlike an immediate noetic intuition or even a mono-logically conducted process of inferential deduction, communicative reason necessarily hesitated before reaching final decisions, keeping open the possibility of future modifications as the process continued and new interlocutors joined the discussion. Although decisionist advocates of leaps of faith were impatient with the often lethargic pace of communicative rationality, pointing out that the luxury of interminable delay was often denied in the real world, communica-tive rationalists responded that sometimes inactive rumination was preferable to rash decisions made without the benefit of sufficient intersubjective reflection.

The standards of deliberative rationality, to cite the analytic philosopher Joseph Raz's formulation, thus

> include much more than standards governing the capacity to discern in-ferential relations, or their absence. They involve, for example, standards by which we judge the proper functioning of abilities to end deliberation when appropriate (and avoid the vices of dithering and indecision), abilities to stick with a conclusion (and avoid the vices of continually changing one's mind, feeling that the grass is always greener on the other side, etc.), as well as the ability to examine one's own conclusions and intentions when appropriate (and avoid dogmatism, pig-headedness, etc.).[56]

Another contrast between consciousness-centered and communicative reason could be found in the register of morality rather than cognition, norms rather than facts. It pitted the subjective notion of practical, deontological reason developed by Kant, the universal sense of duty or obligation felt by each autono-mous individual, against a discourse view of ethics, in which only argument and discussion can help actors intersubjectively weigh moral choices.[57] "Practical reason," Habermas insisted, "can no longer be founded in the transcendental subject. Communicative ethics appeals now only to fundamental norms of rational speech, an ultimate 'fact of reason.'"[58] Communicative rationality does not, however, legislate specific norms, although it provides counterfactual ideal-izations of the procedures through which they might be reached. Rather than a prescriptive blueprint for right action, it can clarify the discursive networks in which such decisions can be more lucidly made. As Habermas explained in his 1992 *Between Facts and Norms*, "communicative rationality is expressed in a de-centered complex of pervasive, transcendentally enabling structural conditions, but it is not a subjective capacity that would tell actors what they *ought* to do."[59]

An explicit target of Habermas's critique of consciousness-centered subjec-tivity was the so-called praxis philosophy, derived from the young Marx and promulgated by twentieth-century Marxists like Antonio Gramsci,[60] that had continued the quest for a concrete metasubject of history, a collective agent that would consciously and rationally make the world and know what it had made, a materialist version of Vico's *verum-factum* principle.[61] The image of man as *homo faber* (man the maker), whose productive labor was the principle source of the world around him, was no longer viable. As I have already noted, as early as the 1960s Habermas criticized the ideal of an unalienated labor as an alternative to its inevitable entanglement in the logic of instrumentality.[62] Although the material conditions of the lifeworld remain central to any social analysis, "the critical theory of society must no longer rely on the normative contents of the expressivist model of alienation and reappropriation of essential powers."[63] Here the metanarrative of a singular reason that alienated itself in the apparent contingencies of history and then recognized them as its own manifestations in a grand affirmative reconciliation could no longer be counted on to heal the wounds of diremption. Reason could not be understood in terms of a narcissistic mirroring that underlay an identity philosophy of the kind Adorno had so powerfully criticized in *Negative Dialectics* and elsewhere. "Modern lifeworlds," Habermas insisted, "are differentiated and should remain so in order that the reflexivity of traditions, the individuation of the social subject, and the universalistic foundations of the social subject do not all go to hell."[64]

(4) *The desublimation of reason.* Along with the detranscendentalization of reason went its embeddedness in the historical realities of the world. Although in many respects he admired Kant, with whose limits on reason he sympathized, Habermas was closer to Hegel in rejecting any attempt to posit a transcendental subject or noumenal self outside of the actual historical constitution of concrete subjects who were doing the arguing in concrete circumstances, circumstances that always impeded the perfect leveling of the playing field and full symmetry of participation. Even when he had posited three general human interests—in dominating nature, intersubjective understanding, and emancipation from unjust social relations—in his early work of 1968, *Knowledge and Human Interests*, Habermas characterized them as only "quasi-transcendental," a locution he was soon quietly to abandon along with the philosophical anthropology they implied. If there is a tension between what is and what should be, Habermas claimed, it has to be located within various forms of life, specific social practices, and concrete institutions, not beyond them. "The theory of communicative action *integrates* the transcendental tension between the intelligible and the world of appearances in communicative everyday praxis," he explained, "yet does not thereby *level* it out."[65] What results is not transcendental in any strict sense of the term, because it is always possible to use language for noncommunicative purposes and without fulfilling its idealized potential. Thus the point

d'appui of critique, as the earlier Frankfurt School had understood, must be more immanent than transcendent.[66]

Although acknowledging that modern philosophy since Descartes had been dominated by a mentalist or consciousness-centered subjectivity in one form or another, Habermas argued that a promising counterdiscourse had also emerged, which he discerned, inter alia, in Wilhelm von Humboldt's distinction between language as *ergon* (work) and language as *energeia* (activity),[67] and the dialectic of recognition that had underpinned the early Hegel's phenomenology. Although regrettably Hegel himself had then subsumed it under his philosophy of the absolute spirit, in which a rational metasubject both constructed the world and recognized itself in its construction, the alternative version of communicative reason remained a potential that could be fully actualized only after the "linguistic turn" had redirected philosophical inquiry away from interior mind and toward symbolic interaction in the world.[68] Understood on the level of utterance rather than deep structures or what deconstruction called "arche-writing," it did not mean turning the subjects in a dialogic relationship into derivative effects of an impersonal structure, matrix of power, or cultural unconscious. For by focusing on the pragmatic level of language, the level of speech acts or utterances, rather than on the grammatical or semiotic rules that subtended them, one could maintain that link between reason and freedom that had been one of rationalism's most fundamental assumptions.[69] As George Herbert Mead in particular had demonstrated, self and other were mutually implicated, institutions and roles were equiprimordial with the subjects that inhabited them.[70] As Wittgenstein had shown, although actions were governed by rules that were not reducible to conscious decisions that founded them ex nihilo, once one entered a language game, it was possible to act freely within them.

Communicative rationality could thus itself be called an "other" of the dominant tradition of reason, whether understood subjectively or objectively, but one that was not "outside" of reason more capaciously construed. Unlike the vital forces of the body or madness or the imagination or the senses, which had been allegedly repressed by a coercive, exclusivist reason and once unleashed, promised liberation, this "other" was able to avoid a romantic celebration of allegedly rapturous limit-experiences and the defiantly irrational. *Pace* Adorno, it was not restricted to the enclave of the aesthetic, where it kept the faith with a primal mimetic experience prior to reason itself. For rather than understanding mimesis as an external supplement to the rational moment in art, Habermas contended that mimesis itself was internal to rationality when it was discursively rather than monologically understood. That is, insofar as communicative rationality involved a dialogic exchange rather than a conceptual subsumption, it did not efface nonidentity in the service of a single rational truth. Even an ideal consensus was not like a unified concept, which could be held in the mind of an individual consciousness, but was more an interactive exchange among participants whose individuality was not fully canceled out by their agreement. This point is nicely articulated by Wellmer:

> That which in "true" reason goes beyond instrumental reason—Adorno calls it "mimesis"—he can only conceive as being extraterritorial to the sphere of conceptual thought. When linguistic philosophy decenters the subject, by contrast, it shows that there is a communicative-mimetic dimension *at the heart* of discursive reason—which is always more than formal logic, instrumental reason, or a compulsion to systematize.[71]

In other words, the nondominating logic of mimesis, which involves the imitation of the other by the self, can be discerned in a communicative rationality, which functions as much through listening to and learning from the arguments of others as trying to persuade them of the validity of your own.

As a result, communicative reason did not serve, as had some of its more restricted variants, to enforce rigid boundaries in order to fend off pollution by what it had abjected. In fact, rather than itself dismissing these "others" as utterly heterogeneous to reason and inhabiting a realm that could only be damned as "irrational," communicative rationality could include them in the discursive process itself, at least as producing alternative content worth arguing about.[72] In principle, there was nothing that could not be grist for the process of discursive reasoning. Although this was not the same as finding an occulted logos in mythos, the capacious position upheld by broad church rationalists, it did mean that attention had to be paid to the valuable material originally expressed in nonrational form. Habermas's late openness to incorporating religion into the political discourse of his day testified to this imperative.

In addition to reason's embeddedness in history, Habermas came to appreciate that it was even more fundamentally embedded in nature, understood in terms of Darwinian evolution. Citing a formulation from Adorno's *Negative Dialectics*—"That reason is different from nature and yet a moment of the latter is its prehistory become its immanent determination"—he acknowledged that "even subjects who are guided by reason, and hence act freely, by no means stand above the course of nature. They cannot sever themselves from their natural origins by transporting themselves into an intelligible original position [*Ursprungsort*]."[73] Of course, once the species develops the capacity to argue and act on the basis of rational choices, it leaves behind its total dependence on instincts and the laws of nature, but without entirely overcoming its somatic "inner nature" with all of its desires, urges, needs, and fears. One consequence of this entanglement, Habermas argued with the memory of Nazi eugenics in mind, is a prudent hesitation before tinkering with our genetic heritage, which provides a bulwark against external control over the unique lived bodies that we carry into the world at birth.[74]

(5) *The pluralization of reason.* Unlike the comprehensive type of reason that earlier Critical Theorists in their more Hegelian moods had championed, this new paradigm of reason could not lay claim to a totalizing sublation of all differences, including those dividing various types of reason themselves.[75] Pace neo-Aristotelian critics such as Rüdiger Bubner, the hope for a fully rational form of life in which abstract moral norms and concrete ethical values were reconciled in a substantively meaningful way was vain.[76] The pluralization of reason was not for Habermas a flaw to be overcome, a symptom of the fragmentation of something that once was whole. "It must be made clear," he insisted, "that the purism of pure reason is not resurrected in communicative reason."[77] *Im*pure reason instead meant the imperative to give reasons, whatever the context, in an unending quest for a general consensus that would remain forever counterfactual, not the attainment of a single perfectly consistent state of full rationality. In fact, actually achieving the ideal of perfect rationality would undermine the very foundation of communicative reason, which implied the ongoing, never-ending activity of reasoning among finite, fallible human beings with all of their corporeal and historical differences.

There was, moreover, no overarching way to integrate and reconcile what modernity had differentiated. "Philosophy," Habermas stressed, "must operate under conditions of rationality that it has not chosen."[78] As Kant and Weber had shown, distinct value spheres had developed their own relative autonomy, following a unique logic and institutional development, and although they were not watertight or unconnected from the less differentiated lifeworld out of which they had emerged, they could not be entirely reintegrated. Ironically, by valorizing such pluralization, Habermas found common ground with some of his poststructuralist critics, such as Foucault, who once said, "I think the word *rationalization* is dangerous. What we have to do is analyze specific rationalities rather than always invoking the progress of rationalization in general."[79]

It was in the service of such an imperative that Habermas posited fundamental differences in the underlying logic of different kinds of rationalization. Whereas rationalization in terms of instrumental rationality meant the accumulation of knowledge about the world based on scientific and technological experience, the rationalizable aspect of communicative action has nothing to do with propositional truth; but it has everything to do with the truthfulness of intentional expressions and with the rightness of norms. . . . *Rationalization* here means extirpating those relations of force that are inconspicuously set in the very structures of communication and that prevent conscious settlement of conflicts, and consensual regulation of conflicts, by means of intrapsychic as well as interpersonal communicative barriers.[80]

But because there was no overarching metaconcept of reason, a superior "healthy" version that would allow us to stigmatize others as "diseased" or "pathological," there was, *pace* the older Frankfurt School, a legitimate role for an objectifying relationship both to the world and the self, alongside a more intersubjective or hermeneutic one. Instrumental rationality and the strategic use of language had their place, as not all action geared to success could be folded into interaction geared to mutual understanding and agreement.

Or to use the terms Habermas borrowed with certain reservations from the British sociologist David Lockwood via their development by the German systems theorist Niklas Luhmann, there was a need for "system" as well as "social integration."[81] System integration refers to those structures and institutions, such as the market economy and state bureaucracy, that have become detached from the immediacy of the lifeworld, gaining relative autonomy, and are regulated by impersonal steering mechanisms, perhaps even becoming reified and alienated in the traditional Marxist sense of those terms. Less functionalist and more dispositional in inclination, social integration involves direct, experiential interaction among actors through cultural norms, values, and intersubjective practices, the locus of what he had earlier called "symbolically mediated interaction." Although sometimes Habermas seemed to be conflating the latter with the predifferentiated lifeworld per se, in modernity specialized institutions of social integration, such as the educational system, had developed in ways that transcended the prereflexive practices of the lifeworld. Thus, the latent communicative rationality of those practices had become the more manifestly self-consciously discursive protocols of modern life.

Habermas's use of Lockwood and Luhmann has been the subject of considerable critical discussion,[82] but the simple point to make here is that he granted both social and system integration their share of rationality. Thus, while privileging communicative reasoning in the ways we have outlined, he also acknowledged the legitimate role of instrumental, functionalist, technological rationality in the modern differentiated world, while protesting against the illegitimate ways it had expanded that role beyond its proper boundaries.

A comparable tolerance marked his attitude toward the place of formal reason in a pluralized modernity. However much Horkheimer and his colleagues had bemoaned the formalization of reason as a symptom of its "disease," there was also a place for formalism in, say, modern legal systems that could not be folded into a higher level substantive justice. "It never occurred to Horkheimer," Habermas pointedly remarked, "that there might be a difference between 'instrumental' and 'formal' reason. Moreover, he unceremoniously assimilated procedural reason—which no longer makes the validity of its results dependent on the rational organization of the world but on the rationality of the procedures through which is solves its problems—to instrumental reason."[83]

(6) *The proceduralization of reason.* In fact, in one sense the formal dimension of reason—its following certain procedural rules—was essential from the beginning. For it can be found in the communicative nature of language itself. Against the structural formalism that disparaged the pragmatic level of usage in favor of deep structures, Habermas insisted that "not only language but speech too—that is, the employment of sentences in utterances—is accessible to formal analysis."[84] Formal, it should be understood, did not mean a relationship between or among propositions, which traditional Aristotelian logic had identified with the syllogistic forms of sentences, but rather the procedures of rational argumentation, where contradictions were performative rather than semantic. As Albrecht Wellmer has noted, "through the notion of communicative rationality, the law of noncontradiction is, as it were, projected back from the one-dimensional space of logical relationships between propositions (and actions) onto the two-dimensional space of dialogical relationships between different speakers."[85] Understood in this way, there was, *pace* Horkheimer, a normative dimension to formal qua procedural reason.

What precisely was the procedure in question? Locating its initial institutional embodiment in seventeenth-century science and eighteenth-century legal and constitutional practices, Habermas identified it with the idea of "discourse," a second-order level of rational reflexivity, which he defined in the following way:

> that form of communication that is removed from contexts of experience and action and whose structure assures us: that the bracketed validity claims of assertions, recommendations, or warnings are the exclusive object of discussion; that participants, themes and contributions are not restricted except with reference to the goal of testing the validity claims in question; that no force except that of the better argument is exercised; and

that, as a result, all motives except that of the cooperative search for truth are excluded.[86]

Later he would further clarify the distinction between communicative interaction per se, which is unselfconsciously inherent in speech, and genuine reflective discourse in the following way:

> In *communicative action*, we proceed naively, as it were, whereas in *discourse*
> we exchange reasons in order to assess validity claims that have become
> problematic. Rational discourse borrows this reflexivity from the written
> word, that is to say, from the published article, or the scholarly treatise,
> because discourse is designed to include everyone concerned and to create
> a third platform on which all pertinent contributions are heard.[87]

If a consensus is reached discursively and generalized interests are established that go beyond the mere strategic agreement of compromise, then the result can be understood, as noted earlier, to express what can be called a "rational will." Although such a goal is, as we have seen, regulative and counterfactual, it can serve as a standard against which actually existing democracy can be measured.[88]

For Habermas, the radical opposition between substantive and formal reason, borrowed from Weber, was itself "a false alternative" based on the premise that

> the disenchantment of religious-metaphysical world views robs rationality,
> along with the contents of tradition, of all substantive connotations and
> thereby strips it of its power to have a structure-forming influence on the
> lifeworld beyond the purposive-rational organization of means. I would
> like to insist that, despite its purely procedural character as disburdened
> of all religious and metaphysical mortgages, communicative reason is
> directly implicated in social life-processes insofar as acts of mutual under-
> standing take on the role of a mechanism for coordinating action.[89]

But coordination did not mean complete fusion or total reconciliation. From the very beginning, one of the distinguishing marks of any rational as opposed to magical or mythical way of thinking—and Habermas, as we have noted, had little patience for attempts to find in myth a more capacious notion of reason—had been the ability to discriminate differences rather than confuse categories and merge everything into a turgid whole.[90] Modernity meant an acceleration of this process, which now had institutional expression. "Kant's three *Critiques*," Habermas wrote, "were a reaction to the emerging independence of distinct complexes of rationality. Since the eighteenth century, the forms of argumentation specializing in objectivating knowledge, moral-practical insights, and aesthetic judgment have diverged from one another. This has moreover occurred within institutions that could take upon themselves, without contradiction, the authority of defining the relevant criteria of validity."[91]

Did, however, the valorization of modern differentiation and the ineradicable plurality of forms of life threaten to undermine even a weakened claim to the universality that reason had always defended? Although respecting the more intransigent universalism of his colleague Karl-Otto Apel, with whom he had a friendly dialogue on the issue,[92] Habermas sought a way to retain the critical power of transcendental norms but within the diverse practices of everyday life. As early as his 1973 postscript to *Knowledge and Human Interests*, he had drawn on Peirce's consensus theory of truth to argue that "the *unity of argumentative reasoning* is compatible with this *differential meaning-constitution of object domains*. In all sciences argumentation is subject to the same conditions for the discursive redemption of truth claims."[93] In an essay of 1992 titled "The Unity of Reason in the Diversity of Its Voices," Habermas conceded a great deal to the antifoundationalist critics of an emphatic concept of substantive reason, such as the one still sought by the earlier generation of Critical Theorists. Agreeing with radical contextualists like Richard Rorty and Jean-François Lyotard that reason cannot be disembedded from its contingent historical embodiments, he admitted that if there is a unified rationality it exists only in those diverse manifestations that resist subsumption under a single, comprehensive model. Even science in its postempirical guise can no longer posit such a unity: "In the wake of [Thomas] Kuhn, [Paul] Feyerabend, [Yehuda] Elkana, and others, unifying reason has been deprived of its last domain, physics."[94] That is, there is no purely cognitive notion of reason that a subject, individual or collective, could have in relation to an object of knowledge.

But serving as what Kant would have called a regulative ideal with normative force, an "*idea* of reason" rather than rational *knowledge*, it is impossible to abandon it entirely.[95] In his vivid metaphor, communicative rationality is "a rocking hull—but it does not go under in the sea of contingencies, even if shuddering in high seas is the only mode in which it 'copes' with these contingencies."[96] Drawing on the response of the American philosopher Hilary Putnam to Richard Rorty's radical ethnocentric contextualism and Gadamer's ideal of harmoniously fusing horizons, Habermas argued that it was wrong simply to equate unity with the coercive repression of difference and particularity.[97] For although truth claims may emerge from within specific contexts, they can transcend their putative boundaries. Rather than hovering above specific subvariants, a genuine rational universality could only be built in the negotiations between and among them:

> Even in the most difficult processes of reaching understanding, all parties appeal to the common reference point of a possible consensus, even if this reference point is projected in each case from within their own contexts. For, although they may be interpreted in various ways and applied according to different criteria, concepts like truth, rationality, or justification play the *same* grammatical role in *every* linguistic community. . . . Reason is, in this sense, both immanent (not to be found outside of concrete language games and institutions) and transcendent (a regulative idea that we use to criticize the conduct of all activities and institutions).[98]

Through a more frankly proceduralist version—what he called "a weak but not defeatist concept of linguistically embodied reason"[99]—it would be possible to avoid having to choose between Kant's ahistorical transcendentalism and Hegel's teleological historical holism. As a result, it allows us to abandon any illusions of ever reaching a final utopian state of full rationality or final consensus in which the world and reason are completely reconciled: "Because the idealizing presuppositions of communicative action must not be hypostasized into the ideal of a future condition in which a definitive understanding has been reached, this concept must be approached in a sufficiently skeptical manner."[100] Often misinterpreted as advocating a rational utopia because of his early use of the phrase "the ideal speech situation," Habermas dropped it as the implicit telos of communicative rationality. In *Between Facts and Norms*, he explicitly repudiated its "essentialist" misinterpretation, claiming it had only been a "thought experiment" and a "methodological fiction" acting as a "foil against which the substratum of *unavoidable* societal complexity becomes visible."[101]

If then there is a possible unity of reason, it is not to be achieved at the cost of overcoming the differentiated cultural spheres but rather in the more primordial "communicative practice of everyday life, in which cognitive explanations, moral expectations, expressions and evaluations interpenetrate [and] this unity is in a certain way *always already* established. That need for reconciliation which Hegel registered against Kant springs from one-sided rationalization of this everyday practice."[102] In other words, there still remained a residue of the mutually beneficial interaction among the various modalities of reason in a predifferentiated lifeworld, despite the development of distinct value spheres in modernity. Although threatened by the domination of one of them—the instrumental rationality and system integration identified with the market economy and bureaucratic steering mechanisms—it might be possible to restore a balance without, however, losing the achievements of the differentiation. As Habermas noted in one of his many responses to his critics, "The yardstick thus used intuitively to measure the deformation of forms of life consists of the idea of the free interplay of the cognitive-instrumental with both the moral-practical and the aesthetic-expressive, within an everyday practice which must be open to an *uninhibited* and *balanced* interpenetration of cognitive interpretation, moral expectations, expressions and values."[103] Such free interplay would require what Martin Seel has called the exercise of an *"interrational* judgment which itself cannot in turn be explained as the form of an excessive logic of argumentation. . . . Its principle is liberation from false limitations and equally from false delimitations."[104]

(7) *The temporalization of reason.* Although always already latent in communicative interaction in the prereflexive lifeworld, the actualization of a fully achieved discursive rationality in institutional terms as a form of life realizing the dream of democratic politics was inherently counterfactual. As in his defense of the "uncompleted project of modernity," the title of his 1980 Adorno Prize address,[105] Habermas was not, *pace* his critics, calling for a fully rational—or completely "modern"—society, but rather an unending process of reasoning communicatively about the issues of the day. "Nothing makes me more nervous," he insisted, "than the imputation—repeated in a number of different versions and in the most peculiar contexts—that because the theory of communicative action focuses attention on the social facticity of recognized validity claims, it proposes, or at least suggests, a rationalistic utopian society."[106] Modernity was not merely uncompleted; it was by definition uncompletable in the sense that total rationality was a never-attainable goal, but served instead as a perpetual regulative ideal in Kant's sense of the term.[107] Reason was thus located in a future that would never be fully realized, rather than in a past that might be recaptured. Although it was not indifferent to what the theologian Johann Baptist Metz, drawing on Walter Benjamin, had called "anamnestic rationality,"[108] it had to free itself from that excessive respect for tradition that Gadamer had posited as the primary source of legitimation. Although common *understandings* of meaning might well emerge out of the lifeworld of pre-reflective beliefs and norms into which we were all thrown, where language's main function was what Heidegger had called "world-disclosing," rational *agreements* could only follow from a process of validity testing. "Discursive rationality," Habermas explained, "owes its special position not to its foundational but to its integrative role."[109] This did not mean, however, a wholesale repudiation of all traditions as inherently irrational. As Jan-Werner Müller has correctly put it, "the cold light of reason is not supposed to be a permanent glare, in which the dimly and warmly perceived objects of tradition appear as naked and

insufficient, but rather a searchlight that is employed from time to time to examine and, if necessary, clean up the complex store of ideas, styles and normative frameworks that shape our lives, not very consciously, for the most part."[110]

Reason in this sense implies a humble humanism that is not equivalent to the self-assertion of a species-wide rational subject seeking to overcome or reintegrate the alienated otherness of nature or different cultures. It is also a humanism that does not posit a sovereign subject at either the origin or the conclusion of the process, a subject who could make a "decision" to follow rational procedures or not. For such a subject would be situated in an impossible place outside of or prior to the communicative rationality entailed by symbolic interaction itself, and as such would not be fully human. When the child matures into a user of language, activating his or her potential for communicative competence, he or she must tacitly assume the inherent protocols of all languages, which necessarily make claims about the validity of their assertions (at least in their most fundamental mode). In this sense, there is a moment of passivity and even heteronomy in the entrance into communicative rationality.

But however modest, it is still a rationalism that avoids the reverse error of a negative metaphysics evoking a reality beyond discursive argumentation, in which the world is entirely negated as pure irrational contingency and the only antidote to meaninglessness is the return of mythic belief. That disenchantment of the world Weber had correctly seen as a handmaiden of its rationalization did not mean either relativist nihilism or the authoritarian assertion of ungrounded belief as its desperate antidotes, which were really two sides of the same coin. Among the latter was the faith in the immanent rationalization of history, for example Hegelian or orthodox Marxist, in which reason was necessarily embedded in the telos of development. With Habermas's more modest procedural version of rationality, in which "the rationality of content evaporates into the validity of results," there was no longer a guarantee of "an *antecedent* unity in the manifold of appearances."[111] The best that could be hoped for, without any guarantee of success, was an interaction among the various rational discourses, which would enrich each without fully integrating them into one metadiscourse based on single emphatic concept of reason.

(8) *The "as if" narrativization of reason.* The first generation of the Frankfurt School entertained a number of conflicting historical metanarratives—the Marxist succession of modes of production, the repetitive circularity of deep patterns beneath ephemeral surface changes, the declension story that led, as Adorno famously put it, from "the slingshot to the megaton bomb"[112]—but never settled on a single candidate and claimed it accurately described the collective fate of mankind. If they had a philosophy of history, it was expressed only negatively.[113] While not turning entirely against the idea of progress, in

the manner of conservative culture critics, they never accepted the optimistic belief that the rationalization of the world could be read in anything but bitterly ironic terms.[114]

Rejecting a substantive philosophy of history as a dubious exercise in false prophecy, Habermas warned that "an historicization of reason means neither the apotheosis of the existing in the name of reason, nor the liquidation of reason in the name of the existing."[115] To foster its critical potential required instead reaching back before Hegel to Kant, to posit an evolutionary model of rationalization with cross-cultural validity, a hypothetical narrative of species-wide development. Although admittedly speculative, such an exercise might have its practical uses, as Kant had suggested in his essay of 1784, "Idea for a Universal History with a Cosmopolitan Aim." Kant, it will be recalled, had invested nature with a teleological purpose—the historical realization of practical reason—that would seem at first glance to be grounded in too metaphysical a premise for Habermas. But rather than positing that teleology as an empirical fact known cognitively through a synthetic a priori judgment, a dangerous assumption that would restrict the human freedom to act in history, Kant had been careful to call it only an "idea" in the sense of being *thinkable* but not *knowable*, like the imperatives of practical reason themselves. Any philosophical attempt to write such a history was therefore not to be confused with an objective account of the disparate facts of history as it unfolded in reality or might do so in the future, facts that could be understood providentially as effects of a latent super-individual subject of history making itself manifest in them, as it would be for Hegel. Instead, it was an "as if" fiction—Kant even compared it to a novel—that must be "considered possible and even helpful to this intention of nature."[116] The result, as Axel Honneth has put it, was a "moderate de-transcendentalization" of practical reason that avoided Hegel's stronger notion of "an objective teleology of the historical process."[117] The future was not fore-ordained but had to be made by the autonomous wills of humankind, guided and inspired by such imaginary stories.

Habermas's version of this noncognitive narrative was what he called a "rational reconstruction,"[118] which would give us a heuristic device—at once descriptive and normative—to make sense of the process of rationalization in all of its forms without, however, either confusing the model with empirical reality or seeing it as a substantive force in history understood as a causal law. Replacing a no longer adequate historical materialist scheme of successive modes of production, it would provide an always revisable normative standard against which actual historical change occurs without serving as a prophecy of where it must necessarily go.[119] It seeks to lay bare the hidden generative structures that make possible actual performances in the real historical world, as, for example, the deep linguistic competences posited by Chomsky make possible the specific speech acts in different languages.

It also posits a logic of potential developmental stages through which a culture, indeed the species as a whole, might pass. As Honneth has noted, "it appears as the diachronic counterpart to the synchronically laid-out theory of communicative action. Whereas the latter reconstructs the implicit rule systems of social action in the form of a universal pragmatics, the former is supposed to analyze the stage-like development in the phylogenetic dimension of the history of the species."[120] Although Habermas may have refrained from calling it a self-conscious fictionalization, it was more of a hypothetical thought experiment than Marxist historical materialism had been, intuitively positing the existence of a pre-theoretical and pre-reflective learning process with potential universal scope, but always dependent on a posteriori empirical and discursive validation on the part of those who participate in the process. At best, it rested only on what Habermas called a "weak naturalism" in which human learning can be understood as continuous with the biological processes limned by Darwin.[121] "The fundamental mechanism for social evolution in general," he wrote, "is to be found in an automatic inability not to learn. Not *learning*, but *not-learning* is the phenomenon that calls for explanation at the socio-cultural state of development. Therein lies, if you will, the rationality of man. Only against this background does the overpowering irrationality of the history of the species become visible."[122] In the terms I have earlier borrowed from Bernard Williams, this was a form of genealogy more vindicatory than unmasking.

Taking his cue from sociologists like Émile Durkheim and Niklas Luhmann, psychologists like Jean Piaget and Lawrence Kohlberg, and linguists like Noam Chomsky, Habermas sought to locate the latent developmental competences that existed for communicative rationality and moral maturation, which were then capable of being realized both on the individual and social levels (indeed could only be realized if both levels were involved). "This is not a macro-process happening to a generic subject," he made clear. "Bearers of evolution are society itself and also the subjects of action integrated in it. Evolution can be deciphered from a rationally reconstructable pattern of hierarchy of ever more comprehensive structures. If we separate these structures from the events with which the empirical substrata change, we need not assume univocity, nor *continuity*, nor *necessity*, nor *irreversibility* of the course of history."[123] Although the potential to evolve was there in a developmental logic that revealed itself retro-actively, the actual achievement of each stage was itself dependent on contingent historical factors and the ways in which crises were resolved and problems overcome. These had to be tested empirically. Some problems may appear to be solved, but it was always possible to regress to an earlier stage of development, as the emergence of twentieth-century totalitarian politics so vividly demonstrated. When trying to flesh this all out with reference to the capitalist downturn of the 1970s, for example, Habermas remained enough of a materialist to accord primary responsibility to economic crises, which triggered administrative or "rationality" crises, leading to "motivation" and "legitimation crises."[124] This was, in other words, an evolutionary model, an "as if" narrative, that did not posit a smooth or inevitable transition to higher stages, allowed for regressions, and was meant more as an aspirational guide than a prophecy of future developments.

Without rehearsing in detail all of the evolutionary stages of Habermas's rational reconstructions of cognitive and moral learning, both on the individual and the social level, we have to ask nonetheless in what senses did he understand them as rational? At its most fundamental, Habermas employed rational reconstruction to arrive at the principles of universal pragmatics themselves. An inborn, species-wide communicative competence—a variant of Chomsky's theory of linguistic competence in grammatical terms—develops over time into the discursive skills that allow participants in discussions to proffer and weigh the better argument and reach an agreement based on reflection and persuasion, or at least inherently to strive toward that end, rather than merely reach agreement through coercion, seduction, or the compromise of still opposing positions and interests. Individual communicative competence is intertwined with intersubjective, mutual practices, which can produce a more sustained institutional setting for enhanced rational communication and sustained practices of discursive deliberation. Nonreflexive, naïve learning without discursive validation can be succeeded by reflexive learning, which "takes place through discourses in which we thematize practical validity claims that have become problematic or have been rendered problematic through institutional doubt, and redeem or dismiss them on the basis of arguments."[125] The bourgeois public sphere, whose rise and fall he had traced in his earliest major work, could thus be placed in an evolutionary pattern, which was susceptible to empirical regressions but tendentially moving in one direction. Following the lead of Kant and Weber, Habermas included in this reconstruction the pluralization of reason into different subvariants such as instrumental-purposive, strategic, and communicative, each with its own institutional embodiments. In *Knowledge and Human Interests*, he had designated the instrumental domination of nature realized through technology as one of the "quasi-transcendental" interests of the species—along with a hermeneutic interest in meaning and an emancipatory interest in liberation from unjust social constraints—that were anthropological constants. Although he backed away from that precise formulation, Habermas continued to accept the necessity of its continuing role. "Communicative rationality," he stressed, "remains on a level with epistemic and teleological rationality. Communicative rationality does not constitute the overarching structure of rationality but rather one of the three core structures that are, however, interwoven with one another by way of the discursive rationality that emerges out of communicative rationality."[126]

Against the Idealist hope for a totalized integration, his evolutionary model valorized differentiation. Against the privileging of one variant, such as Luhmann's elevation of systems-rationality above all others, he argued for honoring the distinct varieties that had emerged out of the practices of the life-world.[127] Thus, for example, the evolution of moral or in Kant's sense practical reason would follow its own course. According to Habermas, "morality refers to practical questions which can be decided with reasons—to conflicts of action which can be resolved through consensus. Only those questions are moral in a strict sense which can be answered in a meaningful way from the Kantian standpoint of universalization—of what *all* could wish for."[128] This procedural notion of morality was thinner than substantive ethics, which emerged out of concrete forms of life and might well resist being turned into universal, binding norms. The crucial point was that moral intuitions should be discursively re-deemed through communicative interaction rather than blindly obeyed, as they were in traditional or charismatically legitimated cultures. Such interaction involved the ability to exchange roles and understand the point of view of the other involved in the intersubjective validation of moral judgments. Rather than willing without contradiction what could be a universal law, as the categorical imperative had defined moral obligation, it meant willing what could be agreed upon by the participants in the discussion. Although deontological rather than consequentialist, moral obligations could not be derived in an a priori way. Autonomy meant that agents had to be accountable for their judgments, able to defend their actions through giving reasons that others might find persuasive.[129] Building on the ontogenetic models of Piaget and Kohlberg, Habermas rationally reconstructed an intersubjective, social progression from preconventional through conventional to postconventional levels of moral reasoning, culminating in universal, comprehensive, and consistent principles like the golden rule or categorical imperative. Understood heuristically as cumulative learning processes, but always subject to transgression, they could come to inform cultural and legal institutions that transmitted them to posterity and made them available for unending rational discussion.[130]

A similar rational reconstruction might also be applied to a third differentiated area of modern culture, which Habermas, following Kant's scheme of three Critiques as elaborated by Weber's sociological insights into the institutionalization of distinct value spheres, identified with the aesthetic.[131] Although distancing himself from Adorno's reliance on the aesthetic as a placeholder of an emphatic, still metaphysical concept of reason and warning against what he saw as the poststructuralist leveling of the genre distinction between philosophical and literary language, he nonetheless was not ready to cede the aesthetic to the counter-Enlightenment defenders of the "other" of reason. In his history of the bourgeois public sphere, it will be recalled, Habermas had included public discussions of literary and other artistic genres in his account of its early manifestations. As Kant had argued in the *Critique of Judgment*, aesthetic judgments were not subsumable under universal, binding rules, as were the determinant judgments of cognition and morality, but were made reflectively instead, based on paradigmatic examples, analogical reasoning, and the wisdom of accumulated experience. But insofar as they entailed argumentation and the giving of reasons, rather than simply being expressions of idiosyncratic taste, they involved rational discourse. Thus, for example, the Enlightenment recognition that aesthetic pleasure was disinterested in a way that normal corporeal pleasure was not demonstrated an ability to make salient rational discriminations, as did the formal isolation of works from their ideological or functional contexts of genesis and reception.

Works of art themselves or at least the genres in which they were placed, Habermas also came to believe, could be understood as undergoing a process of rationalization. The preservation of the expressive or semantic content of the lifeworld, including that mimetic relationship to nature extolled by Benjamin and Adorno, could be rationally developed: "Art becomes a laboratory, the critic an expert, the development of art the medium of a learning process—here, naturally not in the sense of an accumulation of epistemic *contents*, or an aesthetic 'progress'—which is possible only in individual dimensions—but nonetheless in the sense of a concentrically expanding, advancing exploration of a realm of possibilities structurally opened with the autonomization of art."[132]

Because rational reconstruction means that reasoning can be employed with hindsight to posit the innate potential for its own development, it may seem to court the charge of circularity. It was, however, Habermas's argument, following Hans Blumenberg's analysis of the legitimacy of the modern age, that modernity, and along with it, modern reason, had to *"create its normativity out of itself."*[133] Whereas ancient notions of reason were grounded outside of themselves, in for example intelligible forms put into the world by God, modern ones were without external foundations. For all his willingness to engage in a respectful dialogue with religious traditions—he even had a productive exchange with Pope Benedict XVI[134]—Habermas had no doubt that secularization paved the way for the self-grounding of reason:

> Only with the transition to modernity does the knowing and morally judging subject appropriate the divine standpoint, insofar as it assumes

two highly significant forms of idealization. On the one side, the subject objectifies external nature as the totality of states of affairs and events that are connected in a law-like manner. On the other, the subject expands the familiar social world into an unbounded community of all responsibly acting persons. In this way, the door is opened for reason to penetrate the opaque world in both dimensions—in the form of the cognitive rationalization of an objectified nature, and the social-cognitive rationalization of the totality of morally regulated interpersonal relationships.[135]

In a way, we might note in conclusion, Habermas's theory was an updated version of Kant's critique *of* pure reason, in which reason was both the object of the critique and the tool through which critique was itself conducted. Ever since his doctoral dissertation on Schelling, he had been skeptical of attempts to posit ultimate foundations, whether in natural philosophy, transcendental idealism, or identity philosophy.[136] As a result, the reconstruction he attempted was both that of a model of evolutionary development toward greater rationality, which might be observed from an imagined position outside of it, and a participatory, discursive process of arguing rationally about the applicability of that very model. As such, it combined a moment of consciousness-centered subjective reason, cognitively appraising the world from afar, with another based on intersubjective communicative rationality where everyone is a participant. As in the case of the interpretation of psychoanalysis in *Knowledge and Human Interests* as a model of an emancipatory science, although without the dubious parallel between psychological individual and social metasubject, it involved a mixture of third-person observation with second-person recognition and interaction. To maximize the potential for a robust rationalism in a postmetaphysical era, the interaction of its diverse voices had to be fostered, even if there were no chance of their fully harmonizing into a single unified song. Although, to adopt one of his key oppositions, social integration based on intersubjective communication could regain some of the ground it had lost in modernity to system integration based on impersonal functionalist processes, it would be a vain hope to wish for the full incorporation of the latter into the former.

The best that one could hope for was a restoration of the balance that had been lost when modernity privileged purposive rationality, system integration, and steering mechanisms like money and administration over communicative rationality, social integration, and the participatory involvement of the lifeworld. Reason after its eclipse, Habermas cautiously concluded, would never regain its full power to illuminate the world and light humankind's path to a rational utopia. But it still had the potential to move us beyond a world of dark forces clashing violently in an endless night.

# 7

# Habermas
# and His Critics

As might be imagined, a system as bold and ambitious as Habermas's has engendered an enormous critical response, which touches on each and every aspect of his argument.[1] Some commentators, hostile to the Frankfurt School tradition as a whole and suspicious of rationalism in any form, have scorned the very attempt to mount a new defense of reason as a dangerous search for a discredited universalism wisely abandoned by honest historicists and contextualists undaunted by cultural relativism.[2] Rehearsing the traditional psychologistic argument against logism, they contend that his "de-transcendentalization" of reason has not gone far enough to avoid the charge of latent gender bias or Eurocentrism.[3] Even without such accusations, soi-disant "anarcho-rationalists" have argued that different "styles of reasoning" may well undercut the quest for something as basic as neutral observation sentences, let alone more ambitious philosophical systems.[4]

At the opposite end of the spectrum are those defenders of an unapologetically universalist position who urge Habermas to embrace a more explicitly transcendental justification of his critical standpoint, and thus find a way to ground reason more firmly than he has in the hard-wired characteristics of the human condition.[5] For them, he has wrongly overcome his healthy Kantian instincts and relied too heavily on the power of immanent critique to provide the point d'appui for radical negation of the status quo. Not even the "quasi-transcendental interests" he had posited in his early work—and then tacitly abandoned—go far enough, they contend, toward a more fundamental grounding of rational critique.

Deriving inspiration from thinkers on the right like Martin Heidegger or the left like Cornelius Castoriadis, other critics lament Habermas's proceduralist and formalist notion of reason as too thin and bloodless.[6] Deploring his evisceration of the Freudian tradition, whose acknowledgment of the power of libido and fantasy they admire in the utopian musings of Marcuse and Adorno, still other commentators claim that his overly cognitivist version of action and over-reliance on the virtues of "linguistification" lead him to underplay affective and nonrational motivations for human behavior, which cannot be reduced to the argumentative procedures of discursive validity-testing.[7] Even more frankly metaphysical approaches, such as the neo-Thomist Aristotelianism defended by Alasdair MacIntyre, have been revived by those who want to ground a holistic, undifferentiated notion of reason in the scholastic tradition, stressing virtues over rights.[8] Unrepentant Hegelians belittle his abandonment of the dialectical rationalism of Western Marxism in its glory days.[9] His increasing reliance on the Pragmatist tradition, which he praised for combing fallibilism with anti-skepticism and anti-scientistic naturalism, seem to some too comfortably situated within the prevailing order.[10] Without a stronger substantively rational concept of the good life, perhaps even a resolutely utopian one, so these commentators worry, the motivation for critique is lacking. *Verständigung* (common understanding of meaning) as the tacit telos of all communication is not sufficient to bear this weight, they argue, even in the stronger sense of *Einverständnis* (consensual agreement) rather than the mere understanding of meaning.[11]

Still others, drawing on Sartre or defending Idealist philosophies of the subject, have challenged Habermas's granting of logical and psychological priority to intersubjectivity and communicative interaction, arguing that not every version of the subject must imply the domination of the object or the privileging of cognition over recognition.[12] Nor has his version of the "linguistification" of reason gone unchallenged by those who privilege the noncommunicative functions of language, which are harder to reconcile with even a post-consciousness-centered version of reason. The role of language in the unconscious may well be very different from the one it plays in conscious communication, as Jacques Lacan in particular has insisted.[13] Some champions of poststructuralism have even explained the difference in national terms, faulting Habermas for imposing a German narrative—where modernity and rationality are understandably an urgent and ongoing project in the wake of Nazism—on a French one, where rationality was already tried in politics with disastrous consequences during the French Revolution.[14]

There have also been spirited debates about aspects of Habermas's work from within the Frankfurt School tradition, broadly understood. Some adherents of the first generation of Critical Theory remain convinced by Adorno's arguments for art as the placeholder of a lost objective notion of reason.[15] Others, preferring Marcuse's "reason and revolution" to Habermas's "reason and evolution," have lamented the latter's anti-utopian acceptance of at least some instrumental rationalism and domination of the natural world.[16] The rational reconstruction of an "as if" evolutionary development for the cognitive and normative spheres of modern life has not convinced those who fear it smuggles in covert Western values in the guise of universalism, and also misses what has been lamentably "unlearnt" as history has moved on, destroying the past.[17] Western notions of deliberative democracy and legal formalism become, so these critics also worry, too easily turned into the telos of a species-wide project. The "passionate rationality" of "constitutional patriotism" may be preferable to the ardor of national tribalism only in a polity like the post-Nazi Germany Habermas sought so doggedly to liberate from its traumatic past, but not necessarily elsewhere.[18] The parallel between individual ontogenetic development and species learning is for others perhaps too quickly drawn, as is the attribution of communicative rationality to the pre-reflective lifeworld before the crystallization of the reflexive, specialist discourses that emerge from it.[19] While some critics worry that Habermas reifies the differentiated value spheres of modernity, and thus tacitly endorses the alleged functionalist rationality of the capitalist economy, others charge that his attempt to overcome that very differentiation, which he metaphorically characterizes as a "free play" between the spheres, is under-theorized.[20] Other commentators further complain that the normative ground of the ideal balance among the differentiated spheres has not been sufficiently developed.[21] Who, moreover, are the concrete social actors who will struggle to restore the balance between the types of rationalization, based on an action-theoretical notion of power?[22] In addressing that question, can one ignore the issue of gender, they wonder, in contrasting social and system integration—the former traditionally coded female and the latter male—and tallying the costs of colonization of the lifeworld?[23]

Even the ideal of rational agreement or consensus as a sufficient basis for democratic deliberation has been questioned by some of Habermas's most loyal champions.[24] Instead, they argue for a more modest willingness to generalize rather than universalize norms, accept the necessity of agreeing to disagree, and search for areas of meaningful agreement on the level of hermeneutic rather than fully rational grounds.[25] Resisting the idealization of a single rational public sphere, a few even champion a more agonistic and unequal "civil society" in which no fully open "space of reasons" exists in which democratic politics—which is more than the search for rationally discursive will formation, because it acknowledges human rights—can be practiced.[26] It may even be the case, some commentators have speculated, that democratic politics cannot be purged of a certain measure of hypocrisy, insincerity, even mendacity in the building of fragile coalitions and relations with adversaries of various kinds.[27]

It would be easy to multiply other qualms made by friendly as well as hostile critics. If Habermas's elaborate system with all its appropriations of different insights from so many philosophical, sociological, linguistic, psychological, and anthropological sources were only as strong as its weakest link, it would be seriously compromised. For many of the objections raised to the component parts have been telling, requiring him tacitly or explicitly to abandon some of his initial arguments and formulations and modify others. Habermas himself, however, has been tireless in his willingness to learn from the criticisms and attempt to meet them responsibly, thus manifestly embodying the values of the fallibilist communicative rationality he champions. It is hard to think of another major thinker who has engaged in as many forums over the years devoted to the critical examination of his or her work. As a result, the identification of reason with an ongoing process of reasoning among equals with better arguments outweighing the authority of those who make them has been at least performatively confirmed in his own practice, which itself has been a learning process shared by all those who have accompanied him on the voyage. And beyond purely academic discussions among experts, Habermas has also consistently and often courageously engaged in the heated political debates of his day, demonstrating the importance of the practical application of his ideas.[28]

It may well therefore be justified to conclude with Seyla Benhabib that "the fact that the theory of communicative action has not provided the answer to all these questions is not an argument *against* it, but *for* it. . . . The issue is: does it succeed in generating future research hypotheses which are fruitful and subject to refutation."[29] Despite the still ongoing debate about his work—indeed as evidenced by that very debate—it is fair to say that a paradigm shift has occurred in our appreciation of the stakes involved in defending reason as a ground of critique against those who have reduced it to a tool in the service of some deeper purpose, such as power or self-preservation. If it could be put in a nutshell, it might be said—or at least plausibly hoped—that both the Enlightenment Age of Reason and the Counter-Enlightenment Age of Reason's Other have been left behind, and in their place is dawning a new Age of Reason*s*. Here that "space" of which Wilfrid Sellars spoke is becoming more than just a metaphor, but being given increasing institutional embodiment in the political, cultural, legal, scientific, and other public spheres of modern life. In the phrase of the literary critic Amanda Anderson, it is a space in which "argument as ethos" prevails, fostering a kind of "postconventional *Sittlichkeit*."[30] Or to put it in the terms of Friedrich Kambartel, it is reason as a "culture, not a criterion."[31]

The ethos of that culture is distant, it bears repeating, from the identitarian logic of the traditional version of rationalism. As Albrecht Wellmer has put it, "argumentation, which by definition implies a plurality of subjects (even where it takes the form of internalized reflections), not only does not possess the linearity of deductive relationships between statements, it also lacks the stability of 'rigid' meanings."[32] In temporal terms, it also is open-ended because the process of reasoning, based on a fallibilist notion of truth, is understood never to reach a final point of arrival. Modernity is not a completable project for Habermas, and that is ultimately a good thing. The temporal center of gravity of giving reasons is the regulative ideal of a future potential consensus rather than a recovery of a past foundation or ground, even if it is a future that may never be fully realized. As Habermas put it, "the idea of a procedural, future-oriented popular sovereignty along these lines renders meaningless the demand to tie political will-formation to the substantive *a priori* of a past, pre-politically established consensus among homogeneous members of a nation."[33] Although it would certainly be easy to amass evidence to refute the optimism of this narrative and return to the bleak prognosis of the earlier Frankfurt School in the 1940s, there is no less warrant for hope that the trajectory of events may be moving, however haltingly, in a more positive direction.

If one were to focus in conclusion on one particularly crucial dimension of Habermas's effort to rescue reason after its eclipse, it would perhaps be most productive to look at the notion of "giving reasons" itself, which is so essential in the process of validity testing inherent in communicative rationality. To make sense of it we have to back up a bit and recall an earlier moment in the history of thinking about reason. In the version of the "principle of sufficient reason" or *principium ratione* favored by Enlightenment Rationalists like Spinoza and Leibniz, there was no explicit distinction made between cause—efficient, formal, material, or final—and reason.[34] Both were included in the key phrase *nihil est sine ratione* (nothing is without a reason), a metaphysical version of a theological premise, which is that everything made by God is made for a reason. When Heidegger came to write *Der Satz vom Grund* in 1957, translated as *The Principle of Reason*, he noted that "Leibniz obviously posits the principle of reason and the principle of causality as being equivalent."[35] Both were implied by the German *Grund*, which also could be used for base and foundation.

Whereas, however, discerning a "cause" suggests a cognitive relationship between individual or transcendental subject and external object in which reason involved discovering and explaining causes that already existed in nature or the social world, giving a "reason" implied instead an intersubjective interaction between those who argued about what those causes might be. As Habermas was to put it, "the speaker cannot intend her aim as something to be effected

causally, because the 'yes' and 'no' of the hearer is a rationally motivated position; participants in communication enjoy the freedom of being able to say
'no.'"[36] In other words, although the distinction later speech act theorists were
to make between the locutionary and illocutionary dimensions of utterances
was implicit, it was not yet thematized in the principle of sufficient reason as it
was understood in the Age of Reason. Attempts made by some contemporary
cognitive naturalists to restore the unity of cause and reason, by interpreting
the latter as merely the "subjective" expression of "objective" causes, have
regressed to this position. As Habermas points out, "the correct concept of conditioned freedom does not lend support to the overhasty ontological monism
that declares that reasons and causes are two aspects of a single phenomenon.
On this conception, reasons represent the subjective side—the 'experiential
form'—of neurologically observable processes."[37] What this reduction fails to
understand is that rather than being a faculty of the individual mind, reasoning
is a social activity between or among people who offer and consider arguments.[38]

The distinction between cause and reason also roughly corresponded to
another crucial dichotomy, which had shadowed rationalism from the beginning: the opposition between necessity and freedom. As Kant famously argued,
humans could be understood as divided beings, at once beholden to the causal
laws of nature that determined their animal existence, and yet free to obey or
disobey the moral obligations that practical reason told them they ought to
follow. Insofar as *Grund* indicated cause it suggested determinism; insofar as it
meant giving a reason—and the ability to weigh the reasons given by others—
it connoted autonomy and freedom, the freedom of the rational will.

It was perhaps not until Arthur Schopenhauer's *Fourfold Root of the Principle
of Sufficient Reason* of 1813 that the distinction was explicitly drawn.[39] Heidegger,
however, had already discerned a certain slippage in the direction of subjects
giving reasons in the extended version of the Latin phrase, which was *principium
reddendae rationis suffientis* (the principle of rendering sufficient reasons). This
means, he wrote, that "reason as such demands to be given back *as* reasons—
namely back (*re*) in the direction of the representing, cognizing subject, *by* this
subject and *for* this subject."[40] Although Heidegger was by no means a champion
of causal determinism, he found this slippage disastrous, as it opened the way
for a humanist alienation from the world, a loss of our immersion in "being":
"the unique unleashing of the demand to render reasons threatens everything
of humans' being-at-home and robs them of the roots of their subsistence, the
roots from out of which every great human age, every world-opening spirit,
every molding of the human form has thus far grown."[41]

Now if one had to characterize Habermas's distance from Heidegger,
under whose spell he was at the very beginning of his career, one could do

worse than point to his opposition to this judgment. The development of that weak, nondominating humanism mentioned above was due to the need to render reasons, make them public, take seriously the reasons rendered by others, and argue about their merits, rather than merely waiting for God's inherent reasons *cum* causes to reveal themselves. Its logic is not that of an authoritative commandment but rather of an invitation to participate in a focused conversation in which everyone is, at least ideally, an equal participant.[42] To put it another way, communicative rationality is foundationless in the sense of no longer needing a firm ground prior to the process of reasoning itself, a transcendent and unconditioned point d'appui outside the infinite open-ended argument about its own sufficiency. Its center of gravity is not a past decision or act of founding but rather the possibility of a future agreement. What we might call the "principle of sufficient reason*s*" supplants the Leibnizian formula *nihil est sine ratione*. As a result, it avoids the dark conclusion drawn by those ever since Schelling who took the undermining of a metaphysical notion of reason to mean that without a firm, unconditioned *Grund* like the principle of sufficient reason, all that remained was the *Abgrund* or *Ungrund*, the abyss.[43]

But a challenge remained nonetheless: how to establish which reasons can be deemed "sufficient" to allow us to say that the *outcome* of the argumentation process is worthy of the honor of being called rational? It may be rational to seek a consensus based on the better argument in a discourse among equals that approaches the ideal speech situation, but is there a way to decide if that consensus produces a rational *result*? What are the criteria used to distinguish a consensus based on dubious rhetoric, appeals to emotion, demagogic charisma, and so on from one that justifiably might be rooted in unprejudiced validity testing based on the persuasive force of "the better argument"? What are the criteria of a rational reason as opposed to an irrational one? Although implicit in the idea of such a reason is the telos of it being voluntarily accepted by all with the argumentative skills, capacity for discernment, and access to relevant information (as well perhaps as the empathetic ability to see beyond one's own narrow vantage point), can these criteria ever be realized practically in real-life discussions or are they doomed to be eternally regulative rather than fully actualized? Will the conditions, moreover, be the same in cognitive, moral, and aesthetic discourses, where persuasion may depend on different kinds of evidence and logic?

Defenders of the norms of traditional cultures in Weber's sense of the term can and do, after all, give reasons for their legitimacy: these norms have always existed, they are given by divine authority, they are grounded in nature and so on. Interestingly, Kant, who is often seen as privileging ahistorical formal rationality, understood that in the child's initial acquisition of reason, there is dependence on traditional authority. In his work on pedagogy, to cite Axel Honneth's gloss, he argued that "the child's reason is formed through the internalization of the social reserve of knowledge that is amassed in the society in which the child grows to maturity with the help of his or her parents or other primary caregivers."[44] Gadamer would have contended that such traditional reasons warrant respect even for adults, but Habermas argues against granting it to them without a test of their validity. But can there be a meta-argumentative standard by which one knows which reasons meet the test? Can we say there is a pathology of reason*s* comparable to the "pathology of reason" that reduces it to solely its instrumental variant or, as Husserl and Derrida argued, tries to ground it transcendentally?[45] Or is to claim that there is such a pathology really only to stigmatize in advance what people may believe justifies their consent? What, in other words, justifies a reason being called "rational?"

To put it somewhat differently, can we find a single mode of judgment to characterize a reason as more or less rational? Does it entail following rules in the sense of Kant's notion of "determinant judgment," in which specific cases are subsumed under general principles? Or is it closer to what he called "reflective judgments" in which there are no rules but rather analogies and paradigmatic cases acting as our less rigorous guides?[46] Is deciding what is a rational reason a matter of what Aristotle would have called *phronesis* or practical wisdom? And if so, is it clear that all participants in a symmetrically organized speech situation possess it to the same degree, or are there "enlightened tutors" and "immature minors" as Kant had implied in his famous answer to the question "what is Enlightenment?"[47] When Habermas argued that "the rational acceptability of validity claims is *ultimately* based only on reasons that withstand objections under certain demanding conditions of communication" that allow, "if possible, all relevant information and explanations to be brought up and weighted,"[48] his critics wondered when and by whose judgment that final point would be reached.

In acknowledging this criticism, Habermas resisted any implication of elitism by pointedly substituting the "republic of rational beings" for Kant's "kingdom of ends."[49] In this egalitarian republic, "whether reasons are 'good reasons' can be ascertained only in the performative attitude of a *participant* in argumentation, and not through the neutral *observation* of what this or that participant in a discourse holds to be good reasons."[50] At different moments in history, there will be different criteria for what constitutes a "good reason," which themselves can be argued about and only justified through discourse. Denying any discursive God's-eye view meant that "the different forms of argumentation form a system precisely to the extent that they *refer internally to one another* owing to their need for supplementation. . . . The *manner* in which the transition is effected is regulated by the logic of argumentation; *whether* and *when* we are supposed to accomplish it depends on the faculty of judgment inherent in communicative action itself." Then he added, "There are no meta-discourses for this. There are in fact no meta-discourses whatsoever; every discourse is, so to speak, equally close to God."[51] There is, in other words, no hierarchy of reasons, no final court of judgment: "which reason counts as a good or indeed as the better reason for what object in what context has to be assessed in terms of standards which under certain conditions become problematical and in turn require justification."[52]

The only certain quality of a "good" reason, one worthy of the honorific "rational," is its ability to persuade those involved in the intersubjective process of judging, but only, as Maeve Cooke has noted, "in the context of their intuitions, expectations, commitments, convictions, and experiences as a whole. In other words, to see something as a good reason, human subjects must be capable of integrating it into the affectively imbued constellation of reasons that are formative of their identities."[53] The result is that reasons become good only when they are validated by others. In Cooke's pithy formulation, "reasons are not *owned* by the self but *owed* to others; moreover, they are not *protected from* the critical gaze of others but *opened up* to their critical judgments."[54]

Albrecht Wellmer seconded this point, admitting that no extra-argumentative criterion for a rational reason can be found:

> The concept of a "good reason" is attached, in an irreducible way, to the perspective of the one "persuaded" by good reasons. One cannot describe from a meta-perspective which "qualities" reasons must have in order to be *really* good reasons. To call reasons "good" is not the ascription of an "objective" quality, rather it is the adoption of an attitude with normative consequences. These reasons compel *me* to accept that p [a proposition] as true. And naturally these are often the reasons that another brings up; in this sense, linguistic communication is, among other things, also a medium for progress in knowledge.[55]

Discarding the fantasy of a metadiscourse or metaperspective and acknowledging at least some contextual situatedness would thus help guard against an elitist, monologic, logocentric notion of reason, one open to the charge of implicit authoritarianism.

But, so Habermas's unassuaged critics still worried, is the idea of being "compelled" really sufficient, insofar as empirical compulsion is not always a sign of sober persuasion? I can, after all, be compelled by my emotions just as easily as by logic or evidence. As Habermas himself conceded, "pragmatically, 'irresistible' reasons are not 'compelling' reasons in the sense of logical validity."[56]

What allows us to decide which consensus is based on rational persuasion and which on irrational seduction, especially if we are denied a disinterested observer's position outside of the context of discussion? When do we know when "no arguments have been suppressed and that none of the participants has been prevented from putting forward relevant counterarguments?"[57] Is it, moreover, something that happens in the process of judging or only as a long-term effect, which cannot be determined until time has passed through a kind of rational reconstruction of the narrative in which the decision can be situated?

For one commentator, third-generation Critical Theorist Rainer Forst, the criteria of reciprocity and generality are the answer, allowing us to reach outcomes that will be legitimately binding on all. "Principles of reason," he writes, "are principles acceptable to a plurality of actors on the basis of 'reasonable' reasons, i.e., reasons that can be reciprocally and generally shaped or, to use [Thomas] Scanlon's phrase: that cannot reciprocally and generally be rejected."[58] The latter reformulation allows us still to debate different versions of "reasonable" reasons without seeking a single answer. Because generality is tempered by reciprocity, such reasons have to acknowledge the particular qualities of individuals in the debate rather than assume that there is an overarching general principle, an abstract universal rule, that can flatten them out. Or to put it in terms familiar from the sociology of George Herbert Mead, the "concrete" as well as "general" other must be taken into account.

Seyla Benhabib makes the same point still more emphatically when she argues that even if the reasons adduced are religious or utilitarian, Kantian or Nietzschean, they nonetheless "presuppose the capacity of our conversation partner to assent or dissent from our claims on the basis of reasons the validity of which she comprehends. 'Justificatory universalism' is at the heart of reason as a reason-giving enterprise and so is the recognition of the other as a being capable of communicative freedom and of the right to have rights."[59] As a result, there is an intrinsic connection between the universalist claim for justification, the contingent practice of giving and expecting reasons, and the discourse of human rights in general.

Here, however, we are still operating only at the level of justification, and bracketing the issue of what is decided by those who enter the debate. We are also relying on a counterfactual faith that the general and particular can ultimately be reconciled, that the negative dialectic embraced by Adorno as an antidote to forced sublations coercing nonidentity into an extorted unity can in fact become positive. Forst is explicit in his embrace of a reason that is "the uncoerced integration of the individual and the whole,"[60] but it is not clear how we are to treat those outliers who refuse to let themselves be persuaded that their reasons are not really generalizable, or even who makes the decision when to declare that "reasons that *can* reciprocally and generally be shared" really *are* embraced by all. Forst acknowledges that the process is open-ended and infinitely revisable, but it is difficult to apply the criteria of reciprocity and generalizablity when they are perpetually counterfactional. As Hent de Vries has skeptically put it, with regard to the criterion of generalizability, "who exactly is included and excluded in this set? Who judges whom is fit for inclusion and on what 'grounds'? The answer is as simple as it is mind-boggling: *all* relevant others, the omni-inclusive community of autonomous humans, capable of speech and communication."[61] And if we think beyond the human species, what about Kant's broader community of all "intelligible beings" or the non-human animals included by Adorno and Derrida? Who decides whether or not they are relevant?

An additional obstacle to the full realization of the superiority of the better argument is the stubborn intractability of first principles or implicit premises underlying every worldview, which may well present an obstacle to reasonable doubt. This makes the deciding rationally among, for example, basic philosophical positions especially difficult. "An argument for a Platonist is unconvincing for an Aristotelian," as Agnes Heller skeptically notes, because assuming that the better argument can induce conversion from one to another "presupposes that a philosophy can be falsified by good arguments. Perhaps it can be, but this does not hurt a philosophy at all. Did it hurt Plato that Aristotle refuted him with good arguments, or did it hurt Spinoza that Leibniz refuted him, or Leibniz that Kant refuted him, or Kant that Hegel falsified him—all of them with good arguments?"[62] Each specific philosophical argument takes place, moreover, in the context of a system that cannot be conclusively refuted as a whole by a superior argument discrediting a part. In this sense, philosophy may be more like an aesthetic movement than a scientific tradition in which a Galen is, in fact, refuted by later medical research, and Johann Joachim Becher and Georg Ernst Stahl's theory of phlogiston is decisively superseded by Antoine Lavoisier's discovery of combustible oxygen.

But if not for competing philosophies and aesthetic fashions, might something closer to scientific "progress in knowledge" still serve as a viable criterion for the ideal of a "reasonable" reason in at least some areas of human cognitive development? Invoking it as the outcome of rational deliberation inevitably raises the thorny question of the relationship between what is accepted after all the arguments are made and the participants persuaded of their validity, on the one hand, and the truth of what is the case cognitively, on the other. For epistemic justification and objective truth are not necessarily the same. There is, after all, built into the process of discursive reasoning about cognitive claims the understanding that today's justified consensus will possibly be improved, perhaps even surpassed, by future ones ad infinitum. Although absolute truth may forever be beyond human ken, the ideal of asymptotically approaching it drives the process forward.

Habermas's own position on this issue, it should be noted, underwent a crucial evolution. Originally, because of his suspicion of positivism and embrace of universal pragmatics, he focused his attention almost entirely on the illocutionary rather than locutionary or perlocutionary aspect of speech acts, only, that is, on the process of discursive justification of an assertion rather than its extradiscursive *truth*. Rationality involved only the former, when it employed the procedures of disinterested validity testing that approached the conditions of the ideal speech situation. Thus, in 1982, he could explicitly advocate a distinction between rationality and cognition:

> I do not think it makes sense to speak at all of the rationality of knowledge; we should rather reserve the predicate "rational" for the *use* of knowledge in linguistic utterances and in actions. *Communication* and *purposive activity* stand in internal relation to grounds or reasons, because subjects capable of speech and action employ knowledge in speaking and acting, and connect with their utterances, at least implicitly, claims to validity (or to success).[63]

Statements like these allowed commentators to conclude that Habermas was arguing that

> one can give up cognitivism without having to contest that rational utterances of actions as a rule purport to follow good reasons and stand the test of an objective assessment. The standards for this cannot be sought in the truth of the knowledge involved, but in the rules of consensus formation through argumentation. This is indeed the approach taken by Habermas.[64]

Or in the words of another, "the theories of truth and justification that Habermas develops are both, in a broad sense, anti-realist."[65]

But in time, Habermas came to recognize the dangers in the anti-realism of linguistic conventionalists like Rorty, and distinguished more sharply between a consensus, even one rationally achieved, and what might be the extradiscursive truth beyond that consensus. Whereas in an early essay titled "Theories of Truth" of 1972, he had defended a "consensus theory of truth," by the time of *Truth and Justification* in 1999, he had abandoned this premise, going so far as to

call the communicative and representational functions of language "equiprimordial."[66] In so doing, he restored more of a balance between the locutionary,
illocutionary, and perlocutionary, or communicative and representational,
functions of speech acts. As he conceded in his reply to critics of *The Theory of
Communicative Action*: "I do not understand the discourse theory of truth to mean
that the consensus achieved discursively is a criterion of truth (as was the case in
some of my earlier statements)."[67] True beliefs, after all, can be held irrationally
and without justification, and conversely, "the rationality of a judgment does
not imply its truth but merely its justified acceptability in a given context."[68]
Against radical conventionalists like Rorty, who blithely identified truth entirely
with the discursive justification of a finite community, Habermas argued that a
world external to our construction of it made learning possible by stubbornly
resisting false explanations.[69] Truth is not merely a function of discursive
consensus or "rational acceptability" but also has a pragmatic value that extends
beyond whether or not it is achieved by reasoned argumentation.

Here, interestingly, it was the perlocutionary effect of speech acts—what
they effected in the world in terms of solving problems—that emerged as a
consideration beyond the illocutionary intention of those involved in the discourse.[70] Habermas had earlier considered the former only from the perspective
of strategic action with its telos of success, which was inferior to the goal of
agreement. But he came to appreciate that there was an inextricable link between language and action, which involved testing our rationally achieved
justifications against a world that was always more than our discursive constructions. "In everyday practices, we cannot use language without *acting*.
Speech itself is effected in the mode of speech acts that for their part are embedded in contexts of interaction and entwined with instrumental actions. As
actors, that is, as interacting and intervening subjects, we are always already in
contact with things about which we can make statements."[71] We can never
have certain knowledge of those things, or access to causes without the mediation
of the reasons we offer discursively for believing in them. But without their
resistance, we could not get beyond whatever consensus happened to be
reached, even by the most rational argumentation, if the result were mistaken.
That is, knowledge would not be fallible and amenable to correction if the
world were nothing but an effect of our discursive constructions, or to put it in
other terms, if reference were entirely a function of meaning.[72] Rather than
solely focusing on intersubjective "I-thou" relations, as he had done in his
battle with subject-centered mentalist philosophies of consciousness, Habermas
realized it was necessary to restore at least a rough balance with "I-it" relations.
Without falling back on the empiricist or positivist epistemology he had joined
with Adorno in criticizing during the dispute with Popper and his followers,

Habermas now acknowledged that a pragmatism that fails to take into account the recalcitrant givens of the world could not hope to solve the problems they posed.[73]

Whatever the implications these considerations might have for a theory of truth, they appear no less significant for a theory of reason, although precisely what they were remains contested. One approach has stressed the continued importance of keeping reason apart from strong truth claims, supporting the early inclination of Habermas to distinguish them sharply. A major difference between cognitive statements, especially those made by science, and rational judgments, Raymond Geuss has argued, is that

> "truth" and "falsity" as used in science do not admit of degrees; a proposition is true or false, and *tertium non datur* [no third possibility is given]. But rationality is not like that. Decisions, preferences, attitudes, etc., can be more or less rational; agents can have stronger or weaker warrant for their actions, can be more or less aware of their own motives, can be more or less enlightened in their normative beliefs.[74]

Charles Taylor has advocated something similar with his idea of "reasoning in transitions," which involves comparative rather than absolute judgments, in which one may be superior to the other but not itself perfectly true.[75]

A very different reading, however, can be found in other commentators, such as Cristina Lafont, who responds to the statements in Habermas's later work that suggest there is a vital cognitive moment as well in a more robust notion of rationality.[76] She notes, for example, that the chapter on "Rationality—A Preliminary Determination of the Concept," in *Theory of Communicative Action*, begins by stressing the closeness between knowledge and reason, even if Habermas then bracketed the former in order to focus on the latter.[77] By the 1990s, Habermas was carefully arguing against both the collapse of truth into rational discursive justification—a purely consensus theory of truth—and their absolute separation: "although we cannot sever the connection of truth and justification, this *epistemically unavoidable* connection must not be turned into a *conceptually inseparable* connection in the form of an epistemic concept of truth."[78]

Bringing back the cognitivist moment entangled with rational deliberation helped avoid the conclusion that language alone is the locus of rationality after its eclipse. It gets us beyond linguistic conventionalism or idealism, which bedevils certain pragmatists like Rorty, and restores the link with a world that is more than what we make of it, more than our justifications for a truth that is not equivalent to a mere epistemic consensus alone. "In losing the regulative idea of truth," Habermas warned, "the practice of justification loses that point of orientation by means of which standards of justification are distinguished from 'customary' norms. The sociologizing of the practice of justification means a naturalization of reason."[79] Even under the ideal conditions of argumentation at its most open, symmetrical, and inclusive, reasons may, after all, prove fallible and conclusions open to revision. For Habermas, Peirce's understanding of the irreducibility of the things of the world to their semiotic representations and efforts to categorize them, developed in our own day in Putnam's nominalist defense of "internal realism,"[80] shows the value of a pragmatism that refuses to collapse everything into our epistemic understandings or linguistic categorizations. It knows the difference between "propositions" and "facts," on the one hand, and the "things" that are prior to them, on the other, things that can be referred to under different descriptions. As Lafont stresses, acknowledging this distinction links reason once again to an unending learning process, based on problem-solving, about something that is not reducible to cultural immanence and linguistic relativism. Or to put it another way, conclusions reached by discursive validity testing have to be tested further in action, and can always be revised in the future. As Habermas put it in his late essay "Communicative Action and the Detranscendentalized 'Use of Reason,'" "Even after the knowing subject is detranscendentalized, a gap remains between what is true and what is warranted or rationally acceptable to us. Although this gap cannot be definitively closed within discourse, it can be closed pragmatically through a rationally motivated transition from discourse to action."[81]

In the idiom of the older generation of the Frankfurt School, Habermas's growing appreciation of the limits of discursive rationality recalls Adorno's stress on the "object's preponderance" in *Negative Dialectics*.[82] As Wellmer noted, despite the problematic messianic residues in Adorno's notion of reason as redemptive reconciliation, "perhaps it is possible to justify Adorno's insistence on a subject-object model of cognition. . . . Concealed within Adorno's use of this model, there are perhaps elements of a concept of rationality that is not aimed at reconciliation, but at the possibility of conceiving reason without the hope of ultimate reconciliation."[83] Whereas Adorno may have sought the limits of monologic conceptual domination in works of art whose mimetically resonant particulars resisted subsumption under coercively rational categories, the later Habermas sought a parallel limit to the intersubjective discursive domination of the things of the world.[84] In both instances, it was not a matter of reason, or more precisely, reasoning, and its other(s) as a simple opposition, but rather an understanding of both the necessity and the limitations of rationality, however it might be defined.

Or at least so it seems in the realm of cognition, the sphere of modernity most closely identified with science that had differentiated itself off from the lifeworld and the other expert spheres. Here an endless learning process can measure itself against an external reality irreducible to rationally warranted assertions about its truth. But is there a comparable distinction between norms held intersubjectively in a particular community and a more objective moral or ethical standard outside them? By assuming there is such a normative standard in, for example, natural law or religious dogma, do we risk succumbing to deontological absolutism in order to avoid the dangers of moral relativism?

Habermas, in fact, admitted there was no ontological ground for normative rightness, although individual morality had at least the standard of intersubjective ethical values against which it could measure itself. But he also acknowledged that communal ethics (Hegel's *Sittlichkeit*) could itself be coercive, arbitrary, and unjust. Perhaps the only way out, at least in political terms, was a legal constitutional order in which values could be constantly discussed and debated: "the democratic state today provides the legal-political framework for the core of rational morality—a core that can and needs to be institutionalized."[85] Whether or not this solution sufficed to provide a comparable normative standard to the cognitive defense of ontological "things" over discursive "facts" for morality is not clear. For even constitutions of liberal democratic states are subject to the political pressures that create and emend them, which are by no means inherently moral, even in the nondeontological sense of discourse ethics. At times, Habermas seemed to recognize its inadequacy and advanced a stronger test of "universalizability" to identify moral truths, for example when he drew on and extended Lawrence Kohlberg's stage theory of moral development understood as a "rational reconstruction" not open to empirical verification or falsification.[86] But how such an essentially cognitive model can be applied to the positive ethical imperatives of different cultures is not self-evident, nor perhaps is how it might serve as a gender neutral standard, as feminist critics of Kohlberg such as Carol Gilligan, promoting an alternative "ethics of care," have argued.[87] There remains a gap between formal procedures, which may work toward building a just society, and various notions of the good life or substantive virtue. Similar issues haunt the discourse of aesthetic rationalization as well, where the "external" standard of value beyond discursive consensus is even harder to establish.

In short, the struggle to harness the critical function of reason continues unabated, as Habermas's legacy is subjected to new arguments and counterarguments, some seeking to demolish it and others to defend it on less vulnerable grounds. And this is as it should be according to the tenets of communicative rationality itself, which never seeks a steady state of rest and completion, despite the regulative telos of consensus produced by the better argument. In fact, what survives all temporary agreement, however enabled by rational discourse, is the inevitability of asking new questions and raising new objections. Refutation of mistakes, fallacies, ideologies, and unreflected prejudices is as much its aim as is confirmation of positive truth. As Stephen White has pointed out,

> the notion of communicative action is conceived around not just the idea of understanding or agreement, but also around the individual *utterance* and its capacity to *interrupt* ongoing, unproblematic frames of action, coordination, whether they are strategically or normatively structured. . . . Utterances, in short, carry a rational force that disturbs, as well as lubricates, designs.[88]

In this sense, the naïve utopia of perfect social and political unity that some have seen latent in the ideal speech situation is not really a threat, and even less a desideratum. It is better, we might say, recalling Kant's celebrated distinction, to remain perpetually in an "age of enlightenment" rather than seek to live in a fully realized "enlightened age." For as Kant had understood, reason was both the source of critique and its object, both the wound and its cure.

What then, might we ask in conclusion, is the function of a restored but chastened reason after its eclipse? When the term "rationalization" is extended into the social realm, as Habermas, following Weber, thought it must be, it alerts us to the functional purpose of reason, its nondispositional potential. Forms of life, such as the public sphere or democratic political institutions, can be called rational, he writes, "to the degree that they are *conducive* to the solution of problems that arise. To this extent, although forms of life qualify as candidates for the term 'rational,' they do so only in the indirect sense that they constitute the more or less 'congenial' background for establishing discursive procedures and for developing reflexive capacities. In this way, they can promote capacities for problem solving that for their part enable rational beliefs, actions and communications."[89] "Solving problems" may have been the terminology of the pragmatism that the early Frankfurt School had scorned, but Habermas was unafraid to learn from the "Kantian pragmatism" of contemporary figures like Hilary Putnam and Robert Brandom.[90] In *Theory of Communicative Action*, he had distinguished between instrumental and functionalist rationality, moving away from the earlier Frankfurt School collapse of the two. Drawing on Luhmann, he had acknowledged the role functional reason could play in the subsystems of administration and the economy, maintaining them without drawing on the intentionality of agents, as in instrumental reason. In the terminology introduced by Schnädelbach, it allowed him to posit both a "dispositional" and "nondispositional" view of reason, the former attributing it only to persons, the latter to systems.[91] Although this opened him to the criticism that he had conceded too much to impersonal systems theory in his conceptualization of modernity,[92] it did raise the question of the larger function fulfilled by communicative reason as well.

It has been recently argued by the behavioral scientists Hugo Mercier and Dan Sperber, tacitly recalling the claims of Nietzsche and Foucault, that in the evolutionary process, argumentative reason did not have the original function of arriving at better beliefs and sounder decisions, let alone giving us access to the truth. Instead it was merely a tool in persuading one's opponents, an instrument in an adversarial game of power.[93] Flawed reasoning, rather than being a defect, could itself be functional in that outcome, as could confirmation bias evident in using reason to support prior opinions and beliefs. But even supporters of this view, which draws on the "strong naturalism" that Habermas has criticized in the name of a weaker version,[94] concede that it can transcend this initial function, especially when group reasoning supplants monological or logocentric inferential ratiocination. Avoiding the genetic fallacy means, after all, refusing to trace the meaning of an idea or a practice to its roots and denying it an opportunity to grow beyond them. Moreover, contemporary cognitive science has made it possible to appreciate the role intentional training in reasoning can have in fostering the skills developed through natural evolution, even to the point of changing the neural patterns of the brain.[95]

Habermas has not been a starry-eyed utopian when it comes to the realization of a fully rational form of life, nor has he lost sight of the ways in which strategic thinking and instrumental reason can vie for prominence with communicative rationality. He has admitted that "reason" has no concrete social addressee to replace the proletariat in the Marxist imaginary; indeed, "it has no body, cannot suffer, and also arouses no passion."[96] If one asks what the function of communicative rationality itself might be, the only answer can come from exploring the ways in which it has functioned in the practices that have developed as our species grapples with the inadequacies of our instinctual life. Among those, as the Frankfurt School always knew, however much its members may have disagreed over the nature of reason itself, was critique of the inadequate solutions of the past and consideration of possible superior solutions for the future.

"Communicative rationality," Habermas insisted, "operates in history as an avenging force,"[97] refusing to affirm what cries out to be criticized, inspiring us to transcend the fatalism of our condition. In this sense, its most basic function is not system-maintenance or even solutions to local or immediate problems but rather the imagination of radical alternatives to the flawed status quo and the damaged lives it produces. Or to put it in terms that suggest Habermas never did identify entirely with the pragmatist tradition, communicative reason has to diagnose the level where root causes of a problem might be and have the courage to contemplate solutions that transcend the immediate normative context that blocks fundamental responses. Indeed, it includes an acknowledgment that even the terminology of "problems" and "solutions" is inadequate when it comes to the no less exigent questions of meaning that human culture inevitably poses and endlessly struggles to answer. The stakes are therefore very high. For as the most distinguished theorist of the Frankfurt School's third generation, Axel Honneth, noted in assessing the legacy of Critical Theory, in a warning we can emphatically endorse:

> only as long as the theory can count on such a rational impulse for its grounding will it be able to relate itself reflexively to a potential practice in which the explanation it offers is implemented with a view to liberation from suffering. Critical Theory will only be able to continue in the form in which it has developed from Horkheimer to Habermas if it does not forsake the proof of such interests. Without a realistic concept of "emancipatory interest" that puts at its center the idea of an indestructible core of rational responsiveness on the part of subjects, this critical project will have no future.[98]

# Notes

## Preface

1. George L. Mosse, *The Crisis of German Ideology: Intellectual Origins of the Third Reich* (New York, 1964), 13.

2. It is important to acknowledge that alternative traditions may well have very different histories of terms like "reason," and perhaps not even precise equivalents in their vocabularies. As shown by the very suggestive series of *Keywords* edited by Nadia Tazi for Zone Books in English and translated into several other languages, no universal usage can be assumed. The ones treated in the series, which has essays from scholars in different regions of the world, are "gender," "experience," "truth," "identity," and "nature." Unfortunately, there is none yet for "reason." For one attempt to tackle this issue head on, see Wolfgang Schluchter, "Rationality—A Specifically European Characteristic?," in *The Cultural Values of Europe*, ed. Hans Joas and Klaus Wiegandt, trans. Alex Skinner (Liverpool, 2008), 166–86.

3. William Edward Hartpole Lecky, *History of the Rise and Influence of the Spirit of Rationalism in Europe*, 2 vols. (London, 1865). It immediately occasioned rebuttals by defenders of religion, e.g., John F. Hurst, *History of Rationalism: Embracing a Survey of the Present State of Protestant Theology* (New York, 1865). Among the most critical reviewers from a nonreligious point of view was the novelist George Eliot, who objected to Lecky's idealist assumption of a rationalist spirit coursing through history. See her "The Influence of Rationalism," in *The Essays of George Eliot*, ed. Nathan Sheppard (London, 1883), 257–71.

4. Wolfgang Welsch, *Vernunft: Die zeitgenössische Vernunftkritik und das Konzept der transversalen Vernunft* (Frankfurt, 1995).

5. Theodor W. Adorno, *Philosophische Terminologie* (Frankfurt, 1973), 1:18.

6. Ibid.

## Chapter 1. From the Greeks to the Enlightenment

1. Or the "Good." See Plato, *The Republic* VI, 507b–509c.

2. Not all solar myths, however, were so closely identified with reason. In Roy Willis, ed., *World Mythology: The Illustrated Guide* (Oxford, 2006), there are discussions of Aztec, Egyptian, Chinese, Hindu, and other sun deities, but none stresses their connection with a rational ideal.

3. For a now classic account, see Wilhelm Nestle, *Vom Mythos zum Logos: Die Selbstentfaltung des griechischen Denkens von Homer bis auf die Sophistik und Sokrates* (Stuttgart, 1940). For trenchant considerations of its limitations, see Richard Buxton, ed., *From Myth to Reason? Studies in the Development of Greek Thought* (Oxford, 1999), and Kathryn A. Morgan, *Myth and Philosophy from the Presocratics to Plato* (Cambridge, 2003). For another attempt to explain the origins of Greek rationality, see Helmut Heit, *Der Ursprungsmythos der Vernunft: Zur philosophiehistorischen Genealogie des griechischen Wunders* (Würzburg, 2007) and his "Vom Mythos zum Logos—ein Methodenwandel?," in *Sprache-Kultur-Darstellungsformen: Methodenprobleme in der Philosophie*, ed. Bettina Kremberg and Rainer Totzke (Leipzig, 2010), 219–40.

4. For an extensive analysis of what he calls the "intertextuality" of philosophy and myth in this dialogue, see Daniel S. Werner, *Myth and Philosophy in Plato's "Phaedrus"* (Cambridge, 2012).

5. See Morgan, *Myth and Philosophy*, for a thorough discussion of the linguistic stakes involved in the debate over myth.

6. The term also refers to comparable changes in other fields, for example, the emergence of evidence-based historiography in the work of Herodotus and Thucydides, who sought to go beyond legendary accounts of the past, and the development of a protoscientific medical practice by Hippocratus.

7. For a discussion of this distinction, see Luc Brisson, *Plato the Mythmaker*, ed. and trans. Gerard Naddaf (Chicago, IL, 1998), chs. 9 and 10.

8. Stanley Cavell, *The Claim of Reason: Wittgenstein, Skepticism, Morality, and Tragedy* (Oxford, 1982), 366.

9. Rodolphe Gasché, *The Honor of Thinking: Critique, Theory, Philosophy* (Stanford, CA, 2007), 351.

10. Logos can also mean "speech," "discourse," arithmetical ratio, and even musical interval. See Daniel Heller-Roazen, *Dark Tongues: The Art of Rogues and Riddlers* (New York, 2013), 9. The linkage with the divine word continues to animate theology in our own time. See, for example, the discussion of different forms of religious logocentrism in Graham Ward, *Barth, Derrida, and the Language of Theology* (Cambridge, 1995).

11. Under certain circumstances, however, logos also could mean narrative accounts of historical events, as it did in the work of the first Greek historian, Herodotus, whose *Histories* had nine books and twenty-eight logoi (e.g., on "The Story of King Croesus," "The Rise of Cyrus," etc.). What distinguished his historical accounts from mythical narratives was their reliance on the critical sifting of evidence and the plausible explanation of events in human terms, rather than as effects of the intervention of the gods.

12. See Umberto Eco, *The Search for the Perfect Language*, trans. James Fentress (Cambridge, MA, 1995). For a discussion of the complicated role of mathematics in Plato, see Ian Mueller, "Mathematical Method and Philosophical Truth," in *The Cambridge Companion to Plato*, ed. Richard Kraut (Cambridge, 1992), 170–99.

13. The literature on the Greek idea of logos is very extensive. For a comprehensive view from a sociologist's perspective, see Barry Sandywell's series of "logological investigations": *Reflexivity and the Crisis of Western Reason* (New York, 1996); *The Beginnings of European Theorizing: Reflexivity in the Archaic Age* (New York, 1996); *Presocratic Reflexivity: The Construction of Philosophical Discourse* (New York, 1996). The fourth volume, *The Greek Enlightenment: Culture, Thought, and Reflexivity*, is in press. For a useful overview of its uses, see the entry *"Logos"* in F. E. Peters, *Greek Philosophical Terms: A Historical Lexicon* (New York, 1967). Aristotle claimed in his *Metaphysics* that it was Thales of Milet who has the honor of being the first pre-Socratic who thought about nature rationally. For a critique of this claim, see Helmut Heit, "Did Rationality Originate in Ancient Ionia?," *Skepsis* 15, nos. 2–3 (2004): 359–71. See also Herbert Schnädelbach, *Vernunft* (Stuttgart, 2007), ch. 1.

14. See G. S. Kirk and J. E. Raven, *The Presocratic Philosophers: A Critical History with a Selection of Texts* (Cambridge, 1963), 188–89 and 88.

15. For a helpful account of Plato's late thoughts on the relationship between logos and true knowledge, see Alexander Nehamas, *Virtues of Authenticity: Essays on Plato and Socrates* (Princeton, NJ, 1999), ch. 11.

16. For a discussion of Plato's position at different moments in his career, see Nicholas P. White, "Plato's Metaphysical Epistemology," in Kraut, *Cambridge Companion to Plato*, 277–310.

17. Aristotle, *Politics*, 1253a 9f. Significantly, "rationale," like "reason" and "ratio," is derived from the Latin verb *reor*, which means counting or calculating. The translation from Greek into Latin thus may well have given the concept a bias toward calculation. It should also be noted that not all Greeks agreed that man was the only rational animal. Plutarch in particular argued that animal intelligence could at times be understood as rational too. See the discussion in Stephen Thomas Newmyer, *Animals, Rights, and Reason in Plutarch and Modern Ethics* (New York, 2006), which shows the link between Plutarch's treatises on animals and modern animal rights theory.

18. Hans-Georg Gadamer, *Reason in the Age of Science*, trans. Frederick G. Lawrence (Cambridge, MA, 1983), 35.

19. Leo Strauss, *Natural Right and History* (Chicago, IL, 1999); Ernst Bloch, *Natural Law and Human Dignity*, trans. Dennis J. Schmidt (Cambridge, MA, 1987).

20. Cavell, *The Claim of Reason*, 365.

21. Plato's critique of myth can be found, among other places, in *Phaedrus* 61b and *Timaeus* 26e, but he himself used them in a number of places in his own argument, e.g., *The Republic*, allowing F. M. Cornford to remark that "in his 'mythical' manner, Plato amplifies and reinterprets the famous doctrine of Anaxagoras: 'All things were confounded together, when Reason came and introduced distinction and order.' Reason takes the place of Zeus, as Zeus had taken the place of *Moira* [fate]." *From Religion to Philosophy: A Study in the Origins of Western Speculation* (New York, 1957), 36. See also Julia

Annas, "Plato's Myths of Judgment," *Phronesis* 27, no. 2 (1982): 119–43, which argues for the inclusion of the myths at the end of *Gorgias, Phaedo,* and *The Republic* in any discussion of Plato's thought.

22. For a discussion of this linkage, see Schnädelbach, *Vernunft,* 20.

23. Jan Assmann, *Of God and Gods: Egypt, Israel, and the Rise of Monotheism* (Madison, WI, 2008), 13.

24. Lawrence W. Cahoone, *Cultural Revolutions: Reason versus Culture in Philosophy, Politics, and Jihad* (University Park, PA, 2005), 206.

25. See Robert Nozick, *The Nature of Rationality* (Princeton, NJ, 1993). For a discussion of the controversy it raised, see Geoffrey Galt Harpham, "Of Rats and Men; or, Reason in Our Time," in *Shadows of Ethics: Criticism and the Just Society* (Durham, NC, 1999), 99–119.

26. See Martin Kusch, *Psychologism: A Case Study in the Sociology of Philosophical Knowledge* (London, 1995), and his entry on "Psychologism" in the *Stanford Encyclopedia of Philosophy,* Spring 2014 ed., ed. Edward N. Zalta, http://plato.stanford.edu/archives/spr2014 /entries/psychologism/, which brings the dispute up to the present. The term, introduced in the late nineteenth century by Gottlob Frege and Edmund Husserl, refers disparagingly to all allegedly extralogical grounds of logic. Another variant of the reduction came to be called "genealogy," developed in particular by Friedrich Nietzsche and Michel Foucault to expose the extrarational sources of reason in contingent, historically variable networks of power relations. For discussions of genealogy, see Jeffrey Minson, *Genealogies of Morals: Nietzsche, Foucault, Donzelot, and the Eccentricity of Ethics* (London, 1985), and Béatrice Han, *Foucault's Critical Project: Between the Transcendental and the Historical,* trans. Edward Pile (Stanford, CA, 2002). According to Hubert L. Dreyfus and Paul Rabinow, *Michel Foucault: Beyond Structuralism and Hermeneutics* (Chicago, IL, 1983), "Foucault is not attacking reason but rather showing how a historical form of rationality has operated" (133). But like Nietzsche, he was determined to subvert the claim of reason to have transcendental, ahistorical grounds. A similar effort was made by Jacques Derrida in his *Edmund Husserl's Origin of Geometry: An Introduction,* trans. John P. Leavey Jr. (Lincoln, NE, 1989).

27. A. A. Long, *Greek Models of Mind and Self* (Cambridge, MA, 2015), ch. 1.

28. For a feminist critique of its legacy, see Genevieve Lloyd, *The Man of Reason: "Male" and "Female" in Western Philosophy* (Minneapolis, MN, 1984).

29. See Kusch, *Psychologism,* 84. A later, more restricted definition of "logicism" referred only to the reduction of all of mathematics to logic, which was attempted by Frege and Bertrand Russell and then undermined by Gödel's Theorem. See Neil Tennant, "Logicism and Neologicism," in the *Stanford Encyclopedia of Philosophy,* Fall 2014 ed., ed. Edward N. Zalta, http://plato.stanford.edu/archives/fall2014/entries/logicism/.

30. The British philosopher R. G. Collingwood sought to restore the question and answer matrix out of which logic emerged. For discussions, see Christopher Fear, "Collingwood's Logic of Question and Answer against the Relativization of Reason," and Giuseppina D'Oro, "The Logocentric Predicament and the Logic of Question and Answer," both in *Other Logics: Alternatives to Formal Logic in the History of Thought and Contemporary Philosophy,* ed. Admir Skodo (Leiden, 2014), 81–101 and 221–35.

31. For a recent attempt to find a hard-wired, universally human psychological source for logic that tries to overcome the alternative between psychologism and logicism, see Robert Hanna, *Rationality and Logic* (Cambridge, MA, 2006). He argues for a cognitive protologic that is innate rather than learned.

32. For an example of its continuing power, see the attempts by twentieth-century French "philosophers of the concept" to defend the integrity of reason, derived largely from Spinoza, against "philosophers of experience." The distinction was made by Michel Foucault in "Life: Experience and Science," in *The Essential Foucault: Selections from Essential Works of Foucault, 1954–1984*, ed. Paul Rabinow and Nikola S. Rose (New York, 2003), 465–78, to distinguish epistemologists like Jean Cavaillès and Georges Canguilhem from Henri Bergson, Maurice Merleau-Ponty, and Jean-Paul Sartre. In *Logics of Worlds, Being and Event*, vol. 2, trans. Alberto Toscano (London, 2009), Alain Badiou would employ the same distinction. For an account of the abiding power of Spinoza in recent French thought, see Knox Peden, *Spinoza contra Phenomenology: French Rationalism from Cavaillès to Deleuze* (Stanford, CA, 2014).

33. John Searle, *Rationality in Action* (Cambridge, MA, 2001), xiv.

34. Bernard Williams, *Truth and Truthfulness: An Essay in Genealogy* (Princeton, NJ, 2002), 36–37.

35. Dante, *The Inferno*, canto 4.

36. The period saw the appearance of Confucius and Lao-tse in China, the Buddha and the Upanishads in India, the philosophers, historians, and poets of Hellenic Greece, and the Hebrew prophets. For a discussion, see John D. Boy and John Torpey, "Inventing the Axial Age: The Origins and Uses of a Historical Concept," *Theory and Society* 42, no. 3 (May 2013): 241–59.

37. For analysis and critique of the intricate relationship between power and reason from a qualified Heideggerian perspective, see Dominique Janicaud, *Powers of the Rational: Science, Technology, and the Future of Thought*, trans. Peg Birmingham and Elizabeth Birmingham (Bloomington, IN, 1994).

38. See Burton Feldman and Robert B. Richardson, *The Rise of Modern Mythology, 1680–1860* (Bloomington, IN, 1972), for an anthology of texts exploring the meaning of myth. For a more analytic account, see Hans Blumenberg, *Work on Myth*, trans. Robert Wallace (Cambridge, MA, 1985).

39. For discussions of the troubling implications of the modern search for myth, focusing on the German case, see George S. Williamson, *The Longing for Myth in Germany: Religion and Aesthetic Culture from Romanticism to Nietzsche* (Chicago, IL, 2004), and Jean-Luc Nancy and Philippe Lacoue-Labarthe, *Le mythe nazi* (Paris, 1991). Both discuss Alfred Rosenberg's *Myth of the Twentieth Century* as an example of the sinister evocation of myth against the Enlightenment tradition.

40. The most influential advocate of this position was Claude Lévi-Strauss, *The Savage Mind*, trans. John Weightman and Doreen Weightman (Chicago, IL, 1966).

41. See Glenn W. Most, "From Logos to Mythos," in Buxton, *From Myth to Reason?*, 40. He traces this argument back to the eighteenth-century German classicist Christian Gottlob Heyne.

42. For some of the Greeks, logoi designated any kind of discourse, rather than a philosophical one utterly distinguished from a rhetorical one. See the discussion in James Allen, "Aristotle on the Value of 'Probability,' Persuasiveness, and Verisimilitude in Rhetorical Argument," in *Probabilities, Hypotheticals, and Counterfactuals in Ancient Greek Thought*, ed. Victoria Wohl (Cambridge, 2014), 47–64. Other essays in the volume show the ways in which probable reasoning (*eikos*) could also be accepted as valid, anticipating the more rigorous exploration of probability in the seventeenth century.

43. Hans Blumenberg, "An Anthropological Approach to the Contemporary Significance of Rhetoric," in *After Philosophy: End or Transformation?*, ed. Kenneth Baynes, James Bohman, and Thomas McCarthy (Cambridge, MA, 1987), 447.

44. Ibid., 448.

45. Ibid., 452.

46. Nicolas F. Gier, *Wittgenstein and Phenomenology: A Comparative Study of the Later Wittgenstein, Husserl, Heidegger, and Merleau-Ponty* (Albany, NY, 1981), 187.

47. Ute Guzzoni, "Reason—A Different Reason—Something Different than Reason? Wondering about the Concept of a Different Reason in Adorno, Lyotard, and Sloterdijk," in *The Actuality of Adorno: Critical Essays on Adorno and the Postmodern*, ed. Max Pensky (Albany, NY, 1997), 27–28. For a similar distinction between substantive "reason" and instrumental "rationality," albeit from a neo-Thomist perspective, see Jeffery L. Nicholas, *Reason, Tradition, and the Good: MacIntyre's Tradition-Constituted Reason and Frankfurt School Critical Theory* (Notre Dame, IN, 2012), 10.

48. Guzzoni, "Reason," 28.

49. Hartmut Böhme and Gernot Böhme, "The Battle of Reason with the Imagination," in *What Is Enlightenment? Eighteenth-Century Answers and Twentieth-Century Questions*, ed. James Schmidt (Berkeley, CA, 1996), 436–37.

50. Gernot Böhme, "Beyond the Radical Critique of Reason," in *Reason and Its Other: Rationality in Modern German Philosophy and Culture*, ed. Dieter Freundlieb and Wayne Hudson (Providence, RI, 1993), 93.

51. Nikolas Kompridis, *Critique and Disclosure: Critical Theory between Past and Future* (Cambridge, MA, 2006).

52. Richard Campbell, "Reconceiving Truth and Reason," in Freundlieb and Hudson, *Reason and Its Other*, 133–62.

53. Paget Henry, *Caliban's Reason: Introducing Afro-Caribbean Philosophy* (New York, 2000), 180. Not all African philosophers identify reason with a Eurocentric imposition on local values. See, for example, Emmanuel Chukwudi Eze, *On Reason: Rationality in a World of Cultural Conflict and Racism* (Durham, NC, 2008).

54. For a defense of "rationality," understood largely in functional terms, against "reason," see Niklas Luhmann, "Social Theory without 'Reason': Luhmann and the Challenge of Systems Theory; An Interview," in Freundlieb and Hudson, *Reason and Its Other*. There is also no agreement about the meaning of a distinction between "reason" and "rationality." Thus, for example, reason sometimes gets confusingly conflated with "reasonable," which has its own extensive baggage of connotations. Take, for example, the dichotomy posited by Harpham in "Of Rats and Men": "Make a first cut, placing

on one side an acceptance of traditions, customs, conventions, institutions, the intricacies of the human heart, and context in general as factors in understanding and assessment and call this 'reasonablilty.' What's left on the other side is the kind of understanding that recognizes the force of necessity, of laws without appeal, a faculty of comparison, demarcation, differentiation, logical entailment, and computation that may be called 'rationality'" (111). He then concludes, reasonably enough, that "each by itself is not just incomplete but unworthy. Unadulterated reasonableness would be spineless, inconsistent, unaccountable, pious, flaccid, indifferent; pure rationality would be imperial, rigid, narcissistic, terroristic, autistic" (113). There is much to be said for this argument, but the distinction he posits does not easily map on to other dichotomies with the same terms.

55. For a discussion of Schelling and myth, see Markus Gabriel, *Der Mensch im Mythos: Untersuchungen über Ontotheologie, Anthropologie und Selbstbewußtseinsgeschichte in Schellings Philosophie der Mythologie* (Berlin, 2005), and Gabriel and Slavoj Žižek, *Mythology, Madness, and Laughter: Subjectivity in German Idealism* (London, 2009). This expanded notion of reason is not the same as the simple Romantic reversal of the superiority of logos over mythos, which as Hans-Georg Gadamer pointed out, "actually perpetuates the abstract contrast between myth and reason." See *Truth and Method* (New York, 1986), 243.

56. Martin Heidegger, *The Principle of Reason*, trans. Reginald Lilly (Bloomington, IN, 1996), 110. ἀρχαί, αἴται means principles.

57. Ibid. Heidegger identified *ratio* with reckoning based on the call for grounds and reasons. See the discussion in Hans Sluga, "Heidegger and the Critique of Reason," in *What's Left of Enlightenment? A Postmodern Question*, ed. Keith Michael Baker and Peter Hanns Reill (Stanford, CA, 2001), 50–70.

58. Jacques Derrida, "The Principle of Reason: The University in the Eyes of Its Pupils," *Diacritics* 13, no. 3 (Autumn 1983): 7.

59. Ernst Bloch was another Western Marxist advocate of a broad notion of reason; see his discussion of the "Logos-Myth," in *Atheism in Christianity: The Religion of the Exodus and the Kingdom*, trans. J. T. Swann (London, 2009), 192–203. There were, of course, comparable theorists on the right, for example Leo Strauss, who also faulted what they saw as the narrow and impoverished version of reason typical of modernity in general and the Enlightenment in particular. See Strauss, *The Rebirth of Classical Political Rationalism*, ed. Thomas L. Pangle (Chicago, IL, 1989), and Corine Pelluchon, *Leo Strauss and the Crisis of Rationalism: Another Reason, Another Enlightenment*, trans. Robert Howse (Albany, NY, 2014). For a defense of a Straussian concept of "reason" as "wisdom" against "nihilistic" relativism, see Stanley Rosen, *Nihilism: A Philosophical Essay* (New Haven, CT, 1969).

60. There is a substantial literature debating the putative overlap in the philosophies of Heidegger and Adorno in particular. See, for example, Hermann Mörchen, *Adorno und Heidegger: Untersuchung einer philosophischen Kommunikationsverweigerung* (Stuttgart, 1981); Iain Macdonald and Krzysztof Ziarek, eds., *Adorno and Heidegger: Philosophical Questions* (Stanford, CA, 2007); Jan Rosiek, *Maintaining the Sublime: Heidegger and Adorno* (Bern, 2000); and Alexander Garcia Düttmann, *The Memory of Thought: An Essay on Heidegger and Adorno* (London, 2002). Marcuse's debts to Heidegger, with whom he studied in the 1920s, are also widely acknowledged. See, for example, Andrew Feenberg, *Heidegger and*

*Marcuse: The Catastrophe and Redemption of History* (New York, 2005); Richard Wolin, *Heidegger's Children: Hannah Arendt, Karl Löwith, Hans Jonas, and Herbert Marcuse* (Princeton, NJ, 2003); and the early texts collected in Herbert Marcuse, *Heideggerian Marxism*, ed. Richard Wolin and John Abromeit (Lincoln, NE, 2005).

61. Max Horkheimer, "Reason against Itself: Some Remarks on Enlightenment," in Schmidt, *What Is Enlightenment?*, 360.

62. Max Horkheimer and Theodor W. Adorno, *Dialectic of Enlightenment: Philosophical Fragments*, ed. Gunzelin Schmid Noerr, trans. Edmund Jephcott (Stanford, CA, 2002), 5. It should be acknowledged that Horkheimer and Adorno often criticize myth as a false or phantasmatic way of coping with the mysteries of existence, which needs to be debunked and replaced by rational explanation. For a discussion of this ambivalence, see Bo Earle, "Putting the Dialectic Back in *Negative Dialectics*: Modern Melancholia and Adornian Ethical Aesthetics," *New German Critique* 35, no. 2 104 (Summer 2008): 40–46.

63. Theodor W. Adorno, *History and Freedom: Lectures 1964–1965*, ed. Rolf Tiedemann, trans. Rodney Livingstone (Cambridge, 2006), 150.

64. Ibid., 257.

65. Theodor W. Adorno, *Metaphysics: Concepts and Problems*, ed. Rolf Tiedemann, trans. Edmund Jephcott (Stanford, CA, 2000), 19.

66. Jürgen Habermas, *The Philosophical Discourse of Modernity: Twelve Lectures*, trans. Frederick Lawrence (Cambridge, MA, 1987), 309.

67. For much of contemporary analytic philosophy, dianoetic reasoning is privileged. See, for example, the essays in Jacqueline P. Leighton and Robert J. Sternberg, eds., *The Nature of Reasoning* (Cambridge, 2004), where "reasoning is broadly defined as the process of drawing conclusions. Moreover, these conclusions inform problem-solving and decision-making endeavors because human beings are goal driven, and the conclusions they draw are ultimately drawn to help them serve and meet their goals" (3–4). Continental philosophy, however, has more often been amenable to noetic intuition to one degree or another.

68. For a helpful overview, see the entries on "noesis" and "diánoia" in Peters, *Greek Philosophical Terms*. Michael Morgan, in a personal communication to the author on December 24, 2014, cautions against turning the opposition into distinct technical terms with fixed meanings and stresses the infrequent use of the latter term in Plato. At times, he notes, noesis can include propositional, inferential, and definitional knowledge, as well as direct and immediate intuition.

69. Plato, *The Republic*, 508 c/d. The relationship between sight, the alleged "noblest of the senses," and reason has often been remarked. For recent discussions, see Jean-Jacques Wunenburger, "Thinking with the Eyes: Philosophical Rationality and Visual Matrices," and Frederik Stjernfelt, "Forgotten Twins: Reason and Visuality," both in *Transvisuality: The Cultural Dimension of Visuality*, vol. 1, *Boundaries and Creative Openings*, ed. Tore Kristensen, Anders Michelsen, and Frauke Wiegand (Liverpool, 2013), 46–58 and 75–86. For a study of the cultural origins of visually oriented "theory" in religious pilgrimages to see sacred sites and objects, see Andrea Nightingale, *Spectacles of Truth in Classical Greek Philosophy: Theoria in Its Cultural Context* (Cambridge, 2009). On the less

conventional relationship between hearing and reason, which goes against the typical Enlightenment assumption of its link with vision, see Veit Erlmann, *Reason and Resonance: A History of Modern Aurality* (New York, 2014).

70. Parmenides, fragment 3.

71. For a discussion of the principle, in both Greek and contemporary thought, see Christopher Watkin, "Proving the Principle of Logic: Quentin Meillassoux, Jean-Luc Nancy, and the Anhypothetical," in Skodo, *Other Logics*, 17–32.

72. Geometry was so important to the Greeks because it could exemplify both noetic and dianoetic reasoning. The triangle as an eternal form was accessible to the intuition and not dependent on mere sense experience, while Pythagoras's theorem (in any right-angled triangle, the square of the hypotenuse [the side opposite the right angle] is equal to the sum of the squares of the other two sides) was amenable to many different inferential proofs.

73. Aristotle, *Nicomachean Ethics*, trans. Roger Crisp (Cambridge, 2000).

74. Herbert Schnädelbach, "Observations on Rationality and Language," in Freundlieb and Hudson, *Reason and Its Other*, 53. The reference to Gilbert Ryle is to *The Concept of Mind* (London, 1949), which defines a category mistake as a semantic error in which things of one kind are presented as if they belonged to another, or a property is ascribed to a thing that could not possibly share that property. Thus if you have a dispositional view of reason, it is a category mistake to attribute rationality to an impersonal system rather than a personal action. For another discussion of the distinction between dispositional and nondispositional notions of reason, see Schnädelbach, "The Transformation of Critical Theory," in *Communicative Action: Essays on Jürgen Habermas's "The Theory of Communicative Action,"* ed. Axel Honneth and Hans Joas, trans. Jeremy Gaines and Doris L. Jones (Cambridge, MA, 1991), 11. In most Anglo-American discussions of rationality, a dispositional model is assumed. See, for example, the essays in Leighton and Sternberg, *The Nature of Reasoning*.

75. Markus Gabriel remarks that Johann Gottlieb Fichte, Hegel, and Schelling all realized that "the postulate of an intellectual intuition does not help because it is itself formulated in a discursive, non-intuitive language, i.e., with the range of subject and object presupposed in every theory that is not thoroughly self-referential." *Mythology, Madness, and Laughter*, 23. For a critical discussion of the complex interplay of noesis and dianoesis in Wittgenstein, see Rosen, *Nihilism*, ch. 1.

76. Herbert Schnädelbach, "Dialektik als Vernunftkritik," in *Adorno-Konferenz 1983*, ed. Ludwig von Friedeburg and Jürgen Habermas (Frankfurt, 1983), 75.

77. Theodor W. Adorno and Max Horkheimer, *Towards a New Manifesto*, trans. Rodney Livingstone (New York, 2011).

78. Ibid., 73.

79. Herbert Marcuse, *One-Dimensional Man: Studies in the Ideology of Advanced Industrial Society* (Boston, MA, 1964), 125–26.

80. Michael Inwood, *A Heidegger Dictionary* (Oxford, 1999), 217.

81. Ibid.

82. Heidegger, *The Principle of Reason*, 28–30.

83. The complexity of the Scholastic attitude toward reason is nicely captured in Walter J. Ong's gloss on Peter of Spain's thirteenth-century treatise *De locis* (*On Places*): "Peter discusses the various senses in which the term *ratio* is used. It can mean the definition or description of a thing or a power of the soul, or speech making something manifest (as in English, 'the *reason* why this is done,' etc.), or form as opposed to matter, or an essence. Finally, it can mean 'a means for inferring a conclusion.' This is the sense in which Peter takes it." He adds, however, that Peter understands this to mean the creation of conviction, which suggests that "the key word in Peter's explanation of *ratio* is thus not truth at all, but confidence or trust." Thus, although in many respects anticipating the eighteenth-century Rationalists, Peter's *ratio* "is supported not on the pillars of science, but on the topics or arguments of a merely probable dialectic or rhetoric." *Ramus, Method, and the Decay of Dialogue* (Cambridge, MA, 1983), 65.

84. See G. H. R. Parkinson, ed., *The Renaissance and Seventeenth-Century Rationalism* (London, 2003). The humanists' preference for Plato over Aristotle did not necessarily mean a return to Platonic rationalism. Humanists like Marsilio Ficino understood Plato as supporting a vision of God as an artificer, whose divine will had created the world. His student Pico della Mirandola saw humans as imitating God's free will and thus capable of self-fashioning. The renewed appreciation for rhetoric in the Renaissance also moved it closer to Plato's enemies, the Sophists. For a discussion of the importance of Stoic rationalism for the humanist tradition, see William J. Bouwsma, *A Usable Past: Essays in European Cultural History* (Berkeley, CA, 1990), ch. 1.

85. See Robert Voitle, "The Reason of the English Enlightenment," *Studies on Voltaire and the Eighteenth Century* 27 (1963): 1735–74, and Frederick C. Beiser, *The Sovereignty of Reason: The Defense of Rationality in the Early English Enlightenment* (Princeton, NJ, 1996).

86. Ian Hacking, *The Emergence of Probability: A Philosophical Study of Early Ideas about Probability, Induction, and Statistical Inference* (London, 2006); Lorraine Daston, *Classical Probability in the Enlightenment* (Princeton, NJ, 1988).

87. Martin Luther, "Last Sermon in Wittenberg," January 17, 1546, in *Werke: Kritische Gesamtsausgabe*, ed. Georg Buchwald, Gustav Kawerau, et al. (Weimar, 1914), 51:126. For an account of the various compromises offered in Catholic, Protestant, and Jewish circles during this era, see David Sorkin, *The Religious Enlightenment: Protestants, Jews, and Catholics from London to Vienna* (Princeton, NJ, 2008).

88. Beiser, *The Sovereignty of Reason*, 3.

89. Tom Paine, *The Age of Reason: Being an Investigation of True and Fabulous Theology* (London, 1996). The first edition appeared in 1794, and two subsequent editions with additional material were published in 1795 and 1807. The term "critique" came into popular use with Pierre Bayle's encyclopedic *Dictionnaire Historique et Critique* of 1697. For a metacritique of the role of critique in the Enlightenment, see Reinhart Koselleck, *Critique and Crisis: Enlightenment and the Pathogenesis of Modern Society* (Cambridge, MA, 1988).

90. Immanuel Kant, *Critique of Pure Reason*, trans. Werner S. Pluhar (Indianapolis, IN, 1996), 8.

91. Theodor W. Adorno, *Kant's "Critique of Pure Reason,"* ed. Rolf Tiedemann, trans. Rodney Livingstone (Stanford, CA, 2001), 54. These lectures on the first Critique,

delivered in 1959, were more sympathetic to Kant than Adorno's discussion (with Hork-heimer) in *Dialectic of Enlightenment*. For an account of his changing attitude, see Peter Uwe Hohendahl, *The Fleeting Promise of Art: Adorno's Aesthetic Theory Revisited* (Ithaca, NY, 2013), ch. 1.

92. For a discussion, see Wolfgang Welsch, *Vernunft: Die zeitgenössische Vernunftkritik und das Konzept der transversalen Vernunft* (Frankfurt, 1995), 32–33.

93. The assumption that the body is inherently unruly and only the mind is rational has had its recent critics, who point to the lessons of cognitive science. See, for example, Mark L. Johnson, "Embodied Reason," in *Perspectives on Embodiment: The Intersections of Nature and Culture*, ed. Gail Weiss and Honi Fern Haber (New York, 1999), 81–102. He argues that rational concepts are grounded in image schemas that derive from corporeal orientation, movement, and interactions. Thus, to take an example, the logic of moving through the steps of an inferential argument reflects the movement of the body through space. Although such a connection might be useful in helping us understand concept formation and the processes of reasoning, it is less helpful in grounding a notion of ratio-nality based on the obligation to give and consider reasons for actions.

94. Long, *Greek Models*, ch. 4. The political implications of Plato's rationalism have, of course, been heatedly debated for many years, with critics like Karl Popper going so far as to call him proto-totalitarian. See Popper, *The Open Society and Its Enemies*, vol. 1, *The Spell of Plato* (Princeton, NJ, 1971). For a very different view, drawing on Hans-Georg Gadamer's interpretation, see Lawrence J. Biskowski, "Reason in Politics: Arendt and Gadamer on the Role of the *Eide*," *Polity* 31, no. 2 (1998): 217–44.

95. Seneca, *Epistles*, 66:32; *Ad Lucilium Epistulae Morales*, trans. Richard M. Gummere (London, 1917), 2:23.

96. Bouwsma, *A Usable Past*, 399.

97. For discussions of Weber's thoughts on rationalization, see Wolfgang Schluchter, *The Rise of Western Rationalism: Max Weber's Developmental History*, trans. Guenther Roth (Berkeley, CA, 1981), and Sam Whimster and Scott Lash, eds., *Max Weber, Rationality and Modernity* (London, 1987). For an account of the rise and fall of "modernization theory," see Nils Gilman, *Mandarins of the Future: Modernization Theory in Cold War America* (Baltimore, MD, 2003).

98. Max Weber, *The Protestant Ethic and the Spirit of Capitalism*, trans. Talcott Parsons (New York, 1958); for a selection of responses, see Robert W. Green, *Protestantism, Capital-ism, and Social Science: The Weber Thesis Controversy* (Lexington, MA, 1973). For a discussion of Weber's response to Werner Sombart's claim of the Jewish rather than Protestant origins of capitalist rationality, see Gary A. Abraham, *Max Weber and the Jewish Question: A Study of the Social Outlook of His Sociology* (Urbana, IL, 1992), ch. 6.

99. See Michael Walzer, *The Revolution of the Saints: A Study in the Origins of Radical Politics* (Cambridge, MA, 1982). He shows the ways in which the ascetic activism of seventeenth-century Puritans anticipated the vanguard parties of nineteenth- and twentieth-century socialism.

100. Beiser, *The Sovereignty of Reason*. He argues that the attempt of Cambridge Platonists and others to generate a rational theology to justify the moral teachings of the

Anglican Church amounted to a defense of medieval notions of natural law and a failure to understand the practical rationality developed later by Kant.

101. For a defense of the necessary embeddedness of rationality in tradition, see Alasdair MacIntyre, *Whose Justice? Which Rationality?* (Notre Dame, IN, 1988).

102. These distinctions could, however, be challenged by those who argue conceptually against the possibility of instrumental reason being distinguished from the deliberative processes that also help form beliefs and intentions. See, for example, Joseph Raz, "The Myth of Instrumental Rationality," *Journal of Ethics and Social Philosophy* 1, no. 1 (April 2005): 2–28. Raz ignores the historical arguments of Weber and the Frankfurt School, confining himself entirely to debates within analytic philosophy.

103. Max Weber, *The Theory of Social and Economic Organization*, ed. Talcott Parsons, trans. A. M. Henderson and Talcott Parsons (New York, 1947), 324–92.

104. Ibid., 343.

105. Ibid., 339.

106. Ibid., 328.

107. The issue of who makes the rules in the first place, lending legitimacy to legality, is, of course, a difficult one. The debate in legal and political theory generated by Carl Schmitt's assertion that constitutive law is always made in a state of exception in which unconstrained decision founds what are later binding rules and procedures continues to rage. It replays the contest between will and reason that theologians and philosophers fought out in nonpolitical terms for millennia. For discussions of Schmitt's legacy, see David Dyzenhaus, ed., *Law and Politics: Carl Schmitt's Critique of Liberalism* (Durham, NC, 1998); William Scheuerman, *Carl Schmitt: The End of Law* (Lanham, MD, 1999); and Jan-Werner Müller, *A Dangerous Mind: Carl Schmitt in Post-War European Thought* (New Haven, CT, 2003).

108. For critiques of the disenchantment hypothesis, see Jane Bennett, *The Enchantment of Modern Life: Attachments, Crossings, and Ethics* (Princeton, NJ, 2001), and Joshua Landy and Michael Saler, eds., *The Re-Enchantment of the World: Secular Magic in a Rational Age* (Stanford, CA, 2009).

109. Michel Foucault, "Politics and Reason," in *Politics, Philosophy, Culture: Interviews and Other Writings, 1977–1984*, ed. Lawrence D. Kritzman (New York, 1988), 75. Foucault was deeply hostile to what he saw as the pernicious impact of political rationality: "It first took its stand on the idea of pastoral power, then on that of reason of state. Its inevitable effects are both individualization and totalization. Liberation can only come from attacking, not just one of these two effects, but political rationality's very roots" (85). For a more positive assessment of the idea of "reason of state," see Friedrich Meinecke, *Machiavellism: The Doctrine of Raison d'État and Its Place in Modern History*, trans. Douglas Scott (New York, 1965). The Westphalian system, as it came to be known, recognized state sovereignty in opposition to the claims of the Church, allowing each state the right to declare its own official religion.

110. For an account, see Howard Caygill, *Art of Judgment* (Oxford, 1989), ch. 3, and Meinecke, *Machiavellism*, ch. 12. In Germany, it replaced what is called a *Ständestaat*, a corporate state in which traditional estates were more powerful than any centralized

monarchy. For an argument that they nonetheless remained important during the *Aufklärung* (the German Enlightenment) and were even imbued with a certain notion of rationality by the popular Enlightenment movement, see Jonathan Knudsen, "On Enlightenment for the Common Man," in Schmidt, *What Is Enlightenment?*, 270–90. Later, Hegel would attempt to reconcile the residues of the corporate state tradition with the bureaucratic rationalism of the *Polizeistaat*, rather than pit one against the other.

111. A succinct account of the controversies over Wolff's ideas can be found in Jonathan I. Israel, *Radical Enlightenment: Philosophy and the Making of Modernity, 1650–1750* (Oxford, 2001), 544–52. Wolff was banned from teaching in any Prussian university in 1723 by a royal decree of the reactionary King Friedrich Wilhelm I, and then reinstated to his old position in Halle with the accession of Frederick the Great in 1740.

112. Caygill, *Art of Judgment*, 107. Hans-Georg Gadamer stresses the pedigree of the tradition of jurisprudence, "which means sagacity in legal affairs. The very word itself recalls the heritage of practical philosophy that considered *prudential* the highest virtue of practical rationality." *Reason*, 127. Kant, in contrast, would reduce prudence to a more modest, instrumental cleverness, contrasting it with the more elevated demands of moral obligation.

113. Foucault, "Politics and Reason," 71.

114. For discussions of the concept in Foucault and after, see Mitchell Dean, *Governmentality: Power and Rule in Modern Society* (London, 2004), and David Owen, *Maturity and Modernity: Nietzsche, Weber, Foucault, and the Ambivalence of Reason* (London, 1994), ch. 9.

115. For advocates of soft governmental paternalism, see Richard H. Thaler and Cass R. Sunstein, *Nudge: Improving Decisions about Health, Wealth, and Happiness* (New Haven, CT, 2008), and Cass R. Sunstein, *Why Nudge? The Politics of Libertarian Paternalism* (New Haven, CT, 2014).

116. For a helpful overview, see John Cottingham, *The Rationalists* (Oxford, 1988). The period also saw many challenges to the hegemony of the Rationalist position, for example from such defenders of a God defined by his omnipotent will rather than his rational essence as the Jansenist Antoine Arnauld. For an account of Arnauld's battles with Rationalists like Leibniz and Malebranche, see Steven Nadler, *The Best of All Possible Worlds: A Story of Philosophers, God, and Evil in the Age of Reason* (Princeton, NJ, 2010). The voluntarist alternative to a rational God had periodically emerged during the Middle Ages as well, initially in the Augustinian tradition and then by nominalists such as William of Ockham. Bouwsma notes that "Augustianism tended to replace the monarchy of reason in the human personality with a kind of corporate democracy. The primary organ in Aristotelian anthropology is not so much that which is highest as that which is central; it is literally the heart (*cor*) whose quality determines the quality of the whole. And that this quality is not a function of rational enlightenment is seen as a matter of common experience. The will is not, after all, an obedient servant of the reason." *A Usable Past*, 25–26. During the Middle Ages, the classical Greek residue in Christianity seems to have grown more threatening to theologians with the rise of Islam, which had more faithfully preserved the Aristotelian heritage. One result was the nominalist critique of rationalist realism in the thirteenth century. For accounts of the rise of nominalism

and its abiding influence in secular modernity, see Hans Blumenberg, *The Legitimacy of the Modern Age*, trans. Robert M. Wallace (Cambridge, MA, 1983); Amos Funkenstein, *Theology and the Scientific Imagination from the Middle Ages to the Seventeenth Century* (Princeton, NJ, 1986); and Michael Allen Gillespie, *The Theological Origins of Modernity* (Chicago, IL, 2008).

117. Perhaps the main dissenter at this time was Christian Thomasius, who, although embracing Samuel von Pufendorf's teaching about natural law, was more of an empiricist and sensationalist than a believer in deductive rationalism in the manner of Wolff or Leibniz.

118. There were variations in the relationship between intuition and reason in their work, for example in that of Spinoza. For one consideration of this issue, see Spencer Carr, "Spinoza's Distinction between Rational and Intuitive Knowledge," *The Philosophical Review* 87, no. 2 (April 1978): 241–52.

119. Leibniz did stress individual monads over abstract principles, and has been called a nominalist as a result. See Benson Mates, *The Philosophy of Leibniz: Metaphysics and Language* (New York, 1986), ch. 10. See also Daniel Garber, *Leibniz: Body, Substance, Monad* (New York, 2009), for a discussion of the continuities and discontinuities between his early materialist notion of corporeal substances and his later theory of monads as the basic building blocks of the universe. Spinoza, to acknowledge another difference within the Rationalist camp, preferred the idea of "common notions" to "universal notions." See the discussion in Stuart Hampshire, *Spinoza* (Harmondsworth, 1976), ch. 3.

120. In his *Novum Organum*, the second part of his *Great Instauration* of 1620, Francis Bacon made a celebrated analogy between empiricists, who "like ants, merely collect things and use them," and Rationalists, who "like spiders, spin webs out of themselves," preferring instead the bee, "who gathers its material from the flowers of the garden and field, but then transforms and digests it by a power of its own." *Novum Organum*, trans. and ed. Peter Urbach and John Gibson (Chicago, IL, 1995), 105. The later Enlightenment Rationalists were in many respects more spiders than bees.

121. Although mathematics is often understood to be the epitome of rationality, for example by recent French Spinozans, it is important to recognize that even here one can locate an expression of its limits. Thus, the existence of so-called irrational numbers, like π or √2, which cannot be written as simple fractions, suggest that mathematics resists being contained in a completely coherent system. Supposedly, when Pythagoras's student Hippasus discovered their existence, his teacher was so upset that he drowned the messenger (or perhaps, it is said, the gods did the deed).

122. Here Spinoza is perhaps the best example. As Chiara Bottici has noted, in his thought "there is no 'reason versus myth' dichotomy because there cannot be any radical separation between objective reality and a subject who faces it. It is this eccentric ontology that enables Spinoza to recognize that myth and imagination are already a form of Enlightenment and can therefore play an important cognitive, ethical and political role." "Another Enlightenment: Spinoza on Myth and Imagination," *Constellations* 19, no. 4 (December 2012): 604.

123. Koselleck, *Critique and Crisis*, 109–13.

124. Margaret C. Jacob, *The Radical Enlightenment: Pantheists, Freemasons, and Republicans* (London, 1981). The case for Spinoza is made by Israel, *Radical Enlightenment*. Precisely what in Spinoza fueled his reputation as a radical Enlightener has been the source of endless discussion. His critique of the divine origins of the Bible, plea for religious tolerance, disdain for miracles, and immanentist materialism were all threats to received wisdom, both theological and political. But his equation of God with a nature that was eternal, infinite, unchanging, and determined, and his uncompromisingly rationalist reading of existing reality, could be warrant for an uncritical affirmation of the status quo. Israel's impassioned and erudite, if controversial, defense of Spinoza's influence continued in several subsequent volumes: *Enlightenment Contested: Philosophy, Modernity, and the Emancipation of Man, 1650–1752* (New York, 2006); *Democratic Enlightenment: Philosophy, Revolution, and Human Rights, 1750–1790* (New York, 2011); and *A Revolution of the Mind: Radical Enlightenment and the Intellectual Origins of Modern Democracy* (Princeton, NJ, 2011).

125. For a compact discussion, see Leonard Krieger, *Kings and Philosophers, 1689–1789* (New York, 1970), ch. 7. He stresses the connection between their rationalist politics and their enthusiasm for science, especially in its materialist and mathematical form.

126. For an account, see Martin Jay, *Downcast Eyes: The Denigration of Vision in Twentieth-Century French Thought* (Berkeley, CA, 1993), ch. 2.

127. Jean Starobinski, *1789: The Emblems of Reason*, trans. Barbara Bray (Charlottesville, VA, 1982), 43–45. See also Hubertus Kohl and Rolf Reichardt, *Visualizing the Revolution: Politics and Pictorial Arts in Late Eighteenth-Century France* (London, 2008).

128. For an account that treats the cult and festival as events in the struggle for symbolic power during the Revolution, see Lynn Hunt, *Politics, Culture, and Class in the French Revolution* (Berkeley, CA, 1984), 62–66. One of the ironies of depicting reason as a goddess was the bias against women as rational participants in public life during the Revolution. See the discussion in Joan B. Landes, *Women and the Public Sphere in the Age of the French Revolution* (Ithaca, NY, 1988).

129. Burke, in fact, had seen a link with revolution even before the "Cult of Reason" in his *Reflections on the Revolution in France*, which appeared in 1790. As Darrin M. McMahon has shown, it was already a staple of religiously inflected counter-Enlightenment thought, indebted to Pascal, during the *ancien régime*. See his *Enemies of the Enlightenment: The French Counter-Enlightenment and the Making of Modernity* (Oxford, 2001).

130. For some critics of the French Revolution, such as Alexis de Tocqueville, it was the fateful continuity between the rationalization from above of the *ancien régime* and the democratic rationalization of the Revolution that undermined the pluralist underpinnings of liberty. He located the latter in the aristocratic institutions, such as the *parlements*, that had resisted monarchical centralization. See his *The Old Régime and the Revolution*, trans. Stuart Gilbert (New York, 1955). Burke's defense of the unreformed British Parliament against the assertions of power by the crown anticipated in certain respects Tocqueville's critique. In both cases, rationalization from above and below were seen as equally threatening.

131. For some commentators, Samuel von Pufendorf and Christian Thomasius, who were not squarely in the Rationalist tradition, were also important for the development

of the German *Polizeistaat*. See Ian Hunter, *Rival Enlightenments: Civil and Metaphysical Philosophy in Early Modern Germany* (Cambridge, 2001) and *The Secularisation of the Confessional State: The Political Thought of Christian Thomasius* (Cambridge, 2007). It should also not be assumed that the transition from a *Polizeistaat* model to a *Rechtsstaat* model was the simple replacement of one by the other. European states in one degree or another balanced the two, and there were later intellectuals who defended the ethical claims of common welfare. See, for example, the chapter on "The Ethics of Rational Benevolence" in James T. Kloppenberg's *Uncertain Victory: Social Democracy and Progressivism in European and American Thought, 1870–1920* (Oxford, 1986), which deals with late nineteenth-century moral theorists like Henry Sidgwick, who tried to combine insights from utilitarianism with those of Kantian ethics.

132. See Frederick C. Beiser, *The Fate of Reason: German Philosophy from Kant to Fichte* (Cambridge, MA, 1987), ch. 2.

133. For a recent account, see Stefanie Buchenau, *The Founding of Aesthetics in the German Enlightenment: The Art of Invention and the Invention of Art* (Cambridge, 2013). For a discussion of aesthetic discourse in France, see Francis S. J. Colemen, *The Aesthetic Thought of the French Enlightenment* (Pittsburgh, PA, 1971). The importance of the turn to the aesthetic in the later Enlightenment was recognized as early as Ernst Cassirer's classic study, *The Philosophy of the Enlightenment*, trans. Fritz C. A. Koelln and James P. Pettegrove (Boston, MA, 1951), which significantly concludes with the lengthy chapter "Fundamental Problems of Aesthetics."

134. Not all the senses, however, were given equal weight, as sight still remained the "noblest." The more proximate senses, especially smell, were understood as more base, a designation against which Horkheimer and Adorno protested in *Dialectic of Enlightenment*. For a consideration of this issue, see Bradley Butterfield, "Enlightenment's Other in Patrick Süskind's 'Das Parfum': Adorno and the Ineffable Utopia of Modern Art," *Comparative Literature Studies* 32, no. 3 (1995): 410–18.

135. Voitle, "Reason," 1751. He notes that reckoning and calculation were understood by some as synonymous with discourse, or the dianoetic reasoning we have seen pitted against the noetic in classical Greece. It might, however, be more useful to distinguish calculation from the process of giving and judging reasons, which has a more intersubjective and less instrumental implication.

136. Thomas Hobbes, *Leviathan; or, the Matter, Form, and Power of a Commonwealth Ecclesiastical and Civil*, ed. Michael Oakeshott (New York, 1962), where he says "when a man *reasoneth*, he does nothing else but conceive a sum total, from *addition* of parcels; or conceive a remainder, from *subtraction* of one sum from another; which if it be done by words, is conceiving of the consequence of the names of all the parts, to the name of the whole, or from the names of the whole and one part, to the name of the other part. . . . REASON, in this sense, is nothing but *reckoning*" (41). As Reinhart Koselleck observed, for Hobbes, "the rationally construed State was not a pure 'state of reason' like the one looked forward to in the next century; it was a State for people who would act against reason as frequently as reason would speak against them. . . . To Hobbes, reason was the

ending of civil war—a line that can also be reversed in its historical meaning: the ending of the religious civil wars is 'reason.'" *Critique and Crisis*, 32–33.

137.  See Jonathan Sheehan and Dror Wahrman, *Invisible Hands: Self-Organization and the Eighteenth Century* (Chicago, IL, 2015).

138.  For a general history of the rational choice movement, see S. M. Amadae, *Rationalizing Capitalist Democracy: The Cold War Origins of Rational Choice Liberalism* (Chicago, IL, 2003). For selections of relevant texts, see Jon Elster, ed., *Rational Choice* (New York, 1986). For a critique of the claim that rational choices are made about preformed desires, rather than included in the process of determining those desires, see Searle, *Rationality in Action*.

139.  How self-interest lost its negative valence and escaped being grouped with avarice and greed, which had been stigmatized by the medieval Church, is explained in Albert O. Hirschman, *The Passion and the Interests: Political Arguments for Capitalism before Its Triumph* (Princeton, NJ, 1977).

140.  A. V. Dicey, *An Introduction to the Study of the Law of the Constitution* (London, 1885). He stressed three basic principles: no one can be punished except for breaking the law as proven in a court of law; no one is above the law and everyone is equal before it; the rights of private persons are safeguarded by judicial decisions.

141.  See Aldo Schiavone, *The Invention of Law in the West*, trans. Jeremy Carden and Antony Shugaar (Cambridge, MA, 2012). He shows that Roman law was protected by an elite cadre of expert jurists who resisted political pressure but believed the source of the law was in tradition rather than current legislation. They also failed to extend their notion of the individual with legal rights to slaves.

142.  For a consideration of its strengths and weaknesses, written by an associate of the Institut für Sozialforschung, see Otto Kirchheimer, "The *Rechtsstaat* as Magic Wall," in *The Critical Spirit: Essays in Honor of Herbert Marcuse*, ed. Kurt H. Wolff and Barrington Moore Jr. (Boston, MA, 1967), 287–312.

143.  See John D. Schaeffer, *Sensus Communis: Vico, Rhetoric, and the Limits of Relativism* (Durham, NC, 1990). By the eighteenth century, he notes, it came to mean "an organizing sense, an unreflective opinion shared by most people, the manners or social values of a community, the first principle of reflection, an innate capacity for simple, logical reasoning" (3).

144.  Sophia Rosenfeld, *Common Sense: A Political History* (Cambridge, MA, 2011), 92. She shows that "common sense" could be marshaled both to affirm the status quo and to criticize it. While in the American context, it was predominantly critical, in that of the French Revolution, it was more often invoked in right-wing critiques of the allegedly rationalist utopianism of the revolutionaries.

145.  As the historian George Clark noted, "the 'reason' of Voltaire and Diderot, the acid solvent which prepared the way for the French Revolution by discrediting the prejudices, the traditions, and the stability of an uncriticized social order, was not the rationalism of the physicists. It was merely common sense." *The Seventeenth Century* (New York, 1961), 264.

146. Carl Becker, *The Heavenly City of the Eighteenth-Century Philosophers* (New Haven, CT, 1932), which was the target of an influential rebuttal by Peter Gay in "Carl Becker's Heavenly City," *Political Science Quarterly* 72, no. 2 (June 1957): 182–99. For a more recent appreciation of its argument that ties Becker to postmodernist critiques of the Enlightenment, see Johnson Kent Wright, "The Pre-Postmodernism of Carl Becker," in *Postmodernism and the Enlightenment: New Perspectives in Eighteenth-Century French Intellectual History*, ed. Daniel Gordon (New York, 2001), 161–77. It remained, however, a staple of conservative thought to condemn the eighteenth-century philosophes as utopian Rationalists. See, for example, Michael Oakeshott, *Rationalism in Politics and Other Essays* (New York, 1962).

147. "Reason," in *The Encyclopedia of Diderot & d'Alembert Collaborative Translation Project*, trans. Felix Vo, http://quod.lib.umich.edu/cgi/t/text/text-idx?c=did;cc=did;rgn=main;view=text;idno=did2222.0001.157.

148. Ibid.

149. Cassirer, *Philosophy of the Enlightenment*, 8. The contrast had been first formulated by d'Alembert and Condillac.

150. For a good overview of the reception, see Johnson Kent Wright, "'A Bright Clear Mirror': Cassirer's *The Philosophy of the Enlightenment*," in Baker and Reill, *What's Left of Enlightenment?*, 71–101. He has been variously accused of writing high intellectual history only from above, ignoring questions of the social history of ideas, neglecting the relationship between the Enlightenment and political despotism, and underplaying the dark sides of the Enlightenment, including its domination of nature and gender bias.

151. Cassirer, *Philosophy of the Enlightenment*, 13–14.

## Chapter 2. Kant

1. For an excellent account of Kant's pre-critical works in the context of German metaphysical rationalism, which also shows his complicated relationship to the "popular philosophy" and proto-anthropology of the period, see John H. Zammito, *Kant, Herder, and the Birth of Anthropology* (Chicago, IL, 2002). It should be noted that Kant was among the first to extend the charge of "dogmatism" from theology to metaphysics.

2. Cited approvingly in Immanuel Kant, "An Answer to the Question: What Is Enlightenment?," in *What Is Enlightenment? Eighteenth-Century Answers and Twentieth-Century Questions*, ed. James Schmidt (Berkeley, CA, 1996), 39. Kant distinguished here between what he called the "public use of reason," by which he meant the use made by scholars before the reading public, and the "private use," which was the use made in the role of a functionary of the state (or a priest in a church). Whereas the former is free, the latter is subordinated to decisions made by the ruler, and thus not. The distinction sounds less odd if we think of the former as the open-ended process of generating laws through discourse and the latter as subsequent obedience to the laws that have been legitimately enacted.

3. Immanuel Kant, "Theory and Practice Concerning the Common Saying: This May Be True in Theory but Does Not Apply to Practice," in *The Philosophy of Kant*, ed. Carl J. Friedrich (New York, 1949), 422–23.

4. Reinhart Koselleck, *Critique and Crisis: Enlightenment and the Pathogenesis of Modern Society* (Cambridge, MA, 1988), 121. Koselleck, who was then very much in thrall to Carl Schmitt, did not, however, himself embrace Kant's position, which he saw as an affront to the sovereign authority of "the political."

5. See, in particular, Hannah Arendt, *Lectures on Kant's Political Philosophy*, ed. Ronald Beiner (Chicago, IL, 1989).

6. On the Scottish Enlightenment, see Christopher J. Berry, *Social Theory of the Scottish Enlightenment* (Edinburgh, 1997). Kant's maternal grandfather, it is often noted, was of Scottish origin.

7. See Samuel Fleischacker, *A Third Concept of Liberty: Judgment and Freedom in Kant and Adam Smith* (Princeton, NJ, 1999), and Mark D. White, "Adam Smith and Immanuel Kant: On Markets, Duties, and Moral Sentiments," *Forum for Social Economics* 39, no. 1 (2010): 53–60. The latter focuses on Smith's *Theory of Moral Sentiments* rather than *The Wealth of Nations*.

8. Sophia Rosenfeld, *Common Sense: A Political History* (Cambridge, MA, 2011), 221–24.

9. Onora O'Neill, *Constructions of Reason: Explorations of Kant's Practical Philosophy* (Cambridge, 1989).

10. See Knox Peden, *Spinoza contra Phenomenology: French Rationalism from Cavaillès to Deleuze* (Stanford, CA, 2014).

11. On the long and vexed history of the idea of happiness, see Darrin M. McMahon, *Happiness: A History* (New York, 2006).

12. Perhaps the first statement of the principle came in Spinoza's 1663 geometrical exposition of Descartes's *Principles of Philosophy*. Part 1, axiom 11, says: "Nothing exists of which it cannot be asked, what is the cause (or reason) [*causa (sive ratio)*], why it exists." Baruch Spinoza, *Principles of Cartesian Philosophy* and *Metaphysical Thoughts*, in *Complete Works*, ed. Michael L. Morgan, trans. Samuel Shirley (Indianapolis, IN, 2002), 108–212. For an account of the centrality of the principle in Spinoza's philosophy, see Michael Della Rocca, *Spinoza* (New York, 2008). He shows that Spinoza's naturalism was based on the privileging of causal explanation of a world that was inherently intelligible, a world in which teleology played no role. He argues for the two-fold use of the principle in Spinoza: a demand for an explanation of a given fact and an explanation of that fact in terms of explanation itself. For example, a thing's goodness is not self-evident but demands an explanation in terms of its essential nature. The causal power of a thing's nature to determine its qualities must then itself require explanation, which is found in the intelligibility of causation.

13. See Benson Mates, *The Philosophy of Leibniz: Metaphysics and Language* (New York, 1986), 158–59. Mates argues that causes should be distinguished from reasons because the latter "belong to the category of *propositions* (thoughts, the senses of declarative sentences); they are good or bad, true or false, and they stand in logical relations to one another and to that for which they are the reasons. Causes, on the other hand, would seem to be things or events or circumstances—with all of which, unlike reasons, it makes sense to associate spatiotemporal coordinates" (160).

14. On Leibniz's belief in a natural language in which names and things were one, see Hans Aarsleff, *From Locke to Saussure: Essays on the Study of Language and Intellectual History* (Minneapolis, MN, 1982). Here he rejected the linguistic conventionalism normally associated with the nominalist tradition.

15. Amos Funkenstein, *Theology and the Scientific Imagination from the Middle Ages to the Seventeenth Century* (Princeton, NJ, 1986), 198. Compossibility is Leibniz's term for the compatibility of possible individuals in the same world.

16. See Brandon C. Lock, "Grounding the Principle of Sufficient Reason: Leibnizian Rationalism and the Humean Challenge," in *The Rationalists: Between Tradition and Innovation*, ed. Justin E. H. Smith, Dario Perinetti, and Carlos Fraenkel (Dordrecht, 2011), 201–19. He argues that the derivation of the principle of sufficient reason from the principle of contradiction does provide a foundation for its plausibility, if, that is, we accept the idea of the identitarian containment of a predicate in its subject. Funkenstein is not so sure. See *Theology and the Scientific Imagination*, 197.

17. Vincent Descombes suggestively claims that Leibniz betrays his modern sensibility by basing his optimism on an explicit value hierarchy, "value" itself being a category not available to earlier cultures. "In so doing, it introduces the perspective of a subject who compares options and chooses the best one. The world's beauty is no longer immediately expressed by its order or the musical harmony of its parts. It is established only after passing through an order of values assigned by divine understanding to all the various possibilities available to it." *The Barometer of Modern Reason: On the Philosophies of Current Events*, trans. Stephen Adam Schwartz (New York, 1993), 110. This argument dovetails with Heidegger's complaint that Leibniz introduced subjectivism by stressing the need to "render reasons."

18. This equation will be challenged by later philosophers, such as John Searle, who writes in *Rationality in Action* (Cambridge, MA, 2001), "causes are typically events, reasons are never events. You can give a reason by stating a cause, but it does not follow that the reason and the cause are the same thing" (107).

19. The most celebrated expression of that disillusionment was Voltaire's "Poème sur le désastre de Lisbonne," published in 1756, and *Candide, ou l'Optimisme* of 1759. For a general history of the quake and its aftermath, see Nicholas Shrady, *The Last Day: Wrath, Ruin, and Reason in the Great Lisbon Earthquake of 1755* (New York, 2008). Adorno would later compare its effects with those of the Holocaust, arguing that "the earthquake of Lisbon sufficed to cure Voltaire of the theodicy of Leibniz, and the visible disaster of the first nature was insignificant in comparison with the second, social one, which defies human imagination as it distills a real hell from human evil." *Negative Dialectics*, trans. E. B. Ashton (New York, 1973), 361.

20. See Jacob Viner, *The Role of Providence in the Social Order: An Essay in Intellectual History* (Princeton, NJ, 1976). There were also some philosophes, among them Rousseau, who made defenses of providence against Voltaire. See the discussion in José O. A. Marques, "The Paths of Providence: Voltaire and Rousseau on the Lisbon Earthquake," *Cadernos de História e Filosofia da Ciência*, series 3, 15, no. 1 (January–June 2005): 33–57.

21. Werner Hamacher, "The Quaking of Presentation," in *Premises: Essays on Philosophy and Literature from Kant to Celan* (Stanford, CA, 1999), 261–93.

22. Hume seems not to have specifically mentioned the Lisbon earthquake in his work, but much of it was composed in its shadow.

23. On the issue of "probable reasoning" in Hume, see Claudia M. Schmidt, *David Hume: Reason in History* (University Park, PA, 2003), ch. 3. The major contemporary version of this kind of reasoning has come to be called "Bayesian," from the work of the eighteenth-century mathematician Thomas Bayes. See Luc Bovens and Stephan Hartmann, *Bayesian Epistemology* (Oxford, 2003). It was developed as well by Pierre Joseph Laplace and Jakob Bernoulli, who argued from what later became known as the "principle of insufficient reason"—a different usage than Blumenberg's synonym for rhetoric—or the "principle of indifference." See P. Dupont, "Laplace and the Indifference Principle in the 'Essai philosophique des probabilités,'" *Rendiconti del Seminario Matematico, Universitàe Politecnico Torino* 36 (1977/78): 125–37, and Ian Hacking, "Jacques Bernoulli's Art of Conjecturing," *British Journal of Philosophy of Science* 22 (1971): 209–29.

24. Arthur Schopenhauer, *On the Fourfold Root of the Principle of Sufficient Reason*, trans. E. F. J. Payne (La Salle, IL, 1997).

25. Walter Benjamin, "The Lisbon Earthquake," in *Selected Writings*, vol. 2, *1927–1934*, ed. Michael W. Jennings, Howard Eiland, and Gary Smith, trans. Rodney Livingstone et al. (Cambridge, MA, 1999), 538; see also O. Reinhardt and D. R. Olroyd, "Kant's Theory of Earthquakes and Volcanic Action," *Annals of Science* 40, no. 3 (1983): 247–72.

26. For a discussion of his changing attitudes toward the principle, see Béatrice Longuenesse, "Kant's Deconstruction of the Principle of Sufficient Reason," *The Harvard Review of Philosophy* 9, no. 1 (2001): 67–87. She points out that he distinguished no fewer than four types of reason supporting the principle: *ratio essendi* (reason for the *being* of a thing), *ratio fiendi* (reason for the *coming to be* of a thing), *ratio existendi* (reason for the *existence* of a thing), and *ratio cognoscendi* (reason for our *knowing* that a thing is what it is) (67).

27. For an account of the development of critique in Kant, see Willi Goetschel, *Constituting Critique: Kant's Writing as Critical Practice*, trans. Eric Schwab (Durham, NC, 1994).

28. Theodor W. Adorno, *Kant's "Critique of Pure Reason,"* ed. Rolf Tiedemann, trans. Rodney Livingstone (Stanford, CA, 2001), 120. Translation emended.

29. See George S. Williamson, *The Longing for Myth in Germany: Religion and Aesthetic Culture from Romanticism to Nietzsche* (Chicago, IL, 2004) for the lure of mythology. For a discussion of the temptation of mysticism, see Frederick C. Beiser, *The Romantic Imperative: The Concept of Early German Romanticism* (Cambridge, MA, 2003): "there were at least two competing traditions of mysticism alive in German philosophy in the late eighteenth century. Very crudely, there was the mysticism of the Platonic tradition, which understood mystical insight as *hyperrational*, and which made reason an intuitive power. There was also, however, the mysticism of the Protestant tradition, which saw mystical insight as *suprarational*, and which reduced reason strictly to a discursive power. The mysticism of the Protestant tradition ultimately had its roots in the *via moderna*, the nominalist

tradition of late medieval thought, which traces its roots back to William of Ockham" (63). He shows how important the former was for the early German Romantics.

30. For those who want to be walked through its complicated arguments, see Douglas Burnham and Harvey Young, *Kant's Critique of Pure Reason: An Edinburgh Philosophical Guide* (Edinburg, 2007). The number of different uses comes from Klaus Konhardt, *Die Einheit der Vernunft: Zum Verhältnis von theoretischen und praktischer Vernunft in der Philosophie Kants* (Königstein, 1979), 49.

31. Immanuel Kant, *Critique of Pure Reason*, trans. Werner S. Pluhar (Indianapolis, IN, 1996), 31. It would, however, be mistaken too hastily to identify Kant's defense of faith here as a brief for irrational belief, as it was a paradoxical "faith in reason" that he was applauding.

32. Hannah Arendt, *Thinking*, vol. 1 of *The Life of the Mind* (New York, 1978), 14. As Arendt used it, the word *denken* (in English both the noun "thought" and the verb "to think") not only invoked the Enlightenment notion of *Selbstdenken* (thinking for yourself), which she identified especially with Gotthold Ephraim Lessing, but also the multiple meanings developed by her teacher Martin Heidegger in *What Is Called Thinking?*, trans. Fred D. Wieck and J. Glenn Gray (New York, 1968).

33. Kant, *Critique of Pure Reason*, 5.

34. Ibid., 34.

35. Ibid., 63–64.

36. Ibid., 645.

37. Ibid., 495. The architectural implications of this metaphor, which suggests a foundation or ground as well as a systematic structure, are examined in Daniel Purdy, *On the Ruins of Babel: Architectural Metaphor in German Thought* (Ithaca, NY, 2011), ch. 3. He makes the point that for Kant, "the foundations of metaphysics crack because they are not laid out according to a plan. Far from wanting to establish philosophy on first principles, Kant wanted to demonstrate the futility of laying foundations for a new metaphysics" (58).

38. Kant, *Critique of Pure Reason*, 43.

39. Whether or not Kant was actually closer to Copernicus or to Newton in his view of science is discussed in Robert Hahn, *Kant's Newtonian Revolution in Philosophy* (Carbondale, IL, 1988). In a wider sense, the metaphor was misleading, insofar as Copernicus had replaced a geocentric system with a heliocentric one, which displaced humans from their central place in creation. Kant's critical epistemology, in contrast, moved the center of gravity of philosophy away from objects of knowledge to the subjects who constituted them. Whereas Copernicus can be placed in a narrative of narcissistic wounds, culminating in Darwin and Freud, Kant can be read as pushing back against that narrative, helping to restore human dignity. This reading is even more justified if we include his discussion of moral obligation in the second Critique. See Michael Rosen, *Dignity: Its History and Meaning* (Cambridge, MA, 2012), for Kant's crucial role in the modern understanding of human dignity.

40. Kant, *Critique of Pure Reason*, 64.

41. Ibid., 663. For an argument that Kant was never really a foundationalist, see Arthur Collins, *Possible Experience: Understanding Kant's "Critique of Pure Reason"* (Berkeley, CA, 1999), ch. 8.

42. One of the most complex and contested of all of Kant's procedures, "transcendental deductions" were also applied in the other critiques and in his "Opus posthumum." For the controversy over their meaning and plausibility, see Eckart Förster, ed., *Kant's Transcendental Deductions: The Three "Critiques" and the "Opus postumum"* (Stanford, CA, 1989).

43. Kant, *Critique of Pure Reason*, 303. Although *Verstand* is more often translated as "understanding" than "intellect," Hannah Arendt notes that it was itself Kant's rendering of the Latin *intellectus* and lacks all of the connotations associated with the German verb *verstehen*, which was so important in the hermeneutic tradition stressing the interpretation of meaning. See her *Thinking*, 13–14. For Arendt, *"the need for reason is not inspired by the quest for truth but by the quest for meaning. And truth and meaning are not the same"* (15).

44. Adorno, *Kant's "Critique*," 14.

45. Kant, *Critique of Pure Reason*, 343.

46. Longueness, "Kant's Deconstruction," 76.

47. For an analysis of this issue, see Herbert Schnädelbach, "Observations on Rationality and Language," in *Reason and Its Other: Rationality in Modern German Philosophy and Culture*, ed. Dieter Freundlieb and Wayne Hudson (Providence, RI, 1993), 57–62.

48. W. V. O. Quine, "Two Dogmas of Empiricism," *The Philosophical Review* 60, no. 1 (1951): 20–43, reprinted in his *From a Logical Point of View* (Cambridge, MA, 1953). He identified analytic judgments with propositions that were grounded in meaning and synthetic ones grounded in fact, and then holistically challenged the distinction between meaning and factuality. Or to put it slightly differently, he stressed the inevitability of a linguistic mediation of even the most tautological of identities, which brought with it the subtle variations of meaning that could not be entirely squashed by the most stringent of definitions.

49. Kant, *Critique of Pure Reason*, 678.

50. For a discussion, see Thomas E. Wartenberg, "Reason and the Practice of Science," in *The Cambridge Companion to Kant*, ed. Paul Guyer (Cambridge, 1992), 228–48.

51. Critics of Kant like Nietzsche would urge instead that we abandon the dry land and embark on the ocean, clinging if necessary to the debris of a shipwreck from which we fashion new meanings. See the discussion in Hans Blumenberg, *Shipwreck with Spectator: Paradigm of a Metaphor for Existence*, trans. Steven Rendall (Cambridge, MA, 1997).

52. See, for example, Susan Neiman, *The Unity of Reason: Rereading Kant* (Oxford, 1994), and Konhardt, *Die Einheit der Vernunft*.

53. Neiman, *The Unity of Reason*, 59.

54. See Ernst Cassirer, *Rousseau, Kant, Goethe* (Princeton, NJ, 1945), and Richard Velkley, *Freedom and the End of Reason: On the Moral Foundation of Kant's Critical Philosophy* (Chicago, IL, 1989). Whether or not "all men" included "the fairer sex," whose immaturity he condescendingly described in "What Is Enlightenment?," has been a matter of

some contention. See Robin May Schott, ed., *Feminist Interpretations of Immanuel Kant* (University Park, PA, 1997). Rousseau, of course, was not himself free of misogynist prejudices.

55. For a discussion of Leibniz's distinction, see Mates, *The Philosophy of Leibniz*, 119.

56. See Longueness, "Kant's Deconstruction," 81. For a discussion of Crusius and his criticisms of Wolffian rationalism, see J. B. Schneewind, *The Invention of Autonomy: A History of Modern Moral Philosophy* (Cambridge, 1998), ch. 20.

57. See Frederick C. Beiser, *The Fate of Reason: German Philosophy from Kant to Fichte* (Cambridge, MA, 1987), chs. 2 and 3. On the continuing importance of Spinozism in the response to Kant, see George di Giovanni, "The First Twenty Years of Critique: The Spinoza Connection," in Guyer, *The Cambridge Companion to Kant*, 417–48.

58. According to Beiser, "While Hamann and Herder insisted that we cannot abstract reason from society and history, Jacobi stressed that we cannot separate it from desire and instinct. We have to see reason as part of a single living organism, he argued, where it organizes and directs all its vital functions. Reason is not a disinterested power of contemplation then, but an instrument of the will, which uses it to control and dominate the environment." *The Fate of Reason*, 9. For an attempt to defend Jacobi, see Dale E. Snow, "Jacobi's Critique of the Enlightenment," in Schmidt, *What Is Enlightenment?*, 306–16. He cautions against assuming that Jacobi was simply a counter-Enlightenment obscurantist, noting that "those who think of Jacobi as the apostle of irrationalism would doubtless be surprised to encounter Jacobi's argument that the way to self-mastery is through the use of reason" (310).

59. John H. Zammito, *The Genesis of Kant's "Critique of Judgment"* (Chicago, IL, 1992), 311.

60. "Nothing here can escape us, because what reason brings forth entirely out of itself cannot be hidden, but is brought to light by reason itself as soon as reason's common principle has been discovered" (Kant, *Critique of Pure Reason*, 13). There has been a lively discussion in Kant scholarship about the success of his search for a unifying principle, with contributions by Paul Guyer, Klaus Kohnhardt, Susan Neiman, and others. For a summary discussion, see Pauline Kleingeld, "Kant on the Unity of Theoretical and Practical Reason," *The Review of Metaphysics* 52, no. 2 (December 1998): 500–528. Defenders of the unity usually foreground the primacy of practical reason and see it as also providing the regulative ideal that motivates scientific method in the first Critique. What speaks against the perfect unity of the two, besides Kant's often inconsistent formulations, is the fact that he argues that theoretical reason can lead to transcendental illusions, but practical reason cannot.

61. See note 116 in chapter 1.

62. Although introduced by Aristotle in his *Nicomachean Ethics*, *prohairesis* (προαίρεσις) was most extensively explored in the work of the Stoic Epictetus. For a discussion, see Rosalind Hursthouse, *On Virtue Ethics* (Oxford, 2001). For a general discussion of the will in Western philosophy, see Arendt, *Willing*, vol. 2 of *The Life of the Mind*.

63. Steven Nadler, *The Best of All Possible Worlds: A Story of Philosophers, God, and Evil in the Age of Reason* (Princeton, NJ, 2010), 245.

64. For a good discussion of Kant's attitude toward God and religion, see Allen W. Wood, "Rational Theology, Moral Faith, and Religion," in Guyer, *The Cambridge Companion to Kant*, 394–416.

65. Schneewind, *The Invention of Autonomy*, 515.

66. On the implications of this metaphor in Kant, see Dieter Henrich, *Between Kant and Hegel: Lectures on German Idealism*, trans. David S. Pacini (Cambridge, MA, 2003), ch. 4.

67. Kant, *Metaphysical Foundations of Morals*, in Friedrich, *The Philosophy of Kant*, 206.

68. An example of this usage can be found in the famous principle of Giambattista Vico, "verum et factum convertuntur," which means truth and making are convertible. Kant's claim that reason somehow "makes" us feel obliged, while admitting that we cannot rationally justify that feeling, has been called a "fetishist disavowal" of his recognition of the antinomies of reason by Henrik Jøker Bjerre, "Himself Nothing Beholds Nothing: On Schelling's Ontological Isomorphism," *Filozofski Vestnik* 34, no. 2 (2013): 130. He argues that Schelling was more forthright in acknowledging that reason contained something more real than its practical or moral use.

69. Longueness, "Kant's Deconstruction," 82.

70. Kant, "Was heisst: Sich im Denken orientieren?," in *Werke*, ed. Wilhelm Weischedel (Darmstadt, 1983), 5:277. For a discussion of Kant's notion of "rational faith," see Neiman, *The Unity of Reason*, ch. 4. Adorno notes that Kant's claim that the categorical imperative is simply a given "contains all kinds of grimly authoritarian and irrationalist elements," but then adds approvingly, it also contains "an awareness that the sphere of right action does not coincide with mere rationality, that it has an 'addendum.'" Theodor W. Adorno, *Metaphysics: Concepts and Problems*, ed. Rolf Tiedemann, trans. Edmund Jephcott (Stanford, CA, 2000), 116.

71. Ernst H. Kantorowicz, *The King's Two Bodies: A Study in Medieval Political Thought* (Princeton, NJ, 1957). For a particularly imaginative reading of its implications for democratic theory, see Eric L. Santner, *The Royal Remains: The People's Two Bodies and the Endgames of Sovereignty* (Chicago, IL, 2011).

72. Schneewind, *The Invention of Autonomy*, 501–5.

73. Kant, *Critique of Pure Practical Reason*, in Friedrich, *The Philosophy of Kant*, 239.

74. Ibid., 241. For a devout Christian like Kant and many of the later Idealists, the idea of the transcendent becoming immanent in the world, quintessentially exemplified by the Incarnation, was not hard to fathom.

75. Kant, *Metaphysical Foundations of Morals*, in Friedrich, *The Philosophy of Kant*, 184.

76. Kant, "Theory and Practice," 417. Because the ultimate goal of moral behavior is what Kant followed Cicero in calling the "highest good" (*summum bonum*), which acted like the cognitive ideal of the "unconditioned" as a practical spur to virtuous behavior, it might seem as if he hoped for the unity of happiness and moral righteousness. But, as Neiman notes, "virtue and happiness are too fundamentally heterogeneous to be unifiable. Rational faith is the means that permits us to live with the consciousness of this separation, allowing us to hope that the world will become a place more appropriate to reason's needs." *The Unity of Reason*, 179.

77. Onora O'Neill, "Kant: Rationality as Practical Reason," in *The Oxford Handbook of Rationality*, ed. Alfred R. Mele and Piers Rawling (Oxford, 2004), 100–101.

78. For an attempt to read Kant against the grain and argue that the moral sentiment of respect is inextricably intertwined with the somatic motivations of human behavior, see Jane Bennett, *The Enchantment of Modern Life: Attachments, Crossings, and Ethics* (Princeton, NJ, 2001), 133–37. A similar argument about the erotic underpinnings of Kant's references to reason's "needs," "satisfactions," "strivings," and "affections" can be found in Yirmiyahu Yovel, *Kant and the Philosophy of History* (Princeton, NJ, 1980).

79. Friedrich Nietzsche, *On the Genealogy of Morality*, ed. Keith Ansell-Pearson, trans. Carol Diethe (Cambridge, 1994), 45.

80. Hannah Arendt, "On Humanity in Dark Times: Thoughts about Lessing," in *Men in Dark Times* (New York, 1968), 27.

81. As Susan Meld Shell has noted, "God constitutes the one exception to Kant's principle of 'determining reason' thus understood [as either an antecedent or consequent cause]. God cannot have an antecedent reason for existing; but no being has its ground in itself (for then ground and grounded would absurdly be one); hence God is groundless—he simply *exists*." *The Embodiment of Reason: Kant on Spirit, Generation, and Community* (Chicago, IL, 1996), 36–37.

82. Kant, *Metaphysical Foundations of Morals*, in Friedrich, *The Philosophy of Kant*, 206.

83. Kant, *Critique of Pure Reason*, 771.

84. Ibid., 202. Epigenesis was contrasted with preformationism, the former arguing for the gradual development of mature organisms, the latter for their being already preformed prior to their appearance. For a discussion of Kant's attitude toward this issue, see John Zammito, "Kant's Persistence Ambivalence towards Epigenesis," in *Understanding Purpose: Kant and the Philosophy of Biology*, ed. Philippe Huneman (Rochester, NY, 2007). For a contemporary validation of the epigenetic argument, see Robert Hanna, *Rationality and Logic* (Cambridge, MA, 2006), 86–87.

85. Kant, "An Answer," 58.

86. Michel Foucault, "What Is Critique?," in Schmidt, *What Is Enlightenment?*, 392. For a discussion of Foucault on Kant, see Michael Meranze, "Critique and Government: Michel Foucault and the Question 'What is Enlightenment?,'" in *What's Left of Enlightenment? A Postmodern Question*, ed. Keith Michael Baker and Peter Hanns Reill (Stanford, CA, 2001), 102–12. He suggests a link between Kantian notions of critique and the soft, hegemonic power of what Foucault called "governmentality." According to Robert B. Pippin, however, what really marked Kant's philosophy as a "wholly modern project" was his stress on the self-legislating, spontaneous subject who can critically decide what is a valid claim about the objective world and what is not. See his discussion in *Modernism as a Philosophical Problem: On the Dissatisfactions of High European Culture* (Cambridge, MA, 1991), 47.

87. Jürgen Habermas, *The Structural Transformation of the Public Sphere: An Inquiry into a Category of Bourgeois Society*, trans. Thomas Burger and Frederick Lawrence (Cambridge, MA, 1989), 116.

88. Wilfrid Sellars, *Empiricism and the Philosophy of Mind* (Cambridge, MA, 1997).

89. The essay is included along with a collection of essays devoted to it in Amélie Oksenberg Rorty and James Schmidt, eds., *Kant's "Idea for a Universal History with a Cosmopolitan Aim": A Critical Guide* (Cambridge, 2009).

90. For a discussion, see José Antonio Maravall, *Culture of the Baroque: Analysis of a Historical Structure*, trans. Terry Cochrane (Minneapolis, MN, 1986), 189–90, and Reinhart Koselleck, "Chance as Motivational Trace in Historical Writing," in *Futures Past: On the Semantics of Historical Time*, trans. Keith Tribe (Cambridge, MA, 1985), 116–29. That "fortune" was often coded female—the Greek goddess of luck was Tyche and the Roman was Fortuna—and "reason" male has not escaped the attention of a posterity sensitive to the undercurrent of gender politics in such traditional characterizations. See Hanna Fenichel Pitkin, *Fortune Is a Woman: Gender and Politics in the Thought of Niccolò Machiavelli* (Chicago, IL, 1999).

91. See Viner, *The Role of Providence.*

92. There is an extensive literature on the vicissitudes of the idea of progress. Among the most useful treatments are J. B. Bury, *The Idea of Progress: An Inquiry into Its Origin and Growth* (New York, 1955); Robert Nisbet, *History of the Idea of Progress* (New York, 1980); Sidney Pollard, *The Idea of Progress: History and Society* (Harmondsworth, 1971); W. Warren Wagar, ed., *The Idea of Progress since the Renaissance* (New York, 1969). For an account of its earliest incarnations, see Ludwig Edelstein, *The Idea of Progress in Classical Antiquity* (Baltimore, MD, 1967).

93. According to Koselleck, the idea of a singular, unified species-wide history was developed only in the eighteenth century. See his "History, Histories, and Formal Structures of Time," in *Futures Past*, 92–104. See also Funkenstein, *Theology and the Scientific Imagination*, ch. 2. He argues that "the many versions of reason in history from Vico to Marx are only speculative byproducts of a profound revolution in historical thought in the sixteenth and seventeenth centuries, namely the discovery of history as *contextual reasoning*" (206).

94. For a discussion, see Berry, *Social Theory*, 61–70.

95. Kant, "Idea for a Universal History with a Cosmopolitan Aim," in Rorty and Schmidt, *Kant's "Idea for a Universal History,"* 21.

96. For an attempt to spell out the assumptions behind this claim, see Henry F. Allison, "Teleology and History in Kant: The Critical Foundations of Kant's Philosophy of History," in Rorty and Schmidt, *Kant's "Idea for a Universal History,"* 24–45.

97. Kant, "Idea for a Universal History," 12.

98. Kant's preference for a cosmopolitan federation rather than a single, universal world state indicates the pluralist aspect of his rationalism, which resisted the dogmatic belief that there is only one way to order the world rationally. For discussions of this issue, which has once again become very current, see the essays in Garrett Wallace Brown and David Held, eds., *The Cosmopolitanism Reader* (Cambridge, 2010). Several stress the debt owed by Kant and contemporary cosmopolitan thinking to Stoic notions of universal human rationality.

99. Kant, "Idea for a Universal History," 14. For insightful accounts of "unsocial sociability" as a theme in early modern philosophy, see J. B. Schneewind, "Good out of

Evil: Kant and the Idea of Unsocial Sociability," and Allen Wood, "Kant's Fourth Proposition: The Unsocial Sociability of Human Nature," both in Rorty and Schmidt, *Kant's "Idea for a Universal History,"* 94–111 and 112–28.

100. Kant, "Idea for a Universal History," 16. This phrase has been often appropriated by moderates hostile to the Enlightenment program of perfectibility, e.g., Isaiah Berlin, *The Crooked Timber of Humanity: Chapters in the History of Ideas*, ed. Henry Hardy (Princeton, NJ, 1998). For a discussion, see Paul Guyer, "The Crooked Timber of Mankind," in Rorty and Schmidt, *Kant's "Idea for a Universal History,"* 129–49.

101. Axel Honneth, *Pathologies of Reason: On the Legacy of Critical Theory*, trans. James Ingram et al. (New York, 2009), 14.

102. Immanuel Kant, "Of Beauty as the Symbol of Morality," in *Critique of Judgment*, trans. Werner Pluhar (Indianapolis, 1987), § 59. Significantly, the link he posits between the aesthetic and the ethical is symbolic, not discursive or cognitive.

103. Kant, "Idea for a Universal History," 22.

## Chapter 3. Hegel and Marx

1. The tangled history of Kant's early reception is well told in Frederick C. Beiser, *The Fate of Reason: German Philosophy from Kant to Fichte* (Cambridge, MA, 1987). See also Dieter Henrich, *Between Kant and Hegel: Lectures on German Idealism*, trans. David S. Pacini (Cambridge, MA, 2003), and Paul Frank, *All or Nothing: Systematicity, Transcendental Arguments, and Skepticism in German Idealism* (Cambridge, MA, 2005). For a discussion of the ways Kant's ideas about history were developed in particular by Karl Leonard Reinhold, see Karl Ameriks, *Kant and the Historical Turn: Philosophy as Critical Interpretation* (Oxford, 2006).

2. Although sporadically used before, the word "nihilism" was popularized by F. J. Jacobi as a rebuke to the subjective solipsism he saw in Kant and Fichte. For accounts, see Andrew Bowie, *From Romanticism to Critical Theory: The Philosophy of German Literary Theory* (London, 1997), ch. 1; Beiser, *The Fate of Reason*, ch. 2; and Michael Allen Gillespie, *Nihilism before Nietzsche* (Chicago, IL, 1996).

3. For an account, see Frederick C. Beiser, *The Romantic Imperative: The Concept of Early German Romanticism* (Cambridge, MA, 2003), especially ch. 9. See also his *German Idealism: The Struggle against Subjectivism, 1781–1801* (Cambridge, MA, 2008), which argues that if subjectivism is understood as believing in the primacy of consciousness over the world or epistemology over ontology, the Idealists were not really subjectivists. Theirs, he claims, was closer to a Platonic idealism in which ideas were objective, not subjective.

4. Herbert Marcuse, *Hegel's Ontology and the Theory of Historicity*, trans. Seyla Benhabib (Cambridge, MA, 1987); Herbert Marcuse, *Reason and Revolution: Hegel and the Rise of Social Theory* (Boston, MA, 1960); Theodor W. Adorno, *Hegel: Three Studies*, trans. Shierry Weber Nicholsen (Cambridge, MA, 1993). Although Marcuse's first book on Hegel was written under the direction of Martin Heidegger and was thus prior to his involvement with the Institute for Social Research, it anticipates a number of his later concerns. For an overview of his attempt to marry Heidegger and Marx, and his ultimate abandonment

of that quest, see the essays collected in Herbert Marcuse, *Heideggerian Marxism*, ed. Richard Wolin and John Abromeit (Lincoln, NE, 2005).

5. For a discussion of Adorno's debts to Schelling, see Andrew Bowie, "'Non-Identity': The German Romantics, Schelling and Adorno," in *Intersections: Nineteenth-Century Philosophy and Contemporary Theory*, ed. Tilottama Rajan and David L. Clark (Albany, NY, 1995). For a discussion of Horkheimer's early debts to Schopenhauer, see John Abromeit, *Max Horkheimer and the Foundations of the Frankfurt School* (Cambridge, 2011). Horkheimer's continued interest is demonstrated in his 1955 essay "Schopenhauer and Society," *Qui Parle* 15, no. 1 (Fall–Winter 2004): 85–96, and his 1960 lecture "Schopenhauer Today," in *The Critical Spirit: Essays in Honor of Herbert Marcuse*, ed. Kurt H. Wolff and Barrington Moore Jr. (Boston, MA, 1967), 55–71.

6. Marcuse, *Reason and Revolution*, 5. In the section of the *Phenomenology* where Hegel discusses the Revolution, entitled "Absolute Freedom and Terror," he cites the Robespierrean cult, but, *pace* Marcuse, not positively. The universal consciousness and will underlying the Terror "hovers over the corpse of the vanished independence of real being, or the being of faith, merely as the exhalation of a stale gas, of the vacuous *Être suprême*." *Phenomenology of Spirit*, trans. A. V. Miller (Oxford, 1979), 358.

What is, however, perhaps inadvertently expressed in this comparison with Robespierre is the continuing importance of religion in Hegel's understanding of reason. Whereas Kant had limited reason to make room for faith, Hegel claimed that "religion must be understood as rational. For religion is the work of reason as it reveals itself, indeed it is reason's highest and most rational work." *The Philosophy of History*, in *The Philosophy of Hegel*, ed. Carl J. Friedrich (New York, 1954), 168. For a discussion of Hegel on religion, see Emil L. Fackenheim, *The Religious Dimension in Hegel's Thought* (Boston, MA, 1967). He cites the claim in Hegel's *Encyclopedia*, "there is but one Reason. There is no second super-human Reason. Reason is the Divine in man" (223).

7. See, for example, Robert Wokler, "Contextualizing Hegel's Phenomenology of the French Revolution and the Terror," *Political Theory* 26, no. 1 (February 1998): 33–55, and Rebecca Comay, *Mourning Sickness: Hegel and the French Revolution* (Stanford, CA, 2010). For an earlier and still useful study of his attitude, see Joachim Ritter, *Hegel und die französische Revolution* (Frankfurt, 1965).

8. Susan Buck-Morss, *Hegel, Haiti, and Universal History* (Pittsburgh, PA, 2009). Christoph Menke, however, notes that the Haitian rebellion was a struggle to secure rights that were already recognized, whereas the Hegelian dialectic of recognition was the precondition for the establishment of rights in the first place. See his "Hegels Theorie der Befreiung: Gesetz, Freiheit, Geschichte, Gesellschaft," in *Können Wir der Geschichte Entkommen? Geschichtsphilosophie am Beginn des 21. Jahrhunderts*, ed. Christian Schmidt (Frankfurt, 2013), 73.

9. Jürgen Habermas, "Hegel's Critique of the French Revolution," in *Theory and Practice*, trans. John Viertel (London, 1974), 139.

10. In the preface to *Phenomenology of Spirit*, Hegel followed this celebrated claim by explaining that "the whole is nothing other than the essence consummating itself through its development" (11). Accordingly, a serious account of Hegel's thought

would have to follow its evolution over his career, although it might be questioned whether or not there was an "essence" at the beginning that was merely developing over time.

11. Adorno, *Hegel*, 140–41. Hegel's argument against argumentation is made most explicitly in the *Phenomenology* (36–37), where he says it works only to destroy what it refutes, rather than seeing the partial truth in what is negated, and it presupposes a fixed subject that is not itself changed by the process of dialectical exchange between subject and object. Ironically, he seems to be contradicting himself here by making an argument to defend his refusal to argue. But, of course, Hegel's point is precisely that contradiction itself is not an error but a way to the truth, which means his self-contradiction is performatively consistent with what he is arguing!

12. Beiser, *The Romantic Imperative*, ch. 4.

13. See Hans-Georg Gadamer, *Hegel's Dialectic: Five Hermeneutical Studies*, trans. P. Christopher Smith (New Haven, CT, 1976), ch. 4. For a consideration of his rejection of the ideal of linguistic clarity, see Adorno, "Skoteinos, or How to Read Hegel," in *Hegel*, 89–148.

14. Hegel, *Phenomenology of Spirit*, 22.

15. According to Habermas, the early Hegel did entertain the possibility of interpreting ethical community in terms of intersubjective communication in the lifeworld but ultimately abandoned this alternative in favor of a notion of a rational absolute spirit equiprimordially present in subject and object. See Jürgen Habermas, *The Philosophical Discourse of Modernity: Twelve Lectures*, trans. Frederick Lawrence (Cambridge, MA, 1987), ch. 2.

16. According to Beiser, it was Karl Leonard Reinhold who first moved in a meta-epistemological, phenomenological direction in his *Elementarphilosophie*, developed in the early 1790s. See *The Fate of Reason*, ch. 8.

17. Hegel's early insights are rescued in Axel Honneth, *The Struggle for Recognition: The Moral Grammar of Social Conflicts*, trans. Joel Anderson (Cambridge, MA, 1995), although he admits that "the consciousness-theoretic architectonics ultimately do prevail over the 'recognition-theoretic' substance of the work. Hegel gives in to the pressure to project into the organization of the ethical community the hierarchical schema of the whole and its parts, in terms of which he had already laid out the constitution of the ethical community in Spirit's act of reflection upon its own moments of externalization" (58). For a defense of the continuing importance of a dialogic notion of reason in the mature Hegel, see Pirmin Stekeler-Weithofer, "Verstand und Vernunft: Zu den Grundbegriffen der Hegelschen Logik," in *Vernunftkritik nach Hegel: Analytisch-kritische Interpretationen zur Dialektik*, ed. Christoph Demmerling and Friedrich Kambartel (Frankfurt, 1992), 139–97.

18. In the words of the New Testament, "Be merciful, just as your Father is merciful" (Luke 6:36). The metaphor of a tribunal appears again, however, in Hegel's borrowing of the idea that the "history of the world is the world's court of judgment" from Friedrich Schiller, which he cites in *Philosophy of Right* in *Hegel: The Essential Writings*, ed. Frederick G. Weiss (New York, 1974), 306. Here, to the extent that reason is inherent in history, reason is still judging, but the fact that whatever has succeeded historically is judged as rational ultimately weakens the critical claim of reason.

19. Hegel, *The Philosophy of Right*, in Weiss, *Hegel*, 264. The critique of Spinoza's acosmism—which he counterposes to the more familiar complaint that Spinoza was an atheist—comes in the *Logic* in Weiss, *Hegel*, 163.

20. Gadamer, *Hegel's Dialectic*, 56.

21. Hegel, *Philosophy of Mind*, in Weiss, *Hegel*, 251.

22. Hegel, *The Philosophy of History*, in Friedrich, *The Philosophy of Hegel*, 16.

23. Hegel, *The Phenomenology of Spirit*, 16 and 35. The latter phrase is also often translated as "the labor of the concept."

24. See the account of its various uses in ancient Greek thought in F. E. Peters, *Greek Philosophical Terms: A Historical Lexicon* (New York, 1967), 36–37.

25. See, for example, Paul Guyer, "Thought and Being: Hegel's Critique of Kant's Theoretical Philosophy," in *The Cambridge Companion to Hegel*, ed. Frederick C. Beiser (Cambridge, 1993), 171–210.

26. Michael Rosen, *Hegel's Dialectic and Its Criticism* (Cambridge, 1982), 47.

27. Adorno attempted to respond to this charge during the Positivism Dispute of the 1960s by claiming that "if one contaminates by association dialectics and irrationalism then one blinds oneself to the fact that criticism of the logic of non-contradiction does not suspend the latter but rather reflects on it." Theodor W. Adorno, introduction to *The Positivist Dispute in German Sociology*, ed. Theodor W. Adorno et al., trans. Glyn Adey and David Frisby (London, 1976), 66.

28. Despite Kant's arguments for understanding's ability to produce reliable "synthetic a priori" judgments about objects of experience, which went beyond the tautologies of purely analytic truths, Hegel charged that his philosophy remained largely on the level of analysis in the sense that it naturalized distinctions—subject/object, phenomena/noumena, cognitive judgments/moral judgments, etc.—that dialectical reason could overcome.

29. Friedrich Meinecke, *Machiavellism: The Doctrine of Raison d'État and Its Place in Modern History*, trans. Douglas Scott (New York, 1965), 273.

30. Hegel, *Lectures on the Philosophy of World History: Introduction, Reason in History*, trans. H. B. Nisbet (Cambridge, 1975), 78. For a discussion of Hegel's ambivalent attitude toward happiness—he saw the period of the "unhappy consciousness" as only a temporary way station in the journey of the Absolute—see Darrin M. McMahon, *Happiness: A History* (New York, 2006), 367–73.

31. For discussions of the role of desire in Hegel, see Judith Butler, *Subjects of Desire: Hegelian Reflections in Twentieth-Century France* (New York, 1999), and Robert Pippin, *Hegel on Self-Consciousness: Desire and Death in the Phenomenology of Spirit* (Princeton, NJ, 2010).

32. Hegel, *Phenomenology of Spirit*, 118. Hegel's discussion of labor in the "master and slave" section of the *Phenomenology* is one of the mostly frequently analyzed in all of his writings, especially by those who see it anticipating Marx's discussion of alienated labor in his early writings. Whether or not he was referring to real human labor or only metaphorically to the "labor of the concept" is at the heart of the debate.

33. For a discussion, see Charles Taylor, *Hegel* (Cambridge, 1975), 393.

34. The phrase "saving the appearances" has been traced to Simplicius's sixth-century commentary on Aristotle's *De Caelo*, where it was used to warn against concocted

hypotheses designed less to get at the truth than merely to justify what appeared to be the case. In *Paradise Lost*, Milton refers to God's amusement at attempts by pre-Copernican astronomers to explain the cosmos:

> When they come to model heaven,
> And calculate the stars; how they will wield
> The mighty frame; how build, unbuild, contrive,
> To save the appearances; how gird the sphere
> With centric and eccentric scribbled o'er,
> Cycle and epicycle, orb in orb.

> John Milton, *Paradise Lost*, Book 8
> in *The Portable Milton*, ed. Douglas Bush
> (New York, 1966), 417

35. Hegel, *Philosophy of Right and Law*, in Friedrich, *The Philosophy of Hegel*, 226. For a discussion of the origins of this metaphor in Rosicrucian theology and Luther's evocation of it during the Reformation, as well as the distance between Hegel and Goethe over its implications, see Karl Löwith, *From Hegel to Nietzsche: The Revolution in Nineteenth-Century Thought*, trans. David E. Green (New York, 1967), 13–18. Hegel, he argues, was "the last Christian philosopher before the break between Christianity and philosophy" (47).

36. For an account of the comic emplotment of Hegel's historical narrative, see Hayden White, *Metahistory: The Historical Imagination in Nineteenth-Century Europe* (Baltimore, MD, 1973), ch. 2. The irony in Hegel's account, it should be stressed, was not that of Kierkegaard or other defenders of paradoxical instability, which was much admired by later deconstructionist theorists like Paul de Man. For a discussion of the distinction, see Martin Jay, "Intention and Irony: The Missed Encounter between Hayden White and Quentin Skinner," *History and Theory* 52, no. 1 (February 2013): 32–48.

37. The vicissitudes of his immediate reception are masterfully traced in John Edward Toews, *Hegelianism: The Path toward Dialectical Humanism, 1805–1841* (Cambridge, 1985).

38. Hegel, *The Philosophy of History*, in Friedrich, *The Philosophy of Hegel*, 19.

39. In the early 1780s, Moses Mendelssohn had warned that "the goal of nature is not the perfection of the human race. No! It is the perfection of the human being, the individual. Every single person is to develop his talents and abilities." Letter to August von Henning, June 1782, cited in Manfred Kuehn, "Reason as a Species Characteristic," in *Kant's "Idea for a Universal History with a Cosmopolitan Aim": A Critical Guide*, ed. Amélie Oksenberg Rorty and James Schmidt (Cambridge, 2009), 89. More recently, Barbara Herman referred to the essay's "effacement of the individual moral agent" as the most "puzzling" and "provocative" of Kant's claims. Barbara Herman, "A Habitat for Humanity," in Rorty and Schmidt, *Kant's "Idea for a Universal History,"* 150.

40. Habermas, *Philosophical Discourse*, 42. For "ironic laughter" it might be more accurate to say "comic" instead.

41. Hegel, *Philosophy of Right and Law*, in Friedrich, *The Philosophy of Hegel*, 224.

42. Marcuse, *Reason and Revolution*, 42.

43. This charge was first leveled in an 1821 review by Heinrich Paulus of *The Philosophy of Right*, and became common in subsequent critiques of Hegel made by such hostile interpreters as Bertrand Russell and Karl Popper. See the discussion in Shlomo Avineri, *Hegel's Theory of the Modern State* (Cambridge, 1972), 123.

44. See George Armstrong Kelly, *Idealism, Politics, and History: Sources of Hegelian Thought* (London, 1969), 323–33, for a discussion of the *Verstandesstaat/ Vernunftstaat* distinction. The phrase "emphatic institutionalism" is Dieter Henrich's and is elaborated in Habermas, *Philosophical Discourse*, 40. Gadamer, however, notes that "Hegel defended institutions not in a wholesale fashion but against the pretense of knowing better on the part of the individual. With his overpowering spiritual force, he showed the limits of moralism in social life and the untenability of a purely inward morality that is not made manifest in the objective structures of life that hold human beings together." Hans-Georg Gadamer, *Reason in the Age of Science*, trans. Frederick G. Lawrence (Cambridge, MA, 1983), 30.

45. For a discussion of Fichte's 1813 lecture "Doctrine of the State" with its call for a "realm of reason," see Ernst Bloch, *Natural Law and Human Dignity*, trans. Dennis J. Schmidt (Cambridge, MA, 1986), ch. 12.

46. Henrich, *Between Kant and Hegel*, 326–27.

47. Friedrich Engels, *Ludwig Feuerbach and the End of Classical German Philosophy*, in *Selected Works of Karl Marx and Frederick Engels* (Moscow, 1968), 596–97.

48. Ibid., 597.

49. Ibid.

50. For a recent consideration of the debates over what Hegel's dialectical method might have been, see Michael Forster, "Hegel's Dialectical Method," in Beiser, *Cambridge Companion to Hegel*, 130–70.

51. In *Faust*, Mephistopheles describes himself as "der Geist der stets verneint!" and adds "Und das mit Recht; denn alles, was entsteht, ist wert, daß es zugrunde geht" ("I am the spirit that negates. And rightly so, for all that comes to be deserves to perish wretchedly"). *Goethe's Faust*, trans. Walter Kaufmann (Garden City, NY, 1961), 160–61. A more genuinely Hegelian insight could have been found in Alexis de Tocqueville's famous argument in *The Old Regime and the French Revolution* that many aspects of the *ancien régime* were continued, if in modified form, after 1789.

52. Taylor, *Hegel*, 422.

53. Adorno, *Hegel*, 44.

54. See Richard L. Schacht, "Hegel on Freedom," in *Hegel: A Collection of Critical Essays*, ed. Alasdair MacIntyre (Garden City, NY, 1972), 289–328.

55. See Frederic L. Bender, ed., *The Betrayal of Marx* (New York, 1975). For another consideration, which defends Engels against the charge, see Alvin W. Gouldner, *The Two Marxisms: Contradictions and Anomalies in the Development of Theory* (New York, 1980). For more on their relationship, see Manfred B. Steger and Terrell Carver, eds., *Engels after Marx* (University Park, PA, 1999). For a general consideration of the scientific claims of Marxism, see Paul Thomas, *Marxism and Scientific Socialism: From Engels to Althusser* (London, 2008).

56. See, for example, the more nuanced argument in his letter of September 21–22, 1890, to Josef Bloch, in *The Marx-Engels Reader*, 2nd ed., ed. Robert C. Tucker (New York, 1978), 760–65. When a full-fledged "dialectical materialist" philosophy—the term was coined by Josef Dietzgen and popularized by Georgi Plekhanov—became the mainstay of Soviet ideology, Engels was taken as warrant for its adoption. Ironically, of course, Leninism was itself far more voluntarist, a reversal that has sometimes been attributed to his reading of Hegel during World War I.

57. For an attempt to trace this history, see Martin Jay, *Marxism and Totality: The Adventures of a Concept from Lukács to Habermas* (Berkeley, CA, 1984).

58. For a helpful discussion of the similarities and differences between Althusser and Spinozist rationalism, see Robert Paul Resch, *Althusser and the Renewal of Marxist Social Theory* (Berkeley, CA, 1992), 42–46, and Knox Peden, *Spinoza contra Phenomenology: French Rationalism from Cavaillès to Deleuze* (Stanford, CA, 2014).

59. The foundations of a full-fledged philosophy called "dialectical materialism" can be found in Engels. For the relevant documents, see Bender, *The Betrayal of Marx*, section 1.

60. Marx, "Notes to the Doctoral Dissertation" (1839–41), and *The Poverty of Philosophy: A Reply to Proudhon's "Philosophy of Poverty"* (1847), both in *Writings of the Young Marx on Philosophy and Society*, ed. and trans. Lloyd D. Easton and Kurt H. Guddat (Garden City, NY, 1967), 64–66 and 484–85.

61. Marx, *Economic and Philosophic Manuscripts*, in Tucker, *The Marx-Engels Reader*, 118. He goes on to mock the idea that "reason is at home in unreason as unreason. The man who has recognized that he is leading an alienated life in politics, law, etc., is leading his true human life in this alienated life as such."

62. Friedrich Engels, *Socialism: Utopian and Scientific* (1880), in Tucker, *The Marx-Engels Reader*, 686.

63. Marcuse, *Reason and Revolution*, 293–94.

64. Ibid., 314.

65. Karl Marx, "The Philosophical Manifesto of the Historical School of Law" (1842), in Easton and Guddat, *Writings of the Young Marx*, 99.

66. For discussion of his youthful Romantic period, see David McLellan, *Marx before Marxism* (New York, 1970), ch. 3. For a discussion of his literary interests, see S. S. Prawer, *Karl Marx and World Literature* (Oxford, 1976). On the issue of rhetoric, see James Arnt Aune, *Rhetoric and Marxism* (Boulder, CO, 1994).

67. Among the major contributors were Gerald Cohen, Jon Elster, John Roemer, Erik Olin Wright, and Alan Carling. Its main premise, to cite Carling, was that "societies are composed of human individuals who, being endowed with resources of various kinds, attempt to choose rationally between various courses of action. . . . No longer does the choice lie between agentless structure and structureless agency. It thus seems possible to sum up this whole change of perspective in one phase: the reinstatement of the subject." "Rational Choice Marxism," *New Left Review* 160 (November–December 1986): 27–28. Sometimes also called "analytical Marxists" because they hoped to reconcile Marxism with contemporary analytic philosophy, the defenders of rational choice

Marxism never reached unified conclusions about the implications of their readings of Marx, e.g., over technological determinism in Marx or the role of functionalist teleology in his philosophy of history. For critical analyses of the legacy of rational choice Marxism, see Terrell Carver and Paul Thomas, eds., *Rational Choice Marxism* (University Park, PA, 1995).

68. The debts are made clear in the most sustained and scrupulously documented exposition of the role of reason in Marx's thought: Allan Megill, *Marx: The Burden of Reason (Why Marx Rejected Politics and the Market)* (Lanham, MD, 2002).

69. Karl Marx to Arnold Ruge, Kreuznach, September 1843, in Tucker, *The Marx-Engels Reader*, 14.

70. For a discussion of Marx's critique of Hegel's defense of state bureaucracy, see Henri Lefebvre, *The Sociology of Marx*, trans. Norbert Guterman (New York, 1969), ch. 5, and Wolfgang Schluchter, *Rationalism, Religion, and Domination: A Weberian Perspective*, trans. Neil Solomon (Berkeley, CA, 1989).

71. Louis Althusser, *For Marx*, trans. Ben Brewster (London, 2010).

72. Karl Marx, afterword to *Capital*, vol. 2, in Tucker, *The Marx-Engels Reader*, 302.

73. Megill, *Marx*, 52–53.

74. Once socialism was achieved, however, the proletariat as a distinct class would be dissolved into an emancipated humanity, which was no longer identifiable as a metasubject, having overcome its alienation from the objective world of its creation. In fact, that objective world in the guise of abstract capital had itself served as an alienated metasubject, albeit spawning its negation, the proletariat. In practical terms, before the moment of true universalization came, the socialist movement struggled with the question of how strictly to identify the active agent of revolution with the proletariat (itself a contested category with no fixed boundaries). At various moments in its history, it accepted "popular fronts" with other aggrieved groups—peasants, artisans, intellectuals, even lumpenproletarians—who would accept the lead of the workers in a broad coalition of the oppressed. At such moments, a more communicatively rational potential emerged to challenge that of a metasubject, whose singular consciousness could be embodied in a small, vanguard party.

75. The locus classicus of this assertion is the sixth of the *Theses on Feuerbach* (1845), in which Marx writes, "Feuerbach resolves the religious essence into the human essence. But the human essence is no abstraction inherent in each single individual. In its reality it is the ensemble of social relations." Tucker, *The Marx-Engels Reader*, 145.

76. For a discussion of the distinction between a dialectical contradiction and a "real opposition," see Lucio Colletti, *Tramonto dell'ideologia* (Rome, 1980). There was, to be sure, an alternative notion of contradiction, associated with performativity more than logic, which was important for the communicative rationality developed by Habermas.

77. Habermas, *Philosophical Discourse*, 63. For an imaginative reading of Marx that attempts to rescue him from Habermas's claim that he is beholden to a production paradigm that privileges labor over communicative interaction, see Moishe Postone, *Time, Labor, and Social Domination: A Reinterpretation of Marx's Critical Theory* (Cambridge, 1993), ch. 6. Although he concedes that the foundational role of labor is assumed by

what he calls "traditional Marxism," Postone argues that Marx's own position was more historically complex, identifying the centrality of production and the labor theory of value as a deficit of capitalism, not a virtue of the human condition.

78. For an extensive critique of these implications, see Megill, *Marx*.

79. John Rundell, *Origins of Modernity: The Origins of Modern Social Theory from Kant to Hegel to Marx* (Cambridge, 1987), 192.

80. For a Frankfurt School reading of Marx that contended it did, see Albrecht Wellmer, "Der heimliche Positivismus der Marxschen Geschichtsphilosophie," in *Kritische Gesellschaftstheorie und Positivismus* (Frankfurt, 1969), 69–127.

81. Perhaps the most extensive consideration of this issue can be found in the work of Andrew Feenberg, for example, *Alternative Modernity: The Technical Turn in Philosophy and Social Theory* (Berkeley, CA, 1995); *Questioning Technology* (New York, 1999); and *Transforming Technology: A Critical Theory Revisited* (New York, 2002).

82. Karl Marx, *The Difference between the Democritean and Epicurean Philosophy of Nature*, in *Collected Works* by Karl Marx and Friedrich Engels (Moscow, 1975), 1:25–108. Usually, the dissertation is taken to be on the side of Epicurus rather than Democritus, because of the former's acknowledgment that atoms can "swerve" from their determined course. But according to Warren Breckman, this reading underestimates Marx's critique of subjective idealism and atomistic individualism. See his *Marx, the Young Hegelians, and the Origins of Radical Social Theory: Dethroning the Self* (Cambridge, 1999), 259–71.

83. Postone, *Time, Labor, and Social Domination*, 381.

84. For two recent attempts to breathe new life into the concept of reification, see Timothy Bewes, *Reification, or, The Anxiety of Late Capitalism* (London, 2002), and Axel Honneth, *Reification: A New Look at an Old Idea*, with Judith Butler, Raymond Geuss, and Jonathan Lear, ed. Martin Jay (New York, 2008).

85. Taylor, *Hegel*, 419.

86. Marx, *Capital*, vol. 3, in Tucker, *The Marx-Engels Reader*, 441.

87. For an expression of the fear of the "randomization of history and politics," see Ellen Meiksins Wood, *The Retreat from Class: A New "True" Socialism* (London, 1986), ch. 5. Her target is the post-structuralist Marxism of Ernesto Laclau and Chantal Mouffe.

88. The pattern is repeated later in the century. See, for example, Dick Howard, *From Marx to Kant* (Albany, NY, 1985).

89. Theodor W. Adorno, *Kant's "Critique of Pure Reason*," ed. Rolf Tiedemann, trans. Rodney Livingstone (Stanford, CA, 2001), 120, 66.

90. Theodor W. Adorno, *Minima Moralia: Reflections from Damaged Life*, trans. E. F. N. Jephcott (London, 1974), 151, where he rehearses Walter Benjamin's plea to credit the emancipatory value of "what might be called the waste products and blind spots that have escaped the dialectic."

91. Immanuel Kant, *Metaphysical Foundations of Morals* (1785), in Friedrich, *The Philosophy of Kant*, 142.

92. Hegel, "What Is Philosophy?," from *Logic*, in Weiss, *Hegel*, 29. His immediate examples of misology are those thinkers who claim that knowledge has to be immediate to be true.

93. William Carlos Williams, "Landscape with the Fall of Icarus" (1960), in *Collected Poems*, vol. 2, *1939–1962* (New York, 1986). The other celebrated poetic response to Breughel's painting came in W. H. Auden's 1938 "Musée des Beaux Arts" (in *Another Time* [London, 2007]), which also ponders human indifference to the fall and the suffering it caused.

## Chapter 4. Reason in Crisis

1. Eclipses of the sun are periodic occurrences, so it would certainly be possible to discern prior losses of confidence in rationality. But if we remain within the narrative posited by Horkheimer's *Eclipse of Reason* (New York, 1947), the one most pertinent can be traced in the post-Enlightenment era in the West.

2. Georg Picht, "What Is Enlightened Thinking?," in *What Is Enlightenment? Eighteenth-Century Answers and Twentieth-Century Questions*, ed. James Schmidt (Berkeley, CA, 1996), 373.

3. Positing an inherent opposition between reason and power risks forgetting the ways in which they were so often intertwined. Not only could the social processes of rationalization be defined as extending the power of a certain notion of reason, but reasoning itself could be understood to depend on the power of the better argument. This Habermasian insight is expressed by Rainer Forst, who notes that "power is generated in the realm of reasons, in what people think, in what people believe they should think, in what they feel to be right, and so on. That is where power is generated. So arguments can be more or less powerful, just as theories can be. The argumentative sphere is never a sphere apart from power, regardless of whether good or bad arguments are being exchanged." Wendy Brown and Rainer Forst, *The Power of Tolerance: A Debate*, ed. Luca di Blasi and Christoph F. E. Holzhey (New York, 2014), 55.

4. Johann Georg Hamann, "Metacritique on the Purism of Reason" (1784), in Schmidt, *What Is Enlightenment?*, 154–67. For a sympathetic gloss on Hamann's response to Kant, see Garrett Green, "Modern Culture Comes of Age: Hamann versus Kant on the Root Metaphor of Enlightenment," in Schmidt, *What Is Enlightenment?*, 291–305.

5. Paul R. Harrison, *The Disenchantment of Reason: The Problem of Socrates in Modernity* (Albany, NY, 1994). For another account, see Manfred Frank, "Zwei Jahrhunderte Rationalitäts-Kritik und ihre 'postmoderne' Überbietung," in *Die unvollendete Vernunft: Moderne versus Postmoderne*, ed. Dietmar Kamper and Willem van Reijen (Frankfurt, 1987), 99–121.

6. J. W. Burrow, *The Crisis of Reason: European Thought, 1848–1914* (New Haven, CT, 2000). See also Maurice Mandelbaum, *History, Man, and Reason: A Study in Nineteenth-Century Thought* (Baltimore, MD, 1971), ch. 15, "The Rebellion against Reason."

7. See Thomas E. Willey, *Back to Kant: The Revival of Kantianism in German Social and Historical Thought, 1860–1914* (Detroit, MI, 1978), and Klaus Christian Köhnke, *The Rise of Neo-Kantianism: German Academic Philosophy between Idealism and Positivism*, trans. R. J. Hollingdale (Cambridge, 1991). According to Frederick Beiser, neo-Kantianism was given a mortal blow when its advocates supported the German cause in World War I.

See Beiser, "Weimar Philosophy and the Fate of Neo-Kantianism," in *Weimar Thought: A Contested Legacy*, ed. Peter E. Gordon and John P. McCormick (Princeton, NJ, 2013), 115–32. The coup de grâce was the famous debate in Davos, Switzerland between the neo-Kantian Ernst Cassirer and the phenomenologist Martin Heidegger in 1929, the best account of which can be found in Peter Gordon, *Continental Divide: Heidegger, Cassirer, Davos* (Cambridge, MA, 2010). In interwar France, neo-Kantianism was still a powerful presence in the figures of Léon Brunschvicg and André Lalande. And it should also be acknowledged that there were sporadic renewals of interest in Hegel, for example among late nineteenth-century British philosophers such as T. H. Green, Edward Caird, F. H. Bradley, Harold Joachim, Bernard Bosanquet, D. G. Ritchie, Samuel Alexander, and J. M. E. McTaggart, although their arguments did not survive the critiques of G. E. Moore, Bertrand Russell, and Ludwig Wittgenstein.

8. Martin Kusch, *Psychologism: A Case Study in the Sociology of Philosophical Knowledge* (London, 1995), chs. 7 and 8. He points to the impact of Frege and Husserl. For a discussion of the continuing relevance of logic in another context, that of twentieth-century French thought, see Marcel Boll and Jacques Reinart, "Logic in France in the Twentieth Century," in *Philosophic Thought in France and the United States*, ed. Marvin Farber (Albany, NY, 1968), 181–202.

9. Frederick Brown, *The Embrace of Unreason: France, 1914–1940* (New York, 2014).

10. For analyses of this crisis, see Gerald N. Izenberg, *Impossible Individuality: Romanticism, Revolution, and the Origins of Modern Selfhood, 1787–1802* (Princeton, NJ, 1992), and Jerrold Seigel, *The Idea of the Self: Thought and Experience in Western Europe since the Seventeenth Century* (Cambridge, 2005).

11. See G. S. Rousseau, ed., *Organic Form: The Life of an Idea* (London, 1972). See also the entry on "organic" in Raymond Williams, *Keywords: A Vocabulary of Culture and Society* (New York, 1976), 189–92.

12. That unification was evident in the relationship between life and death and between the mortal individual and the species. In the *Logic*, Hegel noted that "the defect of life lies in its being only the idea implicit or natural; whereas cognition is in an equally one-sided way the merely conscious idea, or the idea for itself. The unity and truth of these two is the Absolute Idea, which is both in itself and for itself." Frederick G. Weiss, ed., *Hegel: The Essential Writings* (New York, 1974), 187. For a discussion of Hegel's early interest in "life," see Herbert Marcuse, *Reason and Revolution: Hegel and the Rise of Social Theory* (Boston, MA, 1960), 37–39.

13. Harrison, *The Disenchantment of Reason*, 188.

14. Peter Hanns Reill, *Vitalizing Nature in the Enlightenment* (Berkeley, CA, 2005).

15. For a discussion of it in the English context, see Raymond Williams, *Culture and Society, 1780–1950* (New York, 1958), where he argues that there are five reasons organic became popular: "to stress an idea of 'wholeness' in society; to stress the growth of a 'people,' as in rising nationalisms; to stress 'natural growth,' as in 'culture,' with particular reference to slow change and adaptation; to reject 'mechanist' and 'materialist' versions of society; to criticize industrialism, in favour of a society 'in close touch with natural processes' (i.e. agriculture)" (264). For a discussion of the continuing relevance of the

organic metaphor in contemporary nationalist and postcolonialist discourse, see Pheng Cheah, *Spectral Nationality: Passages of Freedom from Kant to Postcolonial Literatures of Liberation* (New York, 2003).

16. Johann Wolfgang von Goethe, *Goethe's Faust*, trans. Walter Kaufmann (Garden City, NY, 1961), 207.

17. The misuse of Darwinian evolutionary theory by "social Darwinists" to justify whatever succeeded in a struggle for existence is a familiar story. What needs to be acknowledged, however, is that in some respects it corresponded to Hegel's use of Schiller's dictum that "world history is the world court," insofar as both invest value in the ability to survive the vicissitudes of historical struggle. A further question is the role of reason in the evolutionary struggle for survival, which is argued by commentators such as Robert Nozick, *The Nature of Rationality* (Princeton, NJ, 1993).

18. For an account of Simmel's disdain for Kant and practical reason, see Frederick C. Beiser, *The German Historicist Tradition* (Oxford, 2011), 502–10.

19. Schopenhauer's influence was delayed until his culture was ready for it after 1848, some three decades after his major works. For a discussion, see Rüdiger Safranski, *Schopenhauer and the Wild Years of Philosophy*, trans. Ewald Osers (Cambridge, MA, 1990), ch. 24. Schopenhauer himself rejected the idea that his pessimistic philosophy was somehow an expression of his age, which would have been a capitulation to the Hegelian notion of a unified zeitgeist.

20. Arthur Schopenhauer, "On the Suffering of the World," in *Essays and Aphorisms*, ed. and trans. R. J. Hollingdale (Harmondsworth, 1970), 47–48.

21. Arthur Schopenhauer, *On the Fourfold Root of the Principle of Sufficient Reason*, trans. E. F. J. Payne (La Salle, IL, 1997), 6 and 229. This is a translation of the 1847 second edition, in which Schopenhauer more boldly connects his thesis to his mature philosophy.

22. Schopenhauer, *On the Fourfold Root*, 42.

23. As Heidegger would put it in *The Principle of Reason*, trans. Reginald Lilly (Bloomington, IN, 1996), being appears "not as *ratio*, not as *Ursache* [cause], not as Rational ground and Reason, rather as a letting-lie-present that assembles" (110). Because of Heidegger's suspicion of the biological underpinnings of vitalism, he cannot be grouped as one of its adherents. But he shared in their disdain for rationalism in most of its guises.

24. Harrison, *The Disenchantment of Reason*, 121.

25. As Arthur Danto has pointed out in the case of Nietzsche, "although he is often classified as an antirationalist, Nietzsche in fact opposes reason only when reason is opposed to life, or to whatever makes life possible. Like Hume, he considers that reason is or ought to be the slave of passions. . . . Depreciation of the body motivates depreciation of the senses, and the opposition between sense and reason has its origin in this distrust. Such *theories* of reason, not reason as such, are the target for Nietzsche's antirational attacks." Arthur C. Danto, *Nietzsche as Philosopher* (New York, 1980), 81. For another defense of Nietzsche (and Foucault) against the charge of simple irrationalism, made by critics like Habermas, see Dominique Janicaud, *Rationalities, Historicities*, trans. Nina Belmonte (Atlantic Highlands, NJ, 1997), ch. 3.

Gadamer also notes that "[the vitalist philosopher of history Wilhelm] Dilthey starts with life: life itself is ordered towards reflection. . . . There is knowledge in life itself. . . . Before any scientific objectification, life's natural view of itself is thus developed. It objectivises itself in the wisdom of proverb and legend, but, above all, in the great works of art." Hans-Georg Gadamer, *Truth and Method* (New York, 1986), 207–8. The concept of the "lifeworld" developed by phenomenology and later incorporated into Habermas's notion of "communicative rationality" draws on this understanding of "life" as more than mere biological existence.

26. For a discussion, see Mandelbaum, *History, Man, and Reason*, 312–24.

27. Barbara Hannan, *The Riddle of the World: A Reconsideration of Schopenhauer's Philosophy* (Oxford, 2009), 8.

28. For a recent discussion, see Paul Thagard, "Rationality and Science," in *The Oxford Handbook of Rationality*, ed. Alfred R. Mele and Piers Rawling (Oxford, 2004), 363–79. He discusses controversies over the identification of scientists with "confirmation agents," "falsification agents," "probabilistic agents," and "explanation agents," as well as the role of emotion in scientific judgment and the potential tension between individual and group rationality. Resisting the debunking of science's claims to the disinterested pursuit of truth by "science studies" contextualists, he concludes by arguing that "a useful response to the question 'Is science rational?' is 'Compared to what?'" (379).

29. This phrase became the defiant riposte to "vulgar Marxist" made by Western Marxists such as Georg Lukács and Ernst Bloch. The former, for example, finished the first version of his important essay "What Is Orthodox Marxism?" of 1919 by citing it, and giving Fichte the credit. See Victor Zitta, ed., *Georg Lukács's "Revolution and Counter Revolution (1918–1921)"* (Querétaro, Mexico, 1991), 20. The frequent variation in attribution of the phrase is itself a performative confirmation of its substance.

30. Hans-Georg Gadamer, *Reason in the Age of Science*, trans. Frederick G. Lawrence (Cambridge, MA, 1983), 25.

31. Theodor W. Adorno et al., *The Positivist Dispute in German Sociology*, trans. Glyn Adey and David Frisby (London, 1976).

32. For a discussion of the opposition, see Alvin W. Gouldner, *The Two Marxisms: Contradictions and Anomalies in the Development of Theory* (New York, 1980). He resists the argument that Marx was responsible for "critical" Marxism and Engels for its "scientistic" betrayal, an argument that can be found as early as Lukács's *History and Class Consciousness*.

33. Leszek Kołakowski, *The Alienation of Reason: A History of Positivist Thought*, trans. Norbert Guterman (Garden City, NY, 1969).

34. Marcuse, *Reason and Revolution*, 325–28.

35. Adorno, introduction to *The Positivist Dispute*, 51.

36. Foucault first introduced the concept in *The History of Sexuality*, vol. 1, *An Introduction*, trans. Robert Hurley (New York, 1978), 141–45. It has been developed in numerous ways in connection with his concept of governmentality. It should be noted, however, that Foucault, for all of his stress on the link between knowledge and power, was never a simple irrationalist. Instead, he argued that the main theoretical problem since the eighteenth century has been "*What* is this Reason that we use? What are its historical

effects? What are its limits, and what are its dangers? How can we exist as rational beings, fortunately committed to practicing a rationality that is unfortunately crisscrossed by intrinsic dangers? One should remain as close to this question as possible, keeping in mind that it is both central and extremely difficult to resolve. In addition, if it is extremely dangerous to say that Reason is the enemy that should be eliminated, it is just as dangerous to say that any critical questioning of this rationality risks sending us into irrationality." "Space, Time, and Power," in *The Foucault Reader*, ed. Paul Rabinow (New York, 1984), 249.

37. Georg Lukács, *The Destruction of Reason*, trans. Peter Palmer (Atlantic Highlands, NJ, 1981). Attempts have been made to salvage the value of aspects of its argument, but it is difficult to accept its wholesale condemnation of some of the most subtle minds in European thought. For the most recent defense, see Stanley Aronowitz, "Georg Lukács' *Destruction of Reason*," in Michael J. Thompson, *Georg Lukács Reconsidered: Critical Essays in Politics, Philosophy, and Aesthetics* (New York, 2011).

38. See Nancy Cartwright et al., *Otto Neurath: Philosophy between Science and Politics* (Cambridge, 1996). In the 1930s, when both were in exile in New York, Horkheimer and Neurath had a fraught relationship. See the discussion in Karl-Heinz Barck, "The Neurath-Horkheimer Controversy Reconsidered: Otto Neurath's *Erwiderung* to Max Horkheimer's Attack against the Vienna Circle," in *Otto Neurath and the Unity of Science*, ed. John Symons, Olga Pombo, and Juan Manuel Torres (Dordrecht, 2011), 31–40.

39. H. Stuart Hughes, *Consciousness and Society: The Reorientation of European Social Thought, 1890–1930* (New York, 1958). Not all social scientists during this era, of course, turned their backs on positivism or saw it as incompatible with reason. Émile Durkheim, in fact, contended that "the sole [label] we accept is that of rationalism. Indeed, our chief aim is to extend scientific rationalism to human behavior by showing that, considered in the past, it is reducible to relations of cause and effect—relations that a no less rational operation can then transform into rules of action for the future. Our so-called positivism is nothing but a consequence of this rationalism." Quoted in Steven Lukes, *Émile Durkheim, His Life and Work: A Historical and Critical Study* (London, 1973), 72–73.

40. Hughes spends more time on a nuanced presentation of Croce than Lukács, concluding that "certainly it would be a great error to call Croce a Hegelian. But one can argue that Hegel was responsible for the most doubtful features of Croce's thought—its tendency towards a schematic rationalism and its insistence on the pervasive role of a quasi-deity called 'the spirit.'" Hughes, *Consciousness and Society*, 208.

41. Max Weber, *The Theory of Social and Economic Organization*, ed. Talcott Parsons, trans. A. M. Henderson and Talcott Parsons (New York, 1947), 92. For a comparison of Weber with Nietzsche and Foucault on the question of reason, see David Owen, *Maturity and Modernity: Nietzsche, Weber, Foucault, and the Ambivalence of Reason* (London, 1994).

42. Sigmund Freud, *New Introductory Lectures on Psychoanalysis*, trans. and ed. James Strachey (New York, 1965), 80. In the reception of Freud's theories, there has been, of course, a strong resistance to "ego psychology," which expressed waning confidence in the possibility and even value of a strong rational ego. For a succinct discussion of the difference on this question between "modern" and "postmodern" psychoanalysis, see

Alfred I. Tauber, "Freud's Social Theory: Modernist and Postmodernist Revisions," *History of the Human Sciences* 25, no. 4 (October 2012): 43–72.

43. Freud's uncertain faith in the ultimate triumph of reason can be discerned in his evolving attitude toward the waning of religious faith. The relative optimism of *The Future of an Illusion* (1927) was superseded by the darker conclusions of *Civilization and Its Discontents* (1929), which grew even bleaker with the growing power of fascism.

44. This insight is later repeated by Dominique Janicaud: "The affective responsibilities and quasi-religious investments in rationalism strangely allow it to forget a truth of experience: in reasoning too much (or reasoning tangentially to that which is in question), one falls into the absurd (or even worse); excessive rationality—one could say—is paranoid. Rationality itself *can* be paranoid; does its hubris lie in this originary potentialization—or elsewhere?" *Powers of the Rational: Science, Technology, and the Future of Thought*, trans. Peg Birmingham and Elizabeth Birmingham (Bloomington, IN, 1994), 22–23.

45. According to Gerald Izenberg, Wordsworth wrote in 1805 about "the rationalist fetishizing of reason for defensive purposes, as a disguise for the irrational." *Impossible Individuality*, 191.

46. Ernest Jones, "Rationalization in Every-Day Life," *Journal of Abnormal Psychology* 3, no. 3 (1908): 161–69.

47. Even before the impact of Frederick Winslow Taylor's rationalization of labor in America, a comparable effort was made in Europe. See Anson Rabinbach, *The Human Motor: Energy, Fatigue, and the Origins of Modernity* (Los Angeles, CA, 1992).

48. For a discussion of the pervasive crisis of humanism, which concentrates on interwar France, see Stefanos Geroulanos, *An Atheism That Is Not Humanist Emerges in French Thought* (Stanford, CA, 2010).

49. Julien Benda, *The Treason of the Intellectuals*, trans. Richard Aldington (New York, 2011).

50. Georges Sorel, *Reflections on Violence*, trans. T. E. Hulme (London, 1970). The term "romantic anti-capitalism" was introduced by Lukács, partly to describe his own pre-Marxist inclinations. For an attempt to redeem it, see Robert Sayre and Michel Löwy, "Figures of Romantic Anti-Capitalism," *New German Critique* 32 (Spring–Summer 1984): 42–92.

51. Georges Bataille, "The Solar Anus" and "The Rotten Sun," both in *Visions of Excess: Selected Writings, 1927–1939*, ed. and trans. Allan Stoekl (Minneapolis, MN, 1985), 5–9, 57–58.

52. Siegfried Kracauer, "The Mass Ornament," in *The Mass Ornament: Weimar Essays*, ed. and trans. Thomas Y. Levin (Cambridge, MA, 1995), 81. He went on to say that capitalism's "core defect" is that "it rationalizes not too much but rather *too little*" but did not really spell out what a sufficient rationalization would mean.

53. Peter Sloterdijk, *Critique of Cynical Reason*, trans. Michael Eldred (Minneapolis, MN, 1987), 311.

54. His larger statement is worth citing in full: "Rationality is the capacity to generalize, which beasts don't have: as Locke said, 'Brutes abstract not.' Rationality is a capacity

for following logical arguments, for being consistent, for knowing what means lead to what ends (which is empirical knowledge), for needing to give reasons for what you do, which means giving reasons in terms ultimately of the ends you pursue, which we then examine to consider whether they really are ends which you think you are justified in pursuing, given how many other ends may be excluded. All that is rational, but a rational end which everybody else talks about—a rational purpose which is a well-known philosophical concept (it has existed since Plato's day) is to me not intelligible. I think ends are ends. People pursue what they pursue." Isaiah Berlin, "In Conversation with Steven Lukes," *Salmagundi* 120 (Fall 1998): 118.

55. It appeared as well in anti-Soviet leftist critiques, for example, C. L. R. James and Raya Dunayevskaya, *State Capitalism and World Revolution* (Chicago, IL, 1986), ch. 11, which argues that rationalism is "the philosophy of Stalinism." The book was first published in 1950 and credited to the "Johnson-Forest Tendency," a Trotskyist splinter group.

56. Max Horkheimer, "The Rationalism Debate in Contemporary Philosophy" (1934), in *Between Philosophy and Social Science: Selected Early Writings*, trans. G. Frederick Hunter, Matthew S. Kramer, and John Torpey (Cambridge, MA, 1993).

57. Ibid., 219.

58. This point is forcefully made by John Abromeit in *Max Horkheimer and the Foundations of the Frankfurt School* (Cambridge, 2011), ch. 3, which situates this essay among others he did in the history of Western philosophy at around the same time.

59. Later in the essay, Horkheimer suggests in passing that one of the progressive moments in their work can be found in "the relation of their concept of intuition to the history of rationalism, and in particular to the philosophy of Spinoza." "The Rationalism Debate," 229. This remark suggests a certain sympathy for a noetic as opposed to dianoetic concept of reason.

60. Ibid., 221.

61. Ibid., 222.

62. As he notes later in the essay, "In *Lebensphilosophie*, thought—which it accuses of being destructive—is understood in a particular form, namely as conceptually dissecting, comparative, explanatory, generalizing thought: in short, as analysis. To that extent the critique has a certain justification, for a number of rationalist systems have in fact confused this type of thought with intellectual activity *tout court*." "The Rationalistic Debate," 232.

63. Ibid., 227.

64. Ibid., 250. But then he added later in the essay, "materialist thought cannot offer a view of the problem of sacrifice that is valid once and for all. . . . It is not oriented merely to the self-preservation of the individual. For materialism, existence is by no means the highest or the only end" (258).

65. Ibid., 239.

66. Quoted in ibid., 240.

67. Ibid., 259.

68. Ibid., 260.

69. Ibid., 264.

70. Bertolt Brecht had written of "living in dark times" in his famous 1939 exile poem "An die Nachgeborenen" ("To Posterity"), and Hannah Arendt used it for the title of her *Men in Dark Times*.

## Chapter 5. The Critique of Instrumental Reason

1. For some commentators, the emphatic, objective, or substantive concept should be called "reason," while the instrumental, formal, or subjective alternative is better designated as "rationality," but in the usage of the figures we are discussing, no such terminological distinction was made.

2. For a nuanced account of the role of rationality in Horkheimer's work during this period, see Hauke Brunkhorst, "Dialectical Positivism of Happiness: Max Horkheimer's Materialist Deconstruction of Philosophy," in *On Max Horkheimer: New Perspectives*, ed. Seyla Benhabib, Wolfgang Bonss, and John McCole (Cambridge, MA, 1993), 67–98.

3. Richard Wolin, "Critical Theory and the Dialectic of Rationalism," in *The Terms of Cultural Criticism: The Frankfurt School, Existentialism, Poststructuralism* (New York, 1992), 26. For another overview of the changes in Critical Theory's ideas of reason, see Peter Uwe Hohendahl, "From the Eclipse of Reason to Communicative Rationality and Beyond," in *Critical Theory: Current State and Future Prospects*, ed. Peter Uwe Hohendahl and Jaimey Fisher (New York, 2001), 3–28. It should be noted that one important associate of the Institut für Sozialforschung, Walter Benjamin, never accepted his colleagues' emphasis on reason, preferring, as he put it in his admiring essay of 1929 on "Surrealism," "to win the energies of intoxication for the revolution." *Reflections: Essays, Aphorisms, Autobiographical Writings*, ed. Peter Demetz, trans. Edmund Jephcott (New York, 1978), 189. To be fair to Benjamin, he then added, "to place the accent exclusively on it would be to subordinate the methodical and disciplinary preparation for revolution entirely to a praxis oscillating between fitness exercises and celebration in advance." But significantly, in an earlier letter to his friend Christian Florens Rang (December 9, 1923), he had written about ahistorical "ideas" revealed by works of art in the following way: "the ideas are stars, in contrast to the sun of revelation. They do not appear in the daylight of history; they are at work in history only invisibly. They shine only into the night of nature. Works of art, then, may be defined as the models of a nature that awaits no day, and thus no Judgment Day; they are the models of a nature that is neither the theater of history nor the dwelling place of mankind. The redeemed night." Walter Benjamin, *Selected Writings*, vol. 1, *1913–1926*, ed. Marcus Bullock and Michael W. Jennings (Cambridge, MA, 1996), 389.

4. Max Horkheimer, "The Latest Attack on Metaphysics," in *Critical Theory: Selected Essays*, trans. Matthew O'Connell (New York, 1972), 148.

5. Herbert Marcuse, "Philosophy and Critical Theory," in *Negations: Essays in Critical Theory*, trans. Jeremy J. Shapiro (Boston, MA, 1968), 135.

6. Herbert Marcuse, *Reason and Revolution: Hegel and the Rise of Social Theory* (Boston, MA, 1960), 5. Later in his narrative, Marcuse would argue that the more materialist

Marx had replaced reason with happiness as his governing principle (293), but he himself saw them as fully compatible goals as subsequent works like *Eros and Civilization* (1955) made clear.

7. Karl Marx to Arnold Ruge, September 1843, in *The Portable Karl Marx*, ed. Eugene Kamenka (New York, 1983), 95.

8. On the tensions, which were caused by the Institute's financial situation and need to downsize, as well as by substantive issues, see Rolf Wiggershaus, *The Frankfurt School: Its History, Theories, and Political Significance*, trans. Michael Robertson (Cambridge, MA, 1994), 263–64. Adorno's growing ascendency in the Institute in the early 1940s meant a corresponding marginalization of Marcuse, whose work he privately disparaged. See his letter to Walter Benjamin of April 25, 1937, in Theodor W. Adorno and Walter Benjamin, *The Complete Correspondence, 1928–1940*, ed. Henri Lonitz, trans. Nicholas Walker (Cambridge, MA, 1999), 180. In public, however, the Institute presented a united front against critics like the American pragmatist Sidney Hook. See the discussion in Thomas Wheatland, *The Frankfurt School in Exile* (Minneapolis, MN, 2009), ch. 3.

9. The essay first appeared in the Institute's renamed journal *Studies in Philosophy and Social Science* 9, no. 3 (1941): 366–88. According to Habermas, "Although Adorno was already involved in editing the proofs for 'The End of Reason,' both of the essays Horkheimer published in the Benjamin memorial volume testify to the fact that Horkheimer's interest in a direct collaboration with Adorno arose from the course of his own development." "Remarks on the Development of Horkheimer's Work," in Benhabib, Bonss, and McCole, *On Max Horkheimer*, 55.

10. Max Horkheimer, "The End of Reason," in *The Essential Frankfurt School Reader*, ed. Andrew Arato and Eike Gebhardt (New York, 1978), 26.

11. Ibid., 27.

12. Ibid., 28.

13. Herbert Marcuse, "Some Social Implications of Modern Technology," *Studies in Philosophy and Social Science* 9, no. 3 (1941): 414–39. In *Reason and Revolution*, Marcuse still included the domination of nature in the type of rational control favored by Hegel and Marx. See, for example, his remarks on 254.

14. Horkheimer, "The End of Reason," 28.

15. Ibid., 31.

16. Ibid., 36.

17. Ibid., 46.

18. Ibid., 48. Luxemburg, of course, had contrasted socialism, not freedom, with barbarism, but Horkheimer had grown more circumspect in his American exile. Only a year earlier, in his privately circulated essay "The Authoritarian State," he had more optimistically argued that because "the material conditions for socialism have been realized . . . the alternative depends only on human will." Horkheimer, "The Authoritarian State," in Arato and Gebhardt, *The Essential Frankfurt School Reader*, 116.

19. Max Horkheimer, "Reason against Itself: Some Remarks on Enlightenment," in *What Is Enlightenment? Eighteenth-Century Answers and Twentieth-Century Questions*, ed. James Schmidt (Berkeley, CA, 1996), 359.

20. Ibid., 360.

21. Ibid., 367. For a recent attempt to develop the implications of emancipation from the fear of despair, see Robyn Marasco, *The Highway of Despair: Critical Theory after Hegel* (New York, 2015).

22. The commentary on *Dialectic of Enlightenment* is enormous. There is even a recent guide for beginners titled *How to Read Adorno and Horkheimer's Dialectic of Enlightenment (How to Read Theory)* by Nicholas R. Lawrence (London, 2012).

23. Commenting on alternative titles, James Schmidt writes, "*The Agony of Reason, Subjectivation of Reason* and *Objective and Subjective Reason* were considered and found wanting. *Twilight of Reason* was provisionally adopted, although by February, Horkheimer had misgivings: it was too close to the title of 'The End of Reason,' it reminded him of *Götter-dämmerung*, it was 'too pessimistic.' . . . In the end, Philip Vaudrin, an Oxford editor, suggested the final title." "The *Eclipse of Reason* and the End of the Frankfurt School in America," *New German Critique* 34, no. 1 100 (Winter 2007): 65. In this exhaustively researched essay, Schmidt details the difficulties Horkheimer had in composing the book and the disappointing reception it received on publication.

24. Max Horkheimer, *Eclipse of Reason* (New York, 1947), 6.

25. Ibid., 4. It should be noted that the distinction between subjective and objective reason has not always been understood in precisely the same way. Thus, for example, the French philosopher Dominique Janicaud was to posit the following alternative definitions: "subjective reason does not here mean only the reason, or pseudoreason, of individual subjectivity; and the field of objective reason is not to be limited to apodictic or experimentally proven truths. Rather *subjective reason* is understood here as the relation that rationality as such maintains with itself, the modes of its self-affirmation (traditionally called dogmatism), its skeptical holding-in-suspense, its appropriation of its own contradictions. The Kantian transcendental dialectic elaborates the problematic of subjective reason in this sense. *Objective reason* will designate a concern with the products of collective rational activity and its corresponding institutions: in short all the 'spiritual' formations (in the Hegelian sense) that result, for humanity and in an historically observable form, from the development of a positive scientific rationality." *Rationalities, Historicities*, trans. Nina Belmonte (Atlantic Highlands, NJ, 1997), 22.

26. Horkheimer, *Eclipse of Reason*, 7.

27. Ibid., 11.

28. Ibid., 68.

29. Ibid., 10. Habermas would also find the standard of mere "reasonableness," which was upheld by liberals like John Rawls, too weak as a source of critique. See his "Reconciliation through the Public Use of Reason" and "'Reasonable' Versus 'True,' or the Morality of Worldviews," both in Jürgen Habermas, *The Inclusion of the Other: Studies in Political Theory*, ed. Ciaran Cronin and Pablo De Greiff (Oxford, 2002), 49–101. In legal theory, the appeal to the "reasonable man" has also been subject to serious critique. See Michael Saltman, *The Demise of the "Reasonable Man": A Cross-Cultural Study of a Legal Concept* (New Brunswick, NJ, 1991).

30. Ibid., 176.

31. Georg Lohmann, "The Failure of Self-Realization: An Interpretation of Hork-heimer's *Eclipse of Reason*," in Benhabib, Bonss, and McCole, *On Max Horkheimer*, 407.

32. Horkheimer, *Eclipse of Reason*, 62.

33. Although Kant was a target of Adorno and Horkheimer's scorn in the 1940s, in later years they came to appreciate many of his virtues as a bulwark against Hegel's overly optimistic totalization of reason. For a discussion of Adorno's changing attitudes in particular, see Peter Uwe Hohendahl, *The Fleeting Promise of Art: Adorno's Aesthetic Theory Revisited* (Ithaca, NY, 2013), ch. 1.

34. Horkheimer, *Eclipse of Reason*, 123.

35. Ibid., 133.

36. Ibid., 174.

37. Ibid.

38. Ibid., 187.

39. As Stefan Breuer notes, "it is precisely the idea of objective reason—which Horkheimer himself characterizes as obsolete—around which his own critique of civiliza-tion is organized. . . . The line that separates this conception from conservative cultural criticism is thinner than Horkheimer may have recognized." "The Long Friendship: Theoretical Differences between Horkheimer and Adorno," in Benhabib, Bonss, and McCole, *On Max Horkheimer*, 265–66. Not surprisingly, there was an increased appeal to the religious legacy in the late Horkheimer as a reserve of protest against instrumental reason.

40. Lohmann, "The Failure of Self-Realization," 390.

41. See Herbert Schnädelbach, *Vernunft* (Stuttgart, 2007), 116–19.

42. Seyla Benhabib, *Critique, Norm, and Utopia: A Study of the Foundations of Critical Theory* (New York, 1986), 171.

43. Theodor W. Adorno, *Negative Dialectics*, trans. E. B. Ashton (New York, 1973), 317–18.

44. Ibid.

45. Walter Benjamin, "On the Mimetic Faculty" and "Doctrine of the Similar," both written in 1933, in *Selected Writings*, vol. 2, part 2, ed. Michael W. Jennings, Gary Smith, and Howard Eiland (Cambridge, MA, 2005), 720–22 and 694–98. For discussions of Adorno's development of the argument, see Martin Jay, "Mimesis and Mimetology: Adorno and Lacoue-Labarthe," in *Cultural Semantics: Keywords of Our Time* (Amherst, MA, 1998), 120–37, and Artemy Magun, "Negativity (Dis)embodied: Philippe Lacoue-Labarthe and Theodor W. Adorno on Mimesis," *New German Critique* 40, no. 1 118 (Winter 2013): 119–48.

46. Theodor W. Adorno, *Hegel: Three Studies*, trans. Shierry Weber Nicholsen (Cam-bridge, MA, 1993), 41. *Adaequatio* refers to the Thomist formula *veritas est adaequatio intellec-tus et rei*, truth is the adequation of what is in the mind with the thing.

47. Foucault himself came to see the connection. In an interview he gave to Duccio Trombadori in 1978, he remarked, "Couldn't it be concluded that the promise of *Aufklärung* (Enlightenment), of attaining freedom through the exercise of reason, has been, on the contrary, overturned within the domain of Reason itself, that it is taking

more and more space away from freedom? . . . This problem, as we know, was signaled out by Horkheimer before the others; it was the Frankfurt School that measured its relationship with Marx on the basis of this hypothesis." Michel Foucault, *Remarks on Marx: Conversations with Duccio Trombadori*, trans. R. James Goldstein and James Cascaito (New York, 1991), 118. For cogent comparisons of Foucault with the Frankfurt School, see Axel Honneth, *The Critique of Power: Reflective Stages in a Critical Social Theory*, trans. Kenneth Baynes (Cambridge, MA, 1991); Thomas McCarthy, *Ideals and Illusions: On Reconstruction and Deconstruction in Contemporary Critical Theory* (Cambridge, MA, 1991), ch. 2; and Beatrice Hanssen, "Critical Theory and Post-Structuralism: Habermas and Foucault," in *The Cambridge Companion to Critical Theory*, ed. Fred Rush (Cambridge, 2004), 280–309. The challenge Habermas faced was how to acknowledge the embeddedness of reason in the world without then making it a mere function of power or self-interest or any other more fundamental motivation.

48. Freud, of course, is often taken to be a potent source of the disillusionment with rationality. Thus, for example, Albrecht Wellmer writes, "the psychological critique—in which the central figure is, of course, Freud—consists in demonstrating the *factual* impotence or non-existence of the 'autonomous' subject, and in demonstrating *as fact* the irrational nature of its putative reason. This involves the discovery of an *Other* of reason within the subject and its reason." *The Persistence of Modernity: Essays on Aesthetics, Ethics, and Postmodernism*, trans. David Midgley (Cambridge, MA, 1991), 58.

49. Axel Honneth, "A Social Pathology of Reason: The Legacy of Critical Theory," in *Pathologies of Reason: On the Legacy of Critical Theory*, trans. James Ingram et al. (New York, 2009), 38. Honneth, however, also acknowledges that Horkheimer and other Institute figures like Franz Neumann often adopted a simplistic "psychological rationalism that regards every psychical dissolution, every opening for unregulated affects, as a symptom of relapse into irrational behavior" (152).

50. Marcuse's initial response to *Eclipse of Reason* was a ratification of its bleak prognosis. In a letter to Horkheimer of July 18, 1947, he wrote: "I've read your book. At this point I'll only say that I agree with you completely. If only you could soon fully develop all of the perspectives you could only hint at there—especially those that worry me the most: that idea that reason, which has become total manipulation and power, even then remains reason, that the real horror of the system therefore lies more in rationality than irrationality." Herbert Marcuse, *Technology, War, and Fascism: Collected Papers of Herbert Marcuse*, ed. Douglas Kellner (London, 1998), 1:256.

51. Herbert Marcuse, *Eros and Civilization: A Philosophical Inquiry into Freud* (Boston, MA, 1955), 204. Marcuse's continuing adherence to the assumptions of *Reason and Revolution* are evident, inter alia, in *Soviet Marxism: A Critical Analysis* (New York, 1958), ch. 7, and *One-Dimensional Man: Studies in the Ideology of Advanced Industrial Society* (Boston, MA, 1964), ch. 5. He also mobilized Edmund Husserl's *The Crisis of European Sciences and Transcendental Phenomenology* to make a similar argument. See his "On Science and Phenomenology" (1965), in Arato and Gebhardt, *The Essential Frankfurt School Reader*. His roots in the phenomenological critique of technical rationality, in particular that of his mentor Martin Heidegger, are explored in Andrew Feenberg, *Heidegger and Marcuse: The Catastrophe and*

*Redemption of History* (New York, 2005). Habermas would also acknowledge Husserl's defense of reason against its current variant. See his "The German Idealism of the Jewish Philosophers," in *Religion and Rationality: Essays on Reason, God, and Modernity*, ed. Eduardo Mendieta (Cambridge, MA, 2002), 47.

52. Marcuse, *Eros and Civilization*, 101.

53. Joel Whitebook, *Perversion and Utopia: A Study in Psychoanalysis and Critical Theory* (Cambridge, MA, 1995), 41.

54. Richard J. Bernstein, "Negativity: Themes and Variations," in *Marcuse: Critical Theory and the Promise of Utopia*, ed. Robert Pippin, Andrew Feenberg, and Charles P. Webel (South Hadley, MA, 1988), 23.

55. Habermas's defense of the Enlightenment is widely appreciated, but despite his strong critique in *Dialectic of Enlightenment*, Adorno also drew on that strain in the *Aufklärung* that sought to rescue a notion of rationality by turning to aesthetics. Robert Hullot-Kentor goes as far as to argue that "the division between reason and the aesthetic, which Habermas seeks to establish in Adorno's work, is a division drawn and insisted upon by Habermas, not Adorno. Paradoxically, by insisting on this division Habermas separates himself from the Enlightenment tradition. For throughout the German Enlightenment, and especially since Kant, the defense of reason has been conceived not just as inseparable from but ultimately as dependent on the aesthetic." *Things Beyond Resemblance: Collected Essays on Theodor W. Adorno* (New York, 2006), 32.

56. In his 1956 "Aspects of Hegel's Philosophy," Adorno wondered "whether perhaps the reason one imagines one has attained since Hegel's absolute reason has not in fact long since regressed behind the latter and accommodated to what merely exists, when Hegelian reason tried to set the burden of existence in motion through the reason that obtains even in what exists." *Hegel*, 1. But in his 1964–65 lectures on "History and Freedom," he would write, "The incomparable greatness of Kant consists not least in the way in which he incorruptibly held on to the unity of reason even in its contradictory form: reason as the domination of nature, or in what he called its theoretical, causal-mechanical aspect, and reason as the conciliatory power of judgment that moulds itself to the contours of nature. He rigorously translated the difference between them into the self-limitation of the rationality that dominates nature. . . . This was something that Hegel, the dialectician par excellence, failed to appreciate because, in his belief in a *single* reason, he erased this boundary line and so drifted into the mythical totality that he thought of as 'sublated,' 'reconciled,' in the absolute idea." Theodor W. Adorno, *History and Freedom: Lectures 1964–1965*, ed. Rolf Tiedemann, trans. Rodney Livingstone (Cambridge, 2006), 158. For Habermas's nuanced pitting of Hegel against Kant, see, for example, "From Kant to Hegel and Back Again: The Move toward Detranscendentalization," in *Truth and Justification*, ed. and trans. Barbara Fultner (Cambridge, MA, 2005), 175–212.

57. For accounts of their respective positions, see Hent de Vries, *Minimal Theologies: Critiques of Secular Reason in Adorno and Levinas*, trans. Geoffrey Hale (Baltimore, MD, 2005), and Craig Calhoun, Eduardo Mendieta, and Jonathan Van Antwerpen, eds., *Habermas and Religion* (Cambridge, 2013).

58. Habermas, "Remarks," 58.

59. Habermas, *Religion and Rationality*, 96.

60. Adorno, "Reason and Revelation," in *Critical Models: Interventions and Catchwords*, trans. Henry W. Pickford (New York, 1998), 138.

61. Theodor W. Adorno, *Aesthetic Theory*, ed. Gretel Adorno and Rolf Tiedemann, trans. Robert Hullot-Kentor (Minneapolis, MN, 1997), 305.

62. Adorno, *History and Freedom*, 41.

63. Nietzsche, in fact, had misquoted it as "une promesse *de* bonheur," rather than "*du*," and the Frankfurt School adopted his usage. For a discussion, see James Gordon Finlayson, "The Artwork and the *Promesse du Bonheur* in Adorno," *European Journal of Philosophy* (2012), http://jamesgordonfinlayson.net/the-artwork-and-the-promesse-du-bonheur-in-adorno.

64. J. M. Bernstein, "'The Dead Speaking of Stones and Stars': Adorno's *Aesthetic Theory*," in Rush, *Cambridge Companion to Critical Theory*, 144.

65. Adorno, *Aesthetic Theory*, 306.

66. Ibid., 330.

67. Terry Eagleton, *The Ideology of the Aesthetic* (Oxford, 1990), 351.

68. Adorno, *Aesthetic Theory*, 306.

69. Ibid.

70. Ibid.

71. Ibid., 289.

72. Ibid.

73. The issue of the "other" of reason was brought to the fore in the German debate by Gernot and Hermut Böhme, *Das Andere der Vernunft: Zur Entwicklung von Rationalitäts-strukturen am Beispiel Kant* (Frankfurt, 1985). For further elaborations of the issue, see Dieter Freundlieb and Wayne Hudson, eds., *Reason and Its Other: Rationality in Modern German Philosophy and Culture* (Providence, RI, 1993). Habermas responded to the Böhmes in *The Philosophical Discourse of Modernity: Twelve Lectures*, trans. Frederick Lawrence (Cambridge, MA, 1987), 301–2.

74. Axel Honneth, "A Physiognomy of the Capitalist Form of Life: A Sketch of Adorno's Social Theory," in *Pathologies of Reason*, 61.

75. Ibid.

76. Adorno, *Negative Dialectics*, 183–86.

77. Bernstein, "The Dead Speaking," 155.

78. Adorno, *Negative Dialectics*, 408. For an insightful gloss on the implications of this solidarity, see Albrecht Wellmer, "Metaphysics at the Moment of Its Fall," in *Endgames: The Irreconcilable Nature of Modernity; Essays and Lectures*, trans. David Midgley (Cambridge, MA, 1998).

79. Herbert Schnädelbach, "Dialektik als Vernunftkritik," in *Adorno-Konferenz 1983*, ed. Ludwig von Friedeburg and Jürgen Habermas (Frankfurt, 1983), 75.

80. Theodor W. Adorno, *Minima Moralia: Reflections from Damaged Life*, trans. E. F. N. Jephcott (London, 1974), 70–71.

81. According to the deconstructionist literary critic J. Hillis Miller, commenting on the German word for aphorism, *Sentenz,* "an aphorism lays down the law. . . . An aphorism is an aerolith. It is something hard and self-enclosed that seems to have fallen from the sky, from the silence of infinite spaces, into our human atmosphere." "Aphorism as Instrument of Political Action in Nietzsche," *Parallax* 10, no. 3 (2004): 73. It is, of course, possible to provide a discursive argument for the virtues of aphorisms, as Adorno himself did in his introduction to Heinz Krüger, "Studien über Aphorismus als philosophische Form" (PhD diss., University of Frankfurt, 1956). Alasdair MacIntyre makes the point in *Whose Justice? Which Rationality?* (Notre Dame, IN, 1988) that "an aphorism is not an argument. Gilles Deleuze has called it a 'play of forces' . . ., something by means of which energy is transmitted rather than conclusions reached" (368). For a defense of the noetic quality of Adorno's aphorisms, especially in *Minima Moralia,* see Alexander García Düttmann, *So ist es: Ein philosophischer Kommentar zu Adornos "Minima Moralia"* (Frankfurt, 2004).

82. Theodor W. Adorno and Max Horkheimer, *Towards a New Manifesto,* trans. Rodney Livingstone (New York, 2011).

83. Ibid., 73.

84. Christoph Menke, *The Sovereignty of Art: Aesthetic Negativity in Adorno and Derrida,* trans. Neil Solomon (Cambridge, MA, 1999), 214.

85. Jürgen Habermas, *Postmetaphysical Thinking: Philosophical Essays,* trans. William Mark Hohengarten (Cambridge, MA, 1992), 225.

86. Benhabib, *Critique, Norm, and Utopia,* 218. For a more positive evaluation, see Harro Müller, "Mimetic Rationality: Adorno's Project of a Language of Philosophy," *New German Critique* 36, no. 3 108 (Fall 2009): 85–108.

## Chapter 6. Habermas and the Communicative Turn

1. There were, however, significant tensions between Habermas and both Horkheimer and Adorno during his early years in Frankfurt from 1956 to 1959. For one account, see Matthew G. Specter, *Habermas: An Intellectual Biography* (Cambridge, 2010), 29–34.

2. Jürgen Habermas, *Die Neue Unübersichtlichkeit* (Frankfurt, 1985), 136.

3. Herbert Schnädelbach, "Remarks about Rationality and Language," in *The Communicative Ethics Controversy,* ed. Seyla Benhabib and Fred Dallmayr (Cambridge, MA, 1990), 270. The earlier generation of Critical Theorists were, of course, not indifferent to linguistic issues. Adorno in particular understood the delicate dialectic of form and content in his own writing. For an analysis, see Steven Helmling, *Adorno's Poetics of Critique* (London, 2009). But unlike Habermas, they did not systematically develop a theory of language as the normative source of rationality.

4. It has often been claimed that without the capacity to utter propositional sentences, expressing beliefs that can be judged as rational or not, humans would not be capable of reason. The distinction between rational humans and irrational animals is

sometimes based on the ability to possess language. See the discussion in Kirk Ludwig, "Rationality, Language, and the Principle of Charity," in *The Oxford Handbook of Rationality*, ed. Alfred R. Mele and Piers Rawling (Oxford, 2004), 343–62. But to the extent that language can be understood as an opaque, impersonal system subtending the utterances of its users or a rhetorical tool for the emotional persuasion of interlocutors, it could also be considered an obstacle to rationality.

5. Johann Georg Hamann, "Metacritique on the Purism of Reason" (1784), in *What Is Enlightenment? Eighteenth-Century Answers and Twentieth-Century Questions*, ed. James Schmidt (Berkeley, CA, 1996), 154–67. For a good introduction to Hamann's critique of Kant, see Cristina Lafont, *The Linguistic Turn in Hermeneutic Philosophy*, trans. José Medina (Cambridge, MA, 1999), ch. 1.

6. To their opponents the result was often characterized as dangerously irrationalist, a charge they often rejected. To take only one example, Jacques Derrida would claim that "deconstruction, if something of the sort exists, would remain above all, in my view, an unconditional rationalism that never renounces—and precisely in the name of the Enlightenment to come, in the space to be opened up of a democracy to come—the possibility of suspending in an argued, deliberated, rational fashion, all conditions, hypotheses, conventions and presuppositions, and of criticizing unconditionally all conditionalities, including those that still found the critical idea, namely those of the *krinein*, of the *krisis*, of the binary or dialectical decision or judgment." *Rogues: Two Essays on Reason*, trans. Pascale-Anne Brault and Michael Naas (Stanford, CA, 2005), 142.

7. Max Horkheimer, "Zum Begriff der Vernunft," (1952) in *Gesammelte Schriften*, vol. 7, *Vorträge und Aufzeichnungen, 1949–1973*, ed. Gunzelin Schmid Noerr (Frankfurt, 1985), 30. The only figure in the orbit of the earlier Frankfurt School who had stressed the importance of language was Walter Benjamin, whose remarkable 1916 essay "On Language as Such and on the Language of Man" remained, however, unpublished in his lifetime. Its essentially theological defense of an Adamic language that is more basic than the communicative medium of human interaction sets it very far apart from Habermas's universal pragmatics.

8. See, for example, Theodor W. Adorno, "Subject and Object," in *The Essential Frankfurt School Reader*, ed. Andrew Arato and Eike Gebhardt (New York, 1978), 500. For appreciations of his reflections on language and his own rhetorical practice, see Gerhard Richter, "Aesthetic Theory and Non-Propositional Truth Content in Adorno," and Samir Gandesha, "The 'Aesthetic Dignity of Words': Adorno's Philosophy of Language," *New German Critique* 33, no. 1 97 (Winter 2006): 119–35 and 137–58, respectively.

9. Jürgen Habermas, *Theory and Practice*, trans. John Viertel (London, 1974), 276–82. Popper's falsificationist theory of science was pitted against the verificationist alternative associated with positivism, but the Frankfurt School lumped them together as examples of an impoverished version of undialectical reason excessively beholden to the model of the natural sciences.

10. Jürgen Habermas, "A Reply to My Critics," in *Habermas: Critical Debates*, ed. John B. Thompson and David Held (Cambridge, MA, 1982), 238.

11. Specter, *Habermas*, 88.

12. Jürgen Habermas, *The Structural Transformation of the Public Sphere: An Inquiry into a Category of Bourgeois Society*, trans. Thomas Burger and Frederick Lawrence (Cambridge, MA, 1989). The three-decade delay in its translation into English reflected Habermas's growing dissatisfaction with its concluding description of the decline of the public sphere in the twentieth century because of modern media. For a good account of its seminal importance in the development of his theory of communicative reason, see Peter Uwe Hohendahl, *Reappraisals: Shifting Alignments in Postwar Critical Theory* (Ithaca, NY, 1991), ch. 4.

13. For a very long time Habermas was reluctant to discuss these personal origins, but he finally acknowledged them in his acceptance speech for the 2004 Kyoto Prize given by the Inamori Foundation: "Public Space and Political Public Sphere—The Biographical Roots of Two Motifs in My Thought," in *Between Naturalism and Religion: Philosophical Essays*, trans. Ciaran Cronin (Cambridge, 2008), 11–23.

14. Initially, Habermas did not distinguish very strongly between the German word *Verständigung*, which suggests the more modest goal of simply reaching an agreement about the *meaning* of an utterance, and *Einverständnis*, which means a *consensus* about its validity. But by the time of his 1996 essay "Some Further Clarifications of the Concept of Communicative Rationality," in *On the Pragmatics of Communication*, ed. Maeve Cooke (Cambridge, MA, 1998), he had clearly separated them (320–21).

15. Habermas, *Structural Transformation*, 27.

16. Ibid., 83.

17. Albrecht Wellmer pointed out that Adorno shared with Nietzsche a fear that the generality of concepts was the "*proton pseudos* [original lie] of discursive reason," arguing that "the 'rigidity' of the general concept as Adorno describes it, itself remains in a certain sense a rationalistic fiction. Wittgenstein pointed out that, as a rule, the grammar of our language shows us that words can be used in many and various ways, without our always being able to hit upon a 'fundamental,' 'authentic' or 'primary' meaning of words." *The Persistence of Modernity: Essays on Aesthetics, Ethics, and Postmodernism*, trans. David Midgley (Cambridge, MA, 1991), 71.

18. For one account, see Martin Jay, "Should Intellectual History Take a Linguistic Turn? Reflections on the Habermas-Gadamer Debate," in *Fin-de-Siècle Socialism and Other Essays* (New York, 1988), 17–36.

19. Hans-Georg Gadamer, *Reason in the Age of Science*, trans. Frederick G. Lawrence (Cambridge, MA, 1983), 77.

20. Habermas, *Structural Transformation*, 256.

21. Jürgen Habermas, "Consciousness-Raising or Redemptive Criticism—The Contemporaneity of Walter Benjamin," *New German Critique* 17 (Spring 1979): 43.

22. Habermas, *Theory and Practice*, 265.

23. Jürgen Habermas, in "Discussion on Value Freedom and Objectivity," in *Max Weber and Sociology Today*, ed. Otto Stammer (New York, 1971), 64 and 66. Habermas was, however, also heavily influenced by Weber's theory of modernization. See the discussion in Michael Sukale, "Jürgen Habermas und Max Weber: Eine Studie über Wert und Rationalität," in *Das Interesse der Vernunft: Rückblicke auf das Werk von Jürgen Habermas seit "Erkenntnis und Interesse,"* ed. Stefan Müller-Doohm (Frankfurt, 2000), 344–75.

24. Theodor W. Adorno et al., *The Positivist Dispute in German Sociology*, trans. Glyn Adey and David Frisby (London, 1976). In one of his contributions, "A Positivistically Bisected Rationalism," Habermas argued that facts cannot be separated from values, for "as soon as we discuss a problem at all with the aim of reaching a consensus rationally and without constraint, we find ourselves in a dimension of comprehensive rationality which embraces as its moments language and action, statements and attitudes. Critique is always the transition from one moment to another" (219). A further argument he adopted from Karl-Otto Apel against Popper's Critical Rationalism was its neglect of the pragmatic dimension of language in favor of a semantic-syntactical one, which privileged deductive over discursive reasoning. See Jürgen Habermas, *Legitimation Crisis*, trans. Thomas McCarthy (Boston, MA, 1975), 157–58.

25. For the importance of Habermas's repudiation of the goal of full reconciliation between man and nature and among the various differentiated values spheres of modern life, see Axel Honneth, "Communication and Reconciliation: Habermas' Critique of Adorno," *Telos* 39 (Spring 1979): 45–61.

26. Jürgen Habermas, *Toward a Rational Society: Student Protest, Science, and Politics*, trans. Jeremy J. Shapiro (Boston, MA, 1970), 118.

27. Jürgen Habermas, "Psychic Thermidor and the Rebirth of Rebellious Subjectivity," in *Habermas and Modernity*, ed. Richard J. Bernstein (Cambridge, MA, 1985), 75.

28. Jürgen Habermas, *Autonomy and Solidarity: Interviews*, ed. Peter Dews (London, 1986), 105. For a critique of the conflation of German political conservatives with French and other poststructuralists, see Martin Matuštík, *Jürgen Habermas: A Philosophical-Political Profile* (Lanham, MD, 2001), ch. 5.

29. Habermas's sustained animus toward Nietzsche has been challenged by critics who claim he misses the nuances in the latter's attitude toward reason. Dominique Janicaud, for example, writes, "not only does Habermas fail to understand that Nietzsche's vision of scientific rationalization is not a blunt and brutal critique of reason in the name of a subjective or vital *pathos*, but he also fails to see that, if there is a critique of reason in Nietzsche, it is a *self-critique*." *Rationalities, Historicities*, trans. Nina Belmonte (Atlantic Highlands, NJ, 1997), 48.

30. Habermas, *Autonomy and Solidarity*, 102.

31. Jürgen Habermas, *The Philosophical Discourse of Modernity: Twelve Lectures*, trans. Frederick Lawrence (Cambridge, MA, 1987), 111.

32. Ibid., 110.

33. Ibid. For analyses of the critical role of "performative contradiction" in his debate with the poststructuralists, see Martin J. Matuštík, "Habermas on Communicative Reason and Performative Contradiction," *New German Critique* 47 (Spring–Summer 1989): 143–72; and Martin Jay, "The Debate over Performative Contradiction: Habermas vs. the Post-Structuralists," in *Force Fields: Between Intellectual History and Cultural Critique* (New York, 1993), 25–37.

34. Later, Habermas would pull back from the implication that he was equating Adorno with Heidegger. In an interview in *Le Monde* in 1993, he protested, "I would not mention Adorno and Heidegger in the same breath. . . . Adorno knew that even the

most radical critique of reason is dependent on the power of negation, which derives from reason itself. Unlike Heidegger he never became an opponent of the Enlightenment." Jürgen Habermas, *A Berlin Republic: Writings on Germany*, trans. Steven Rendall (Lincoln, NE, 1997), 59. There is a substantial literature now comparing Heidegger and the Frankfurt School, especially Adorno. See, for example, the essays in *Adorno and Heidegger: Philosophical Questions*, ed. Iain Macdonald and Krzysztof Ziarek (Stanford, CA, 2007). On Adorno's debts to and critique of Nietzsche, see Karin Bauer, *Adorno's Nietzschean Narratives: Critiques of Ideology, Readings of Wagner* (Albany, NY, 1999).

35. Habermas, *Philosophical Discourse*, 149.

36. *Dasein* is a term of art for Heidegger with multiple meanings. See the entry on it in Michael Inwood, *A Heidegger Dictionary* (Oxford, 1999), 42–44.

37. Habermas did concede that Adorno had hinted at a communicative notion of reason in one of his "few affirmative utterances concerning the unspoiled [*nicht-verfehltes*] life. When in *Minima Moralia* Adorno actually tries to explain what he means by a mimetic association, not only with nature but also among people, he refers to [Josef Freiherr von] Eichendorff's 'distant nearness.' So he has recourse to categories of intersubjectivity from which he abstains philosophically." *Autonomy and Solidarity*, 99.

38. Summarizing the changes in Habermas's position, which are made clear in *Between Facts and Norms: Contributions to a Discourse Theory of Law and Democracy*, trans. William Rehg (Cambridge, MA, 1996), Lukas Kaelin writes: "he discards the Hegelian-Marxist picture of the entanglement of state and society as too general; he rejects a holistic conception of society in favor of a functionally differentiated one; and he reevaluates the transformation of the public sphere by emphasizing the impact of secondary education, the critical potential of the public, and the interpretation strategies of the public to deal with media content." "Virtual Ignorance: The Blind Spot in German Public Sphere Theory," *New German Critique* 42, no. 1 124 (February 2015): 190.

39. Although Habermas is perhaps the most notable advocate of communicative reason, he was not the first to defend it. Karl Jaspers, for example, wrote in his 1947 *Von der Wahrheit*, "reason is the *total will to communication*. . . . It wants to make authentic communication possible and, hence, seeks to realize the *honesty* whose attributes are unlimited openness and probing, as well as a sense of *justice* that wants all that arises from primal sources to attain its own validity, though also to let it founder against its limits." *Karl Jaspers: Basic Philosophical Writings*, ed. and trans. Edith Ehrlich, Leonard H. Ehrlich, and George B. Pepper (Atlantic Highlands, NJ, 1994), 181.

40. For a typical Habermasian critique of noesis, see "A Conversation about God and World," where he claims "while mystical contemplation is speechless, privileging a mode of intuition or recollection that repudiates the reasonableness of discursive thought, dialectical thought always criticizes the intellectual intuition, the intuitive access to the (supposedly) immediate." Jürgen Habermas, *Religion and Rationality: Essays on Reason, God, and Morality*, ed. Eduardo Mendieta (Cambridge, MA, 2002), 157.

41. The comparison was already made at the beginning of Habermas's career by George Lichtheim, who wrote that he "seems to have been born with a faculty for digesting the toughest kind of material and then refashioning it into orderly wholes.

Hegel, whom he resembles at least in his appetite for encyclopaedic knowledge, possessed this capacity in the highest degree, but he was cursed with an abominable style and a perverse fondness for obscurity, whereas Habermas writes as clearly and concisely as any empiricist." *From Marx to Hegel* (New York, 1971), 175.

42. Theodor W. Adorno, *Minima Moralia: Reflections from Damaged Life*, trans. E. F. N. Jephcott (London, 1974), 50. For a discussion of the tradition of philosophical miniatures and thought-images in earlier Critical Theory, see Gerhard Richter, *Thought-Images: Frankfurt School Writers' Reflections from Damaged Life* (Stanford, CA, 2007). See also Andreas Huyssens, *Miniature Metropolis: Literature in an Age of Photography and Film* (Cambridge, MA, 2015), for an account of the larger context in modernist writing.

43. Jürgen Habermas, *Postmetaphysical Thinking: Philosophical Essays*, trans. William Mark Hohengarten (Cambridge, MA, 1992).

44. In a 1936 essay, Marcuse had defended this latter position, which he identified with Hegel's phenomenology and contrasted with the intuitive eidetics of later phenomenologists such as Husserl. See "The Concept of Essence," in *Negations: Essays in Critical Theory*, trans. Jeremy J. Shapiro (Boston, MA, 1968), 43–87.

45. Habermas, "The Unity of Reason in the Plurality of Its Voices," in *Postmetaphysical Thinking*, 122.

46. See Michael Allen Gillespie, *The Theological Origins of Modernity* (Chicago, IL, 2008), for a full account of the nominalist revolution's lasting impact on modern thought and its theological roots.

47. Jürgen Habermas, "Questions and Counterquestions," in Bernstein, *Habermas and Modernity*, 197.

48. Habermas, *Philosophical Discourse*, 314.

49. Habermas, "Some Further Clarifications," 311. Here Habermas was responding to the argument of Herbert Schnädelbach that rational dispositions were subjective before they were intersubjective.

50. Jürgen Habermas, "Communicative Action and the Detranscendentalized 'Use of Reason,'" in *Between Naturalism and Religion*, 27.

51. Herbert Schnädelbach, "Observations on Rationality and Language," in *Reason and Its Other: Rationality in Modern German Philosophy and Culture*, ed. Dieter Freundlieb and Wayne Hudson (Oxford, 1993), 59.

52. Jürgen Habermas, "From Kant's 'Ideas' of Pure Reason to the 'Idealizing' Presuppositions of Communicative Action: Reflections on the Detranscendentalized 'Use of Reason,'" in *Pluralism and the Pragmatic Turn: The Transformation of Critical Theory*, ed. William Rehg and James Bohman (Cambridge, MA, 2001), 16.

53. Jürgen Habermas, "Reconstruction and Interpretation in the Social Sciences," in *Moral Consciousness and Communicative Action*, trans. Christian Lenhardt and Shierry Weber Nicholsen (Cambridge, MA, 1990), 31.

54. Wilfrid Sellars, *Empiricism and the Philosophy of Mind* (Cambridge, MA, 1997). The original essay appeared in 1956. See also Robert Brandom and Kevin Scharp, eds., *In the Space of Reasons: Selected Essays of Wilfrid Sellars* (Cambridge, MA, 2007). For an account of its relevance to Critical Theory, see Kenneth Baynes, "Practical Reason, the 'Space of Reasons,' and Public Reason," in Rehg and Bohman, *Pluralism*, 53–86.

55. While Habermas was coming to appreciate the importance of communicative reason, what became known as Cold War rationality, developed in response to the logic of mutually assured destruction in the nuclear age, sought to reduce it instead to an automatic, algorithmic calculation of information with no reference to values, history, ideology, or human rumination. For a critique of its premises, see Paul Erickson et al., *How Reason Almost Lost Its Mind: The Strange Career of Cold War Rationality* (Chicago, IL, 2013).

56. Joseph Raz, "The Myth of Instrumental Rationality," *Journal of Ethics and Social Philosophy* 1, no. 1 (April 2005): 15.

57. See Habermas, *Moral Consciousness*. For discussions of the implications of communicative rationality for ethics, see Seyla Benhabib and Fred Dallmayr, eds., *The Communicative Ethics Controversy* (Cambridge, MA, 1990).

58. Habermas, *Legitimation Crisis*, 120. Kant understood our inevitable feeling of moral obligation—the famous example he gives is the moral scruple felt when a prince asks someone to give false testimony against an honorable man as the price of avoiding execution—to be an unmediated and unjustified "fact of reason," not something that had to be derived from a prior argument. For a defense of the moral "fact of reason" in intersubjective terms, which stresses the immediacy of the obligation to justify an argument to others through reasons, see Rainer Forst, *The Right to Justification: Elements of a Constructive Theory of Justice*, trans. Jeffrey Flynn (New York, 2012), 52–55. The basic premise of both versions is that there can be no prior ground for giving reasons, as such a ground would also itself be a reason.

A typical deconstructionist critique of Habermas—one that echoes Schelling's critique of Hegel—is the claim, as Hent de Vries puts it, that "the motivation and ultimate grounds for argumentation cannot be conceived as argumentation." Hent de Vries, *Minimal Theologies: Critiques of Secular Reason in Adorno and Levinas*, trans. Geoffrey Hale (Baltimore, MD, 2005), 123. But insofar as this assertion itself is based on the assumption that there must be a ground or reason for reasoning, it can be understood to imply the opposite conclusion.

59. Habermas, *Between Facts and Norms*, 4.

60. For an account that includes Lukács and the early Frankfurt School, see Andrew Feenberg, *The Philosophy of Praxis: Marx, Lukács, and the Frankfurt School* (London, 2014). The term also referred to the group of Marxist humanist Yugoslav philosophers grouped around the journal *Praxis* in the 1960s and 1970s. For an account, see Gershon Sher, *Praxis: Marxist Criticism and Dissent in Socialist Yugoslavia* (Bloomington, IN, 1977).

61. On Habermas's rejection of Vico, see Martin Jay, "Vico and Western Marxism," in *Fin-de-Siècle Socialism*, 67–81. Against Habermas's reduction of praxis philosophy to a mistaken notion of a metasubject knowing the world it has made, Axel Honneth has argued that it also can be understood as an alternative "in which the formation of the intersubjective consensus of a society maintained by cooperative efforts represents the guiding model. . . . This theoretical tradition of 'praxis philosophy' cannot be refuted with objections against forms of thought belonging to the philosophy of consciousness, but only with proof of the definitive limits of action theory and thus the unavoidability of systems theory." *The Critique of Power: Reflective Stages in a Critical Social Theory*, trans. Kenneth Baynes (Cambridge, MA, 1991), xxxii.

62. Whether or not he was fair to Marx, even the early Marx, has been a major point of contention among his critics. See, for example, Moishe Postone, *Time, Labor, and Social Domination: A Reinterpretation of Marx's Critical Theory* (Cambridge, 1993).

63. Habermas, *Autonomy and Solidarity*, 177.

64. Ibid., 107.

65. Habermas, *Religion and Rationality*, 91.

66. Habermas may not have embraced the concept of "immanent critique" explicitly, but it characterized much of his work. See Titus Stahl, "Habermas and the Project of Immanent Critique," *Constellations* 20, no. 4 (December 2013): 533–52.

67. See Jürgen Habermas, "Communicative Rationality and the Theories of Meaning and Action," in *On the Pragmatics of Communication*, 183–214, for a discussion of Humboldt, comparing his own understanding of the Humboldtian legacy with that of Charles Taylor. For a helpful account of the general importance of Humboldt's linguistics, see Lafont, *The Linguistic Turn*, ch. 2.

68. Habermas would return to Hegel's mixed legacy in "From Kant to Hegel and Back Again: The Move toward Detranscendentalization," in *Truth and Justification*, trans. Barbara Fultner (Cambridge, MA, 2005), 175–212.

69. See Maeve Cooke, *Language and Reason: A Study of Habermas's Pragmatics* (Cambridge, MA, 1994), for a discussion of this dimension of his work.

70. Jürgen Habermas, "Individuation through Socialization: On George Herbert Mead's Theory of Subjectivity," in *Postmetaphysical Thinking*, 149–204.

71. Wellmer, *The Persistence of Modernity*, 83.

72. Habermas was perhaps clearest on the importance of this function in his 1972 essay "Consciousness-Raising or Redemptive Criticism," where he pondered the possibility that an expanded discursive will-formation in the future might have nothing to discuss unless content from traditional sources was redeemed: "Without the store of those semantic energies with which Benjamin's redemptive criticism was concerned, there would necessarily be a stagnation of the structures of practical discourse that had finally prevailed" (59).

73. Habermas, "'I Myself Am Part of Nature'—Adorno on the Intrication of Reason in Nature: Reflections on the Relation between Freedom and Unavailability," in *Between Naturalism and Religion*, 182.

74. Jürgen Habermas, *The Future of Human Nature*, trans. Max Pensky, Helen Beister, and William Rehg (Malden, MA, 2003).

75. Marcuse's residual Hegelianism was readily apparent in many of his works, but even Horkheimer could advocate as late as 1952 the "sublation of diremption" and the "unity of subjective and objective reason" as the result of the "work of the social totality, of historical activity." "Zum Begriff der Vernunft," 34.

76. Habermas, "Was macht eine Lebensform 'rational'?," in *Erläuterungen zur Diskursethik* (Frankfurt, 1991), 31–48. "The substance of a form of life," he wrote, "can never be justified from a universalistic point of view. That also explains why a rationalization of a life world doesn't necessarily—or even normally—make those effected *happier*" (48).

77. Habermas, *Philosophical Discourse*, 301. For an argument that Habermas's position nonetheless presupposes a holistic, comprehensive notion of reason, at least as a telos, see David Ingram, *Habermas and the Dialectic of Reason* (New Haven, CT, 1987).

78. Habermas, "Metaphysics after Kant," in *Postmetaphysical Thinking*, 18.

79. Michel Foucault, "How Is Power Exercised?," trans. Leslie Sawyer, in Hubert L. Dreyfus and Paul Rabinow, *Michel Foucault: Beyond Structuralism and Hermeneutics* (Chicago, IL, 1983), 210.

80. Jürgen Habermas, *Communication and the Evolution of Society*, trans. Thomas McCarthy (Boston, MA, 1979), 119–20. The reference to intrapsychic barriers alluded to Habermas's understanding of Freud in terms of the internal distorted communication that produced symptoms, which could be alleviated through a process of self-reflection, affective re-experiencing, and the objective analysis of a therapist armed with psychoanalytic theory. He developed this argument in *Knowledge and Human Interests*, where psychoanalysis was seen as a model of emancipatory practice.

81. David Lockwood, "Social Integration and System Integration," in *Explorations in Social Change*, ed. G. K. Zollschan and W. Hirsch (London, 1964), 244–57.

82. See Nicos Mouzelis, "Social and System Integration: Habermas's View," *British Journal of Sociology* 43, no. 2 (1992): 267–88, and "Social System and Integration: Lockwood, Habermas, and Giddens," *Sociology* 31, no. 1 (February 1997): 111–97.

83. Habermas, *Religion and Rationality*, 95. For Habermas to defend a procedural notion of reason, it was necessary to extend its meaning beyond the scientific method that was established by Descartes and others in the early modern period. For a discussion of the links between the Cartesian subject, science, and proceduralism, see Charles Taylor, "Inwardness and the Culture of Modernity," in *Philosophical Interventions in the Unfinished Project of Enlightenment*, ed. Axel Honneth et al., trans. William Rehg (Cambridge, MA, 1992), 97–98.

84. Habermas, "What is Universal Pragmatics?," in *Communication*, 6.

85. Albrecht Wellmer, "Reason, Utopia, and Enlightenment," in Bernstein, *Habermas and Modernity*, 53.

86. Habermas, *Legitimation Crisis*, 108.

87. Habermas, "Public Space," 16.

88. Traditionally, democracy meant the rule of popular will, but did not entail a necessarily rational component. For this reason, liberals were often highly distrustful of its irrationalist potential as mob rule. Indeed, for a long time "liberal democracy" was understood as an oxymoron. Habermas, in contrast, contends that rational will can be achieved discursively, overcoming the decisionist implications of irrationalist popular sovereignty.

89. Habermas, *Philosophical Discourse*, 315–16.

90. For an exhaustive list of the types of distinctions that magical thinking failed to register, see Thomas McCarthy, "Reason and Rationalization: Habermas' 'Overcoming' of Hermeneutics," in *Ideals and Illusions: On Reconstruction and Deconstruction in Contemporary Critical Theory* (Cambridge, MA, 1991), 136. The contemporary version of the same deficiency, Habermas argued, could be discerned in the poststructuralist

leveling of the genre difference between philosophy and literature. See *Philosophical Discourse*, 185–210.

91. Habermas, "Metaphysics after Kant," 17.

92. See Karl-Otto Apel, "Normatively Grounding 'Critical Theory' through Recourse to the Lifeworld? A Transcendental-Pragmatic Attempt to Think with Habermas against Habermas," in Honneth et al., *Philosophical Interventions*, 125–70. For Apel's general position, see Karl-Otto Apel, *Selected Essays*, vol. 2, *Ethics and the Theory of Rationality*, ed. Eduardo Mendieta (Atlantic Highlands, NJ, 1996). For a recent updating of his difference with Apel, see Habermas, "On the Architecture of Discursive Differentiation: A Brief Response to a Major Controversy," in *Between Naturalism and Religion*, 77–98. For an insightful discussion of their differences, see Peter Dews, "A Question of Grounding: Reconstruction and Strict Reflexion in Habermas and Apel," in *Critical Theory: Current State and Future Prospects*, ed. Peter Uwe Hohendahl and Jaimey Fisher (New York, 2001), 205–28.

93. Jürgen Habermas, "A Postscript to *Knowledge and Human Interests*," *Philosophy of the Social Sciences* 3, no. 1 (1975): 171–72. It should be noted that one of the major differences between Horkheimer and Habermas was their contrasting evaluations of the pragmatist tradition. *Eclipse of Reason* reduces Peirce to a scientistic experimentalist and claims that William James and John Dewey reflected the business culture of their era when being practical meant anti-intellectual instrumentalism. That Horkheimer may have rightly sensed something dismissive in at least James's attitude toward reason may be shown by the latter's remark in *Varieties of Religious Experience: A Study in Human Nature* (Harmondsworth, UK, 1982) that among our mental faculties reason "has the *prestige* undoubtedly, for it has the loquacity, it can challenge you for proofs, and chop logic, and put you down with words. But it will fail to convince or convert you all the same, if your dumb intuitions are opposed to its conclusions. If you have intuitions at all, they come from a deeper level of your nature than the loquacious level which rationalism inhabits" (73).

94. Habermas, "The Unity of Reason," 133.

95. Habermas hesitated to call the ideal of rational consensus fully regulative because he considered the expectation of communicative rationality an unavoidable pragmatic presupposition of speech. As a result, he argued that it overcame the Kantian distinction between constitutive and regulative. See Jürgen Habermas, *Die nachholende Revolution* (Frankfurt, 1990), 132. Still, the critical force came from its being a future possibility, not an inherent quality of the world.

96. Habermas, "The Unity of Reason," 144.

97. For Hilary Putnam's argument against the naturalization or contextualization of reason, see his "Why Reason Can't Be Naturalized," in *After Philosophy: End or Transformation?*, ed. Ken Baynes, James Bohman, and Thomas McCarthy (Cambridge, MA, 1987), 222–44. He concludes: "If reason is both transcendent and immanent, then philosophy, as culture-bound reflection and argument about eternal questions, is both in time and in eternity. We don't have an Archimedean point; we always speak the language of a time and place; but the rightness and wrongness of what we say is not *just* for a time and place" (242).

98. Habermas, "The Unity of Reason," 138–39.

99. Ibid., 142.

100. Ibid., 144.

101. Habermas, *Between Facts and Norms*, 323.

102. Habermas, "A Reply to My Critics," 250.

103. Jürgen Habermas, "A Reply," in *Communicative Action: Essays on Jürgen Habermas's "The Theory of Communicative Action,"* ed. Axel Honneth and Hans Joas, trans. Jeremy Gaines and Doris L. Jones (Cambridge, MA, 1991), 225–26.

104. Martin Seel, "The Two Meanings of 'Communicative' Rationality: Remarks on Habermas's Critique of a Plural Concept of Reason," in Honneth and Joas, *Communicative Action*, 46–47.

105. Jürgen Habermas, "Modernity versus Postmodernity," *New German Critique* 22 (Winter 1981): 3–14. The original German title was "Die Moderne: Ein unvollendetes Projekt." For a selection of essays discussing his complicated attitude toward modernity with a response by Habermas, see Bernstein, *Habermas and Modernity*.

106. Habermas, "A Reply to My Critics," 235. Some of his supporters nonetheless urged him not to give up the utopian dimension of the earlier Critical Theory tradition. See Seyla Benhabib, "The Utopian Dimension in Communicative Ethics," *New German Critique* 35 (Spring–Summer 1985): 83–96.

107. It has been argued by Gernot Böhme that it is first "through Kant [that] reason becomes a project. It is not a human gift but a discipline. The human being is not an *animal rationale*, but an *animal rationabile*, an animal that must civilize, cultivate and moralize itself in order to become a human being." "Beyond the Radical Critique of Reason," in Freundlieb and Hudson, *Reason and Its Other*, 89.

108. Johann Baptist Metz, "Anamnestic Reason: A Theologian's Remarks on the Crisis of the Geisteswissenschaften," in *The Frankfurt School on Religion: Key Writings by the Major Thinkers*, ed. Eduardo Mendieta (New York, 2005), 285–92; for Habermas's response, see his "Transcendence from Within, Transcendence in this World," and "Israel or Athens: Where does Anamnestic Reason Belong?" both in *Religion and Rationality*, 67–94 and 129–38. The link between reason and anamnesis, which goes back at least to Plato, also informed Marcuse's stress on re-membering what had been sundered in the modern, alienated world. See Martin Jay, *Marxism and Totality: The Adventures of a Concept from Lukács to Habermas* (Berkeley, CA, 1984), ch. 7. Metz's version did not mean the recovery of forgotten atemporal forms but rather the remembrance of the victims of the past.

109. Habermas, "Some Further Clarifications," 309.

110. Jan-Werner Müller, *Constitutional Patriotism* (Princeton, NJ, 2007), 28.

111. Habermas, "Themes in Postmetaphysical Thinking," in *Postmetaphysical Thinking*, 55.

112. Theodor W. Adorno, *Negative Dialectics*, trans. E. B. Ashton (New York, 1973), 320.

113. See Peggy H. Breitenstein, "Negative Geschichtsphilosophie nach Adorno," in *Können Wir der Geschichte Entkommen? Geschichtsphilosophie am Beginn des 21. Jahrhunderts*, ed. Christian Schmidt (Frankfurt, 2013), 82–105.

114. The complexity of their attitude toward the idea of progress is best expressed in Adorno's 1962 essay "Progress," in *Critical Models: Interventions and Catchwords*, trans. Henry W. Pickford (New York, 1998).

115. Habermas, "Was macht eine Lebensform 'rational'?," 47.

116. Immanuel Kant, "Idea for a Universal History with a Cosmopolitan Aim," in *Kant's "Idea for a Universal History with a Cosmopolitan Aim": A Critical Guide*, ed. Amélie Oksenberg Rorty and James Schmidt (Cambridge, 2009), 21.

117. Axel Honneth, *Pathologies of Reason: On the Legacy of Critical Theory*, trans. James Ingram et al. (New York, 2009), 11.

118. The concept was already in use in analytical philosophy, for example by Rudolf Carnap and Hans Reichenbach, as well as in Imre Lakatos's philosophy of science. For a discussion of Habermas's usage, see Jørgen Pederson, "Habermas' Method: Rational Reconstruction," *Philosophy of the Social Sciences* 38 (December 2008): 457–85.

119. Jürgen Habermas, *Communication*, and "History and Evolution," *Telos* 39 (Spring 1979): 5–44. For a useful summary and critique of the argument, see Michael Schmid, "Habermas's Theory of Social Evolution," in Thompson and Held, *Habermas*, 162–80, and Pederson, "Habermas' Method."

120. Honneth, *Critique of Power*, 282.

121. Jürgen Habermas, *Justification and Application*, trans. Barbara Fultner (Cambridge, MA, 2003), 27–28.

122. Habermas, *Legitimation Crisis*, 15.

123. Habermas, "History and Evolution," 42.

124. Habermas, *Legitimation Crisis*. In this work, the concept of a "rationality crisis" is reserved entirely for administrative rationality, not communicative. It is caused when "contradictory steering imperatives, which cause the unplanned, nature-like development of an anarchistic commodity production and its crisis-ridden growth, are then operative within the administrative system" (62).

125. Ibid., 15.

126. Habermas, "Some Further Clarifications," 309.

127. Habermas, *Legitimation Crisis*, 142.

128. Habermas, *Autonomy and Solidarity*, 170.

129. For a sustained discussion of the importance of rational accountability in Habermas, see Maeve Cooke, *Re-Presenting the Good Society* (Cambridge, MA, 2006).

130. For a lucid presentation of Habermas's evolutionary models and their problems, see Thomas McCarthy, *The Critical Theory of Jürgen Habermas* (Cambridge, MA, 1978), ch. 3, section 6.

131. For discussions, see David Ingram, "Habermas on Aesthetics and Rationality: Completing the Project of Enlightenment," *New German Critique* 53 (Spring–Summer 1991): 67–103; Pieter Duvenage, *Habermas and Aesthetics: The Limits of Communicative Reason* (Malden, MA, 2003); David Colclasure, *Habermas and Literary Rationality* (New York, 2010). For my own earlier consideration of these issues, see Martin Jay, "Habermas and Modernism," and Habermas's response in "Questions and Counterquestions," both in Bernstein, *Habermas and Modernity*, 125–39 and 192–216.

132. Habermas, "Questions and Counterquestions," 201.

133. Habermas, *Philosophical Discourse*, 7.

134. Jürgen Habermas and Josef Ratzinger, *The Dialectics of Secularization: On Reason and Religion*, trans. Brian McNeil (San Francisco, CA, 2006). See also Habermas, introduction to *Between Naturalism and Religion*, where he concedes that Hegel was right to think that "the major world religions belong to the history of reason itself" (6); Michael Reder and Josef Schmidt, eds., *Ein Bewusstsein von dem, was fehlt: Eine Diskussion mit Jürgen Habermas* (Frankfurt, 2008); and Craig Calhoun, Eduardo Mendieta, and Jonathan Van Antwerpen, eds., *Habermas and Religion* (Cambridge, 2013). Mendieta provides an appendix tracing Habermas's growing interest in religion during his career.

135. Habermas, *Religion and Rationality*, 148.

136. Jürgen Habermas, *Das Absolute und die Geschichte: Von der Zweispältigkeit in Schellings Denken* (Bonn, 1954). For a different reading of Schelling, see Peter Douglas, "Habermas, Schelling, and Nature," in *Critical Theory after Habermas: Encounters and Departures*, ed. Dieter Freundlieb, Wayne Hudson, and John Rundell (Leiden, 2004), 155–80.

## Chapter 7. Habermas and His Critics

1. The extraordinary extent of the response is shown by the appearance in 1982 of René Görtzen, *Jürgen Habermas: Eine Bibliographie seiner Schriften und der Sekundärliteratur 1952–1981* (Frankfurt, l982), which was over two hundred pages long.

2. A prime example would be Richard Rorty. See, for example, his "Habermas and Lyotard on Postmodernism," in *Habermas and Modernism*, ed. Richard J. Bernstein (Cambridge, MA, 1985), 161–75.

3. Marie Fleming, *Emancipation and Illusion: Rationality and Gender in Habermas's Theory of Modernity* (University Park, PA, 1997), and Paget Henry, *Caliban's Reason: Introducing Afro-Caribbean Philosophy* (New York, 2000).

4. Ian Hacking, "Styles of Scientific Reasoning," in *Post-Analytic Philosophy*, ed. John Rajchman and Cornell West (New York, 1985), 145–65. To be fair to Hacking, it should be noted that he follows Donald Davidson in denying the absolute incommensurability of all conceptual schemes, while distinguishing between classes of assertions that can be reasoned about and are thus amenable to translation into other cultural vocabularies, and those that are not.

5. See, for example, Karl-Otto Apel, "Normatively Grounding 'Critical Theory' through Recourse to the Lifeworld? A Transcendental-Pragmatic Attempt to Think with Habermas against Habermas," in *Philosophical Interventions in the Unfinished Project of Enlightenment*, ed. Axel Honneth, Thomas McCarthy, Claus Offe, and Albrecht Wellmer, trans. William Rehg (Cambridge, MA, 1992), 125–70. Other friendly critics like Richard J. Bernstein urge him to split the difference between Apel and Rorty by combining Kant and Dewey. See, for example, his "Jürgen Habermas's Kantian Pragmatism," in *The Pragmatic Turn* (Malden, MA, 2010), 168–99.

6. See, for example, Nicolas Kompridis, "Heidegger's Challenge to the Future of Critical Theory," in *Habermas: A Critical Reader*, ed. Peter Dews (Oxford, 1999), 118–52,

and Kenneth MacKendrick, "The Moral Imaginary of Discourse Ethics," and John Rundell, "Imaginary Turns in Critical Theory: Imaginary Subjects in Tension," both in *Critical Theory after Habermas: Encounters and Departures*, ed. Dieter Freundlieb, Wayne Hudson, and John Rundell (Leiden, 2004), 280–306 and 307–43. The complaint against his proceduralism continues to be voiced by friendly critics as well, for example, David Ingram, *Habermas: Introduction and Analysis* (Ithaca, NY, 2010), chs. 8 and 9.

7. See, for example, Joel Whitebook, *Perversion and Utopia: A Study in Psychoanalysis and Critical Theory* (Cambridge, MA, 1995).

8. See, for example, Jeffrey L. Nicholas, *Reason, Tradition, and the Good: MacIntyre's Tradition-Constituted Reason and Frankfurt School Critical Theory* (Notre Dame, IN, 2012). For another defense of the necessity of metaphysics, see Dieter Henrich, "What Is Metaphysics?—What Is Modernity? Twelve Theses against Jürgen Habermas," in Dews, *Habermas*, 291–319.

9. See, for example, Gillian Rose, *Hegel contra Sociology* (Athlone, NJ, 1981).

10. For assessments, both favorable and critical, of his debts to Pragmatism, see the essays in *Habermas and Pragmatism*, ed. Mitchell Aboulafia, Myra Bookman, and Catherine Kemp (New York, 2002).

11. See, for example, Allen W. Wood, "Habermas' Defense of Rationalism," *New German Critique* 35 (Spring–Summer 1985): 145–64.

12. See, for example, Dieter Freundlieb, "Why Subjectivity Matters: Critical Theory and the Philosophy of the Subject," Dieter Henrich, "Subjectivity as Philosophical Principle," and Manfred Frank, "Against *a priori* Intersubjectivism: An Alternative Inspired by Sartre," all in Freundlieb, Hudson, and Rundell, *Critical Theory after Habermas*, 211–32, 233–58, 259–79.

13. For a comparison between Habermas and Lacan as theorists of language, see Peter Dews, "Communicative Paradigms and the Question of Subjectivity: Habermas, Mead, and Lacan," in Dews, *Habermas*, 87–117.

14. See Vincent Descombes, *The Barometer of Modern Reason: On the Philosophies of Current Events*, trans. Stephen Adam Schwartz (New York, 1993). The simplistic opposition between French poststructuralism and German Critical Theory, always a bit of a caricature, was even further undermined when Habermas moved away from the more tendentious equations of poststructuralism with conservative irrationalism he had made in the 1970s and early 1980s. He came to acknowledge certain strengths in Foucault's work, and entered into a constructive dialogue with Derrida near the end of the latter's life. In fact, when he died, Habermas wrote a tribute titled "A Last Farewell: Derrida's Enlightening Impact," in *The Derrida-Habermas Reader*, ed. Lasse Thomassen (Chicago, IL, 2006), 307–8.

15. See, for example, J. M. Bernstein, *Recovering Ethical Life: Jürgen Habermas and the Future of Critical Theory* (London, 1995); David Ingram, *Habermas and the Dialectic of Reason* (New Haven, CT, 1987); Robert Hullot-Kentor, *Things Beyond Resemblance: Collected Essays on Theodor W. Adorno* (New York, 2006); Martin Morris, *Rethinking the Communicative Turn: Adorno, Habermas, and the Problem of Communicative Freedom* (Albany, NY, 2001); and Deborah Cook, *Adorno, Habermas, and the Search for a Rational Society* (New York, 2004). Albrecht

Wellmer has also urged a more generous understanding of the rational potential in art, which cannot be subsumed under communicative rationality. See, for example, his "Truth, Semblance, Reconciliation: Adorno's Aesthetic Redemption of Modernity," in *The Persistence of Modernity: Essays on Aesthetics, Ethics, and Postmodernism*, trans. David Midgley (Cambridge, MA, 1991), 1–35.

16. See, for example, Andrew Feenberg, "Marcuse or Habermas: Two Critiques of Technology," *Inquiry* 39 (1996): 45–70; Andrew Feenberg, *Alternative Modernity: The Technical Turn in Philosophy and Social Theory* (Berkeley, CA, 1995); Steven Vogel, *Against Nature: The Concept of Nature in Critical Theory* (Albany, NY, 1996); and Samir Gandesha, "Marcuse, Habermas, and the Critique of Technology," in *Herbert Marcuse: A Critical Reader*, ed. John Abromeit and W. Mark Cobb (New York, 2004), 188–208.

17. See, for example, Thomas McCarthy, "Reason and Rationalization: Habermas's 'Overcoming' of Hermeneutics," in *Ideals and Illusions: On Reconstruction and Deconstruction in Contemporary Critical Theory* (Cambridge, MA, 1991), 127–51, and Anthony Giddens, "Reason without Revolution? Habermas's *Theorie des kommunikativen Handelns*," in Bernstein, *Habermas and Modernism*, 95–124. More recently, McCarthy has extended his analysis by focusing on the legacy of imperialism and colonialism, which was generally ignored by earlier Critical Theory. See his *Race, Empire, and the Idea of Human Development* (Cambridge, 2009).

18. For a discussion of Habermas's unsuccessful attempt to convince his compatriots of the need for "constitutional patriotism" in the reunification of Germany, see Jan-Werner Müller, *Constitutional Patriotism* (Princeton, NJ, 2007). According to Müller, the term "passionate rationality" was actually coined by Dolf Sternberger, who was first to float the idea in 1971 (21).

19. Cristina Lafont points out that understood holistically, the background meanings inherent in the lifeworld cannot be reduced to the types of isolated propositional claims that can be tested for validity. See *The Linguistic Turn in Hermeneutic Philosophy*, trans. José Medina (Cambridge, MA, 1999), 222. Habermas has come increasingly to acknowledge the importance of pre-reflective meanings in the lifeworld, which cannot all be reflectively validated. As a result, one commentator has gone so far as to call his position a tacit "neo-primitivism" because of its reliance on premodern, prerationalized worldviews to generate the substance that is discursively validated. See Victor Li, "Rationality and Loss: Habermas and the Recovery of the Pre-Modern Other," *Parallax* 11, no. 3 (July–September 2005): 84.

20. For an example of the reification charge, see Axel Honneth, *The Critique of Power: Reflective Stages in a Critical Social Theory*, trans. Kenneth Baynes (Cambridge, MA, 1991). For the claim that the reconciliation is undertheorized, see Martin Seel, "The Two Meanings of 'Communicative' Rationality: Remarks on Habermas's Critique of a Plural Concept of Reason," in *Communicative Action: Essays on Jürgen Habermas's "Theory of Communicative Action,"* ed. Axel Honneth and Hans Joas, trans. Jeremey Gaines and Doris L. Jones (Cambridge, MA, 1991), 36–48. For an attempt to conceptualize the interaction, see the discussion of "transversal" reason by Wolfgang Welsch in *Vernunft: Die zeitgenössische Vernunftkritik und das Konzept der transversalen Vernunft* (Frankfurt, 1995).

21. Maeve Cooke, *Re-Presenting the Good Society* (Cambridge, MA, 2006), 53.

22. Honneth, *The Critique of Power*, ch. 9.

23. Nancy Fraser, *Unruly Practices: Power, Discourse, and Gender in Contemporary Social Theory* (Minneapolis, MN, 1989), ch. 6, and Fleming, *Emancipation and Illusion*. For another issue raised by feminist critics, the gender dimension of the ideal of an autonomous self, see Maeve Cooke, "Habermas, Feminism, and the Question of Autonomy," in Dews, *Habermas*, 178–210.

24. For example, Thomas McCarthy argues that "*rationally motivated* agreement as a moral-political alternative to coercion may well involve elements of conciliation, compromise, consent, accommodation, and the like." "Practical Discourse: On the Relation of Morality to Politics," in *Ideals and Illusions*, 197. Albrecht Wellmer argues that "contrary to what Habermas assumed until recently, the conditions of a rational discourse are not identical with the conditions of a *democratic* discourse. The former can be formulated with the help of a metaprinciple of rational dialogue; the latter only with the help of a principle of equal individual *rights*; but the category of individual rights cannot be conceptually derived from any principle of rationality." "Models of Freedom in the Modern World," in *Endgames: The Irreconcilable Nature of Modernity; Essays and Lectures*, trans. David Midgley (Cambridge, MA, 1998), 27.

25. Albena Azmanova, *The Scandal of Reason: A Critical Theory of Political Judgment* (New York, 2012).

26. Jodi Dean, "Civil Society in the Information Age: Beyond the Public Sphere," in *Critical Theory: Current State and Future Prospects*, ed. Peter Uwe Hohendahl and Jaimey Fisher (New York, 2005), 154–74.

27. David Runciman, *Political Hypocrisy: The Mask of Power, from Hobbes to Orwell and Beyond* (Princeton, NJ, 2008), and Martin Jay, *The Virtues of Mendacity: On Lying in Politics* (Charlottesville, VA, 2010).

28. For overviews of these interventions, see Robert C. Holub, *Jürgen Habermas: Critic in the Public Sphere* (London, 1991); Martin Matuštík, *Jürgen Habermas: A Philosophical-Political Profile* (Lanham, MD, 2001); and Matthew G. Specter, *Habermas: An Intellectual Biography* (Cambridge, 2010). For a general overview of his career, see Stefan Müller-Doohm, *Jürgen Habermas: Eine Biographie* (Berlin, 2014).

29. Seyla Benhabib, *Critique, Norm, and Utopia: A Study of the Foundations of Critical Theory* (New York, 1986), 252–53.

30. Amanda Anderson, *The Way We Argue Now: A Study in the Cultures of Theory* (Princeton, NJ, 2006), 173 and 176. She wants to rescue the concept of an "ethos" from those who identify it only with authenticity and charisma. It is, of course, always hazardous to speak of "our" situation, as if there were a single story to be told. There are, in fact, many reversals and hesitations in the empirical record, but if we accept the necessity of some sort of rational reconstruction, then perhaps these kinds of generalizations are not without their merit.

31. Friedrich Kambartel, "Vernunft: Kriterion oder Kultur?," in *Philosophie der humanen Welt: Abhandlungen* (Frankfurt, 1989), 27–43.

32. Wellmer, *The Persistence of Modernity*, 81.

33. Habermas, "On the Relation between the Nation, the Rule of Law, and Democracy," in *The Inclusion of the Other: Studies in Political Theory*, ed. Ciaran Cronin and Pablo de Greiff (Cambridge, MA, 1998), 137. Perhaps his main target here was the legacy of Carl Schmitt, which had two different implications. One was the inevitability of adversarial friend/foe relations, which meant that dissensus was a permanent feature of political life, either in existentially antagonistic form or in a more benign agonistic variety. The second was the positing of a homogeneity within the category of "friend," which implied a prepolitical consensus that existed on the basis of some given communal solidarity (such as that posited by the Nazis).

34. For a general account of the seventeenth-century debate about the principle of sufficient reason, see Stephen Nadler, *The Best of All Possible Worlds: A Story of Philosophers, God, and Evil in the Age of Reason* (Princeton, NJ, 2010).

35. Martin Heidegger, *The Principle of Reason*, trans. Reginald Lilly (Bloomington, IN, 1996), 21.

36. Jürgen Habermas, "Some Further Clarifications of the Concept of Communicative Rationality," in *On the Pragmatics of Communication*, ed. Maeve Cooke (Cambridge, MA, 1998), 316.

37. Jürgen Habermas, "Freedom and Determinism," in *Between Naturalism and Religion: Philosophical Essays*, trans. Ciaran Cronin (Cambridge, 2008), 158.

38. For a recent account of reasoning that expands this point, see Anthony Simon Laden, *Reasoning: A Social Picture* (Oxford, 2012).

39. Arthur Schopenhauer, *On the Fourfold Root of the Principle of Sufficient Reason*, trans. E. F. J. Payne (La Salle, IL, 1997). The first root invokes causes or *Gründe*, which involve a change in the physical relationship not between isolated objects but between states of the complex relations among them. The second is "logical" and works with concepts and their entailments. The third, which Schopenhauer treated more cursorily, is "mathematical," by which he meant arithmetic and geometry. The fourth root was the most suggestive, because it was linked with Schopenhauer's own later emphasis on the central importance of the will. It is the "moral" root in the Kantian sense of freely determining action and is grounded in the inner sense of subjective volition. Although lacking any serious demonstration that the will might be itself guided by rational deliberation or an obligation to follow formal principles such as the categorical imperative, Schopenhauer's inclusion of it as a root of sufficient reason for action had the virtue of continuing the connection between reason and freedom that was so much a part of the Kantian legacy. Here we have a fully dispositional notion of reason as expressed only in human cognition and will, and thus directly opposed to the tradition that began with Anaxagoras, in which nature was itself ruled by rational laws.

40. Heidegger, *The Principle of Reason*, 26–27.

41. Ibid., 30.

42. See Laden, *Reasoning*, for more on the distinction between command and invitation. It also should be noted that the invitation is to enter into a special kind of conversation, one based on an earnest search for common ground and submission to the better argument, not a conversation based on competitive repartee, polysemic irony, and playful

wit. Perhaps the criticisms made by French poststructuralists of communicative rationality reflect the abiding tradition of *esprit* that retains much of its power today in France. Ironically, during the heyday of Descartes, baroque *acutezze* (wit) was the target of critics like Dominque Bouhours. See the discussion in John Schaeffer, *Sensus Communis: Vico, Rhetoric, and the Limits of Relativism* (Durham, NC, 1990), 63. But by the time of the salon culture of the Enlightenment, with its stress on sociability and conversation, *esprit* had won out. See Dena Goodman, *The Republic of Letters: A Cultural History of the French Enlightenment* (Ithaca, NY, 1994).

By contrast, the weaker German tradition of *Witz* (wit), which developed in the *Aufklärung* as a response to French charges of lugubrious German earnestness, has had less of an impact. For a discussion of Habermas's understanding of its ambivalent role in the early public sphere, as both a rebuke to scholarly pedantry and the preserve of an educated elite, see Carl Hill, *The Soul of Wit: Joke Theory from Grimm to Freud* (Lincoln, NE, 1993), 18–19.

43. Friedrich Schelling, *The Abyss of Freedom: Ages of the World*, ed. Slavoj Žižek, trans. Judith Norman (Ann Arbor, MI, 1997).

44. Axel Honneth, *Pathologies of Reason: On the Legacy of Critical Theory*, trans. James Ingram et al. (New York, 2009), 14.

45. The rhetoric of pathology is, of course, highly charged, drawing as it does on normative models of "health" and "illness" that may well hide culturally particular investments. But lest it be seen as a problem for the Critical Theory tradition alone, it should be noted that it is also used by both Husserl and Derrida to denounce an objectivist notion of reason based on a dubious transcendentalism. See Derrida's discussion, which is based on Husserl's *Crisis of the European Sciences*, in Jacques Derrida, *Rogues: Two Essays on Reason*, trans. Pascale-Anne Brault and Michael Naas (Stanford, CA, 2005), 124–25.

46. The relationship between judgment, both determinant and reflective, and dianoetic reason is a source of some controversy. For a powerful rebuttal of the attempt made by Hannah Arendt to differentiate reason from reflective judgment, see Albrecht Wellmer, "Hannah Arendt on Judgment: The Unwritten Doctrine of Reason," in *Hannah Arendt: Twenty Years Later*, ed. Larry May and Jerome Kohn (Cambridge, MA, 1997), 33–52. He argues that "there was no place in her thought for a broader conception of rationality that would have allowed her to tie reflective judgments to rational argument. Such a conception of rationality would have to be located, as it were, in between the formal rationality of logical demonstration and the speculative rationality of what she called 'thinking'—in between, that is, the rationality of intellect and the rationality of reason. For Arendt, what is in between these two rationalities, or one might even say, what mediates between them, is the rationality of judgment" (38–39).

47. Immanuel Kant, "An Answer to the Question: What Is Enlightenment?," in *What Is Enlightenment? Eighteenth-Century Answers and Twentieth-Century Questions*, ed. James Schmidt (Berkeley, CA, 1996), 58–64. The elitist implications of Kant's notion of a tutelary relationship between those who were the self-designated enlighteners and those who

were in need of liberation from their "self-incurred immaturity" was already criticized by Hamann and others in his day.

48. Jürgen Habermas, "Communicative Action and the Detranscendentalized 'Use of Reason,'" in *Between Naturalism and Religion*, 49.

49. Ibid., 47.

50. Jürgen Habermas, *Communication and the Evolution of Society*, trans. Thomas McCarthy (Boston, MA, 1979), 200.

51. Habermas, "A Reply," in Honneth and Joas, *Communicative Action*, 226.

52. Ibid., 231.

53. Cooke, *Re-Presenting the Good Society*, 17.

54. Ibid., 142.

55. Albrecht Wellmer, "The Debate about Truth: Pragmatism without Regulative Ideas," in Freundlieb, Hudson, and Rundell, *Critical Theory after Habermas*, 198–99.

56. Jürgen Habermas, "Introduction: Realism after the Linguistic Turn," in *Truth and Justification*, trans. Barbara Fultner (Cambridge, MA, 2005), 38.

57. Albrecht Wellmer, "Truth, Contingency, and Modernity," in *Endgames*, 143. He adds: "This again is a performative idealization which may always turn out to be wrong, since retrospectively we might discover some external or internal constraints which prevented some—or all—of the speakers from saying what otherwise they could have said."

58. Rainer Forst, "Justice, Reason, and Critique: Basic Concepts of Critical Theory," in *The Handbook of Critical Theory*, ed. David M. Rasmussen (Cambridge, MA, 1996), 153.

59. Seyla Benhabib, *Dignity in Adversity: Human Rights in Troubled Times* (Cambridge, 2011), 71.

60. Forst, "Justice, Reason, and Critique," 149.

61. Hent de Vries, *Minimal Theologies: Critiques of Secular Reason in Adorno and Levinas*, trans. Geoffrey Hale (Baltimore, MD, 2005), 118. The book as a whole argues for the restoration of a nonbisected rationality in which noetic and dianoetic moments coexist, with the former explicitly indebted to a *"minimal, albeit nonnaturalist, realism of the ab-solute—of ab-solutes, since we must think of the singularity in question as inherently plural"* (109). Against the goal of a postmetaphysical reason, de Vries shares with Adorno a solidarity with metaphysics—and theology—at the moment of its—their—fall.

62. Agnes Heller, "Philosophy as a Literary Genre," *Thesis Eleven* 110 (June 2012): 18.

63. Jürgen Habermas, "A Reply to My Critics," in *Habermas: Critical Debates*, ed. John B. Thompson and David Held (Cambridge, MA, 1982), 234.

64. Herbert Schnädelbach, "The Transformation of Critical Theory," in Honneth and Joas, *Communicative Action*, 13.

65. Joseph Heath, *Communicative Action and Rational Choice* (Cambridge, MA, 2003), 8.

66. Habermas, "Wahrheitstheorien" (1972), reprinted in *Vorstudien zur Ergänzungen zur Theorie des kommunikativen Handelns* (Frankfurt, 1984), 127–86, and Habermas, *Truth and Justification*, 5.

67. Habermas, "A Reply," in Honneth and Joas, *Communicative Action*, 232.

68. Habermas, "Some Further Clarifications," 312.

69. Habermas, "Richard Rorty's Pragmatic Turn," in *On the Pragmatics of Communication*, 343–82. Rorty also objected to what he saw as Habermas's ambiguous use of rationality as a both cognitive and moral term. See his "The Ambiguity of 'Rationality,'" in *Pluralism and the Pragmatic Turn: The Transformation of Critical Theory*, ed. William Rehg and James Bohman (Cambridge, MA, 2001), 41–52. This is an odd objection to make by a critic who has long abandoned the analytical philosophical fetish of clearly defined and monosemic language.

70. Allen Wood, in "Habermas' Defense of Rationalism," had criticized his excessive hostility to the perlocutionary dimension of speech acts (191), and Habermas took his criticism to heart. See his "Toward a Theory of Meaning," in *Postmetaphysical Thinking: Philosophical Essays*, trans. William Mark Hohengarten (Cambridge, MA, 1992), 86–87.

71. Habermas, "Richard Rorty's Pragmatic Turn," 359.

72. See Lafont, *The Linguistic Turn*, for an extensive discussion of the dangers of reducing reference to nothing but an effect of meaning.

73. Albrecht Wellmer spells out the differences between Popper's falsificationist theory and Habermas's fallibilist theory, in "What Is a Pragmatic Theory of Meaning? Variations on the Proposition 'We Understand a Speech Act When We Know What Makes It Acceptable,'" in Honneth et al., *Philosophical Interventions*, 191–92.

74. Raymond Geuss, *The Idea of a Critical Theory: Habermas and the Frankfurt School* (Cambridge, 1981), 31.

75. Charles Taylor, *Sources of the Self: The Making of Modern Identity* (Cambridge, MA, 1989), 72.

76. Lafont, *The Linguistic Turn in Hermeneutic Philosophy*, ch. 6. She adopts Hilary Putnam's concept of "internal realism" to describe Habermas's later position.

77. Jürgen Habermas, *Theorie des kommunikativen Handelns*, 2 vols. (Frankfurt, 1981), 1:25.

78. Jürgen Habermas, "Introduction: Realism after the Linguistic Turn," in *Truth and Justification*, 38. In his 1989 essay, "What Is a Pragmatic Theory of Meaning? Variations on the Proposition 'We Understand a Speech Act When We Know What Makes It Acceptable,'" in *Philosophical Interventions*, Wellmer had already pushed Habermas to adopt a cognitivist fallibilism that went beyond justification by rational consensus. See also his more extensive discussion of this issue in "Ethics and Dialogue: Elements of Moral Judgement in Kant and Discourse Ethics," in *The Persistence of Modernity*, 113–231.

79. Habermas, "Richard Rorty's Pragmatic Turn," 375.

80. "Internal realism" means that within the linguistic system there are universal categories that are taken to be real, but the world beyond is understood to be composed of things that cannot be subsumed with no remainder under those categories. Ontological nominalism is more plausible than ontological realism.

81. Habermas, "Communicative Action," 34.

82. Theodor W. Adorno, *Negative Dialectics*, trans. E. B. Ashton (New York, 1973), 183–86. For a discussion of this theme in his work, see Brian O'Connor, *Adorno's Negative Dialectic: Philosophy and the Possibility of Critical Rationality* (Cambridge, MA, 2004), ch. 2.

It also might be possible to see a residue of Schelling's resistance to Hegel's pan-rationalist philosophy of immanence, about which Habermas had written in his doctoral dissertation. For a discussion of Habermas's relation to Schelling, see Andrew Bowie, *Schelling and Modern European Philosophy: An Introduction* (London, 1993). He argues that "Habermas admits that the semantic potential of both religious and aesthetic articulation poses challenges that cannot be answered by philosophical discourse, but then defuses this challenge by giving essentially Hegelian priority to that discourse" (189). Bowie contends that Habermas needs more of a balance between the world-disclosing and problem-solving functions of language.

83. Wellmer, "The Significance of the Frankfurt School Today: Five Theses," in *Endgames*, 262.

84. Another way to reconcile Adorno's vision of reason with Habermas's has been suggested by Gregg Daniel Miller in *Mimesis and Reason: Habermas's Political Philosophy* (Albany, NY, 2011). He draws on Mead's theory of intersubjectivity and Benjamin's notion of experience to flesh out the possible role of mimesis in an expanded Habermasian idea of communicative reason.

85. Habermas, "Introduction: Realism after the Linguistic Turn," in *Truth and Justification*, 46.

86. Habermas, *Communication and the Evolution of Society*, and Jürgen Habermas, *Moral Consciousness and Communicative Action*, trans. Christian Lenhardt and Shierry Weber Nicholsen (Cambridge, MA, 1990).

87. For an overview of the controversy, see Leena Kakkori and Rauno Huttunen, "The Gilligan-Kohlberg Controversy and Its Philosophico-Historical Roots," in *The Encyclopaedia of Educational Philosophy and Theory*, ed. Michael Peters et al. (2010), http://eepat.net/doku.php?id=the_gilligan_kohlberg_controversy_and_its_philosophico historical_roots.

88. Stephen K. White, "The Very Idea of a Critical Social Science: A Pragmatist Turn," in *The Cambridge Companion to Critical Theory*, ed. Fred Rush (Cambridge, 2004), 330.

89. Habermas, "Some Further Clarifications," 334.

90. Jürgen Habermas, "Norms and Values: On Hilary Putnam's Kantian Pragmatism," in *Truth and Justification*, 213–36, and Jürgen Habermas, "Communicative Action and the Detranscendentalized 'Use of Reason,'" in *Between Naturalism and Religion*, 24–76.

91. Schnädelbach, "The Transformation of Critical Theory," 11.

92. According, for example, to Honneth, Habermas's turn away from his quasi-transcendental anthropology of interests meant "he no longer interprets the processes of rationalization, in which he attempts to conceive the evolution of society, as a process of the will-formation of the human species; rather he understands them as a supra-subjective learning process carried by the social system." *The Critique of Power*, 284.

93. Hugo Mercier and Dan Sperber, "Why Do Humans Reason? Arguments for an Argumentative Theory," *Behavioral and Brain Sciences* 34 (2011): 57–111, and the symposium of responses to the essay.

94. Habermas, *Truth and Justification*, 22–30. He distinguishes "weak" from "strong" naturalism, exemplified by Quine, because the latter adopts a scientific method that has

no place for transcendental questions, even in their post-Kantian, postmentalist form. Weak naturalism does not forget the place of the validity-testing functions of the life-world in justifying the objective claims about external nature.

95. A. P. Mackey, A. T. Miller Singley, and S. A. Bunge, "Intensive Reasoning Training Alters Patterns of Brain Connectivity at Rest," *Journal of Neuroscience* 33, no. 11 (2013): 4796–803.

96. Habermas, "A Reply to My Critics," 221.

97. Ibid., 227.

98. Honneth, *Pathologies of Reason*, 41–42. Even if one questions the terminology of emancipatory interest, which harkens back to Habermas's earlier formulation in *Knowledge and Human Interests*, the force of Honneth's linkage between a viable understanding of rationality and the future of critical theory is, as I hope this book has shown, hard to gainsay.

# Index

adaequatio, 104, 211n46

Adorno, Gretel, 17, 112

Adorno, Theodor W., 118–19, 123, 128–29, 137–38, 143, 146, 154–55, 157, 159, 171–72, 180, 184, 189, 195, 200, 209, 211, 213, 215, 217, 219, 221; "additional factor" (*Hinzutretende*), 14; *Aesthetic Theory*, 107, 110 (*see also* aesthetic: theory); on Comte, 88; on *Critique of Pure Reason*, 79; *Dialectic of Enlightenment*, 13, 20, 89, 100–102, 112, 117, 120; on dialectics and irrationalism, 195n27; on Enlightenment, 20, 106, 117, 121; on Hegel, 61–62, 70, 104, 108, 111, 213n56; and Heidegger, 14, 17, 112, 171n60; and intersubjectivity, 219 (*see also* intersubjectivity); on Kant, 41, 44, 79; on Kant and Hegel, 211n33; on mimesis, 130; on myth, 172n62; on negative dialectics, 17, 79; and Nietzsche, 217n17, 218n29, 218–19n34; on noetic and dianoetic reason, 112; on reason, 13, 98, 100, 103–4, 107–12, 114–17

aesthetic, 23, 30, 34, 54, 82, 83, 108, 120, 129, 142, 143; contemplation, 86; disinterestedness, 58, 108; disinterestedness, 58, 108; experience, 107, 112; judgment, 37, 135, 143; movement, 88, 155; as a placeholder of an emphatic, 142; pleasure, 143; ratio, 110; rationality, 108, 113, 125; rationalization, 160; reasoning, 30, 37; theory, 30, 33, 106, 214. *See also* Adorno: *Aesthetic Theory*; Schopenhauer: and aesthetic contemplation

affect, 24, 111–12

Al-Farabi, 18

Al-Ghazali, 18

alienation, 88, 128, 150, 199

allegory, 3, 6, 13

Althusser, Louis, 71, 73

analytic: tautologies, 46; philosopher, 127; philosophy, 73, 172, 176, 199, 227

anamnestic: rationality, 137; reason, 225

anarcho-rationalists, 145

Anaxagoras, 65, 66, 167, 231

Anderson, Amanda, 148, 230n30

anthropology, 128, Aristotelian, 177n116

Aquinas, Thomas, 18

Arendt, Hannah, 42, 54; on *Denken*, 186n32; on Kant, 53, 187n43; on Kant's *Verstand*, 187n43; on judgment, 232n46

Aristotle, 5, 6, 7, 15, 18, 32, 84, 152, 155, 167n13

Arnauld, Antoine, 50, 177n116

# George L. Mosse Series in Modern European Cultural and Intellectual History

## Series Editors

Steven E. Aschheim, Stanley G. Payne, Mary Louise Roberts, and David J. Sorkin

## Advisory Board

Ofer Ashkenazi
*Hebrew University of Jerusalem*

Annette Becker
*Université Paris X–Nanterre*

Christopher Browning
*University of North Carolina at Chapel Hill*

Natalie Zemon Davis
*University of Toronto*

Saul Friedländer
*University of California, Los Angeles*

Emilio Gentile
*Università di Roma "La Sapienza"*

Anson Rabinbach
*Princeton University*

John S. Tortorice
*University of Wisconsin–Madison*

Joan Wallach Scott
*Institute for Advanced Study*

Jay Winter
*Yale University*

# Series Books

*Of God and Gods: Egypt, Israel, and the Rise of Monotheism*
Jan Assmann

*The Enemy of the New Man: Homosexuality in Fascist Italy*
Lorenzo Benadusi; translated by Suzanne Dingee and Jennifer Pudney

*The Holocaust and the West German Historians: Historical Interpretation and
Autobiographical Memory*
Nicolas Berg; translated and edited by Joel Golb

*Collected Memories: Holocaust History and Postwar Testimony*
Christopher R. Browning

*Cataclysms: A History of the Twentieth Century from Europe's Edge*
Dan Diner; translated by William Templer with Joel Golb

*La Grande Italia: The Myth of the Nation in the Twentieth Century*
Emilio Gentile; translated by Suzanne Dingee and Jennifer Pudney

*Carl Schmitt and the Jews: The "Jewish Question," the Holocaust, and
German Legal Theory*
Raphael Gross; translated by Joel Golb

*Reason after Its Eclipse: On Late Critical Theory*
Jay Martin

*Some Measure of Justice: The Holocaust Era Restitution Campaign of the 1990s*
Michael R. Marrus

*Confronting History: A Memoir*
George L. Mosse

*Nazi Culture: Intellectual, Cultural, and Social Life in the Third Reich*
George L. Mosse

*What History Tells: George L. Mosse and the Culture of Modern Europe*
Edited by Stanley G. Payne, David J. Sorkin, and John S. Tortorice